THE EDUCATIONAL
INNOVATORS

1750–1880

W. A. C. STEWART

AND

W. P. McCANN

MACMILLAN

London · Melbourne · Toronto

ST MARTIN'S PRESS

New York

1967

MACMILLAN AND COMPANY LIMITED
Little Essex Street London WC 2
also Bombay Calcutta Madras Melbourne

THE MACMILLAN COMPANY OF CANADA LIMITED
70 Bond Street Toronto 2

ST MARTIN'S PRESS INC
175 Fifth Avenue New York NY 10010

Library of Congress catalog card no. 67-25981

PRINTED IN GREAT BRITAIN
BY R. & R. CLARK, LTD., EDINBURGH

Contents

vi *Contents*

List of Illustrations

Preface and Acknowledgements

In the present century schools have come into existence to express particular beliefs about education and by these assertions to voice criticism of and opposition to certain educational principles and practices. A good deal has been written about individual schools or educational experiments but no thorough study has been made of unorthodoxy in English education, and when beginning on such an inquiry one needs to find reasonable justification for choosing a starting-point as well as for the criteria by which to select the innovators who are to be considered.

It is common to say that identifiably modern ideas in education may be traced to Rousseau, especially to the influence of *Émile*, published in 1762. While the claim has substance, evidence exists to show that there were innovators in British educational theory and practice before 1762, and it is these who provide us with a starting-point.

This is the first of a two-volume study on educational innovation from about 1750 to the present time. The span of the first volume reaches to approximately 1880 and the second volume will continue from there.

I wish to make warm acknowledgement to the Leverhulme Trust, whose financial support made it possible for me to have Dr. Phillip McCann as my collaborator in this first volume. The research and most of the initial writing of this volume were undertaken by Dr. McCann. Responsibility for the final plan and drafting, however, rests with me.

I also wish to thank Professor W. H. G. Armytage for help in the early stages of planning this volume ; Professor J. F. C. Harrison for critical discussion of Robert Owen and the Owenites ; Dr. K. Silber of Edinburgh University for copies of manuscript material relating to Dr. Charles Mayo ; Mrs. Hester Burton for information on Barbara Bodichon's school ; Mr. A. S. Wainscot, Librarian of the Swedenborg Society, for access to rare material on Samuel Wilderspin and the New Church; and Mrs. June Taylor, who was responsible for the typing of all the early drafts of the manuscript.

Keele   W. A. C. S.

Introduction

I

THE present pattern of compulsory schooling in England is less than a century old, and an immense increase in educational provision took place in the last quarter of the last century. To bring about such expansion some degree of control and standardization was inevitable, and there seems to have been a broad consensus on how children should be treated and how they should be taught. Children as pupils were supposed to be dependent upon the authority of the adult. Knowledge was organized as material to be taught and learned, and the learner had to match himself against what the teacher (or the examiner) required and to prepare himself accordingly. Schools were instruments of induction for the young and of supremacy for the adults, while the induction itself was in morals, obedience, and piety as well as in the three R's or more sophisticated subjects. These are the sketch-lines of the average, orthodox view on schools in the period 1750–1870, leaving out of account the quality of education given or the degree of devotion or neglect shown by teachers or pupils. Evidence exists, however, of unorthodox theory and practice over the same period, minority opinion that merits attention.

Some people who have had ideas and theories about dealing with children and the kinds of knowledge that are important have started schools to practise what they preach, and there are plenty of examples of teacher-innovators in the pages that follow. Others have interested themselves in unorthodoxy in education by writing about it, often as part of a larger social or philosophical analysis ; it was so with Locke, with Rousseau, and with Owen. There are also those who backed new schools with money as sympathizers while not themselves originating the ideas or taking an active part in the day-to-day conduct of affairs.

Right at the start there are three main problems — of definition, of coverage, of terminology. How do we define the question we have to examine ? How far does this scrutiny extend ? What words shall we use to name the unorthodoxy we are considering ? After these, there is the fourth question of the method we use to examine the examples we choose.

First, to consider definition and coverage. Before we can talk of unorthodoxy in education there have to be enough schools to have established a prevailing mood and practice, an orthodoxy, and while we could take this a long way back, we shall start at 1750 before the dramatic expansion of education in the nineteenth century and a few years before the publication of *Émile*. We could consider theorists, philanthropists, and practitioners expressing unorthodox ideas about education, but for the most part we shall examine only those principles that reached a sufficient degree of definiteness to be worked out in a school. Yet we do not list every unorthodox school in the country throughout the period, for this is not a commentary of that kind. It is our intention to consider unorthodox principles of substance, with evidence from schools to support the argument, and the coverage will be almost entirely in England. However, no analysis of this kind can entirely ignore Germany, Switzerland, and France, but these are mentioned mainly in connection with the work of Froebel, Pestalozzi, Fellenberg, and Rousseau.

To turn now to the matter of terminology. Rousseau is often considered the father of progressive education, but we have avoided this term as far as possible because it begs too many questions — has unorthodoxy always and necessarily a claim to represent progress ? What is progress in any case and how is it assessed ? We have given serious consideration to calling these unorthodox schools 'experimental' or 'radical', but neither word is appropriate for different reasons. 'Experimental' implies rather more readiness to test out a hypothesis, and if necessary reject it on evidence supplied, than most of these schools were willing to accept. If they had to close, as they all did in time, it was usually because teachers, pupils, or money were not forthcoming ; it was not because checking had shown that principles and practice were not producing the desired results. Again, 'radical' has a shifting significance, suggesting at one time a political revolutionary, at another a non-aligned, original thinker of liberal intention.

It is true that here and there we use the terms 'progressive', 'experimental', and 'radical' almost interchangeably, but where stricter definition is involved we have used some variant of the term 'innovating' as this represents a more accurately neutral description of much of the educational practice, however radical the theory sometimes was. Thus our main concern is with the educational innovators and their unorthodoxies in theory and practice, and it must be admitted at once that what is thought to be a deviation in 1800 is likely to be much less so in 1850 or 1900.

II

Where, then, will educational innovation in schools be seen sufficiently clearly ? Obviously in the area of knowledge, and this means predominantly in the curriculum both in the range and content of subject-matter and in the consideration given to children's individual differences, particularly in the subjects taught to them and the methods of learning encouraged. If a school in the nineteenth century, for rationally worked-out reasons, is prepared to diverge in its curriculum from common practice, here is cause for attention. If, in addition, it pays heed to the aptitudes and interests of the pupils before prescribing a programme of studies, this is another unusual feature.

If knowledge and curriculum is an obvious area of innovation, so too is the territory of personal relationships, especially those between teachers and pupils. This will appear particularly clearly in the forms of authority and discipline and punishment. Where the dominance of adults was taken for granted it was customary for them to punish with severity and confidence and correspondingly unusual for children to be expected to form a jury to assess the guilt of their fellows and to decide on the appropriate punishments to be applied.

Unorthodox teaching methods are another index of innovation and novel practices were quite often based on ideas that had been tried out by Pestalozzi or Fellenberg or some other Continental pioneer.

The schools included here, then, have to be markedly original in their approach to what is taught and how it is taught ; in their recognition of the pupil as initiator and the teacher as guide rather than authoritarian ; in their concern for the humane organization of the school community to these ends. Not all the schools included would score equally under each of these headings, but it has not usually proved difficult to identify the kind of innovation we have in mind. Some schools exemplify reform, but were not really regarded as radical ; Rugby under Arnold and Shrewsbury under Butler would be two good examples of these. Neither of them at any time ran a serious risk of being separated from the public schools but instead modified and reformed the system from within rather than broke through into being a quite different kind of school. Mack, speaking of Hazelwood, founded by the brothers Hill early in the nineteenth century and one of the schools considered later, makes this point clear :

> [Hazelwood's] ideas were too new and its break with the past too abrupt to appeal to most upper-class Englishmen so long as a more moderate substitute could be found. Middle-class attachment to the Hills' doctrine was predicated on despair of such a substitute. But at the end of the twenties Arnold provided a solution of the moral problem which did not necessitate destruction of the [public] schools or involve a thorough-going liberalism, and thus it was Arnold and not the Hills who has lived as England's great educator.[1]

The norms Hazelwood assumed both for the society for which it was educating and for the methods of education practised in the school were implicitly and explicitly different from those of the public schools, even the reformed public schools.

There are a few cases where inclusion or exclusion is not easy to decide, but these examples will show themselves. The question is always the same : do these schools seem to be so far from what was thought normal in education *at that time* that they can be classed as innovators ? A school may sometimes show unusual and symptomatic features, such as rejecting corporal punishment or excluding religious instruction, without really changing fundamentally the whole organization ; it could still have a limited view of the curriculum or the relationship of school to society and such a school is not included here as an innovator.

Education and schools are, admittedly, part of a wider and deeper panorama of ideas and institutions. However, the focus in this book is on the working-out in practice of unorthodox educational ideas, and the linking social and economic themes arise from these.

---

[1] E. C. Mack, *Public Schools and British Opinion, 1780–1860* (London, 1938), pp.168–169.

Part One

1750–1850

E.I.—B

Section One

THE EIGHTEENTH CENTURY: EXPERIMENT AND ENLIGHTENMENT

1. Early Experiments: William Gilpin and David Manson

THE work of at least two educationalists, begun as early as the 1750s, foreshadowed some of the experiments usually ascribed to the new school of educationalists inspired by Rousseau. These pioneers were William Gilpin of Cheam School and David Manson of Belfast. Unknown to each other, they made some highly original reforms in school discipline, organization, and teaching method. Their innovations were the expression of a critical attitude to traditional forms of education, but neither Gilpin nor Manson was influenced by Continental theorists. They did not consciously start a movement, yet they were the pioneers of the whole progressive tradition in England. It is to William Gilpin that we turn first of all.

William Gilpin of Cheam School

William Gilpin, who became headmaster of Cheam School in Surrey in 1752, was the first English schoolmaster decisively to break with the public-school traditions of fagging, corporal punishment, and the supremacy of classical studies. Much of his work was a reaction against the moral atmosphere and authoritarian regime of these schools. He also believed that the work of public schools could be more closely related to society, or, more accurately, to that section of society to which his pupils would eventually belong. Many of his pupils he

3

expected to become 'landholders, tradesmen and public officers',[1] and he was not averse from introducing commercial principles and practice into the school curriculum. 'I consider my school', he wrote, 'in the light of something between a school to qualify for business, and the public school, in which classical learning only is attended to.'[2] He considered his methods a better preparation for life for the directing classes of society than those pursued in the more conventional classical boarding-schools.

Gilpin was opposed to the concentration on the classics and the lack of moral training found in these establishments. He believed that their pupils,

> having lost the only kind of improvement they came in quest of, which is classical accuracy . . . leave school rude and unfurnished with ideas or principles, and if they have not the good fortune to fall into good company, their minds are ready to catch the first incidental impressions of vice or folly.[3]

'Let them candidly own', he wrote of the public schools, 'whether it may not be worth while to try some new method ; and to endeavour, if possible, to bring early habit, in the common instances of life, to fight in the causes of virtue and good manners.' Gilpin, far more conscious than most schoolmasters of his time of the importance of early childhood in the formation of character, was not content to pass over the bullying by older boys of the younger as 'schoolboys' tricks' ; he believed that such practices, together with arbitrary discipline exercised by the masters, could lead to a permanently hardened cast of mind and might be the 'foundation for knavery' in later life.[4]

With this critical assessment of the public schools in mind, Gilpin was determined to reform the organization at Cheam as soon as he was able. He had started teaching there, as an assistant usher, in 1750 ; two years later he was the principal assistant. The school was then conducted by the Rev. James Sanxay, whose wife, it appeared, was unwilling to undertake the duties connected with the domestic side of the establishment. Sanxay decided to give up the school, and made

---

[1] 'An Account of the Rev. Mr. Gilpin', in W. Gilpin, *Memoirs of Dr. Richard Gilpin* (London, 1879), p. 127.

[2] Cited in C. P. Barbier, 'Gilpin, Master of Cheam', *Glasgow Herald*, 14 Sept. 1957.

[3] Cited in [C. P. Barbier], 'Submerged by Dr. Syntax : William Gilpin of Cheam'. *Times Educational Supplement*, no. 2226, 17 Jan. 1958, p. 67 (hereafter *T.E.S.*).

[4] Gilpin, *Memoirs*, p. 128.

it over to Gilpin, who, with capital provided by Sanxay's brother, and with the help of a newly married wife, became principal of Cheam in 1752.[5]

His success, however, was not instantaneous. 'Immediately on his taking the school it sank', he admitted, writing of himself in the third person. 'It was low before ; but it now fell to fifteen boys. The omen was bad : but it was yet too soon to despond.'[6] And so it proved. Within a few years the numbers had risen to eighty, sufficient test of the popularity and effectiveness of his innovations.[7]

His first 'new scheme', as he called it, was to frame a code of laws for the whole school, with specific punishments for each transgression. These laws were publicly read at stated times before the whole school, and also strictly observed by Gilpin himself. Punishments were, however, carried out by the principal, but a safeguard was added in that if he carried out the punishment more severely than the law enjoined, he would listen to complaints, and if a sufficient number of 'good witnesses' appeared, then he would recompense the boy who had suffered. In doubtful cases which the existing law did not sufficiently cover, or where the offence was not sufficiently proved, a jury of twelve boys was empanelled to decide upon the case.[8]

These innovations, which foreshadow later schemes of self-government instituted by David Williams and the Hill family, were not justified on any of the theoretical or psychological grounds familiar to later educationalists. Gilpin merely hoped that by associating his pupils with the maintenance of school discipline he would accomplish two things — impress on the boys' minds 'an early love of order, law and liberty', and make corporal punishment virtually unnecessary. The latter was, in fact, administered only in extreme cases, for 'vice or obstinate idleness'.

The main punishments were fines and imprisonment. The latter consisted of confinement to the dining-room on holiday afternoons. Fines were deducted from the boys' weekly allowance, and an account of them was kept by a Secretary in books that were always open to inspection. At times the sum deriving from fines might reach a total of £70. The money was spent on books or sports equipment ; an extensive fives court was paved, for instance, and a school library

[5] W. D. Templeman, *The Life and Work of William Gilpin* (Urbana, Ill., 1939), pp. 58–59.
[6] Gilpin, *Memoirs*, p. 123.   [7] Templeman, p. 60.   [8] Gilpin, *Memoirs*, p. 123.

built up. The Librarian was one of the two Officers of State in the school, the other being the Secretary.[9] About £5 of the money accruing from fines, however, was spent twice a year on bread for the poor. This had a moral purpose, for Gilpin hoped that it would have a good effect on the future conduct of the boys. Nevertheless, the scene as described by Gilpin had that somewhat degrading air that charity always suggests :

> The boys were seated in the dining room ; and the loaves were piled up, on a long table in the middle of the room. One of the seniors then standing up with his list, called in each of the poor people in rotation, to receive the number of loaves allotted to him. . . . They were given to understand, at the same time, this was the young gentlemen's charity whom they were to thank.[10]

Gilpin often referred to the school society as a 'state'. But the state that he had in mind was an ideal one, specifically designed to overcome the oligarchy of the older boys so prevalent in schools of this type. Gilpin soon discovered the powerful influence that the leading boys could have on the school. As in so many of the schemes of delegated discipline, his methods aimed at opposing despotic tendencies and equalizing public responsibility by making every boy personally accountable for his role in the miniature state. Instead of a powerful group of older boys, and a dependent mass of younger pupils, he sought to substitute a corporate consciousness, based on the acceptance of moral laws, under which each boy was equally and personally responsible to the community as a whole.

On one occasion only did he record a failure, and that was with a group of boys who had been sent to him because other schools had despaired of reforming them, a circumstance of which Gilpin was not fully aware at the time. However, despite some suspicions about their behaviour, Gilpin hoped to be able to integrate them into his system. The new boys, however, with the object of resisting the 'orderly manner' of the prevailing democratic system, soon gathered round themselves a group of younger boys, over whom they maintained a despotic power. This was really the bullying and fagging that Gilpin's system was designed to prevent. The cook complained to the principal that she had been forced to double the meat ration because some of the younger boys had suddenly developed enormous appetites, coming back for second and even third helpings of meat at dinner. Gilpin

[9] Gilpin, *Memoirs*, p. 124.   [10] Ibid.

kept a close watch and soon discovered why. The older boys were paying the juniors to get the meat, which was being fed to a pack of hounds that the former were keeping secretly in the nearby village. Faced with such well-organized opposition to his democratic system, and feeling that the boys were too old to be reformed, Gilpin expelled them. After this he refused to admit to Cheam older boys from other public schools.[11]

With the normal run of boys, however, Gilpin was nearly always successful and a good example of his method was his treatment of the country rambles on holiday afternoons. To most schoolmasters these would serve as a means of ensuring healthy exercise by the boys, not to mention an opportunity of getting rid of them for the afternoon. Gilpin, however, saw these walks primarily as 'an instrument of exciting truth, honour and integrity'. When the boys returned from vacation, they were given the option of promising never to go out of bounds without leave. Those who made the promise were allowed, on written application to the principal, to go for country walks on leave, provided they agreed not to enter any house and to return by a stated time. Those who did not promise ran the risk of being caught ; if they were caught, they merely suffered the usual penalties for being out of bounds, for no breach of promise was involved. The promises and the punishments resulting from breaking bounds were entered in a book. One such entry reads :

> August 22 [1760]. I have been caught out of bounds, and not chusing to promise am justly condemned to a month's imprisonment in the inner yard.
>
> [signed] John Lewis.[12]

Gilpin claimed that there were rarely more than half a dozen offenders a year, and that these eventually begged to be admitted to the promise. Whether these boys had come to see, as he thought, the advantages of 'orderly liberty' over 'dangerous licence', or whether they merely wanted to be on the same footing as the rest is an open question. In any case it is an interesting example of moral persuasion, for those who went out of bounds after promising not to were punished far more severely than those who committed the same offence without having given the undertaking.[13]

---

[11] Ibid., pp. 130–1   [12] Cited in Barbier, *Glasgow Herald*.
[13] Gilpin, *Memoirs*, pp. 125–6.

A great deal of the organization of the school was directed towards character-building of this kind. The type of person whom Gilpin aimed to produce was 'the honourable man', well fitted to take his place among the politically and socially active upper classes. Cheam at this period represented one of the first attempts by a public school at a progressive development of the organization and curriculum that would enable it to fulfil these aims. 'The formation of manners being the grand point I have in view,' Gilpin wrote to a parent, 'the information of the mind I consider as subordinate to it.'[14] One of his early biographers described the principles on which the school was conducted as 'the fear of disgrace, the spirit of emulation, and the praise of desert', which encouraged the nobler sentiments of the mind and created 'that dignity of character in youth, which is the surest foundation of honourable and virtuous conduct in after life'.[15] Gilpin himself thought that the first objects of education should be 'the great truths of religion, and virtue'.[16]

One of his inflexible rules was never to accept a boy unless his parents were prepared to agree with Gilpin's views on education, and no matter how exalted the father Gilpin would hold to this. On one occasion he conducted an argument with Sir Thomas Frankland over an account for the son's fees, until Frankland apologized and paid up. Later he stood firm against the jurist, Sir William Blackstone, on the health rules of the school, in the end until Blackstone removed his two sons.[17] On occasion Gilpin could also be ironic, as when he informed the father of Henry Addington, later Viscount Sidmouth :

> Harry is a genius ; and I may add, he takes the licence of a genius — he trusts more to his parts than his industry . . . he is exceedingly retentive of what he appears to get merely by intuition.[18]

Some of Gilpin's innovations were designed to reproduce in microcosm certain aspects of the outside world that his pupils might experience when they left school. Boys were allowed to keep small shops,

---

[14] Cited in [Barbier], *T.E.S.*
[15] 'Biographical Sketch of the late Rev. W. Gilpin', in Rev. Richard Warner, *Miscellanies* (Bath, 2 vols., 1819), ii, p. 155. Substantially the same account of Gilpin's work at Cheam appears in this author's *Literary Recollections* (London, 2 vols., 1830), i, pp. 330–2.
[16] W. Gilpin, *Lectures on the Catechism of the Church of England* (London, 1779), p. x.
[17] Gilpin, *Memoirs*, pp. 132–4.
[18] G. Pellew, *The Life and Correspondence of the Rt. Hon. Henry Addington, First Viscount Sidmouth* (London, 3 vols., 1847), i, p. 13.

in which trade was done in gingerbread, cakes, apples, and similar commodities, but this concession to Mammon was modified by the medieval Christian practice of the just price. A legalized scale of profit per article was laid down, and any violation of this meant that the individual concerned was not allowed to continue in business. Gilpin recalled one case of transgression by a school Secretary, who, as we have seen, was in charge of the boys' finances, paying out to them their weekly allowances. This boy, taking a somewhat literal reading of the values of private enterprise, had the idea of displaying the goods in his shop at one end of the table whilst he paid the boys their allowances at the other. 'This was taking so unfair an advantage by leading them into temptations which they could not possibly resist', observed Gilpin, 'that he was not only forbidden to open his shop again, but was turned out of his high office with disgrace.' [19]

Another strictly regulated introduction to economics was by means of the cultivation of garden plots. Templeman, in his biography of Gilpin, represents the introduction of gardening into the curriculum as a pioneering attempt that anticipated similar efforts in the mid-nineteenth century by almost a hundred years.[20] Gilpin probably had a different aim in view, and an introduction to economics was very likely as much in his mind as the value of gardening. The borders of the playground were divided into some thirty strips of soil, on which the boys tried to grow melons, cucumbers, onions, and other vegetables for domestic consumption. The cultivation was mainly in the hands of the older boys, who used the younger ones as assistants, and it was the custom of the former, when they left school, to bequeath the plots to their assistants by means of a will. This sometimes resulted in some of the more popular and active boys possessing, by means of inheritance, quite large 'estates', portions of which they could lease or sell. Often the size of their estates outran their ability to cultivate them, for the number of assistants was not unlimited and in cases like this the boy who owned the land lost those portions that were neglected, for it was obligatory that all land should be under cultivation. 'It was a law of the state', wrote Gilpin, 'that whatever was neglected, escheated to the Lord; who gave it to those who would make a better use of it.' [21]

If Gilpin's notions of commercial practice had a somewhat feudal

---

[19] Gilpin, *Memoirs*, pp. 127-8.   [20] Templeman, p. 67.
[21] Gilpin, *Memoirs*, p. 127.

ring, his attitude to study and learning was decidedly modern. In relation to classics and religion he justly claimed some innovations in teaching method. As we have seen, he was very much opposed to the supremacy of the classics, as he frequently told the pupils and parents, among them William Mitford, later to become the historian of Greece.[22] It seemed to Gilpin a waste of time to learn a dead language with critical exactness, to give precise attention to the significance of each word and expression, or to compose verses in it. In fact, he bluntly informed parents that if they wanted their sons to achieve critical exactness in Greek and Latin, then his school was not for them. Proficiency in the usual exercises of construing and versification, he thought, added little to a man's knowledge, or to his appreciation of a classical author. It was of much more use to his pupils to learn their own language with accuracy than to study a dead one. To a parent who wished his son to study more Latin poetry he wrote :

> It is my endeavour, rather to rein the *imagination* of boys, and to spur their reason. It is my wish to improve their *sense*, and if possible to add *judgement*. And as a vehicle for their thoughts, I think I cannot do better than to teach them to write their own language in plain prose.[23]

His object was merely to train boys to read the writers of Greece and Rome 'with ease and pleasure'. Even this was going too far in some cases, he felt, particularly if a boy did not continue this reading after leaving school.

It is therefore not surprising to find that Gilpin was opposed to the memorizing of words and formulae in the study of Greek and Latin. Instead he concentrated on getting his pupils to keep at a translation until they had mastered the sense of it, translating and re-translating several times if necessary.[24] At all times he tried to give them 'a delicacy of taste and a feeling of the beauties of the authors'.[25]

Gilpin also claimed that he practised a new mode of explaining the Scriptures. On Sunday mornings he would dictate to the older boys explanations of the Scriptures in contemporary language, and on

---

[22] W. Mitford, *An Inquiry into the Principles of Harmony in Language* (London, 1804). The reminiscence occurs in the dedication to Gilpin's son, John.

[23] Cited in [Barbier], *T.E.S.*   [24] Gilpin, *Memoirs*, p. 132.

[25] Warner, *Miscellanies*, ii, p. 155.

Sunday evenings he gave lectures to the school on the same subject, encouraging the pupils to ask questions afterwards on all points of difficulty. On weekday mornings, the Scriptures were read for an hour during the period when the boys were taken out one by one for their daily washing and combing. The New Testament and a large part of the Old Testament were thus read over several times each year, and in this way their understanding and knowledge of the Bible were slowly built up.[26]

The curriculum at Cheam was reasonably wide and included, in addition to Greek and Latin, English, arithmetic, geography, religious instruction, drawing, and dancing. The boys played football and cricket, went riding and rambling, and also had a large range of extra-curricular activities — drama, indoor hobbies, the keeping of pets, and, as we have seen, the running of miniature shops and gardens. Geography was apparently taught in part by fitting together pieces of a jigsaw map of Britain, and in 1765 a pupil wrote to his parents complaining that he had lost Flintshire and asking for a replacement.[27]

Gilpin himself, together with his brother Sawrey, taught drawing. Boys were allowed to make expeditions into the surrounding district to draw from nature, and a pupil named Thomas Grimston, whose draughtsmanship, it is to be hoped, was better than his spelling, described such an outing :

> I went into the Town at Cheam this morning to draw some Houses or any thing that I liked, with some more of my fellow Schoolboys. They tyed one of Mr Robt Sanxay's Horses up and d[rew] it but they finding it hard to do all leaft of but one, and they drew a barn an a house. I drew Mr Sanxay's house and Mr Sorey Gilpin said it was very well done.[28]

Not unexpectedly, much of Gilpin's success seems to have been due to his personal qualities. According to a contemporary biographer, he had 'a commanding person, dignified manners and a deep sonorous voice'.[29] His person could strike his pupils with terror at times, but Gilpin was renowned for his absolute fairness and integrity, and there

---

[26] Gilpin, *Memoirs*, pp. 129–30.   [27] [Barbier], *T.E.S.*

[28] Cited in C. P. Barbier, *William Gilpin, His Drawings, Teaching and Theory of the Picturesque* (Oxford, 1963), p. 37.

[29] 'W.H.G.', *A Memoir of the Late Rev. William Gilpin, M.A.* (Lymington, 1851), p. 17. According to Templeman (p. 13), 'W.H.G.' were the initials of W. Henry Grove of Lymington. An engraving of Gilpin is reproduced below, facing p. 48.

can be no doubt of the respect the boys had for him. An instance of this occurred over the village green. The pupils had the use of the green for cricket, on the understanding that the rule of 'first come, first served' was adhered to. If the village boys were in possession, the scholars had to leave, but if the Cheam boys were the first occupiers they were to give way to nobody. One day some local farmers disputed the possession of the green, and during the altercation one of them threw a ball which injured one of the boys. Gilpin's reaction was to inform the farmer concerned that if he gave a guinea to the poor and publicly begged the boy's pardon the incident would be closed. The farmer paid his guinea readily enough, but jibbed at the apology, so Gilpin returned the money with a warning that the incident would be taken further. In view of Gilpin's intransigence the farmer had second thoughts, repaid the money, and made a public apology before the whole school. However, Gilpin was equally fair to the villagers and investigated all the complaints of the local inhabitants, and was diligent in seeing that recompense was made to anyone in the parish who suffered because of the bad behaviour of any of his pupils.[30]

It was actions of this kind that endeared him to his pupils, and resulted in many of them keeping in touch with him when they had left school. They visited him and sent him letters from all over the world. Several of his pupils became eminent in public life, and at the turn of the century Cheam's old boys included a Prime Minister, a Lord Chancellor of Ireland, two secretaries of the Treasury, and one at the War Office.[31]

Gilpin's original method of conducting Cheam School had brought him a good deal of fame. When public men like Bishop Newton or Dr. Weatherall, President of University College, Oxford, wished to enter their sons at Cheam, they had to take their place at the end of a long waiting-list.[32] The school was for many years celebrated as one of the best known in Surrey.[33] Gilpin's friend, Richard Glover, acknowledged in his own day as a poet, dramatist, and scholar, was for ever asking him about the progress of the school and enthusiastically recounting Gilpin's achievements to his friends.[34] It is probable that Glover's proselytizing gave rise to the remarkable account of a progressive school, with features very similar to those of Cheam, in

[30] Gilpin, *Memoirs*, p. 125.   [31] [Barbier], *T.E.S.*   [32] Ibid.
[33] 'W.H.G.', *A Memoir*, p. 9.   [34] Templeman, p. 68.

Tobias Smollett's *Peregrine Pickle*. Templeman, the most recent biographer of Gilpin, in this piece of literary detection makes a good,
though circumstantial, case for Smollett having heard of Gilpin's
innovations through Glover or his friends.[35]

Peregrine Pickle, at the age of six, was sent to 'a boarding school
not far from London, which was kept by a certain person very eminent
for his successful method of education'. The school was, in fact, run
by an assistant named Jennings, though nominally in charge of 'an
old illiterate German quack' named Keypstick. Jennings, 'a man of
learning, probity and good sense', had brought the school its reputation single-handed. He enacted a body of laws 'suited to the age and
comprehension of every individual . . . each transgression was fairly
tried by his peers, and punished according to the verdict of the jury'.
No one was scourged for want of ability, but a spirit of emulation was
engendered by 'well-timed praise and artful comparison' and maintained by the distribution of small prizes for the industrious, clever,
or well behaved.[36] The resemblance between this description and
Gilpin's practice is striking, but if Smollett was really basing his fictional school at Cheam, then Gilpin must have introduced some of
his measures of self-government whilst working under Sanxay, for
Peregrine Pickle was published in 1751.

Gilpin retired from Cheam in 1777, having achieved his ambition
of saving £10,000,[37] a remarkable result in view of the moderate fees
he charged — £25 a year, with an additional £5 or £6 for extras in
school equipment.[38] Colonel William Mitford offered Gilpin the living
of Boldre on the edge of the New Forest in Hampshire. In April 1777
he became, and remained for the rest of his life, Vicar of Boldre, in a
parish of wretched and poverty-stricken forest dwellers.

Gilpin made heroic and largely successful efforts to civilize his
parishioners. To this end he founded two schools of industry, one
for boys and one for girls.[39] He gave most of his time to drawing,
however, and made a second reputation as a topographer, developing
a landscape style that had a considerable influence on English taste for
the two following generations.[40] He died in 1804 in his eightieth year.

[35] Ibid., pp. 68–71.
[36] [Tobias Smollett,] *The Adventures of Peregrine Pickle* (London, 4 vols., 1751), i,
pp. 85 ff.   [37] Warner, *Miscellanies*, ii, p. 157.
[38] Sir H. C. M. Lambert, 'A Cheam School Bill in 1766', *Surrey Archaeological
Transactions*, xxv (1924), pp. 80–84.   [39] Templeman, pp. 194 ff.
[40] Barbier, *William Gilpin*, p. 98.

David Manson and the Belfast Play School

Very different from William Gilpin was the mercurial Irishman, David Manson, brewer, inventor, and schoolteacher. His school, which opened in 1752 and ran for some forty years, was one of the first to modify the normal school routine by combining lessons with play and amusement and devising a system of pupil self-government based on a complex gradation of rank. His elaborate series of rewards and punishments, and his rejection of corporal punishment in an age when its use was almost universal, predated by nearly seventy years a similar system used by the Hills in Hazelwood School. In addition, his organization of one scholar instructing another anticipated the monitorial system of Bell and Lancaster. Manson's reputation, which was extremely high in his home town of Belfast and throughout Ireland in his lifetime, never spread very widely in England, although his name was known in Scottish educational circles in the early nineteenth century. Elizabeth Hamilton, the Scottish writer and educationalist, in her novel, *The Cottagers of Glenburnie*, published in 1808, made one of the characters say :

> I will show you a book written by one Mr. David Manson, a school-master in the North of Ireland, which contains an account of what he calls his play-school ; the regulations of which are so excellent, that every scholar must have been made insensibly to teach himself, while he all the time considered himself assisting the master in teaching others.[41]

She added in a footnote that during his lifetime he was considered little more than 'an amiable visionary, who, in toys given to his scholars, foolishly squandered the profits of his profession', but she also spoke of his 'unwearied and disinterested zeal in the cause of education',[42] and this judgement by one of the earliest British pioneers of the theories of Pestalozzi must be considered worthy of respect.

Manson's early education and training were in the tradition of the hedge school, that peculiar form of educational self-help which arose in Ireland in the period following the penal code of William III. Forbidden to teach in school in the normal way, schoolmasters took their pupils under a hedge or bank and gave them lessons in the open air. In the later eighteenth century, when the laws were less strictly en-

[41] Elizabeth Hamilton, *The Cottagers of Glenburnie* (Edinburgh, 1808), pp. 374–5.
[42] Ibid., pp. 375–6.

forced, the school might be taught in a barn, cabin, or other building, but they retained the name of hedge school.[43] The Irish novelist William Carleton has left an unforgettable picture of these hedge schoolmasters, their high erudition, and the veneration in which they were held by the peasantry.[44]

Manson was born in Cairncastle, Co. Antrim, in 1726, and started work as a farmer's boy.[45] His quickness and intelligence attracted the attention of a neighbouring clergyman, who took charge of his education. It was common in Ireland, at that time and for long after, for intelligent peasant boys to rise to the position of schoolmaster with the help of well-disposed scholars and the support of their families. Manson qualified as a teacher and began teaching in his home parish as a hedge schoolmaster. His first school was in a cowshed, but his subsequent work, in different parts of the country, was less restricted. For a short while he gave up teaching in Ireland in order to follow the more profitable occupation of tutoring sailors in Liverpool in mathematical navigation, at a fee of 6*d*. an hour.

In 1752 his mother's illness and his own approaching marriage caused him to return to Belfast and, in the same year he opened a brewery. Shortly afterwards, however, he started an evening school at his house, where he taught grammar, reading, and spelling, and the number of his scholars eventually rose to twenty. The first of these was Helen Joy, the daughter of Henry Joy, an owner of the *Belfast News Letter*, who aided Manson in many ways, not least by giving publicity to his method. Another pupil was Elizabeth Hamilton's eldest sister, Catherine, from whom Elizabeth gained her knowledge of Manson's work.[46]

After the success of this evening school, Manson established a day school. In 1760 he added a boarding-school, whose opening was announced in the following advertisement :

> 1760, March, 20, — David Manson begs leave to inform the publick that he inclines to board a few children from the first of May next, having taken a convenient front house in High Street, Belfast, for

---

[43] P. J. Dowling, *The Hedge Schools of Ireland* (Dublin, n.d.), pp. 1, 45–46.

[44] W. Carleton, *Traits and Stories of the Irish Peasantry* (Dublin, 2 vols., 1830), ii, pp. 109 ff.

[45] J. J. Marshall, 'David Manson, Schoolmaster in Belfast', *Ulster Journal of Archaeology*, vol. xiv (1908), p. 59.

[46] Elizabeth Hamilton herself was educated by a schoolmaster also named Manson, of Stirling : A. Gordon, 'Elizabeth Hamilton', ibid., vol. i (1895), p. 26.

that purpose. They will be taught to read and understand the English tongue, without the discipline of the rod, by intermixing pleasurable and healthful exercise with their instruction. As virtue is preferable to learning, due regard will be had to their morals ; good nature, truth, and integrity always encouraged, and the contrary vices exposed wherever their symptoms appear. The credit of the school is supported by the constant application of the undertaker and three careful assistants, who have their classes in separate apartments to prevent confusion.[47]

A few years later, when the school was again moved, this time to Donegall Street, it was run in conjunction with a school immediately opposite, and the hours were so arranged that the pupils could attend the latter in order to learn writing and mathematics without interfering with Manson's timetable. An advertisement of 1 July 1768 shows that, in addition to the lessons, Manson provided recreation out of school hours for his pupils :

Children and youths are boarded, and taught the English language by David Manson, at his house in Donegall Street, Belfast, which is large and commodious, being built on purpose where there is a healthful air and a delightful prospect of land and water. The boarders are permitted to go out without a guide. They have for their amusement a large yard behind the house, the use of the Linen Hall off market hours, and a bowling green about half a mile out of town (Lilliput), to which they repair in the summer evenings.[48]

The only account of Manson's teaching methods and school organization is contained in a supplement to his *New Pocket Dictionary*, published in 1762.[49] In this he states that the Play School was first opened in 1752, and in the beginning was restricted to pupils who were completely without education. Later on he took in pupils who had found difficulties at other schools or, as he put it, had been 'accustomed to the rod, and who had contracted an aversion to reading'. The curriculum of the school appears to have been limited to grammar, reading, and spelling, though, as we have seen, he had arrangements with specialist teachers in mathematics, handwriting, and French, so that his pupils could have the advantage of other studies.

The organization of the school was based upon Manson's own esti-

[47] Cited in Marshall, p. 63   [48] Ibid., p. 65.
[49] It has not been possible to obtain a copy of this volume. It is, however, extensively quoted in W. J. McCallister, *The Growth of Freedom in Education* (London, 1931), pp. 331 ff.

mation of the character of children and his belief in their need for freedom. He took issue with Locke over the latter's contention that a child's obstinacy justified punishment by the master. Manson argued that the child was a free individual who had the right to be given a choice of actions rather than be forced to accept a positive command from the teacher. In presenting his wishes to the child as a series of alternative actions the teacher could still maintain his authority, as no refusal of any one of these could be construed as insubordination. Manson was also a great believer in 'shaming', much practised by the Quakers and later by Joseph Lancaster. A crying child, for instance, might be exposed to ridicule by the teacher or mimicked by his companions until he stopped. Moral stories could be recited to the child in order to show him the error of his ways. The main object of this method was to avoid a head-on clash between the teacher and the pupil:

> The rod only quenches the flame, which will break out afterwards with greater fury than before. Every tutor should endeavour to gain the affections and confidence of the children under his care, and make them sensible of the kindness and friendly concern for their welfare: and when punishment becomes necessary, should guard against passion, and convince them 'tis not their *persons* but their *faults* which he dislikes. The love of LIBERTY is as natural to children as to grown persons: the method, then, to make them easy under a state of discipline is to convince them that they are free; that they act from choice, not compulsion.[50]

Occasionally a child might commit an offence for which in another school he would have been flogged. Flogging of a particularly brutal nature was common in the hedge schools of Manson's time, and William Carleton has given some terrifying examples of it. 'Indeed,' he writes, 'the instances of atrocious cruelty in hedge schools, were almost incredible.' [51] Manson recognized that pupils occasionally needed a more severe form of punishment than the system of loss of merit that he devised. He therefore constructed a wooden figure of a man in a boxing attitude, whom he called the Conqueror. This was placed in a corner of the schoolroom and the miscreant was forced to box a few rounds with the lay figure, skinning his knuckles in the process, a form of self-inflicted punishment that kept within the letter of Manson's theory of non-coercion by the master, but may have

[50] Ibid., p. 332.   [51] Carleton, ii, p. 183.

seemed entirely in the spirit of corporal punishment to the unfortunate victim. The great merit, however, about Manson's whole theory and practice of punishment was that it put the master in the position of a guide and mentor rather than a taskmaster.

Side by side with his reforms in the matter of punishment Manson introduced what today we should call the play-way method of teaching reading and spelling. His scheme bears a close resemblance to that advocated by Comenius, the great seventeenth-century Bohemian educational reformer. He had suggested making lessons more interesting and more closely related to life by the introduction of games based on farming, medicine, war, politics, and so on, and the granting of titles of rank to the most deserving :

> Further in order to encourage them, the mock titles of doctor, licentiate, or student of medicine, may be given to those who make the greatest progress.[52]

The first activity of the morning in Manson's school was the division of the children into ranks on the strength of their performance in repeating a passage of prose that they had been given to learn the previous evening. The amount to be learned, however, was entirely the choice of the child. The boys and girls who could repeat the greatest number of lines based on a standard of twenty-four received rank on the following scale :

24 lines or more	King and Queen
20 lines or more	Princes and Princesses
16 lines or more	Dukes and Duchesses
12 lines or more	Lords and Ladies
8 lines or more	tenants
4 lines or more	undertenants
Less than 4 lines, absentees	sluggards
Less than 4 lines when kept in to do so	dunces

The children in the school were thus sorted into a simplified version of feudal social relationships on the basis of their ability to learn a piece of work by heart. The best children, however, formed an élite that Manson termed the Royal Society. Children in the first four categories of the table were made Fellows of this society and received a ticket

---

[52] J. A. Comenius, *The Great Didactic*, trans. M. W. Keatinge (London, 1896), p. 331.

marked F.R.S. This was given with the proviso that they maintained good behaviour and did not fall below a certain standard in spelling. The King and Queen, however, received two tickets each. There was a great incentive to collect these tickets, for they could be exchanged for valuable prizes, at the rate of ten tickets for a half-guinea medal. Noisy behaviour or bad spelling, however, always meant the loss of tickets already gained. Manson's prodigality in the matter of prizes was held to be one of the causes that led to his removal to smaller premises in Co. Donegal in 1782. He seems to have kept solvent, however, by profits from his brewing business, which he continued to run and to advertise side by side with his school.[53]

To return to the schoolroom. After the children had been examined and sorted into their ranks, the day's lessons proceeded, with children reciting to each other under the supervision of monitors. The children were arranged in seats according to their rank, with the King and Queen at the head and the tenants between the undertenants and landlords, and proceeded, in Manson's words, to 'rehearse each other the back lessons of the Grammar'. Each correct line said by a landlord counted as £1 of rent due by the tenant, and each line correctly recited by a tenant counted as £1 paid. The object of the whole exercise, of course, was for the members of the Royal Society to claim as much rent as possible from the tenants and for the latter, together with the undertenants, to keep out of debt. Manson's account of the detailed working of the system cannot be summarized and is best told in his own words :

> When the royal society exceeds the number of tenants and undertenants the deficiency of one tenant to each is to be made up out of the sluggards ; they being so many pounds in arrear as their landlords have said lines of back-lesson to those who sat next to them : for the sluggards, not having said their morning lessons, are not ready for their back lessons ; and consequently cannot be said to have paid any of their rent. . . . When the tenants, undertenants, and sluggards exceed the number of the royal society, one of the remaining sluggards is given to each of those landlords who have said most lines of back lesson, when the morning lessons are over. But if the tenants and undertenants outnumber the royal society,

[53] In an advertisement of May 1782 he advertised : 'For sale, in barrels and half barrels, fine beer of his own manufacture, which he hopes will be found equal, if not superior, to the famous Burton ale in strength and flavour' : cited in Marshall, p. 69.

each tenant may get an undertenant, till there be none remaining ; the tenant sitting below his landlord, and above his undertenant, that he may be equally ready to pay rent to the one, or receive it from the other ; and if the tenant be in arrear to his landlord, the undertenant must become the debtor for what he owes ; and thus the tenant gets out of debt by having an undertenant . . . the tenants and undertenants may discharge their arrears of rent by *those* who become *their* tenants, when they get into the royal society.[54]

For spelling and reading, which involved the whole school, the pupils were divided into three companies according to their rank, i.e. members of the Royal Society, tenants and undertenants, and sluggards. Each company had its own Chancellor and Vice-Chancellor. The former sat in a high chair and explained any hard words that occurred during a reading lesson. The latter sat in a low chair and corrected any mistakes made by a reader. Both officials had to vacate the chair, however, if any child in the company could get his correction in first.

At the end of each week there was a general reorganization. If a child had kept the office of King or Queen for a week he was given a guinea medal, and had the privilege of calling a parliament after school on Saturday, at which arrears of rent were dealt with ; those in arrears could pay for their discharge, but those who had nothing to give that was acceptable to their landlords had to plead poverty with their feet uncovered and their arrears were discharged 'out of the fund of toys, which were taken from those who used them at improper seasons'. The way was thus clear for new accounts to be opened the following week.

The whole process seems excessively complicated, but would probably have been clearer in the middle of the eighteenth century when feudal rank and obligations were much more familiar to children than they are today. The whole process would probably absorb all the mental and physical energy that the children could give to it, at least for a time, and no doubt many of the children took to it with zest.

However, it was inevitable that some children would sometimes leave their seats or neglect their lessons or show boredom. In order to deal with these, Manson instituted a group called the Trifling Club, a form of punishment from which the children could be freed only by increased diligence towards their lessons ; it was in fact a remedial

[54] Cited in McCallister, p. 336.

measure as much as a punishment, though repeated failure resulted in some form of public censure and shame. The Trifling Club stood in a line at the back of the room, and offenders could only leave this club by successfully reciting their reading and spelling lessons to a partner. Those who failed to win their freedom or who misbehaved in the club itself had to march to their seats with one hand upon their mouth and the other over their left eye to the accompaniment of a 'Ba' or a hiss from the whole class. 'This method of punishment', wrote Manson blandly, 'is never productive of personal resentment ; because all who refused to join in the general censure, would be considered as accomplices and exposed accordingly.'

Manson also introduced the practice of teaching by means of cards. In his day card-playing was an almost universal amusement and taking advantage of this he furnished his pupils with packs of cards similar to playing cards, on which were printed elementary lessons in reading, spelling, and arithmetic, which the children studied as a form of play. This particular project gained great fame ; according to one of his biographers, 'David Manson's cards were long known in Belfast'.[55]

Manson's inventive ability was not confined to the schoolroom. In 1760 he constructed a velocipede, an early form of bicycle, which he leased out to subscribers for use in the mornings and evenings on payment of half a guinea. Manson also gave his pupils free rides on the velocipede as a reward for merit. He invented an improved spinning machine, based on the principle of a spinning wheel which, turned by one man, set in motion twenty spindles. His greatest invention, however, was a 'flying machine'. By means of this machine, he claimed, people would be able 'to raise themselves above the tops of the houses, and thus enjoy a most delightful prospect'. It is almost certain, however, that this machine never got beyond the model stage.[56]

Apart from his talent for invention, Manson took a great interest in social reform. The condition of the handloom weavers attracted his attention and he wrote a book to show that their work need not be done in unhealthy conditions in crowded towns but might be carried on just as well in the pure air of the countryside, in conjunction with a small farm. The book gave detailed instructions on farming techniques and designs for improved dwellings.[57]

Manson wrote two very popular textbooks. The British Museum

[55] Marshall, p. 66.   [56] Ibid., pp. 64–68.   [57] Ibid., p. 68.

has a copy of the 1823 edition of his dictionary entitled *Manson's Pronouncing Dictionary and English Expositor*.[58]   The publishers speak of 'numerous editions' through which the dictionary has passed, which they claimed were 'a strong proof of the intrinsick value of the book, and of the high estimation in which its author was justly held'.[59]   The dictionary measures $5\frac{1}{2}$ inches by $4\frac{1}{2}$ inches, so it is presumably the same as the pocket dictionary first published in 1762.   It contains 208 pages of entries plus a supplementary list containing pronunciation of Biblical names.   The definitions are simple, rarely running into more than five or six words.   The other surviving volume of Manson's is his *Spelling Book*, of which the British Museum has a copy of the 1826 edition ; [60] the preface states that 'many thousand copies are annually sold'.   It is divided into sections of words containing one syllable, of words accented on the first syllable, of words accented on the second syllable, and so on, each section being followed by simple lessons in the use of the words.

Manson's school continued with great success until the last years of his life, when his health failed ; he died on 2 March 1792.   He was described as 'a tall, handsome, clean-skinned, pleasant-looking man, almost always dressed in a drab coat, vest and breeches'.   An oil painting of him, done in his middle years, hangs in the Belfast Academical Institution and shows him looking somewhat like a benevolent Dr. Johnson.[61]   His fame in Belfast was great and his funeral was attended by great crowds.   An eyewitness wrote :

> All classes respected him, and when death called him away, his admirers assembled and insisted on burying him by torchlight.   The vivid scene comes back to me with the fresh recollection of yesterday.   The slow measured tread of the vast multitude, the lights almost endless in profusion, waving, flickering, then stretching out a lurid flame, in which the dark pall of the coffin glistened, as with a ruby hue, the faces thrust out of the windows to see the procession pass, and the shadows thrown upon them by the moving lights — ah, those were times when there were faith and friendship, and appreciation of worth amongst the people of Belfast.[62]

[58] *Manson's Pronouncing Dictionary and English Expositor* (Belfast, 1823).

[59] Ibid., p. iii.

[60] *Manson's Spelling Book, Revised and Corrected for the Use of Schools and Private Families* (Belfast, 1826).

[61] Marshall, pp. 71–72. A water-colour copy of the portrait is reproduced below, facing p. 48.   [62] Ibid., p. 71.

The dynamic of Manson's and Gilpin's work had been a reaction against the educational constrictions of their day — authoritarianism, corporal punishment, the traditional curriculum, and the prevailing attitude that education was a dismal experience, to be enforced by the rod. They based their reforms not on theories but on the way in which a sensible, humane teacher would try to build up good and friendly relationships with children. Their outlook owed nothing to the Enlightenment and they lived before the effects of the Industrial Revolution had influenced educational thought and practice ; some of their schemes have a curiously archaic, semi-feudal air. Nevertheless, they anticipated several aspects of the work of more sophisticated and far more famous successors. William Gilpin and David Manson left no disciples, founded no school of thought, nor did they propound any general theory of education. Those who followed them in the field of educational innovation were to find their inspiration in Continental theory.

2. *Rousseau and English Education in the Late Eighteenth Century*

FEW books have had a greater immediate effect on English educational thought than Rousseau's *Émile*. Coming at a time when new stirrings disturbed the calm waters of eighteenth-century English education, its ideas fused with those of radical and scientific thinkers to create new insights into the nature of children, into methods of teaching, and the scope of the educational process, and these gave new directions to English educational thought. Modern educational methods in England have their origin in the emergence in the late eighteenth century of a new school of theorists who took *Émile* as their guide. Though the group was small in numbers and limited in its immediate effect, its ideas had a slow but steady influence.

A translation of *Émile* first appeared in 1762, in the same year as the French publication. Two further translations appeared in 1763 and the success was great and immediate. This was partly due to the emotional appeal of the book, to its sensibility, a quality greatly prized

in the eighteenth century and which was an essential part of the popularity of all Rousseau's works.[1]   The main appeal of *Émile*, however,
lay in its repudiation of dogmas that were thought to fetter human
development.   Capel Lofft, a political radical and later opponent of
Burke, hailed Rousseau as 'the deliverer of the human mind from many
degrading prejudices destructive of political and private happiness',[2]
and it was this kind of warm tribute that Rousseau won from his
admirers.   Thomas Day rated him as the 'first of humankind',[3] and
devoted an eight-page dedication of the third edition of his anti-slavery
poem *The Dying Negro* to Rousseau, stressing the nobility of his life,
his devotion to his ideals, and his contempt for riches and honours.[4]
William Godwin, a critical admirer, believed that '*Émile* is upon the
whole to be regarded as the principal reservoir of philosophical truth
as yet existing in the world'.[5]   Between the 1760s and 1790s there was,
in fact, an outbreak of Rousseaumania in England.   'Parties are formed
for the destruction and defence of his fame', wrote David Williams, one
of his most judicious followers.[6]   Writers as diverse as Lord Kames,
the Scottish judge, and Mrs. Catherine Macaulay, the radical historian,
wrote admiringly of *Émile*.[7]   As late as the 1790s, the young Wordsworth and Coleridge moved in a circle of enthusiastic Rousseauphiles,
including Charles Lamb, William Hazlitt, and the remarkable Thomas
Poole, a Somerset farmer, self-taught in Latin and French, experimental stock-breeder, founder of a local school, and a supporter of
the French Revolution.[8]   A number of educational novels, with *Émile*
as their model, celebrated in various forms the supremacy of 'natural'
over artificial education ;   they included Henry Brooke's enormously
long *The Fool of Quality* (1766), David Williams's *History of Philo and*

----

[1] J. H. Warner, 'The Basis of J.-J. Rousseau's Contemporary Reputation in
England', *Modern Language Notes*, vol. lv, no. 4 (Apr. 1940), pp. 270–80.

[2] Ibid., p. 274.

[3] R. L. Edgeworth, *Memoirs* (London, 2 vols., 1820), i, p. 226.

[4] T. Day, *The Dying Negro, A Poem* (London, 3rd ed., 1775), p. iv.

[5] W. Godwin, *An Enquiry Concerning Political Justice, and its Influence on General
Virtue and Happiness* (London, 2 vols., 1793), ii, p. 504 n. See also [W. Godwin],
*An Account of the Seminary . . . at Epsom in Surrey for the Instruction of Twelve Pupils
. . .* (London, 1783), p. 4.

[6] D. Williams, *Lectures on Education* (London, 3 vols., 1789), i, pp. 110–11.

[7] Henry Home, Lord Kames, *Loose Hints upon Education* (Edinburgh, 1781), p. 27
and *passim* ; Catherine Macaulay Graham, *Letters on Education* (London, 1790),
passim.

[8] E. Légouis, *The Early Life of William Wordsworth*, trans. J. W. Matthews
(London, 1897), pp. 56, 365–6.

Amelia (1774), Maria Edgeworth's unfinished *Harry and Lucy* (1778), a translation of Madame de Genlis's *Adèle et Théodore* (1783), and the most famous of all, Thomas Day's *Sandford and Merton* (1783–9).

This last near-novel tells the story of the re-education of Tommy Merton, a spoilt, selfish child, corrupted by luxury and idleness. His salvation is brought about by his tutor, Mr. Barlow, and Henry Sandford, a country-bred child of nature. Tommy undergoes a variety of testing experiences, in most of which Day's hatred of aristocratic values, his predilection for bodily hardihood and Sermon on the Mount ethics, and his belief that education should be both useful and elevating, are evident.

Sandford and Merton exemplified the tendency for radicals and reformers who were influenced by Rousseau to focus their interest upon the second book of *Émile*, in which Rousseau's ideal of 'negative education', the physical development of the pupil in natural surroundings, without the benefit of formal lessons, was brilliantly and passionately set out.

Day himself, one of those English radicals who feel it is part of their creed to abandon conventional dress and live simply in the countryside, produced a caricature of Rousseau's injunctions on the hardening of his pupils in the training he gave to Sabrina Sidney, a foundling whom he hoped to make his future wife. Day solemnly believed that in submitting Sabrina to tests of endurance, which included the dropping of hot wax on her bare arms or the firing of pistols close to her ear, he was faithfully following in the footsteps of Rousseau.[9] Others found in *Émile* a sanction for similar experiments.

David Williams confirmed that many attempts were made to educate children as noble savages.[10] He described one child of nature of his acquaintance who, at the age of thirteen, slept on the floor, spoke 'a jargon he had formed out of the several dialects of the family', could not read or write, and appeared to Williams as 'a little emaciated figure ; his countenance betraying marks of premature decay, or depraved passions ; his teeth discoloured, and his hearing almost gone'. Rousseau himself, declared Williams, would have made 'some dreadful exclamation' at the sight.[11]

Richard Lovell Edgeworth, an Irish landowner, educated at Oxford, friend of scientists and industrialists and ceaseless experimenter in

---

[9] G. W. Gignilliat, *The Author of Sandford and Merton: A Life of Thomas Day* (New York, 1932), p. 83.   [10] Williams, i, p. 185.   [11] Ibid., iii, pp. 5–6.

mechanical and educational projects, attempted to bring up his son, Richard Lovell, on an intelligent assessment of the principles of Book II of *Émile*. Between the ages of three and eight the boy led a hardy open-air life, becoming 'bold, free, fearless, generous' and considered by all as very clever. He even passed the critical scrutiny of Rousseau himself, with whom he had a long conversation when Edgeworth visited Paris in 1777. But Edgeworth found in him what seemed to be a flaw : the boy refused to obey anyone but his father. Edgeworth considered the experiment a failure and packed the boy off to boarding-school. He felt the result was partly due to errors in Rousseau's theory, about which he thereafter became less enthusiastic ; but he also admitted his own failure to superintend the boy in the way necessary to make the experiment a success.[12]

Day's *Sandford and Merton* inspired many with its philosophy. The chemist Samuel Galton's daughter, Mary Anne (later Mrs. Schimmel-penninck), took from it an admiration for simple living and a contempt for finery in dress and aristocratic distinctions.[13] Mrs. Gaskell, the biographer of Charlotte Brontë, held that the Reverend Patrick Brontë had formed some of his opinions on the upbringing of his daughters from a reading of Rousseau and Day,[14] and those familiar with the early life of Charlotte, Emily, and Anne hardly need reminding of its Spartan nature. In her life of Charlotte Brontë, Mrs. Gaskell wrote incidentally of the upbringing of an aunt of the Gaskell family, who had been adopted by a disciple of Day's, apparently in the 1790s. The unfor-tunate girl's experiences ranged from being frightened by dressed-up ghosts to being tossed in a blanket ; her otherwise benevolent guard-ians persisted in the blanket-tossing because her obvious dread of it convinced them that they were strengthening her nerves.[15] Robert Southey records a similar regime in early childhood with his Rousseau-phile aunt, Miss Tyler, at Bath.[16]

During the last part of the eighteenth and the early part of the nine-teenth century, these ideas had a widespread influence on the upbring-ing of children. Williams, writing in 1789, maintained that recent

---

[12] Edgeworth, i, pp. 177–9.
[13] C. C. Hankin (ed.), *Life of Mary Anne Schimmelpenninck* (London, 2 vols., 1858), i, p. 10.
[14] E. C. Gaskell, *The Life of Charlotte Brontë* (London, 2 vols., 1857), i, p. 49.
[15] Ibid., p. 50.
[16] Rev. C. C. Southey (ed.), *The Life and Correspondence of the Late Robert Southey* (London, 6 vols., 1849–50), i, p. 70.

alterations and improvements in the management of children and in the discipline of schools had been principally due to the eloquence of Rousseau.[17] Mrs. Gaskell believed that the new ideas had spread widely to all classes of society.[18] No less than thirteen editions of *Sandford and Merton* had been published by 1823, but at least one of its most celebrated readers, the young Charles Dickens, was not impressed. He found Mr. Barlow, 'the instructive monomaniac', too much to bear. 'He knew everything', recalled Dickens in 1869, 'and didactically improved all sorts of occasions, from the consumption of a plate of cherries to the contemplation of a starlight night.' [19]

The didactic element of Day's story inspired a number of moral tales for children in which there was a move away from an appreciation of 'natural' education towards a concern with botanizing and moralizing. Mrs. Trimmer, for instance, wrote a number of stories in which her child heroes collected flowers and grasses, compared and analysed and recorded, while a moralizing parent or tutor was always on hand with lessons on the marvels of God's handiwork and the need for piety and good behaviour.[20]

The same outlook was maintained by Mrs. Barbauld and her brother, John Aikin,[21] and to some extent by Edgeworth's daughter, Maria, in her moral tales. Instead of being allowed to develop at their own pace in natural surroundings under the wise guidance of a tutor, as Rousseau proposed, children became the object of zealous study, and the teacher more intrusive, directing the children's attention to specific aspects of the world around them. The type of instruction exemplified in these volumes tended to overload the child with all the appearances of learning and with wisdom beyond his years, the model satirized by Wordsworth in the *Prelude* :

> A miracle of scientific lore,
> Ships he can guide across the pathless sea,
> And tell you all their cunning ; he can read
> The inside of the earth, and spell the stars ;
> He knows the policies of foreign lands ;

[17] Williams, ii, p. 8.   [18] Gaskell, i, p. 49.

[19] Charles Dickens, 'New Uncommercial Samples : Mr. Barlow', *All the Year Round*, no. 7, N.S., 16 Jan. 1869, pp. 156–9.

[20] Cf. Mrs. Sarah Trimmer, *An Easy Introduction to the Knowledge of Nature, and Reading the Holy Scriptures* (London, 1780).

[21] Cf. [J. Aikin and Mrs. A. L. Barbauld], *Evenings at Home ; or, The Juvenile Budget Opened* (London, 6 vols., 1792–6).

Can string you names of districts, cities, towns,
The whole world over, tight as beads of dew
Upon a gossamer thread ; he sifts, he weighs ;
All things are put to question . . .[22]

This was not the ideal of Rousseau, whose Émile at twelve years of age was healthy and confident, with a free and open manner, untroubled by books or learning.[23] Neither was he, however, the docile young classicist beloved of the more orthodox eighteenth-century educationalists.

What were the leading ideas of Rousseau's *Émile* ? Its originality lay in the fact that it was the first comprehensive attempt to describe a system of education according to nature. The key idea of the book was the possibility of preserving the original perfect nature of the child by means of the careful control of his education and environment, based upon an analysis of the different physical and psychological stages through which he passed from birth to maturity.

Rousseau divided the educative process into four periods, corresponding to the stages of a child's life. 'Every age, every station in life,' he maintained, 'has a perfection, a ripeness of its own.' [24] The first was the period of infancy, from birth to about two years of age, during which the child began to learn to walk and talk and during which he should be free from unnatural restraint. The second period was that of childhood, lasting from two to twelve years, described in Book II of *Émile*. Here Rousseau diverged most from contemporary practice and won for himself the extremes of support and opposition. He argued that this stage should be a time of unrestricted play in natural surroundings, free from intellectual pursuits and external restraint, leaving the child to develop his five senses as he wished. Action should spring from necessity and not from obedience, for the supreme good was not authority but freedom : 'That man is truly free who desires what he is able to perform, and does what he desires. This is my fundamental maxim. Apply it to childhood, and all the rules of education spring from it.' [25] The child should receive no formal academic training, but should be left to make the most of a happy time that would never return : 'the education of the earliest

[22] W. Wordsworth, *The Prelude, or Growth of a Poet's Mind* (London, 1850), bk. v, p. 120.
[23] J.-J. Rousseau, *Émile*, trans. Barbara Foxley (London, 1961), p. 124.
[24] Ibid., p. 122.   [25] Ibid., p. 48.

years should be merely negative', maintained Rousseau. 'It consists, not in teaching virtue or truth, but in preserving the heart from vice and the spirit from error.' [26] This conception of education was only possible if one maintained the fundamental goodness of the child, and Rousseau's expressed belief in this clashed with equally fundamental eighteenth-century orthodoxies concerning the nature of children, and was the chief cause of the vituperation he received from the Church and the establishment :

> Let us lay it down as an incontrovertible rule that the first impulses of nature are always right; there is no original sin in the human heart. . . .[27]

The third period, the pre-adolescent period from twelve to fifteen years, was the age of intelligence for which the previous stage had prepared. The child's appetite for knowledge was now to be whetted through the medium of his present interest and his realization of the useful. Science, geography, and handicraft were among the subjects now to be taken up.

The type of education described in the first three books of *Émile* was specifically designed to free the child from corrupting passions and second-hand opinions, whether emanating from books or from society. His acquaintance would be with the objects of the material world, and necessity and utility would form the spur to discovery. The aim was a child who was 'self-regarding' in the best sense of the term, who was prepared for the next stage of education, his introduction to the moral and social order.

The years after fifteen formed a bridge between childhood and manhood, when the child's moral and social development became the chief concern of his tutor, and to this end the relevance of history, metaphysics, religion, physical training, and sexual knowledge was discussed. Finally, for *Émile* was cast in the form of a novel, came the preparation for marriage, the wedding of Émile and Sophie, and devotion to a life of civic virtue.

These, in brief, are the main points of a work that was destined to change the thinking of whole generations of teachers and to affect educational practice throughout Western Europe. It is often said that Rousseau was the first to put the child firmly in the centre of the educational stage. But he did more than this. In a sense education had always been child-centred, but the child had been seen as an

[26] Ibid., p. 57.   [27] Ibid., p. 56.

object to be operated upon by adults, and made to conform to their rules and methods in order to fit into adult society. Rousseau regarded children as human beings, restored a belief in their essential goodness, and directed attention to the necessity of closely examining their nature and adapting education accordingly. Rousseau's injunction to tutors in the preface to *Émile*, 'Begin thus by making a more careful study of your scholars, for it is clear that you know nothing about them',[28] set the tone for the whole work.

Rousseau's educational views were a product of his discontent with society as a whole. *Émile* was the spearhead of a protest against the stifling formality and elaborate insincerity of the *grand siècle*, a conscious reaction against the artificial child beloved of society families of the time. Taine, the French critic and historian, has painted a remarkable picture of these manikins, the 'embroidered, gilded, dressed up, powdered little gentlemen, decked with sword and sash, carrying the chapeau under the arm, bowing, presenting the hand, rehearsing fine attitudes before a mirror . . .'.[29]

Critics of this conception of life and manners were strongly attracted to an ideal of a simpler and more natural existence which travel and exploration were making popular. The appeal of *Émile* was strengthened by the cult of the noble savage that flourished in the 1770s and 1780s, fed by romantic accounts of the discoveries of the islands of the South Pacific. Commerson's account of Tahiti, and *Hawkesworth's Voyages*, describing Cook's discovery of Polynesia, were two of the many accounts of the ideal natural man that impressed critics of the civilized life.[30] However, Voltaire, in *L'Ingénu*, dared to suggest that a real noble savage might not be well received in civilized France.

In England it was among those concerned with problems of science, industry, public health and education, and philosophical speculation that the ideas of Rousseau found their most receptive audience. The philosophical societies, the majority of whose members stood outside the social, religious, and political establishment, were the focus of the new critical and scientific spirit. Among those associated with the societies were several of the educationalists mentioned earlier in the chapter. Day and Edgeworth, for instance, were among the Lichfield

[28] J.-J. Rousseau, *Émile*, trans. Barbara Foxley, pp. 1–2.
[29] H. A. Taine, *The Ancient Régime*, trans. J. Durand (London, 1876), p. 273.
[30] For an account of the cult of the noble savage see H. N. Fairchild, *The Noble Savage* (New York, 1928) ; C. B. Tinker, *Nature's Simple Plan* (Princeton, 1922).

group who attended meetings of the Birmingham Lunar Society, whose members included the engineers Matthew Boulton and James Watt, as well as Joseph Priestley, Josiah Wedgwood, and Erasmus Darwin, grandfather of Charles. In Manchester a similar group called themselves the Literary and Philosophical Society, whose leading member was Dr. Thomas Percival, pioneer of public-health reform, author of *A Father's Advice to his Daughters*, and a friend of the young Robert Owen. In Liverpool William Roscoe, described as 'banker, politician, poet, historian and art collector', was connected with the Lunar Society and also with William Godwin, Mary Wollstonecraft, and other London radicals.[31]

There were international links as well. Edgeworth, Williams, and Darwin had met Rousseau himself, and Percival was a friend of Diderot and Voltaire. David Williams associated with French and German intellectuals, and was a leading member of the Club of 13 which flourished in the 1770s and 1780s. The members of this body supported the American cause in the War of Independence and corresponded with Franklin and Jefferson; Thomas Day was another member and Priestley and Edgeworth were closely associated with the club.[32] The doctrines of Rousseau could not but find a ready reception in such circles.

Those who were particularly interested in education were Edgeworth, Williams, Day, Priestley, Godwin, Mary Wollstonecraft, Darwin, and Percival, all of whom wrote treatises on the subject more or less influenced by Rousseau. Lord Kames and Mrs. Catherine Macaulay were also, as we have seen, followers of Rousseau, though not members of any philosophical or scientific circle. Edgeworth, Williams, and Day were undoubtedly the most influential protagonists of Rousseau's doctrines and *Sandford and Merton* had a substantial influence on educational thought lasting well into the nineteenth century. David Williams, a radical deist, organized a school run on principles derived from *Émile*, which is more fully described later, and Edgeworth and his daughter Maria are justly celebrated for their *Practical Education*, a work owing much to Rousseau, though Edgeworth himself became, as we know, critical of some of Rousseau's formulations.

---

[31] B. Simon, *Studies in the History of Education, 1780–1870* (London, 1960), pp. 17 ff.

[32] N. Hans, 'Franklin, Jefferson, and the English Radicals at the End of the Eighteenth Century', *Proceedings of the American Philosophical Society*, vol. 98, no. 6 (1954).

The Edgeworths' book influenced, as examples, Robert Owen's practice at New Lanark and some of the teaching methods at Hazelwood
School run by the Hill brothers in Birmingham.

Practical Education was based upon a close and systematic study of
children, those of Edgeworth's second wife, thus exemplifying Rousseau's belief that educational principles should be grounded upon child
nature and that the teaching should conform to their wants, interests,
and feelings. With a variety of ingenious illustrations, Edgeworth
described new and interesting methods of teaching, stressing that education was a happy, creative, and active process.

The impact of *Émile* in English intellectual circles and the rise of a
group of followers alarmed orthodox educationalists who supported
the Anglican public-school and university tradition, and many sprang
to its defence. Vicesimus Knox and John Brown were among the
most representative of the defenders of established educational practice.
Brown, Vicar of Newcastle upon Tyne, man of letters, and critic of
the manners and morals of his day, embodied his views in three sermons
on education published in 1764.[33] The fact that they were published
within two years of the first translation of *Émile* is an indirect tribute
to Rousseau's influence on England.

In opposition to Rousseau, Brown accepted as axiomatic the natural
depravity of youth. The child was naturally evil, and if he was not
taught virtue he would inevitably turn to vice : 'the condition of
human nature inevitably leads him to acquire that which is destructive
of it'.[34] To counteract this, Brown advocated a long training in the
formation of virtuous habits and the eradication of evil passions.[35]
The object was to produce good citizens and to this end Brown was
willing to push his doctrines to extremes :

> even to shackle the mind (if you so please to speak) with salutary
> prejudices, such as may create a conformity of thought and action
> with the established principles on which his native society is built.[36]

Brown did not consider childhood to be an early stage of development
having its own special characteristics in the progress towards a full
personality ; to him, children were incipient adults with unregulated
passions.

A similar view of child nature was taken by Vicesimus Knox, who

[33] J. Brown, *Sermons on Various Subjects* (London, 1764).
[34] Ibid., Sermon I, p. 12.   [35] Ibid., p. 7 ; Sermons II and III, *passim*.
[36] Ibid., Sermon I, pp. 16–17.

succeeded his father as headmaster of Tonbridge School while still in his twenties and whose celebrated defence of classical learning, *Liberal Education*, was published in 1781, before his thirtieth birthday. The book went through nine editions in the following eight years. Knox, described as 'a strenuous supporter of the establishment',[37] wrote as a practical man in opposition to the schemes of Rousseau and the visionaries, and defended 'the ancient system of education, which consists of a classical discipline' precisely because it was coming under attack.[38] The arguments that Knox used have in essentials become the standard defence : the classics make for the 'enlargement, refinement and embellishment of the mind', they have a meliorative effect on the character, and are the best preparation for every liberal pursuit.[39] Hard study of the grammar, followed by the learning of passages by heart, would strengthen the character, but should this fail to stifle 'the vicious propensities of human nature', then corporal punishment should be administered in addition.[40]

If Brown and Knox were content to restate the orthodoxies of the day, others felt that a stronger attack on the visionaries was necessary, and that a much sharper reiteration of the dogma of the innate depravity of the child was essential. The Evangelicals took a leading part in popularizing these doctrines. John Wesley, for instance, described *Émile* as 'the most empty, silly, injudicious thing that a self-conceited infidel wrote', and advocated more religion and stricter control of children, urging 'Break their wills that you may save their soul'.[41] Hannah More, who also saw the enemy in the ideas of Rousseau and the French Enlightenment, consistently stressed the corruption and helplessness of human nature ; the duty of tutors was not only to act upon this belief but also to convey it to young people who, she lamented, 'are peculiarly disposed to turn away from it as a morose, unamiable and gloomy idea'.[42] The whole object of education, she considered, was to counteract the innate depravity of children :

> Is it not a fundamental error to consider children as innocent beings, whose little weaknesses may perhaps want some correction, rather

[37] *Dictionary of National Biography.*
[38] V. Knox, *Liberal Education ; or, A Practical Treatise on the Methods of Acquiring Useful and Polite Learning* (London, 1781), p. 3.
[39] Ibid., pp. 4, 9, 11–12. [40] Ibid., pp. 21, 286, 290.
[41] A. H. Body, *John Wesley and Education* (London, 1936), pp. 19, 52.
[42] Hannah More, *Strictures on the Modern System of Female Education* (London, 2 vols., 1799), ii, p. 255.

than as beings who bring into the world a corrupt nature and evil dispositions, which it should be the great end of education to rectify ? [43]

The whole approach to education as exemplified by these writers has been called the classical-Christian,[44] and it rests on four main propositions : that the child is evil by nature ; that childhood is a preparation for adult life ; that education must therefore consist of that which will be useful to the child when he becomes a man ; and that the value of the subjects taught lies not in their intrinsic interest but in the moral and intellectual training they give.

The mark of the new school of educationalists was that they were prepared to overthrow these assumptions about childhood and child education and begin the study of education afresh on the basis of Rousseau's injunction to make the child and his nature the starting-point. Almost all the leading characteristics of the new school contradicted the classical-Christian presuppositions. The new theorists rejected the almost universal belief that the child was innately wicked, and stressed the desire for knowledge on the part of the child, which it was the function of the tutor to stimulate and direct. They believed in the value of natural virtues and behaviour, and the development of the child according to his own nature rather than in conformity with the artificial qualities demanded by adult society. The importance of interesting the pupil in the educational process was emphasized, with the stress on things rather than on words and memory work. Coercion and authority, of course, had little part to play in the structure of the new education. In the curriculum the emphasis was on the natural sciences rather than on the classical languages and Christian doctrine did not figure largely in their schemes. 'She does not attack religion nor inveigh against it,' said a Baptist minister of Maria Edgeworth and her educational stories, 'but makes it appear unnecessary by exhibiting perfect virtue without it.' [45]

The views and activities of the new school represented, for the first time in modern English educational history, a decisive break with the prevailing ideas of education. Hence the true beginning of modern

[43] Hannah More, i, p. 64.
[44] A. A. Evans, 'The Impact of Rousseau on English Education', *Researches and Studies*, University of Leeds Institute of Education, no. 11 (Jan. 1955), p. 19.
[45] Cited in G. E. Hodgson, *Rationalist English Educators* (London, 1912), p. 162.

progressive education dates from the last quarter of the eighteenth century. Educational thought and practice became polarised round the classical-Christian and what could be called the natural-scientific standpoints. The former had the weight of social approval behind it, the inertia of established practice, and deep roots in the political and religious establishment, and it was a very long time before it was to be dislodged. Despite the fact that the pure gospel of Rousseauism was, in many cases, modified on the one hand into a Spartan-like regime and on the other into the moral tale, nevertheless there remained a noticeable shift of emphasis in the thinking of a significant minority of people. This was towards a greater respect for the personality of the child and for his ability often to initiate his own learning, and away from the mastery of Latin and Greek language and literature, enforced by the rod, as an ideal of education. This change of emphasis took place decisively in the period 1760–1800, but it did not establish itself in England until the nineteenth century and then but rarely, as we shall see. During that century only the radical minority at various levels in society tried the ideas out, and the more general acceptance of the progressive principle in education is only now, two centuries later, becoming possible.

David Williams and the Laurence Street Academy

I

DAVID WILLIAMS, the 'Priest of Nature', radical deist, friend of Franklin and French revolutionary leaders, was the first to put into successful practice the principles of the new school of educationalists inspired by Rousseau. Compared in his own day with Thomas Paine,[1] Williams was the classic case of the political radical turned educational reformer, and in the short-lived school that he opened in Chelsea in 1774 he introduced reforms in organization and discipline, curriculum

---

[1] Madame Roland, *Appeal to Impartial Posterity* (London, 1796), pt. ii, pp. 43–44.

and teaching method, that have been repeated, but scarcely surpassed, from his day to ours.

Williams was a product of the British radical and Dissenting tradition which was itself inspired by the ideals of the European Enlightenment. He was born in Glamorganshire in 1738, the son of a speculator in coal and iron mines. He was educated at Carmarthen Academy and intended for the Dissenting ministry, but on his own testimony he was unsuited by nature for the life of a pastor.[2] He bowed to family pressure, however, and was ordained in 1758, taking up his ministry at Frome in Somerset. Three years later he was invited to Exeter, where he remained for eight years, leaving after disagreements with his congregation to take charge of a Dissenting meeting-house in Highgate, London. In the capital he was able to indulge his love of argument and his fondness for social life. His writings brought him notoriety; following the publication of *Essays on Public Worship* in 1773, he was, according to his first biographer, 'deserted by almost every friend and acquaintance he had in the world'.[3] In 1773 Williams gave up his ministry and decided to set up a school. To aid him in this enterprise he married a girl whom he had long known, took a house in Chelsea, and advertised for pupils. The school was immediately successful and he gave it up only on the death of his wife in 1775.

For the next twenty years Williams played a notable part in the public life of his time as an unrelenting critic of political and religious orthodoxy. He was one of the founder-members of the Club of 13, an organization similar to the Birmingham Lunar Society and the Manchester Literary and Philosophical Society in which other notable educationalists such as Thomas Day, Edgeworth, and Owen had been nurtured. Day, in fact, was also a member of the Club of 13 together with Benjamin Franklin (who first gave Williams the title 'Priest of Nature'), Josiah Wedgwood and his partner Thomas Bentley, Dr. Solander the botanist and Keeper of the Printed Books in the British Museum, and others.[4] One of the first tasks of the club was to help with the drafting of Williams's *Liturgy on the Universal Principles of Religion and Morality*, an early attempt to found a natural religion based upon the essential principles of all religions. In the same year, 1776,

---

[2] *Annual Biography and Obituary for the Year 1818* (London, 1818), p. 18.

[3] T. Morris, *General View of the Life and Writings of the Rev. David Williams* (London, 1792), p. 7.

[4] E. Robinson, 'R. E. Raspe, Franklin's "Club of Thirteen" and the Lunar Society', *Annals of Science*, vol. ii (1955), pp. 142–4.

Williams set up a chapel in Margaret Street, Westminster, where he preached his universal religion, gaining a European reputation both for his ideas and his eloquence.[5] His views were influential in revolutionary France, where they contributed to the cult of the worship of Reason and the Supreme Being in 1793–4.[6] He was made a French citizen, together with Joseph Priestley, Sir James Mackintosh, and other notable Englishmen, helped in the drawing-up of a new constitution, undertook diplomatic missions, and was welcomed to discussions with French philosophers and politicians.[7]

Williams was also in touch with many noted German educationalists, including Dr. K. F. Bahrdt, theologian and deist and head of the Philanthropinum at Heidesheim, and Basedow, the founder of the Dessau Philanthropinum, schools run on the principles of Rousseau. Williams's *Treatise on Education* was translated into German in 1781.[8]

He maintained a large literary output and was responsible for the foundation of the Royal Literary Fund, an institution for helping impecunious authors that is still in being today, and for many years until his death in 1816 Williams helped to advise on and administer this Fund.[9]

II

Williams's decision in 1773 to found a school after relinquishing his career as a Dissenting minister had been maturing in his mind for some time. Soon after arriving in London he had begun the study of education and started taking private pupils.[10] In 1774, he wrote in his autobiography, 'I then took a house at Chelsea and was married, with a view to a plan of education I had long considered'.[11] The house was in Laurence Street, near the river, and was said to have formerly belonged to Mrs. Macaulay Graham, the radical historian and disciple of Rousseau.[12]

Williams had little difficulty in finding pupils and the school was a

[5] Morris, p. 13.
[6] D. Williams, 'More Light on Franklin's Religious Ideas', *American Historical Review*, vol. xliii (July 1938), pp. 803–13.
[7] David Williams's MS. autobiography entitled 'Incidents in My Life', *passim*.
[8] C. J. Phillips, 'The Life and Work of David Williams', unpublished Ph.D. thesis, University of London (1951), pp. 73–80.
[9] E. V. Lucas, *David Williams, Founder of the Royal Literary Fund* (London, 1920), *passim*.   [10] Morris, p. 8.
[11] Williams, MS. autobiography, p. 4.   [12] *Annual Biography, 1818*, p. 20.

success from the first.   During the two years of its existence the number of pupils rose to twenty and several assistants were employed.[13] Most of the pupils were the sons of wealthy or aristocratic parents and some pupils came to Williams from well-known public schools.[14]   His fees were £100 a year, high for that time, but he could hardly ever make the school pay, mainly because he carried out his reforming ideas regardless of cost.[15]   He frequently described his school as 'a family', believing that the educational process was best carried on in a group and not in isolation from society.   Men were formed for mutual assistance, he maintained, and found their happiness not in solitariness but in loving and serving each other.[16]

Williams was determined to avoid the authoritarianism, verbalism, and concentration on the classics that he felt were defects of the average boarding or public school of his day.   The 'superstition', 'mechanic order', and 'iron sceptre of absolute authority' that he saw in these institutions were abhorrent to him, and he felt that their methods of impressing children's minds with maxims, precepts, and rules at an age when they were incapable of apprehending their full significance were a negation of the practice of natural education.[17]   'In all schools', he wrote, 'you may find boys committing parts of Ovid to memory at twelve which they may not understand at forty.'[18]   The popularity of public schools, he thought, was not based upon their educational achievements but on the belief that they encouraged the manly qualities of courage, resolution, and fortitude.[19]

Fundamentally Williams believed in education according to nature and stood four-square on the ground cleared by Rousseau.   He upheld the innate goodness of the child, his educability and perfectibility, and believed that the learning process originated in the impressions made by objects of the natural world upon the human senses.   If a child were brought up according to his normal inclinations in natural surroundings, Williams maintained, he would grow up healthy and with a sound and active mind.[20]   However, he was unwilling to follow Rousseau too far in the matter of natural education, recognizing that the claims of society could not entirely be ignored at any stage in the

[13] D. Williams, *Lectures on Education* (London, 3 vols., 1789), i, p. 236 (hereafter *Lectures*).

[14] Ibid., pp. 165, 236, 260 ; ii, p. 128.

[15] Ibid., i, p. 232.   [16] Ibid., ii, p. 74.   [17] Ibid., i, pp. 59, 97.

[18] D. Williams, *A Treatise on Education* (London, 1774), p. 11 (hereafter *Treatise*).

[19] *Lectures*, ii, p. 204.   [20] *Treatise*, p. 24.

educational process. He believed in the perfectibility and ultimate happiness of man : 'To be happy, and to render others happy is the whole duty of man', he wrote. 'His sensibility, his affections, his reason, are all formed to produce these effects.' [21] Williams conceived that the object of education was to reconcile the claims of nature and the claims of society. Education, he wrote, was 'the art of forming a man on rational principles, and yet making him capable of entering into the community and becoming a useful and good citizen'.[22]

Though Williams accepted the broad outlines of Rousseau's educational theories, he was the first British educationalist to give them searching criticism and to attempt to apply what he considered was valuable in them to the classroom situation. Williams's *Lectures on Education* submitted *Émile* to a thorough examination, and the verdict was on the whole a favourable one. Williams recognized Rousseau's stature, his European influence, and welcomed his criticism of existing educational institutions, his natural and humane attitude to children, and many of his proposals with regard to the curriculum. In fact he confessed that he would deem himself 'mean and reprehensible in an extreme degree' if he withheld 'the tribute of approbation and praise I think due to his memory'.[23] Nevertheless, he could not tolerate Rousseau's tendency 'to speak of everything with passion', nor his 'vague theories and visionary systems'. The latter is perhaps Williams's main criticism of Rousseau. His own object, he declared, was to 'arrange and disentangle' Rousseau's principles, to bring them to the test of experience and to suggest improvements.[24]

Williams's main disagreement was with Rousseau's periodization of child development. That a child should not extend his mental cultivation, develop the use of his reason or his passions, or embrace moral or religious principles between the ages of two and twelve seemed to Williams fanciful and absurd and in no way based upon observation. Because children were not properly employed in schools, argued Williams, it did not mean that they should be allowed to run about 'idly and at hazard', nor, if they grew up as 'prating impertinent puppets', should they be suffered to sink into 'the inattention and stupidity of brutes'.[25] Here Williams obviously had in mind the failure of attempts to rear children of nature mentioned in an earlier

[21] *Lectures*, ii, p. 207.   [22] *Treatise*, p. 15.   [23] *Lectures*, i. pp. 180–2.   [24] Ibid., p. 112.   [25] Ibid., ii, pp. 306–7.

chapter rather than the text of *Émile*. Disgust at contemporary mal-
practices, Williams continued, should not result in a preference for
extreme solutions. A way of teaching children between the ages of
two and twelve could be worked out :

> The common method of confining children to formal lessons to be
> committed to memory, I will allow to be injurious to the under-
> standing, as it is to health. But it does not follow, that children
> are to be left to their own devices, or to obtain information by
> accident. There is a mode of instruction, suitable to the restless
> activity and curiosity of infancy.[26]

Reason and imagination were not innate but ultimately the product
of experience of the external world. The first desire of children, after
food, was for acquaintance with external objects. Reason, in Williams's
view, was the power of comparing objects or ideas of objects, and arose
gradually in children during their early years, and one did not have to
wait, as Rousseau would have it, until 'the moment when reason un-
folds as the sun rises, at a given period'. On the contrary, Williams
maintained, the first twelve years of a child's life was the time when he
most desired and most easily assimilated knowledge. Determined to
prove his point, he had a friend approach Rousseau himself with the
proposition. Rousseau's reply, which could scarcely be considered an
answer, was : 'He had been conversant with artificial children, and I
have referred only to those of nature.' [27]

If by 'artificial children' Rousseau meant children living in society
and hoping to be educated in a school, then his charge was correct.
Williams's concern was with what the tutor could achieve in the school
situation. He conceived the role of the educator to be that of directing
the child's natural curiosity about the world to the proper objects,
and of providing for its 'full and various gratification'. He believed
that the tutor was concerned, in his own expressive phrase, with 'the
management of curiosity'.[28] Each child was born with certain capacities and it was the job of the teacher to lead children into employments and pursuits best suited to those capacities.[29] In this way the
teacher could judiciously aid nature. 'The instructions of nature',
wrote Williams, 'are by trial and experience ; those of education by

---

[26] *Lectures*, p. 307. Williams used the term 'infancy' to denote the period from
birth to twelve years of age.
[27] Ibid., i, pp. 39, 44–45, 54–55 ; ii, p. 308 ; iii, pp. 9, 43.   [28] Ibid., iii, p. 13.
[29] Ibid., i, pp. 101, 186 ; ii, p. 295.

words, maxims and precepts.' [30] The basis of Williams's educational method was thus to contrive incidents in which the effect of a line of conduct could be observed by the child as part of a group. Education became a process that began with the pupil's own situation, and the function of the tutor was not to impose principles by authority but to bring about situations in which the child could learn by means of his own experience. Received ideas, either from books or from the teacher, interfered with this process. Moral conduct depended on the correct perception of the world by the child himself on the basis of his own experience.

Politically Williams was a radical. Though basically a supporter of the Revolution of 1688, he recognized the imperfections of that settlement, which had led to a concentration of political power in the hands of landed proprietors.[31] He believed that the basis of civil and political liberty lay in the 'industry, talents and virtues of the people',[32] and as a 'benevolent reformer' he strove for those reforms that would allow the popular will free play in the state. He was not, he pointed out, a preacher of sedition, but where 'barbarous customs' were waning or 'sanguinary statutes' were crumbling, he would be happy to give his assistance in sweeping them away.[33] He was, however, no democrat in the modern sense. He believed that intellectual liberty based upon the use of reason was possible only for an educated élite, and should not be extended to the mass of the people, who were actuated solely by habit. He further agreed with the view held by many of the radicals of his day that a state system of education would be an interference with political liberty.[34]

Williams was a natural rebel who found it impossible to acquiesce in the political atmosphere and religious orthodoxy of his time. The restraints under which he had been placed as a Dissenting minister gave a sharper edge to his unorthodoxies : 'I was educated among the Saints,' he wrote, 'and now I live, thank God, among sinners.' [35] So great was his contempt for respectable public opinion that at times he encouraged rather than discountenanced scurrilous rumours against

[30] Ibid., i, p. 72.
[31] D. Williams, *Letters on Political Liberty* (London, 1782), pp. 16–18, 21–22 ; *Lectures*, i, p. 153.
[32] *Letters on Political Liberty*, p. 22.
[33] Ibid.   [34] *Lectures*, i, pp. 75 ff. ; *Treatise*, p. 37.
[35] [D. Williams], *Essays on Public Worship, Patriotism, and Projects of Reformation* (London, 1773), p. 25.

himself.[36]   When he began his school, therefore, he was little troubled by the effect that his unusual methods might have on the attitudes of the world at large.   The school soon acquired the reputation of having a principal who 'did nothing like other people'.

The basis of this estimation lay, of course, in Williams's experimental methods and above all in the novelty of his abolition of corporal punishment.   The latter gave rise to some peculiar rumours.   Since it was obvious that no corporal punishment was given in the school itself, it was believed that it was administered privately in a dungeon beneath the house, from which several people allegedly heard the moans and cries of the victims.[37]   Williams, however, was utterly opposed to the view that corporal punishment was necessarily a part of the educational process.   This did not mean that standards of right and wrong were abandoned, or that no penalties existed for transgressions.   On the contrary, he tried to involve the pupils themselves in the creation of a code of conduct and in the reformation of those who did not abide by it.   The basis of his system was a court, consisting entirely of pupils, headed by a magistrate who changed weekly.

Williams, as we have seen, was not the first to introduce student self-government into a school.   His institution of a court had much in common with Gilpin's system.   Unlike Gilpin, however, Williams abolished corporal punishment entirely.   His opposition to it lay not so much in its severity as in the fact that it was often the result of a chance reaction of the child's conduct upon the teacher's feelings, and could thus be arbitrary and brutal.   He put in its place a kind of social contract, to which all subscribed, and by which a transgressor could be punished in accordance with 'equal laws, enacted by general consent, and executed with general approbation'.   In this way boys could not only be stimulated to higher aspirations but also learn to endure severities because they saw justice in them.   The great thing, however, was that the boys themselves should habitually make and exercise the laws and thus experience and appreciate 'habits of regulated liberty and moral virtue'.

Williams was consistent in submitting himself to the rulings of the court and not interfering in their decisions, relying upon experience to correct errors.   At one point the court decided that discretion and responsibility for punishment should be entirely vested in Williams

[36] Morris, p. 19.   [37] *Lectures*, i, pp. 232–5.

himself. But he successfully argued against this, quoting in his favour a case of cruelty by the mother of one of his boys, and pointing out that if not even a mother could be entrusted with the power to punish, then why should it be invested in a tutor ? On the whole, the court worked extremely well, and only occasionally did consistent male-factors form themselves into factions. In proportion that the laws were good, Williams pointed out, fewer sanctions were needed.[38]

Generally speaking the court dealt with day-to-day infractions of school discipline. But sometimes Williams supplied it with a contrived situation. On one occasion he hired a boy from a local workhouse and assured the court that they could have him as a servant if they could cure him of his constant lying. At first the court was convinced that they could never cure him without the use of corporal punishment, but Williams reminded them that whatever was decided upon would be binding both upon himself and on all the pupils. This proposition they debated at such length that supper was long delayed. But Wil-liams was pleased, because they were discussing a situation that affected their own school lives, and he declared that he would rather have heard their debate 'than the most celebrated contest of Greek or Roman eloquence'. But no conclusion was reached. One unlooked-for con-sequence of the debate was, however, the sudden descent upon the school by the father of one of the boys, who removed his son on the grounds that such thoroughgoing insistence on truth would make the boy a dupe of society when he left school.

That particular boy had also been the major cause of the deadlock in the court ; on his departure the members decided to take the work-house boy as their servant and to correct his lying by means of con-trivances rather than punishment, delving into classical and modern authors for suggestions. Though Williams dismissed the boy before the experiment was finished, he considered his purpose achieved. For some time the boys concerned had been 'intensely occupied in the cure of lying', and had thus become 'the instruments of their own correction or improvement, while they appeared to be occupied on the faults of others'. Thus was virtue produced from the lessons of experience.[39]

Williams's remedial methods were not confined to the operations of the court, but included work with boys whose education had been

[38] Ibid., pp. 241-2 ; iii, pp. 46-49, 59-61, 65, 67, 85-91.
[39] Ibid., i, pp. 240-8.

neglected or deficient.   One of his most spectacular successes concerned
a boy, the son of an almost insane father and a mother who had died
young, who was, in Williams's view, 'just beyond the limits of idiot-
ism', and of whom he almost despaired.   'I have sifted every atom of
his frame,' he declared, 'and it is all rubbish.'   Despite having had
educational opportunities greater than 'half the princes in Europe',
the boy did not even fully know the alphabet.   In particular, his
inability to learn four letters of the alphabet defeated every usual
method of teaching him to read.

Williams devised a plan based on the boy's very healthy appetite.
The letters he could not learn were, for one week, to stand for meat,
vegetables, bread, and beer respectively, and these could only be
obtained at table by submitting the appropriate letter.   If a mistake
were made, the article of diet concerned was lost.   In four attempts the
boy failed twice and thus lost half his dinner.   Williams not only
forbade the other boys to help him, but also insisted that their sole
communication with the illiterate youth be made by means of printed
words cut out of dictionaries.   The boys considered it a delightful
game, and within a short time Williams had to restrain his pupils from
cutting up every book in the house.   But the two methods were remarkably effective ; within three months the boy had learned to read
fluently and intelligently, mainly, as Williams pointed out, by the use
of his own abilities, stimulated, of course, by hunger and the need for
communication.   Williams used this method on other backward
readers, always with success.   He also tried using small printing-
presses for the same object but found them less successful, though
excellent remedies for bad spelling.[40]

Once, however, Williams tried an expedient that reads like a parody
of his own methods.   In this case the boy could read but was completely
averse from even opening a book, preferring to indulge his interest in
horses and food.   In order to bring the boy around to books, Williams
proposed two new school laws : that all food (except the minimum
necessary for life) and the use of horses should be forbidden until
comprehensive accounts of the origins of food and the nature and
management of horses were produced from certain suggested books ;
for was it not time to abolish the credulity with which their health was
committed to the care of cooks and the horses to the care of servants ?
On this occasion, however, the boy for whom it was intended saw

[40] *Lectures,* ii, pp. 139–43.

through the stratagem, and parental trouble ensued. Though the parents eventually supported Williams, this was too obvious a case of the teacher pushing a favourite method to absurdity.[41]

All Williams's efforts were infused with moral teaching. In fact he rarely lost an opportunity to point out the moral consequence of any course of action. But his morality had nothing in common with the conventional piety and sentimentality of the Hannah More type. The most important virtue he considered to be truth, which he defined as 'a disposition to represent to others the information and ideas that occur, exactly as they occur'.[42] In this he felt he had an example to set ; every caller at the house was given an answer with scrupulous exactitude and Williams never allowed himself to be represented as 'out' when he was on the premises, no matter how busy he was. Only thus, he felt, could he convince his charges that he was in earnest about the practice of truth, for he realized that 'any ground of suspicion of my sincerity would have been instantly and fairly occupied by the majority'.[43]

In addition to personal example, he tried various methods to cure lying when he found it. On one occasion he cured a boy of falsehood by secretly taking another boy into his confidence, getting him to fight and insult the first youth, and then disbelieving the liar's story when he came seeking help. Not content with this, he asked his confederate's help in seeking to remedy the alleged lack of truth in the other.[44] But, predictably, Williams sometimes was too clever and complicated and suffered the consequences of his own success.

His pupils, with the zealousness of the newly converted, would carry their insistence upon truth at all times home with them in the holidays, frequently to the astonishment and indignation of their families and friends. As a result, the single-minded Williams found that complaints from parents 'poured on me'.[45] In one instance a boastful and talkative boy inclined to romancing had been cured of this tendency by a decision of the court to send him to Coventry for every falsehood. Immediately his parents wished to remove him on the grounds that 'secret severities' must have been used to turn the brilliant raconteur into 'a blunt insufferable brute'. But the boy himself strongly contradicted his parents, declaring his treatment to be 'kind and affectionate', and expressing a desire to return, which he did.[46]

---

[41] Ibid., iii, pp. 46–49.   [42] Ibid., i, p. 32.   [43] Ibid., p. 238.
[44] Ibid., pp. 226–9.   [45] Ibid., pp. 259–60 ; ii, pp. 14–15.
[46] Ibid., i, pp. 260–8.

Perhaps the most revolutionary step was Williams's abdication of the traditional role of teacher. He had early realized, as many a teacher has done since, the difficulty of obtaining the entire confidence and friendship of a class, and he noticed that the confidence of each class centred not on himself but on the leading boy. As Williams believed that the purposes of a rational education were lost without rapport between teacher and pupils, he gradually gave up his position as a teacher and became a member of every class, receiving instruction in common with the pupils and going ahead of them merely in order to stimulate them to further efforts. In this way he found it easy to acquire the pupils' confidence, since he was no longer in a position of power or authority. In addition, he noticed that it kept his assistants up to the mark to find the principal of the Academy a member of their classes ! [47]

At one period, Williams tried a further unorthodox teaching method. This arose from an experiment designed to help a boy who, because of an early infirmity, had never learned to read. Williams put him under the care and tuition of another boy, and was interested to find that he learned more rapidly than by any other method yet tried. From then on the whole school went over to 'reciprocal assistances', as Williams called the method. Though it differed in intention and organization from the later monitorial system of Bell and Lancaster, Williams's method was essentially the same in so far as boys taught boys. Again, the chief sufferers seem to have been the assistants, who were forced to forgo their 'assumed dignity' and step down from their ranks of 'imagined consequence'.[48]

As might be expected from the abandonment of normal teaching methods, Williams's Academy did not adhere to the common practice of having a fixed curriculum, with regular lessons at particular times of the day. In some ways Williams anticipated twentieth-century practice in the integration of subjects and the introduction of what is now called the project method. Nevertheless, the pupils tackled an extremely wide range of subjects, some of which were admittedly included in deference to the usages and customs of society. His Academy offered geography, history, languages — which included Greek, Latin, Italian, and French — natural history, mathematics, astronomy, moral and political philosophy, poetry and eloquence, and science, including the special study of chemistry.[49] Though no rigid division of subjects according to age was made, Williams felt that

[47] *Lectures*, ii, pp. 310–11.   [48] Ibid., pp. 127–31.   [49] Ibid., pp. 121–2.

advanced science, chemistry, and the higher reaches of philosophy were better suited to the twelve to fifteen years age-group.

Williams's most notable break with tradition was to dethrone the classics from first place in the curriculum and substitute the study of natural history. In this he directly followed Bacon, who, he pointed out, was the first to indicate the natural order of the sciences and to postpone until a later date subjects that were incomprehensible to young children.[50] Williams's view that natural history — 'the first pursuit of the human mind', as he called it — was peculiarly suited to the young had been stimulated by his experiences with a six-year-old child in the days before he opened the school. Both tutor and pupil had begun a study of the subject by gathering botanical specimens, and then took part in harvesting and gardening. After this they examined the furniture of the house, classified the wood involved in its making, then constructed their own. They searched for stones and ores, smelted them, and constructed metal objects. The classification and designation of the objects involved the need to practise drawing and arithmetic. The child made progress that astonished Williams ; in his own young days, he confessed, he had 'waded in wretchedness through volumes of arithmetic calculations' without comprehension.[51]

In his school, Williams used natural history as a means of introducing the study of languages ; specimens of flora were obtained from gardens to which they had access, and after the names and properties had been ascertained, the Greek, Latin, Italian, and French equivalents were obtained in that order. Williams employed native Greeks to teach Greek, and Jesuit novitiates to teach Latin, although he said he had a distaste for the alleged 'interference and intrigue' of Jesuit fathers.[52]

Williams's attitude to learning languages was a utilitarian one. 'The only possible use of learning languages,' he wrote, 'is to know what was written in them.' [53] This cut across the prevailing view as put forward by Knox, for instance, that the study of Latin and Greek was useful in itself and its fruits of universal application. Certainly Williams had no objection to the Greek and Latin authors as such — he was steeped in a knowledge of them, and derived many of his educational ideas from this source. But he understood that much of the

[50] Ibid., p. 312.   [51] Ibid., i, pp. 133–40.   [52] Ibid., ii, pp. 122–4.
[53] *Treatise*, p. 124.

classical heritage was beyond the grasp of children. He thought it was painful to hear young children discuss the thoughts of Socrates and Plato when they almost entirely lacked a knowledge of men and the world.[54] Williams liked to use the classical authors as sources of guidance concerning points of law and morality in problems that cropped up in the investigations of his pupils.

Williams was always looking for new approaches in the presentation of subjects. Geography, for instance, was not introduced with astronomy, as Rousseau had advocated, but was taught by what we now call the concentric system, beginning with the survey of a house, then proceeding to a neighbourhood, a district, and so on. Williams's pupils made several excursions for this purpose, thus anticipating the method later used by the Hill brothers at Hazelwood. Once the boys had reached the stage of studying the oceans and the world, then they could proceed from a study of climatic variations to an examination of the solar system. Needless to say, Williams's pupils made their own maps and globes and studied the construction of clocks.[55] But Williams's geography was largely human geography; the divisions of the earth were considered as habitations of man, in relationship one with the other. This logically entailed the study of the history of mankind, beginning with an examination of the 'fabulous origin or settlement of men', and tracing their history from the banks of the Ganges and Euphrates all over the globe.[56] Geography, astronomy, and history thus became in effect a unified study of the history of man in his environment.

All these studies Williams considered suitable for boys up to the age of about twelve. Beyond that age there were facilities for the study of chemistry, hydrostatics, and the construction of air-pumps.[57] But the older boys were encouraged to go beyond mere investigations. A group of them studied the papers of the Royal Society, and finding some of them 'puerile, improbable and foolish', wrote a number of mock-serious questions to that body. For instance :

> Q.1. The Transactions containing an account, of its having rained mice in Iceland, we wish to know, whether they had any qualities or properties different from earthly mice — whether they had the same pilfering disposition, and the same predilection for cheese.[58]

[54] D. Williams, *Lectures on the Universal Principles and Duties of Religion and Morality* (London, 2 vols., 1779), i, p. 195.   [55] *Lectures*, iii, pp. 11–12, 22–25.
[56] Ibid., pp. 26–27.   [57] Ibid., pp. 28–32.   [58] Ibid., p. 35.

William Gilpin

David Manson

David Williams

Children dancing at Robert Owen's school at New Lanark

The South London Rational School at 3 Blackfriars Road. The building was formerly known as the Rotunda. Note the Owenite text above the proscenium arch

This study of the Royal Society's *Transactions* was symptomatic of Williams's encouragement of older boys to study primary sources. Despairing of finding suitable textbooks, he encouraged them to consult the French *Encyclopédie* and the transactions of several European philosophical societies. These were not to be read *seriatim*, but to be looked at only when required for information or for the construction of a particular machine. In this way boys of thirteen or fourteen read the *Transactions* with avidity and understood, for instance, the principles on which heat and cold were measured 'as well as any philosophers in Europe'.[59]

Williams must have been the first modern schoolmaster to teach political economy. Characteristically, he avoided presenting principles or systems, not because of any tendency to impartiality, but because, as we have seen, he believed in the empirical method of beginning with the boys' own situations and status and working from there. Nearly all his pupils came from wealthy or landed families,[60] and at first Williams found it difficult to give them a clear and accurate idea of property (for possession, he noted, did not lead to a clear understanding of claim and right), so he tried several experiments. He divided his annual income into equal portions for a month, a week, and a day, to show how best it could be used for the good of the school. This was after a disastrous attempt to put the whole household economy into the pupils' hands ; the result was 'to render me poor and the young men avaricious'. We are not told what Mrs. Williams's reactions were.[61] On another occasion he put all the allowances and presents of the pupils into a common fund, which led the pupils, by analogy, to divide the country's national income by the total population, and they were astonished to find that this gave no more than 8*d.* a day to each inhabitant, or, excluding Sundays and holidays, no more than 2*d.* a day for the very poorest. This caused some pupils to attempt the experiment of living on 2*d.* a day — until the rumour went round that Williams was keeping his pupils on starvation rations for his own benefit ! Williams noticed, however, that the immediate question that his pupils asked of the national income was : 'Why should it not be equally divided ?' This enabled Williams to put before his pupils the idea of the essential unity of mankind, and to encourage them to search in history for the origins of the division into rich and poor.[62]

[59] Ibid., ii, pp. 316–17 ; iii, pp. 27–32. [60] Ibid., i, pp. 236, 260 ; ii, p. 128.
    [61] Ibid., ii, pp. 265–7. [62] Ibid., iii, pp. 211–12, 218–21.

A third experiment was to declare all the 'raw materials' of the house-hold common property and to make the pupils' skill in converting them to use the only grounds of a claim upon them. Some naturally produced more than others and so could claim more raw material, but since their talents gave general enjoyment and did not result in sub-jecting others to their will, this did not matter. Thus, Williams pointed out, the pupils learned in practice the use of surplus production, 'the spring both of alienation and of social industry', in the fostering of the useful arts.[63] Furthermore, in order to counter the tendency to inequality produced by parents' 'indiscreet and enormous allowances of money' to some pupils, Williams contrived to make the boys give some of their money to charitable causes, and taught them not to expect gratitude, in keeping with his views that actions should be performed for moral and useful reasons and not under the stimulus of reward and punishment.[64]

Williams also gave his pupils some experience of what today we should call sociology. He asked his pupils to examine the rank of society from which they came, and to estimate their place in society and their prospects in the light of the school maxim 'Every idle man is a knave'. Classical authors were also sifted to discover their attitudes to rank, honour, and riches ; the result was a modification in the attachment to these properties by many of the pupils. In fact Williams had to prevent some of the younger pupils from adopting the maxim that 'Goodness is the sister of poverty'. Some of the older pupils, in consequence of their studies, even changed their views on the prospects that their families envisaged for them.[65]

As might be expected from Williams's religious position, the teach-ing of Anglican Christianity found no place in his school. Religious teaching in Williams's Academy was, in effect, the comparative study of world religions. Like most deists, Williams opposed both organized Christianity and atheism ; to him the world was divided between 'the votaries of superstition' and 'those of a coarse contemptuous . . . infidelity',[66] and he had, therefore, no desire to induce his pupils to accept any one religion nor to promote unbelief. His pupils, who included Anglicans and Dissenters, Catholics and Jews,[67] spent their time in 'tracing the pretensions of all sacred systems to their origin', and in critically examining 'ancient and modern miracles'. The

[63] *Lectures,* iii, pp. 77–81.   [64] Ibid., ii, pp. 157–8, 169–71.

[65] Ibid., iii. pp. 138–40.   [66] Ibid., ii, p. 22.   [67] Ibid., p. 46.

estimate of each religion was left to the discrimination of the pupils.

Williams's method in all these studies was to present certain basic human principles and then to examine social and political problems in the light of these. This was particularly useful in the study of social history :

> If you induce youth to start on level ground ; to consider themselves as of a common species ; and to allow the expedience or advantages of general competence and happiness ; which are irrefragable data in the science or philosophy you would cultivate ; you may deduce all the possible sources of inequality, power, or opulence, in a manner extremely favourable to humanity and benevolence.[68]

Thus in the study of history, economics, religion, and associated subjects, Williams confined himself to suggesting universal truths, in the light of which investigations might be carried out, or presenting questions for his pupils to try to answer. In this he was true to his belief that the role of the tutor was to guide and stimulate rather than to issue statements that he expected his pupils to accept unquestioningly.

III

Williams made the first, and indeed the only consistent attempt to apply the basic principles of *Émile* to the education of a group of boys in a classroom situation. As early as the 1770s he raised nearly every problem that later generations of schoolteachers have had to meet, and of all the educationalists described in this volume, Williams has strong claims to be considered the most enterprising and successful experimentalist. His great strength was his use of psychological theory. With Rousseau as a guide he tried to understand the psychology of the child by means of close observation, and to base his teaching upon his theories. Williams saw that it was essential first to observe and understand children and then to contrive situations in which they could learn from their own experience ; the role of the teacher was the management of the child's natural activities and propensities and in practice this meant giving the pupil's initiative full play.

This, of course, involved a good deal of individual tuition and guidance, but Williams did not neglect the group. Some of his teaching

[68] Ibid., iii, pp. 223.

was the earliest example of successful group methods in education. He involved his students in the disciplines and loyalties of group work, particularly in the maintenance of school discipline. The traditional role of the teacher, with its assumed dignity, he more or less abandoned. In one of his most revolutionary experiments he became a member of the student group, exercising leadership not by the authority of his position but by changing the direction and achievements of the group from within.

His experiments in the curriculum and teaching methods anticipated nearly all the innovations that claimed originality in the nineteenth or even the twentieth century. This was particularly true of the introduction of a wide range of subjects, the emphasis on science as opposed to the classics, the introduction of new subjects such as economics and sociology into the curriculum, the integration of subjects, natural methods of language teaching, the project method, the concentric method of geography teaching, and so on.

Though his substitution of the school court in place of corporal punishment was not original, he carried it out more thoroughly and elaborately than had been done before. His remedial work, however, was something new in educational practice. He saw that delinquency originated in psychological disturbance and was remediable by methods based upon close study of the child's nature. Though he was one of the first teachers to recognize the need for a psychological basis for educational practice, he considered that his own work in this field was merely a beginning. He believed that 'great attention should be given to the human mind ; a subject superior to all others, as a matter both of curiosity and importance ; but a subject very little understood'.[69] Williams hoped that a genius would arise who would give to the world 'a simple, compleat, and intelligible idea of a human mind'. With prophetic insight, he continued :

> Till this is done, men in general who are incapable of thinking and forming ideas for themselves, will have no rules to go by in education. They must proceed, as they do now, at random, and apply as well as they can, any directions which fall in their way to the use of their pupils.[70]

[69] *Treatise*, p. 44.   [70] Ibid.

Section Two

THE INDUSTRIAL REVOLUTION

AND AFTER

4. Robert Owen and the New Lanark Schools [1]

I

Owen is probably the best-known educationalist to be considered in this volume. The story of his environmentalist theories, his communitarian colonies, and his educational experiments at New Lanark has been told many times. With what justification can his views and practices be examined once again ? If little can be added to our factual knowledge of Owen's life and philosophy it is still possible for a fresh approach to be made to the problem of Owen as a progressive educationalist. What were the sources of his views on education ? How did they differ from the commonly accepted theories of his time ? In what degree were his experiments radically new and how did they compare with current and preceding practice ? The answers to these questions will help to assess the position of Owen in the progressive tradition.

Owen's life (1771–1858) covers the traditionally accepted time-span of the Industrial Revolution, and he accepted the existence and implications of industrial change. He was born fourteen years before his future father-in-law David Dale set up one of the first cotton-spinning

[1] This chapter owes a great deal to discussions with Prof. J. F. C. Harrison of Wisconsin University. It was completed before the publication of H. Silver's *The Concept of Popular Education* (London, 1965). His views on Robert Owen as an educator and those in this chapter are in broad agreement.

mills in the British Isles at New Lanark, and died seven years after the
Great Exhibition had proclaimed Britain's world industrial supremacy.
His life and fortune as a cotton magnate were bound up in the progress of Britain's industry and he had watched in his own lifetime,
as Wordsworth had, the rise of the towns of industrial England :

> Abodes of men irregularly massed
> Like trees in forests — spread through spacious tracts,
> O'er which the smoke of unremitting fires
> Hangs permanent . . .[2]

Though Owen was aware of the attractions of the pre-industrial
pastoral society,[3] he did not look back upon it with the nostalgia of
Wordsworth, but accepted the new industrial system as the one in
which his life had to be lived. 'He was the first British writer who
grasped the meaning of the Industrial Revolution', wrote Max Beer
in his introduction to Owen's autobiography,[4] and he was impressed
by the possibilities for production of the new industrialism, and how
its new sources of wealth might be used for the benefit of the people.[5]
He realized that the character of the working class had been 'formed
chiefly by circumstances arising from trade, manufactures and commerce',[6] and could only be transformed by a change in society, a
process in which education would play a crucial part.

If the economic potentialities of industrial Britain were one main
element in Owen's outlook, the philosophical thought of the Enlightenment was another that informed his theories, particularly those on
education. The difficulties of tracing the sources of Owen's intellectual
outlook are increased by his own unwillingness to give credit to
others, and by the fact that many of the ideas of the Enlightenment
came to him at second or third hand from friends and acquaintances.

This chapter will suggest that the importance and significance of
Owen's progressivism in education lies in his successful attempt to
unite the broad principles of the new school of educationalists outlined earlier with the actual conditions of the working-class child, a
process that represented a completely new direction in British educa-

---

[2] W. Wordsworth, *The Excursion* (London, 1814), bk. viii, p. 370.
[3] R. Owen, *Observations on the Effects of the Manufacturing System* (London, 1815),
pp. 6–7.
[4] M. Beer, introduction to *The Life of Robert Owen* (London, 1920), pp. v–vi.
[5] R. Owen, *Report to the County of Lanark for a Plan for Relieving Public Distress*
(Glasgow, 1821), pp. 1–4.
[6] Owen, *Observations on the Manufacturing System*, p. 5.

tion. The theories of *les philosophes*, the Émilian experiments, the education of the child according to nature, had formerly been confined to the children of the middle and upper classes. The children of the poor, whether in monitorial, charity, or industrial schools, had been subjected to a narrow curriculum, rote methods of learning, and a conviction that the chief aim of education was the inculcation of habits of social passivity in a narrow vocational context.

Andrew Bell and Joseph Lancaster, originators and popularizers of the monitorial system, had called able children monitors when they were old enough and had set them to instruct, in a more or less mechanical fashion, the less able children in the elements of reading, writing, arithmetic, and religion, and had placed the monitors under the charge of a single master. The Anglican schools of the National Society led by the Rev. Dr. Bell and the Dissenters' schools of the British and Foreign Schools Society led by the Quaker Joseph Lancaster were at the peak of their very considerable popularity when Owen opened his schools at New Lanark in 1816.

The genius of Owen lay in his break with this system and the introduction of the working-class child to the methods of education according to nature. The significance of Owen's contribution can therefore best be understood if we examine the genesis of his educational theories, the way in which they differed from those of Bell and Lancaster, and the manner in which he put his views into practice at New Lanark.

II

The two major influences in Owen's early life were Manchester and Scotland. Having lost his belief in Christianity in his early teens after a study of comparative religion,[7] he came to see human nature 'through a medium different from others'.[8] His scepticism, the improvement in the habits and attitudes of the operatives at Drinkwater's mill in Manchester that his reforms when manager there brought about,[9] combined with a 'study of the history of the human race', gave him 'the early habit of considering man the necessary result of his

---

[7] R. Owen, *The Life of Robert Owen* (London, 2 vols., 1857), i, p. 16 (hereafter *Life*). Owen's autobiography is in two volumes numbered I and IA, but the narrative is entirely in Vol. I, the second volume containing reprints of various pamphlets and documents.   [8] Ibid., p. 30.   [9] Ibid., p. 31.

organization and the conditions by which nature and society surrounded him'.[10]

During his ten years in Manchester in the last decade of the eighteenth century, Owen immersed himself in scientific and philosophical
discussion. At Manchester Academy he argued with John Dalton,
founder of the atomic theory and Professor of Mathematics and Experimental Philosophy there,[11] and also crossed swords with the young
Samuel Taylor Coleridge, then under the influence of Southey's
Rousseauist views.[12] At the Manchester Literary and Philosophical
Society he rapidly became a member of the inner circle, contributing
a paper each session during his residence in Manchester. The Society
had similar aims and purposes to the clubs to which Williams, Edgeworth, Day, and others belonged some years before,[13] and Owen
became friendly with its leading member, Dr. Thomas Percival, a
Unitarian who had studied medicine at Edinburgh University and who
was a close friend of David Hume and a correspondent of the French
philosophers Voltaire, Diderot, Condorcet, and d'Alembert.[14] Owen
also became an active member of the Manchester Board of Health,
another of Percival's concerns, and contributed to the improvement
of the health and sanitation of industrial Manchester. It was in this
connection that Owen first came across the name of David Dale, whose
daughter he later married. In 1796 the Board of Health addressed a
questionnaire to Dale, then the benevolent owner of the New Lanark
cotton mills[15] to the management of which four years later Owen was
to succeed.

Through his acquaintance with Dr. Percival and others the ideas of
French philosophical and educational thought, which directed attention
to the conscious control of the environment in the interests of humanity
and the important role that education would play in this process,[16]

[10] *Life*, p. 30.

[11] Ibid., p. 36; R. A. Smith, *Memoir of John Dalton* (London, 1856), p. 27.

[12] E. K. Chambers, *Samuel Taylor Coleridge* (Oxford, 1938), pp. 25 ff.; E. H.
Coleridge, *Letters of Samuel Taylor Coleridge* (London, 2 vols., 1895), i, p. 79.

[13] See above, Chap. 3.

[14] F. Espinasse, *Lancashire Worthies*, 2nd ser. (London, 1877), pp. 174, 178;
E. M. Fraser, 'Robert Owen in Manchester', *Memoirs and Proceedings of the Manchester
Literary and Philosophical Society*, vol. lxxii (1937–8).

[15] S. E. Maltby, *Manchester and the Movement for National Elementary Education,
1800–1870* (Manchester, 1918), p. 16.

[16] S. E. Ballinger, 'The Idea of Social Progress through Education in the French
Enlightenment Period: Helvétius and Condorcet', *History of Education Journal*, vol.
x (1959), pp. 88–99.

were mediated to Owen, together with a practical realization of the role of science and rational organization in the improvement of public welfare.

Owen's move to New Lanark did not deprive him of similar intellectual stimulation. In Scotland he became 'on the most friendly terms with many of the professors of the Universities of Edinburgh and Glasgow', of whom he mentions two by name, Professors Jardine and Mylne, who sat with him on a platform to welcome Lancaster to Glasgow.[17] George Jardine, Professor of Logic at Glasgow University from 1787 to 1824, was one of the instigators of 'Scottish democracy' in university teaching, and was recently described as one of the greatest examples of the Scottish academic tradition and one of the chief formulators of its ideals.[18] In his youth a friend of Helvétius and d'Alembert,[19] he attempted not only to relate the study of philosophy 'to the business of active life', but also to ground its teaching upon conversational and Socratic methods, and to give the students themselves a part in the running of his courses.[20]

James Mylne was Professor of Moral Philosophy at Glasgow University, a liberal and a supporter of Jardine's system of education.[21] Both these men were part of a university tradition that was based upon philosophy, the exact sciences, and the classics, with philosophy in the commanding position, in contradistinction to the classical specialization of Oxford and the mathematical preoccupations of Cambridge.

The Scottish university tradition, which included the influences of David Hume, Dugald Stewart, Adam Ferguson, and Adam Smith, was instinct with the values of reason and nature, a deistical view of the universe, and an empirical 'common-sense' approach to man and society.[22] Thus, during his early manhood, from the 1790s to the opening of the New Lanark schools in 1816, Owen's educational theories developed in harmony with the views of the Enlightenment and of those who advocated education according to nature. Before this, however, he had a curious flirtation with the monitorial system.

---

[17] *Life*, p. 107.
[18] G. E. Davie, *The Democratic Intellect* (Edinburgh, 1961), p. 10.
[19] *A Biographical Dictionary of Eminent Scotsmen* (London, 3 vols., 1869), ii, p. 388.
[20] Davie, pp. 14–15.   [21] Ibid., p. 39.
[22] Gladys Bryson, *Man and Society: The Scottish Inquiry of the Eighteenth Century* (Princeton, 1945), *passim*.

III

Owen claimed that he first took an interest in education while in Manchester. 'My mind', he wrote later, 'had been early deeply impressed while in Manchester with the importance of education for the human race.' [23]   It was not until he had been some years at New Lanark, however, that he began to take an interest in specific methods of education, when he was attracted to the monitorial system of Bell and Lancaster that was then beginning to sweep the country as the very latest in educational improvements. He was inspired 'to seek out Joseph Lancaster in his obscurity',[24] and to support him with loans and gifts, and a little later to aid Bell in a similar manner.

Owen's donations to Lancaster totalled some £1,000, and he offered a similar sum to Bell if the National Society would make their schools unsectarian, adding a rider that he would reduce the sum to £500 if they failed to do so. The Society accepted the £500 and retained their religious identity, but Owen believed that his offer subsequently induced the Society to adopt a somewhat less strict policy on the matter.[25]

Owen regarded the monitorial systems of Bell and Lancaster as a first step in the preparation of the public mind for the reception of his own educational theories, in so far as it directed attention to 'the beneficial effects on the unresisting young mind of even the limited education which their systems embrace'.[26]

Owen's praise of Lancaster's system was for its effect upon the character of children and not for its formal content, of which there was, of course, very little. In his speech as chairman at a public dinner in Glasgow, to which he had invited Lancaster in 1812, Owen declared that children in a Lancasterian school

> must learn the habits of obedience, order, regularity, industry and constant attention, which are to them of more importance than merely learning to read, write, and account, although we all know and feel the advantages which these have given to each of us.[27]

[23] *Life*, p. 84.
[24] R. Owen, *The New Existence of Man upon the Earth* (London, 1854), pt. ii, p. 1.
[25] *Life*, pp. 84–85.
[26] R. Owen, *A New View of Society ; or, Essays on the Principles of the Formation of the Human Character* (London, 1813–14), Essay First, p. 16.
[27] 'Mr. Owen's Speech at a Public Dinner at Which he Presided, given to Joseph Lancaster at Glasgow in 1812', *Life*, App. A, p. 251.

Thus the importance to Owen of the monitorial system was, as he stressed earlier in his speech, a social one — to remove from the population 'gross ignorance and extreme poverty, with their attendant misery' and to make the workers 'rational, well disposed and well behaved'.[28]

Until the end of 1812 Owen was an admirer of the monitorial system and was even prepared to lavish praise on its founders. At the Glasgow meeting he called Lancaster 'this extraordinary man, whom Providence seems to have created for this great and good purpose',[29] and he and Bell, Owen emphasized in the first essay of *A New View of Society*, would 'for ever be ranked among the most important benefactors of the human race'.[30] Owen was at this time not only on friendly terms with Allen, Place, Mill, and others of the Royal Lancasterian Society, but was also contributing regularly to its funds.[31] The Society itself was convinced that the schoolroom that Owen was building in New Lanark was to be a Lancasterian school. 'At New Lanark', the finance committee of the Society categorically stated, 'at the expense of the New Lanark Company a schoolroom is built for 1000 boys and girls.'[32]

As late as 1838 an account of National and British schools in the Central Society of Education Publications stated that Owen was persuaded to build his schools on Lancaster's instigation while the latter was on a visit to the mills, presumably in 1812.[33] This is an obvious piece of misinformation or exaggeration, but there is nothing inconsistent in the idea that Owen toyed with a scheme for a monitorial school before 1812. Even as late as 1814 Allen managed to embody in the articles of partnership drawn up between himself and Fox, Walker and Owen a clause stating 'that schools should be established on the best models of the British or other approved system to which the partners might agree'.[34]

By 1814, however, Owen had made it clear that he had no intention at all of organizing a school based on the monitorial system. In this year, in the fourth essay of *A New View of Society*, he set out dis-

---

[28] Ibid., p. 250.   [29] Ibid., p. 252.

[30] Owen, *A New View of Society*, Essay First, p. 16.

[31] *Report of the Finance Committee and Trustees of the Royal Lancasterian Institution for the Education of the Poor, for the year 1812* (London, 1813), p. 34. In 1811 Owen contributed £113.   [32] Ibid., p. 10.

[33] Central Society of Education, *Second Publication* (London, 1838), p. 376.

[34] J. Sherman, *Memoir of William Allen, F.R.S.* (London, 1851), p. 91.

enchantment with both the system and its founders. Between 1812 and 1814 Owen's thinking on educational matters had undergone a great change ; it is possible that he had met William Godwin during this period and Enlightenment values had reasserted themselves. Whereas Owen had previously praised the monitorial system for its inculcation of habits of obedience and industry, in 1814, while still giving Bell and Lancaster their due as innovators in the sphere of method, he now denounced 'this mockery of learning' which could render the mind of a child irrational for life.[35] The children of the working class, Owen now argued, should have not only the best manner, but also, and far more important, the best matter of instruction. It was not enough now to teach children to know their place, to become docile and obedient ; they must become rational and useful members of society :

> Either give the poor a rational and useful learning, or mock not their ignorance, their poverty, and their misery, by merely instructing them to become conscious of the extent of the degradation under which they exist. And therefore, in pity to suffering humanity, either keep the poor, if you now can, in the state of the most abject ignorance, as near as possible to animal life, or at once determine to form them into rational beings, into useful and effective members of the state.[36]

No longer were children, in Owen's mind, to be treated as the recipients of those values that the middle and upper classes thought were necessary for them if they were to know their place in society. In future they should have the best possible curriculum and be trained in the most rational habits, with the object of becoming rational beings and useful members of society. It was a decisive break with the old philanthropic attitude to the education of the poor, the tradition in which Bell and Lancaster were firmly rooted, and its importance in the history of British education cannot be overestimated. For the first time the educational outlook that had inspired Edgeworth, Day, and Williams was applied not to upper- or middle-class children but to the children of the poor. Owen's educational principles could almost be summed up as Rousseauism applied to working-class children. He was the first to demonstrate that what later was called elementary education could be based upon affection, imagination, and the full realization of the potentialities of the child.

[35] Owen, *A New View of Society*, Essay Fourth, p. 25.   [36] Ibid., p. 27.

It is not entirely true that Owen's educational views are to be found mainly in *A New View of Society*. More advanced formulations are made, for instance, in the speeches he delivered in Ireland in 1823. However, Owen's educational credo was rooted in the Enlightenment commitment to happiness. 'All that have conscious life', he declared, 'have been created to desire happiness.' [37] For the achievement of this, however, two things were required : 'a superfluity of real wealth at all times for all' and 'a really good character for all from birth to death'.[38] The greatest role in the formation of this character would be played by education.[39]

Owen increasingly liberated himself from the simplified view of the power of education and the environment to which he had subscribed in 1812 at the Lancaster dinner,[40] in which education 'wholly and solely' accounted for 'general bodily and mental differences', a view that was and sometimes still is mistaken for Owen's last word on the subject. Owen's environmental theories, as G. D. H. Cole pointed out, have too often been misrepresented — that an adult's character may forthwith be changed for the better by a sudden improvement in the environment.[41] Owen developed a more subtle conception of the powers of education in relation to the endowment of the child. He stressed the 'endless varieties' of children's aptitudes and the different propensities and qualities that gave individuality and distinctiveness to a person's character, and which would not and could not be obliterated under his system.[42] Education, he pointed out in 1823, 'cannot make human beings all alike'; what it could do would be to make everybody 'good, wise and happy'.[43]

Education in the widest sense began at the moment of birth :

The mother and the nurse must be previously instructed in a knowledge of the influence which surrounding circumstances have upon his health and disposition from the hour of birth, and more

---

[37] *Life*, p. 106.   [38] Ibid., p. 104.
[39] Ibid., p. 106.   [40] Ibid., App. A., pp. 249–50.
[41] G. D. H. Cole, 'The Educational Ideas of Robert Owen', *Hibbert Journal*, vol. xxiii, no. 89 (Oct. 1924), p. 131.
[42] Owen, *Report to the County of Lanark*, pp. 39–40 ; *A New View of Society*, Essay Second, pp. 2–5 ; 'A Sketch of Some of the Errors and Evils Arising from the Past and Present State of Society', pp. 23–24 in R. Owen, *New View of Society* (London, 1818).
[43] R. Owen, *Report of the Proceedings at the Several Public Meetings held in Dublin* (Dublin, 1823), pp. 71–72.

particularly with regard to the effect of their own looks, language, and conduct, when they may be in presence of the child.[44]

In their upbringing parents should teach children impartially and never give any individual reward, and at all times display the greatest kindness in manner and feeling. This parental guidance was essential in the first year or two of the child's life. Then children should be placed in circumstances that would enable them 'to become children of one family, and truly, and indeed, to love one another as brethren'; that is, they should be placed in infant and other schools and reside in dormitories. Suitable arrangements would be made to allow parents to see their children frequently, and indeed, under his proposed communitarian plan, Owen prophesied that parent–child relationships would be much better than those under most existing social arrangements. In all situations the child would be treated kindly, and those with defects of character or physical handicaps would receive increased care and attention.[45]

If parental and social attention was essential in the early part of the child's life, it was no less necessary during his time at a school. Owen made it clear that the education that children would receive under his plan would be based upon the principles of Rousseau and Pestalozzi, whereas under the existing educational system, 'the child goes, half-fed and half-clothed, to learn . . . strange sounds, which convey no meaning to his mind'.[46] At New Lanark a totally different situation existed:

> With regard to the instruction to be given at the schools, it is proposed that the mode of communicating knowledge, by means of sensible signs and of conversations with the teachers, shall supersede, for a considerable period, the usual practice of learning from books, which, if commenced before the child can have acquired an adequate number of correct and useful ideas, is calculated not only to disgust him, but to fill his head with mere words, to which either no ideas, or very erroneous ones are attached, and thus materially to injure his faculties, and retard or prevent his intellectual improvement. In short, in this case, as well as in every other, we must follow, not counteract nature.[47]

Childhood, he continued, was the age of curiosity and children had an intense urge to examine every object around them. If, therefore,

---

[44] Owen, *Report of Meetings in Dublin*, p. 72.   [45] Ibid., pp. 73–79.
[46] Ibid., p. 77.   [47] Ibid., p. 79.

a child's attention was not arrested by the mode of tuition adopted, 'it is our duty to alter and amend our plan'. Children should be presented with 'simple and . . . agreeable facts', and gradually introduced to others 'of a more complex nature'. From birth to the age of twelve, every child should be able to acquire 'a general knowledge of the earth, and of the animal, vegetable and mineral kingdoms — of the useful sciences, and of human nature and its past history' in addition to 'as much both of theory and practices in the arts and sciences, as will afford them full employment and agreeable recreation'.[48]

Strongly reminiscent of the work of David Williams and the new school of educationalists rather than directly of Rousseau, these principles were the ones on which the children of the operatives of New Lanark were educated. In an age when Andrew Bell, Sir Thomas Bernard of the Society for the Betterment of the Poor, Patrick Colquhoun, the economist, and others believed that the education of the poor should properly consist of the three R's together with religion and the formation of habits of order and submission suitable to their station in life,[49] Owen considered he was giving the New Lanark children an education according to nature that would produce 'full-formed men and women, physically and mentally, who would always think and act consistently and rationally'.[50]

IV

When Owen arrived at New Lanark in 1800 to take over the direction of the mills from his father-in-law David Dale his views were still in process of formation, and though he very soon began to put in hand improvements in housing, health, and working conditions in the New Lanark community, he was not able to put into practice his theories on education until sixteen years later, in 1816. In education, as in the community experiments, Owen's starting-point was the situation and conditions he inherited from David Dale.

Dale's treatment of the five hundred or so pauper apprentices on whom the running of the mills depended would not recommend itself to later generations, but compared with fellow mill-owners north and south of the Tweed, his methods were unusually enlightened. The *Annual Register* for 1792 (published in 1799) gave Dale a friendly

[48] Ibid., pp. 79-81.   [49] Cf. below, Chap. 12.   [50] *Life*, p. 134.

notice, praising the provisions that 'this extraordinary man' had made for the health of the children employed by him.[51] Several contemporary accounts by travellers and others mention him as outstanding for his treatment of children. From these and from the detailed reply that he addressed to T. B. Bayley in Manchester, Dale's achievement can be assessed.[52]

Dale established his mills in 1785 in conjunction with Arkwright, later becoming sole owner. By the middle of the 1790s he was employ-over five hundred children between the ages of six and fourteen from the workhouses of Glasgow and Edinburgh. Dale not only justified the use of these children in cotton mills, but also contended that their health and morals were actually improved by their employment and that many of his children 'now have stout healthy bodies, and are of decent behaviour, who in all probability would have been languishing with disease, and pests to society had they not been employed in Lanark cotton mills'.[53]

The children were lodged in six well-ventilated dormitories and though they slept three to a bed, the straw mattresses were changed once a month, and they were provided with sheets and blankets. The dormitories were washed with hot water every week and the walls were limewashed twice a year. The children were dressed in cotton clothes in summer and woollen ones in winter, and these clothes were changed weekly. Their food was nutritious and contained plenty of protein, as the detailed menus available bear out. They began work at 6 a.m. and worked till 7 p.m., with breaks at 9.30 a.m. for breakfast, and 2–3 p.m. for dinner.

After supper at 7 p.m. education commenced and continued until 9 p.m., and while we should nowadays question the wisdom of trying to teach children, however well fed, who had just done eleven hours' continuous work in a factory, it must be said that Dale was virtually alone in making any educational provision at all. He employed sixteen teachers of whom three were full-time and the rest assistants.

---

[51] 'Chronicle', p. 27, in *Annual Register, 1792* (London, 1799).

[52] This account is based upon J. Sinclair, *The Statistical Account of Scotland* (Edinburgh, 21 vols., 1791–9), xv, pp. 34–41 ; Sir Thomas Bernard, 'Extract from an Account of Mr. Dale's Cotton Mills at New Lanark in Scotland', in *Reports of the Society for Bettering the Condition and Increasing the Comforts of the Poor* (London, 2 vols., 1800), ii, pp. 363–74 ; T. Garnett, *Observations on a Tour Through the Highlands* (London, 2 vols., 1800), ii, pp. 231–5 ; 'Extract from Letter of David Dale of New Lanark to T. B. Bayley, 1796', in Maltby, App. iv, pp. 124–7.

[53] Maltby, p. 125.

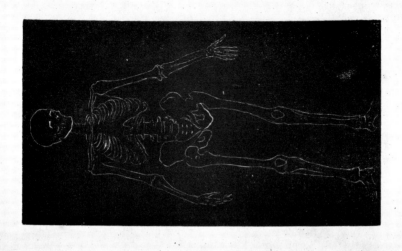

EXERCISES.

[The following Exercises may be used to test the Memory, and as simple Lessons in Grammar and Composition. The Plates will assist the Child to form an idea of the position of parts ; and being drawn in brief outline, encourage him to adopt a similar method of conveying his ideas to others.]

The Bones.

[See p. 6, 7, 8, 9.]

1. State their numbers, qualities, varieties of form, substance, effects produced by fire and muriatic acid.

2. Head—Parts, number of bones in each part, how united (refer to Lesson X).

3. Trunk—How divided. Spine—its extent, form, qualities, contents, division, uses. Vertebræ—their number, form, parts, how connected, how divided.

4. Chest—its position, contents, number of parts, connection of parts, ribs true and false, how connected.

5. Pelvis—form, parts, connection.

6. Upper extremities—parts, position, uses, joints of shoulder, elbow, wrist, hands, fingers.

7. Lower extremities—number of parts, relative position, joints at the trunk, knees, ankles, heels, feet, toes, uses.

In describing joints refer to Lesson X.

Text and illustration from The Human Body Described for the Instruction of the Young of Both Sexes, *a textbook by the Owenite schoolmaster, John Ellis*

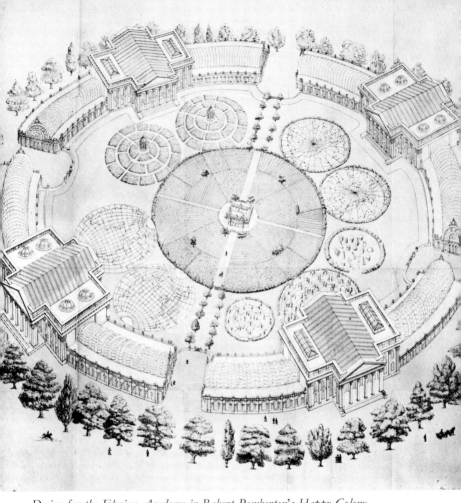

Design for the Elysian Academy in Robert Pemberton's Happy Colony

including the writing master, music master, and sewing mistress. In 1796 there were 507 children divided into eight classes according to merit, and each class had one or more teachers attached to it who received a small premium on the promotion of one of the scholars to a higher class. The educational standards of the school in 1796 were not high, only twelve boys and twelve girls being able to read sufficiently well at that time to proceed to arithmetic and sewing.

The most interesting feature of the New Lanark educational system, however, was the day schools. There were two day schools 'for children too young to work', and since the youngest children employed were six years of age, these schools were what we should call infant and nursery schools. These names were not applied to them, nor were they organized on the basis of any educational theory, but they were nevertheless the first of their kind in the British Isles. The teachers for these schools were full-time dominies, and could not have been called child-minders. Owen does not mention these infant schools in any of his writings, nor is any account given of them in the standard works on the education of young children, but if we are looking for a precursor of Robert Owen's infant school then New Lanark in Dale's time is the place to find it.

What was Owen's criticism of Dale's regime at New Lanark? Though he admitted that the children 'looked fresh, and, to a superficial observer, healthy in their countenances',[54] he assessed Dale's work as 'a very partial experiment', and argued that his kind intentions had been rendered almost nugatory by the fact that the whole scheme depended upon the children working eleven and a half hours a day in the mills. 'The error proceeded from the children being sent from the workhouses at an age much too young for employment', wrote Owen. 'They ought to have been detained four years longer, and educated.' [55] Thus Owen saw that the employment of children at too early an age was the real weakness in Dale's educational scheme, though he recognized that Dale was in a dilemma : he had either to accept children from six years of age into his mills or stop the factory that he was then operating. Owen, by refusing to employ any child before ten years of age and improving the conditions for adult workers in the village, tried to meet this difficulty and was thus enabled to put

[54] *Report from the Select Committee on the State of the Children Employed in the Manufactories of the United Kingdom*, P.P. (1816), iii, p. 20.
[55] *A New View of Society*, Essay Second, pp. 15–16.

into practice educational projects far beyond any that had been envisaged at the time.

Owen's educational system at New Lanark consisted of three schools,
graded according to age ; children between two and six years of age
attended the infant school, those from six to fourteen the day school,
and older children and the adults went to the evening classes. It is
with the first two that we shall be concerned here.

The greatest attraction at New Lanark and one that Owen himself
was most interested in was the infant school.[56] His first conception
of this institution was merely the provision of a playground in which
the children's minds might be properly directed towards co-operation
and living together, which he felt was an essential part of the education
of the young.[57] His first task was to find a suitable teacher, and he
dismissed the old dominie remaining from David Dale's time, who was
opposed to all new methods and even to teaching infants at all, which
would suggest that the infant day school of Dale's time had died out.
Owen looked for a teacher who had the qualifications of love for and
patience with the children, and, what was perhaps more important,
was willing to follow Owen's instructions. His choice fell upon
James Buchanan and, as an assistant, Molly Young, both working
people from the village.

Buchanan has hardly received fair treatment in histories of education. To a great extent this is due to Owen's rather cavalier treatment
of him in his autobiography, in which he stressed Buchanan's low
standard of learning and lack of independent character.[58] Later writers
have enlarged upon this until Buchanan appears in Cullen's *Adventures
in Socialism* as 'a quiet, simple-minded old weaver named Jamie
Buchanan, who could scarcely read, write or spell',[59] but the publication of the *Buchanan Family Records* in 1923 enables a more accurate
picture to be presented. At the opening of the infant schools in 1816
Buchanan was an ex-Serviceman of the Scottish Militia thirty-two
years of age, fully literate as his surviving diaries and letters show ;
indeed, his granddaughter claimed for him an education 'considerably
above the average for the times'.[60] In November 1815, when he was
entrusted by Owen with the future direction of the infant school, he

[56] *Life*, p. 138.
[57] [R. Owen], *A Statement Regarding the New Lanark Establishment* (Edinburgh,
1812), p. 13.   [58] *Life*, p. 139.
[59] A. Cullen, *Adventures in Socialism* (Glasgow, 1910), p. 49.
[60] [B. I. Buchanan], *Buchanan Family Records* (Cape Town, 1923), p. 1.

wrote in his dairy : 'I commenced my new era, and gave up the desire of becoming rich or great, content if my life would be useful.' [61]

On the other hand, Buchanan's usefulness has been somewhat exaggerated by his granddaughter. She states that Owen merely provided him with 'a bare room without even seats, much less toys, pictures, or anything else to occupy, instruct or amuse the children', and that Buchanan's own efforts initiated and carried forward the school, without the aid of apparatus ; [62] but this cannot be accepted as correct. Not only Owen himself, but also his son Robert Dale Owen, described the early days of the infant school, which showed that a definite method of teaching was pursued and that apparatus and pictures were extensively used :

> They were trained to habits of order and cleanliness ; they were taught to abstain from quarrels, to be kind to each other. They were amused with childish games, and with stories suited to their capacity. Two large, airy rooms were set apart, one for those under four years, and one for those from four to six. This last room was furnished with paintings, chiefly of animals, and a few maps. It was also supplied with natural objects from the gardens, fields and woods. These suggested themes for conversation, and brief familiar lectures ; but there was nothing formal, no tasks to be learned, no readings from books.[63]

Owen's instructions to Buchanan were in accordance with his theories already described and give an interesting glimpse of what they were to supersede. Owen insisted that no corporal punishment, threats, or abusive terms were to be used ; that teachers were to adopt a pleasant manner of speech and that they should teach the children to make each other happy. The pupils were not to be 'annoyed with books', but taught the uses and qualities of common things 'by familiar conversation' and, when their curiosity was aroused, to ask questions about them.[64]

Buchanan certainly tried to fulfil Owen's instructions in both the letter and spirit. He began by making the children march round the room to the strains of the flute ; then, like the Pied Piper, he led them through New Lanark village to the river, let them play on the banks of the Clyde, and then marched them back again. He also devised indoor

[61] Ibid., p. 2.   [62] Ibid.
[63] R. D. Owen, *Threading My Way* (London, 1874), p. 90.
[64] *Life*, pp. 139, 140.

amusements for the children, simple gymnastic movements, arm exercises, clapping their hands, to all of which the children counted in numbers. He conducted oral lessons on arithmetical tables, object lessons in which the children did most of the talking, and hymn-singing to the sound of the flute.[65] Buchanan, in fact, gave himself up to the new teaching so unreservedly that it is difficult to see why Owen repeatedly stated that Buchanan did not understand his system.

Buchanan remained at New Lanark for nearly two years, when he left to take up an appointment as head of the first London infant school at Brewer's Green. His successor was a former pupil of the school who, according to Owen, made a rapid advance and improvement in his first year and became 'the best instructor of infants I have ever seen in any part of the world'.[66]

In the day school for older children Owen was not able to carry out his plans as he would have wished. According to his son Robert Dale Owen, if he had had a free hand he would have allowed the children to spend their first seven or eight years in the practical study of natural history, geography, ancient and modern history, chemistry, and astronomy; in doing this they would be 'following the plan prescribed by nature'. Having thus acquired a practical knowledge of the objects of the natural world around him, only then would the child have been taught to read, to use and understand words, 'the artificial signs adopted to represent these objects'. With his background of practical knowledge, the child would then learn to read with increased interest, since knowledge of the language would open up new discoveries in subjects already familiar.[67] This scheme, however, had to be modified because of the parents' insistence on the children learning to read at an earlier age than eight.

The children learned the three R's, natural history, geography, and history. In addition there was religious instruction, dancing and singing, sewing for the girls, and marching for the boys. The day scholars from four to ten years were graded into three groups, each covering a two-year range, and there was a master for each class, a singing and dancing master, a drilling master, and a sewing mistress.[68] Above all, the atmosphere of the school was free from the severe

---

[65] [Buchanan], p. 3.   [66] *Life*, p. 143.

[67] R. D. Owen, *An Outline of the System of Education at New Lanark* (Glasgow, 1824), pp. 34–35 (hereafter *Outline*).

[68] H. G. MacNab, M.D., *The New Views of Mr. Owen of Lanark Impartially Examined* (London, 1819), pp. 221–3 ; *Outline*, p. 31.

discipline and sense of authority traditionally found in educational institutions, as every visitor testified. The good relations between teacher and pupil, the relaxed atmosphere, opportunities for what Owen called 'a good deal of exercise and some amusement',[69] the care devoted to ensuring that the child understood what it was learning — these were what gave the peculiar character to the schools.

The teaching method was founded on Owen's philosophical and psychological theories. The children were led gradually, and with as full an explanation as they could comprehend, from fact to fact, gradually increasing in complexity ; thus 'their powers of reflection and judgement may be habituated to draw accurate conclusions from the facts presented to them'.[70] A high place was given to the study of natural history ; as with David Williams it was considered to be 'almost the first knowledge of which Nature directs an infant to acquire'.[71] It was assiduously taught at New Lanark, even to the infants ; botanical and mineralogical specimens were collected from the surrounding countryside, and scale drawings illustrative of the science were hung around the schoolroom or displayed on canvas rolls.[72] Arithmetic received special attention, and after Owen's visit to Yverdon in 1818 the Pestalozzian method was introduced. The elementary arithmetical processes were taught by the Pestalozzian Table of Units, and the theory of fractions from the Table of Squares, in which each square was divided into a number of equal parts.[73] 'A legible business hand such as shall be useful to them in after life' was taught in the later forms of the school.[74] In the higher classes of the school, however, an ingenious visual aid for teaching grammar was in use. It consisted of a series of emblems which personified the parts of speech and assigned to each its relative importance according to military rank. 'General Noun', wrote an observer, 'figures in his cocked hat, sword, and double epaulettes. By his side stands Colonel Verb, and so on down to Corporal Adverb.' [75]

A surprising feature of the school, in view of the educational traditions that animated it, was that the arts and sciences were taught by means of lectures. Natural history, geography, and history were

[69] *Select Committee on Children Employed in Manufactories*, p. 22.

[70] Owen, *Report to the County of Lanark*, pp. 43–44 ; *A New View of Society*, Essay Third, p. 25.   [71] *Outline*, p. 45.   [72] Ibid., pp. 45–46.

[73] Cullen, pp. 56–57.   [74] *Outline*, pp. 36, 38, 39–40.

[75] 'An Account of a Visit to New Lanark in November 1825', in Owen, *The New Existence*, pt. v, App. B, pp. xl–xli.

usually taught together. At first the lectures were given to as many
as 150 children at once, but this was later reduced to forty or fifty,
still a large enough group. Every effort was made to keep the lectures
simple and interesting, illustrated by as many anecdotes as possible ;
this required, as Robert Dale Owen pointed out, 'great attention,
considerable ability and a correct knowledge of human nature' on the
part of the teacher.[76] In an appendix to the account of the school
there is an outline of the lectures that were given to the older children,
entitled 'Introduction to the Arts and Sciences'. This begins with a
description of the earth and of natural phenomena, and the mineral,
vegetable, and animal kingdoms, followed by the divisions of human
knowledge — astronomy, geography, mathematics, zoology, botany,
mineralogy, other sciences, and the arts, together with agriculture,
manufacture, architecture, drawing, and music.[77]

Despite all efforts made by the teachers to get the children to ask
questions, to discuss and to understand the substance of the lectures,
it would appear that the children might have learned more had they
been able to discover some of the facts for themselves in the way
Williams encouraged his pupils to do, for some of the activity and
bustle was misleading. A visitor noticed that the children marched
to their lessons in time to martial music, arriving at their seats in class
order, and answered all the questions simultaneously, 'with great
precision'.[78] To some extent, however, the passivity on the part of
the children was overcome by the provision of what are now called
visual aids. In addition to those mentioned, a conspectus of history
was provided in the form of seven large wall maps, composed upon
the principle of the Stream of Time, bought from Miss Whitwell, a
London headmistress with Owenite leanings who came to teach at
New Lanark. Each map represented a nation, and each was coloured
differently. The children were drawn into active participation and
discovery by being able to compare the incidents of each century,
enclosed between two horizontal lines, and in this way they could
relate the events of one nation to another chronologically and build up
a comprehensive picture of the world.[79] According to George Combe
the phrenologist, Owen ordered £500 worth of transparent pictures,
'representing objects interesting to the youthful mind', for use in

[76] *Outline*, p. 42.   [77] Ibid., Appendix, pp. 82–103.
[78] 'Visit of August 1822', in Owen, *The New Existence*, pt. v, App. B, p. xxviii.
[79] *Outline*, pp. 50–51.

enabling children 'to form ideas at the same time as they learn words'.[80]

For some geography lessons all the children stood in a circle around one huge map of the world. Cities and towns were marked with circles but not names. One child would ask another to indicate with a pointer the location of places he would call out. As soon as he failed to answer a question, the pointer was given to the questioner, who had to go through the same process, and so on round the group. The children became so adept at this, Owen records, that 'one of our Admirals, who had sailed round the world, said he could not answer many of the questions which some of these children not six years old readily replied to'.[81]

Many of the features of the New Lanark schools derived from a reaction to the uglier aspects of the Industrial Revolution. Owen liked the schoolchildren to be healthy, happy, and clean. He dressed them in white toga-like uniforms, encouraged them to make expeditions to the countryside, and, what was anathema to his Quaker partner William Allen, insisted that dancing and singing were vital to the health and happiness of the children and formed an essential part of the curriculum. His son wrote that the children especially liked 'spirited songs in the bravura style',[82] and Owen described the children dancing 'all the dances of Europe' seventy couples at a time.[83] Recitals by choirs of 150 voices, and military exercises by boys and girls to fife-band music, were frequent occurrences.[84]

As might be expected, these lively pursuits were reinforced by moral teaching whenever the opportunity presented itself. Owen himself considered that the doctrine of the interest and happiness of one being identical with the interest and happiness of all was the beginning and end of teaching, and the teachers never lost an opportunity to 'create enlarged ideas, to repress illiberal or uncharitable sentiments'.[85] Geography lessons became opportunities to break down insularity and nationalist ideas. Religion at New Lanark, although the Scriptures were read and the catechism taught in deference to the parents' and partners' wishes, was really a sustained attempt to present practical moral principles rather than doctrine.[86]

It followed almost as a matter of course that all rewards and

[80] C. Gibbon, *Life of George Combe* (London, 2 vols., 1878), i, p. 132.
[81] *Life*, p. 144.   [82] *Outline*, p. 70.
[83] *Life*, p. 143, see also illustration above, facing p. 49.
[84] Ibid., p. 144.   [85] *Outline*, p. 43.   [86] Ibid., pp. 47, 52–68 *passim*.

punishments were abolished. This was done on the grounds that not only were they unjust but that they tended to enhance deficiencies of character.[87] Even Miss Edgeworth's children's books, though read, were criticized because they contained 'too much of praise and blame'.[88] Following Rousseau, only the 'natural' rewards and punishments in the shape of the necessary consequences of an action were recognized, and standards of right and wrong were fixed in relation to the increase or decrease of happiness of the school community.[89] Owen wanted to get away from the authority and fear inherent in the traditional pupil–teacher relationship ; to this end the New Lanark teachers had to be critical of themselves rather than of the children if a lesson did not go well, and they were expected never to overstep the boundary of kindly admonition when dealing with an offence.[90]

This self-criticism on the part of the teachers was one of the many new notes struck by Owen. In his autobiography he made a list of the ten innovations that he had introduced into the education of young children. They were : the absence of corporal punishment ; kindness on the part of the teachers ; instruction in realities by means of conversation ; the answering of questions in a 'kind and rational manner' ; the abolition of fixed hours and the alternation of lessons and play ; the introduction of music, dancing, and drill into the curriculum ; excursions into the countryside ; the attempt to train children to think and act rationally ; and the placing of children in superior surroundings.[91] Though some of these had been anticipated by David Williams, the total picture is a powerful vindication of Owen's plans, of the methods of the advocates of education according to nature, and represents an astonishing innovation in the education of the working class.

V

Owen's schemes never had the complete backing of his partner William Allen, the Quaker philanthropist and chemist, who found it difficult to reconcile his principles with Owen's free-thinking on religion and libertarian views on children's amusements. In 1819 Allen and another Quaker partner Joseph Foster visited New Lanark to investigate allegations that the religious beliefs of the inhabitants were being

---

[87] *Outline*, pp. 9–10.   [88] Ibid., pp. 35–36.   [89] Ibid., pp. 11–13.
[90] Ibid., pp. 16, 25.   [91] *Life*, pp. 232–3.

undermined. Owen paid little attention at the time to what he called Allen's 'crude and prejudiced notions',[92] but Allen persisted in his opposition to what he considered damaging to religious belief, and to the music-making. Finally, in January 1824, the London partners — Allen, Foster, Michael Gibbs, and Charles Walker — made Owen sign an agreement on the reorganization of the schools, whose terms covered the dismissal of many of the teachers, including the dancing master and Miss Whitwell, and the appointment of a new master, John Daniel, at a salary of £150 a year, to teach on the Lancasterian system. If the parents wished their children to learn dancing, they would have to pay for it themselves. Weekly reading of the Scriptures and 'other religious exercise' was instituted, music and singing (except for instruction in psalmody) were abolished, and the wearing of kilts was banned. The one positive feature was Allen's insistence that lectures in chemistry, mechanics, experimental philosophy, and natural history were to be given twice a week.[93]

Owen rightly believed this document to be an unwarranted interference in his educational schemes, and resigned from active management of the establishment. Thus, after eight years, what MacNab called 'the most valuable establishment in education to be found in this or any other country'[94] came to an end. Owen's 'liberal modes of natural instruction' were replaced by the rote-learning of the Lancasterian system, which Allen, according to Owen, believed to be 'the perfection of education'.[95]

Four years later, in 1828, Matthew Davenport Hill, a founder of Hazelwood, the experimental school at Birmingham, visited New Lanark. He found the children ' more disorderly than I had expected', the master in 'a constant state of painful exertion', and in the habit of striking the children hard in order to maintain 'a very distant approach to silence'.[96] It was a sad transformation of the New Lanark scheme. The last footnote was added by George Jacob Holyoake, the Owenite and Co-operator. Fifty-three years after Owen's experiment had come to an end and nearly twenty years after Owen's own death, he saw in the New Lanark schoolhouse in 1877 the remains of the blackboards

[92] Ibid., p. 236.
[93] 'New Arrangements Respecting the Schools at New Lanark, Determined upon the 21st of January, 1824', in Owen, *The New Existence*, pt. v, App. A, pp. vii–ix.
[94] MacNab, p. 224.   [95] *Life*, p. 235.
[96] R. and F. Davenport-Hill, *The Recorder of Birmingham : A Memoir of Matthew Davenport Hill* (London, 1878), p. 88.

and canvas diagrams 'of immense dimensions . . . well and brightly painted' lying ruined against the walls.[97]

5. The Followers of Owen : Working-class Educators and Utopians

WHILE the New Lanark experiment lasted only eight years, one of the most striking characteristics of the body of social thought known as Owenism was the appeal that it made over several decades to different social groups, whether to Scottish followers of Owen such as Hamilton, Abram Combe, and Captain Donald MacDonald, to gentlemen philanthropists of the type of John Minter Morgan, or to the working-class Co-operators, communitarians, and socialists. Each group tended to take from Owen's philosophy those elements that most suited its aims. Owen's educational theories and practices, in similar fashion, were taken up and modified by individuals and organizations of very varied character.

After the end of Owen's connections with the New Lanark schools, his educational doctrines provided the inspiration for two quite separate movements (leaving aside the rather tenuous connection of Owen with the post-New Lanark infant school developments, which are dealt with in Chapter 15): the working-class Co-operators and socialists of the 1830s and 1840s and a small group of independent middle-class philanthropists, among whom Robert Pemberton and John Minter Morgan were the most important. The former tended to stress the rational and scientific elements of Owenite education, the latter the utopian aspect of his theory.

In propagating his ideas, Owen had pointed out that co-operative communities might be set up by any section of the population in order to relieve themselves of the evils of their condition. It was the working class who responded to the suggestion, and from the early efforts of London printers, who in 1821 formed a 'Co-operative and Economic Society', the Owenite Co-operative movement grew until by 1830

[97] *The Times* 13 Nov. 1877.

there were some three hundred local societies, and two hundred more were opened in the next few years.

These early Co-operators were imbued with a zeal for education that would make each member an efficient producer, fit to assume the duties of the new society that they believed their efforts would bring about. In a practical way many of these Co-operative societies set up schools of their own to hasten this process, and we now turn to examples of Co-operative schools of the early 1830s.

I

Owenite Co-operative Schools

The Second Co-operative Congress in 1831 passed a resolution to set up schools 'for the formation of a superior physical, moral, and intellectual character for the children of Co-operatives'.[1] At the Third Congress, Robert Owen emphasized that these schools should not only give children the necessary education but also give to the subjects taught to them 'an entirely new character'.[2] According to Aubrey Black, whose researches have thrown much light on the early history of Co-operative education, nine societies had set up a school in the twelve months following the Second Congress resolution.[3] Details can be gleaned from Owenite journals and other sources to give some indication of the type of institution the Owenites tried to form, in the face of the greatest difficulties connected with the provision of finance, premises, and teachers.

One of the earliest of these schools was set up in Charlotte Street, London, founded by two leading members of Owenite organizations, T. V. Grettan and B. Portbury. Grettan was secretary of the London branch of the Social Community of Friends of the Rational System of Society,[4] and Portbury secretary of the Moral Union.[5] The school was started on 28 October 1833, on the premises of the Labour Exchange Bazaar in Charlotte Street, the institution at which Co-operators exchanged the goods they had made against labour-notes, which in

---

[1] *Proceedings of the Second Co-operative Congress* (Birmingham, 1831), p. 24.
[2] *Proceedings of the Third Co-operative Congress* (London, 1832), p. 41.
[3] A. Black, 'Early Co-operative Education, 1830–36', unpublished dissertation, University of Manchester (1951), p. 17.
[4] *Crisis*, vol. ii, no. 34, 24 Aug. 1833.
[5] Ibid., vol. iii, no. 13, 23 Nov. 1833.

turn could be used to purchase other articles. The school finances, in fact, seemed to be integrated with the economy of the Labour Exchange, for half the fees of 4*d*. (for those under eight) and 6*d*. (for those above eight years) were payable in labour-notes.

The aims and objects of the school expressed the desire to break with the religious and social basis of existing institutions for the working class. It was to be 'a rational school for the industrious classes', giving 'a sound education unmixed with the peculiar dogmas of any party', to enable 'the working man's child to receive such education as to make him moral, intelligent, virtuous and happy'.[6]

The constitution of the school showed a conscious attempt to elevate the position of the child :

1. Every pupil shall be encouraged to express his or her opinion.
2. No creed or dogma shall be imposed upon any.
3. Admitted facts alone shall be placed before the pupils, from which they shall be allowed to draw their own deductions.
4. No distinction whatever shall exist ; but all be treated with equal kindness.
5. Neither praise nor blame, merit or demerit, rewards nor punishments, shall be awarded to any : kindness and love to be the only ruling powers.
6. Both sexes shall have equal opportunities of acquiring useful knowledge.

Co-education, the absence of corporal punishment, factual teaching, the emphasis on kindliness — all are reminiscent of New Lanark, and show the importance placed upon the formation of character. This was also the concern of the regulations relating to the teachers :

1. To observe that the strictest order prevails.
2. To maintain among the pupils the best social feelings.
3. To create the best possible circumstances for the formation of the best moral, intellectual, and physical characters.
4. To visit on alternate weeks the parents of absentees.

The curriculum was very ambitious, too ambitious for the resources available. It included Latin, French, geography, algebra, gymnastic exercises, music, and dancing. In addition a mistress took needlework and looked after the infants. Great importance was attached to apparatus, though the school did not possess much — merely some

[6] *Crisis,* vol. iii, no. 19, 4 Jan. 1834.

pieces of wood for lessons in geometry, a few balls with which to teach arithmetic, and some infant apparatus. There was no blackboard, and exercises were chalked on the floor.

The school faced some initial difficulties. Co-education had to be abandoned and some children were expelled for bad behaviour, and the shortage of books and apparatus made it difficult to occupy the children. But the main error was to set up the school on the same premises as the Bazaar, for which two walls were being knocked down to enlarge the accommodation, which unsettled the children. The teachers were forced to abandongy mnastics, which had helped to balance the lack of a stove by keeping the children warm, because this disturbed the officials of the Bazaar. So the committee of management gave the school notice to leave on the grounds that a school and a bazaar could not be run on the same premises.

Grettan and Portbury were keenly disappointed, for some of the hundred or so pupils had made 'visible progress' even in the first difficult eight or nine weeks. A meeting was called to review the situation. The running of the school had been on a democratic and business-like basis. It was vested in a committee of ten, chosen from parents and subscribers, equally divided between the sexes. The subscription for the school was 2*s*. 6*d*. a quarter. Monthly meetings were held at which half the committee retired, and new members were elected. The balance-sheet showed that there were thirteen subscribers — a reasonable number if it is remembered how difficult it was for working people to find half a crown at that period. The main expenditure was upon basic school needs — books, slates, pencils, paper, pens, inks. At the meeting to decide the future of the school there was support for carrying it on ; two gentlemen present promised to subscribe two guineas each, and a committee of four was set up to search for new premises.

The search for new premises could not have been easy. But three months after the meeting an advertisement in the Owenite journal *Crisis* announced that Portbury had opened a school in London at 'Portbury's School Rooms', 31 Crown Street, off Oxford Street. This was run on a day and evening basis, the day school at the same fees as formerly. Nothing was said of the way in which the school was to be conducted, except that 'all children will have equal facilities of learning'.[7] But there is no doubt that this was a continuation of the

[7] Ibid., vol. iii, no. 29, 15 Mar. 1834.

Charlotte Street venture. The evening-school curriculum included French, dancing, and gymnastics, for each of which there was an extra charge. In addition, 'Social Festivals' were to be held every alternate Wednesday, and lectures were planned. After this announcement there was no further mention of the school in any Owenite journal.

Three other London schools are mentioned in *Crisis*. One, described as a Free School, was at 6 Broad Street, Golden Square, 'where the children of the disciples of Robert Owen may receive gratuitous instruction'.[8] Another, a girls' school, was announced to commence on 2 June 1834, run by a Mrs. Freeman. The advertisement was addressed to 'the Advocates of Rational Education', and the school offered instruction in 'all useful branches of knowledge, without any mixture of Superstition and Fear, or any of the prejudices usually impressed on the infant mind'.[9]

About the third school we have more information. In November 1833 a letter appeared in *Crisis*, signed by W. Hassell, announcing that a society had been formed in Westminster for the purpose of establishing a school on rational principles, and seeking a schoolmaster and mistress, who should possess 'a knowledge of the social principles combined with sufficient scientific attainments'.[10] A few months later another communication from Hassell described the institution in some detail. The full name was the Westminster Rational School and General Scientific Institution, situated in Grosvenor Street, Millbank, and it comprised a day school, evening classes, a library (with a proposed museum), and provision for periodic lectures and festivals. The objects were in accord with the Owenite philosophy : useful knowledge ; the development of the mental, moral, and physical powers ; emphasis on scientific instruction ; and 'frequent friendly associations and extended rational amusements'. The day school also was typical — co-educational, 'without distinction of class, or sect, or country, or colour' ; no rewards or punishments ; an emphasis on factual and useful knowledge ; and a wide curriculum. The fees were fairly high for the period : children under seven were charged 6*d*. a week ; from seven to ten years 9*d*. ; and above ten years, 1*s*. The Institution was run by a committee of the shareholders,[11]

[8] *Crisis,* vol. ii, no. 34, 24 Aug. 1833.
[9] Ibid., vol. iv, no. 7, 24 May 1834.
[10] Ibid., vol. iii, no. 12, 16 Nov. 1833.
[11] Ibid., vol. iii, no. 20, 11 Jan. 1834.

and shortly after its opening the school announced that it would take
boarders under twelve years of age, at £1 a month, payable in advance,[12]
and advertised for a governess, presumably in order to look after
these children.[13]

Outside London only one school is recorded as having been founded
by Co-operators in this period, but that was the most ambitious and
long-lived of them all — the school at Salford, Lancashire, set up in
1831. E. T. Craig, the Co-operator and educationalist, whose activities
at Ralahine and Ealing Grove School are detailed elsewhere in this
book, gave some details of the founding of this school in his reminiscences of the English socialist movement. The school originated in
a scientific society formed by a number of young men attending Manchester Mechanics' Institute, including Craig himself, Charles Bury,
Joseph Caldwell, and Charles Rowley. The society was set up chiefly
to study chemistry, but languages and mathematics were also included
in the programme.[14] The venture was typical of the great enthusiasm
for self-education that manifested itself among intelligent artisans at
this period.

It was not long before some members of this society, including
Craig himself, became converted to Owen's ideas, especially those to
do with co-operation and education, and became enthusiastic missionaries for the cause. According to Craig :

> the zeal of the advocates of co-operation in those days was power-
> fully stimulated by the great social and educational results antici-
> pated. The men were as earnest as they were effective in spreading
> a knowledge of the principles involved in the social economy which
> contemplated nothing less than a new arrangement of society and
> social life, embracing an organized system of production in connec-
> tion with machinery and the possession of land — a wise distribution,
> educational training, and government.[15]

The members of the society, which according to Black was known
as the Manchester and Salford Association for the Spread of Co-
operative Knowledge,[16] decided to put their aims into practical effect
and to open a Sunday and evening school for the use of the district,
with the chief aim of teaching scientific subjects precisely because

[12] Ibid., vol. iii, no. 25, 15 Feb. 1834.
[13] Ibid., vol. iii, no. 26, 22 Feb. 1834.
[14] E. T. Craig, 'Socialism in England : Historical Reminiscences', *American Socialist*, vol. ii, 13 Dec. 1877, pp. 394–5.
[15] Ibid., vol. iii, 10 Jan. 1878, p. 10   [16] Black (1951), pp. 31–32.

these were not at that time taught to working-class children. The founders hired two large rooms, made the desks themselves, and canvassed from door to door for pupils.[17] Expenses were defrayed by contributions, and Lady Byron gave an annual subscription of £5 towards expenses.[18]

According to Black, the school was established at Christmas 1831 at Bank Parade, Salford, and by the end of 1832 it had become a common school for the Co-operators of the whole district, giving instruction in the evenings and on Sundays to over two hundred pupils. The evening scholars paid low fees and the Sunday school was free.[19] The curriculum was, as usual with Owenite schools, a wide one, with particular emphasis on the sciences. Apart from the three R's, geometry, mathematics, drawing, and political economy were offered ; later geology, astronomy, and chemistry were added, and by 1834 grammar, history, morals, and phrenology were also in the curriculum.[20] There was a tendency, judging by the development of this range of work, for the school to move away from being mainly a children's school towards becoming an adult or semi-adult mechanics' institute, and this is borne out by the fact that at the end of 1834 an investigation by the Manchester Statistical Society found that only 26 out of 150, or 17 per cent, of the evening scholars were under fifteen years of age.[21] But in the first two years or so of its existence it was, as Jones makes clear, obviously a school for young children.

Despite the fact that they had to teach a wide variety of subjects, the teachers, who numbered eight in 1834, were all self-educated working men who gave their services free. Jones himself acted as the writing master,[22] and Charles Bury — 'a good classical scholar' according to Craig — gave lessons in Latin. The school was sometimes visited by Richard Robert Jones, a local eccentric, the son of a bricklayer's labourer, who was reputed to know twenty-five different languages and always wore a huge top-coat, the pockets of which were filled with books. Jones would enter a classroom and write mottoes in the children's notebooks in various languages.[23]

By 1836 the school was doing so well that a committee had been

[17] L. Jones, *The Life, Times, and Labours of Robert Owen* (London, 2nd ed., 1895), pp. 285–7.   [18] Craig, *American Socialist*, 13 Dec. 1877.

[19] Black (1951), p. 32.   [20] Ibid., pp. 37–39.

[21] *Report of a Committee of the Manchester Statistical Society on the State of Education in the Borough of Salford in 1835* (London, 1836), p. 34 (hereafter *Report*).

[22] Jones, p. 287.   [23] Craig, *American Socialist*, 13 Dec. 1877.

formed to raise funds for a more extensive institution, and Lloyd Jones, as the secretary, sent out a circular to this effect. In it he gave further details of the school. He claimed that it was established on principles essentially different from those of any other institution of the kind that had ever been formed, in that it was unconnected with sect or party, and no corporal punishment was administered.[24] In a letter to Owen accompanying the circular, Jones stressed that 'the most particular object of our solicitude' was the implanting of the principles of Owen's social system in the infant mind,[25] but as in all Owenite schools, this was evidently achieved by the happy atmosphere, simple moral injunctions, and the absence of corporal punishment, though Craig mentions that John Minter Morgan's *Revolt of the Bees*, which illustrated the advantages of community over competition, was used as a reading-book.[26] A delegate named James Rigby told the Fifth Co-operative Congress that the children were taught that no individual could love or hate at pleasure, and that his character was created for him by organization and surrounding circumstances,[27] and this, apparently, was as far as the teachings of Owen's principles went. However, Owenites always judged the success of their methods by the extent to which the actual disposition and behaviour of children were changed for the better, and Rigby recounted the story of a visit by the children to some public gardens in Manchester. Other school-children had been barred from entering them because of their rowdy and destructive behaviour, but the Owenite children, because of their responsible bearing, were allowed in, behaved themselves well, and were later complimented on their good behaviour, the teachers after-wards being asked what forms of discipline and corporal punishment were used to obtain such results. 'Other teachers rule their pupils by a rod of iron', declared Rigby; 'our rod is a rod of love. And if we were to turn our backs upon them, they would behave with the same propriety as when our eyes are upon them.' [28]

The creation of an atmosphere of love and trust in the classroom, and the substitution of practical and dynamic methods of teaching for rote-learning from books, were, of course, the hallmarks of the Owen-ite pedagogy and there is evidence that informal teaching methods were

[24] 'For the Erection of a New Co-operative Institution', printed circular, n.d., but Feb. 1836 (Owen correspondence).
[25] Lloyd Jones to Robert Owen, 14 Feb. 1836 (Owen correspondence).
[26] Craig, *American Socialist*, 13 Dec. 1877.
[27] *Crisis*, vol. iii, nos. 7 and 8, 19 Oct. 1833.   [28] Ibid.

E.I.—G

pursued at Salford. Lloyd Jones, in the circular previously mentioned, states that the lessons were 'conveyed to the mind in the most simple and amusing manner'. Much of the instruction was given orally, and often lessons took the form of conversations, although there were also lectures several times a week.[29] The school also aimed, as did Owen's at New Lanark, to provide recreation in the form of music, dancing, and singing, to counterbalance similar attractions in the town, where, as Jones pointed out, they were mixed up with the 'the vicious habit of drinking intoxicating liquors, thereby seducing those who are betrayed by these allurements, to immoral practices and finally to their destruction'.[30]

An unusual feature of the school, judging by previously accepted Owenite standards, was the attempt made to bring the senior pupils (who did not necessarily include the eldest pupils) into the government of the school. The first or most advanced class had a vote on all the transactions of the school, and the other classes had a right to send petitions to the teachers in favour of any reform or in pursuance of any grievance. On one occasion in 1833, the masters had decided to apply for a grant for the school under the terms of the educational grants of the Reform Government. The scholars, perhaps prompted by committed parents, petitioned the staff to abandon this on the grounds that 'it might subject the school to some tyrannical restraint'. The masters acceded and cancelled their resolution. As another example, the senior scholars, on their own initiative, set up a science society for the purpose of training themselves to be teachers.[31]

Unlike New Lanark, where opposition was at first mainly confined to some not very severe prejudices of the parents and some of Owen's partners, the Salford school had to contend with great opposition; 'most men of the present day', wrote Jones in 1895, 'would find it difficult to realise the brute indifference, and the blind hostility, with which the social and industrial reformers of the earlier part of the present century had to contend.' [32] The Salford school came in for particular hostility from clergy and the religious world in general;[33] one minister, Mr. Frost, of St. Stephen's, Salford, stated from the pulpit that parents would go to hell if they sent their children there.[34] This opposition, which had little, if any, effect, sprang from the fact that religion was not part of the curriculum, though the Statistical

[29] *Crisis,* vol. iii, nos. 7 and 8, 19 Oct. 1833.   [30] Ibid.   [31] Ibid.

[32] Jones, pp. 288–9.   [33] *Crisis*, 19 Oct. 1833.   [34] Black (1951), p. 33.

Society noticed that the Bible was used as a class-book. The Society was nevertheless troubled by the non-religious atmosphere of the school, but contented itself by reflecting that there was a majority of adults among the pupils when it made its investigation.[35]

The report of the Statistical Society enables a comparison to be made between the Owenite school and other schools in the borough in 1835. In comparison with other evening schools, the curriculum, the teaching methods, and the status of the pupils of the Owenite school were very much in advance of the rest; in nearly all of the latter reading, writing, and accounts formed the staple of the instruction. Sunday schools in the borough gave a limited range of subjects, most of them teaching reading only; writing, arithmetic, and other subjects were taught in only a small proportion. The standard of education in the whole borough was very poor in the Committee's view. 'Little or nothing' was learned in the many dame-schools; in the day schools little more than the three R's were taught, and that 'in a very slovenly and mechanical manner'.[36] The quality of the teachers was very low, and they were in general, says the report, suspicious of any modern improvements in teaching methods.[37] Only in the infant schools, where Wilderspin's methods were universally adopted, and in a few private schools, did the method of teaching, or the width of the curriculum, approach that of the Co-operative school.

There is no record of how long the Salford school existed, but it did not outlast the 1830s. According to Craig it gave birth to two divergent agencies — the Salford Mechanics' Institute, or Lyceum, and a social club sponsored by Joseph Smith, a local tradesman.[38] The Co-operative school we have described, however, was essentially a product of the upsurge of Co-operation of the early 1830s, as were those in London, and this had lost its impetus long before the end of the decade.

II

The Rational Schools

The schools of the Co-operative societies were regarded mainly as a means whereby the ideals and methods of Co-operation might more speedily be achieved. The schools that we shall consider in the

---

[35] *Report*, p. 28.   [36] Ibid., pp. 15, 16, 19.   [37] Ibid., p. 10.
[38] Craig, *American Socialist*, 13 Dec. 1877.

section that now follows were the product of the missionary zeal of the Rational Religionists, a quasi-socialist body which flourished from 1839 to 1845, and whose schools were more numerous, better organized, and more effective than those of the Co-operators. As J. F. C. Harrison emphasizes, the Co-operative and trade-union upsurge of the early 1830s was largely a political, economic, and social movement; that of the late 1830s and early 1840s was primarily a movement of ideas, which aroused the fear and horror of many respectable people, particularly of the clergy.[39]

The Universal Community Society of Rational Religionists was formed in May 1839 by the amalgamation of two existing Owenite bodies, the Association of All Classes and All Nations (founded 1835) and the National Community Friendly Society (founded 1837). The latter body had been registered under the Friendly Societies Acts, and as Owen's paper *Union* pointed out, 'the shield of the law was thereby thrown over the proceedings of the socialists'.[40] The Rational Religionists were therefore in a much stronger position than previous Owenite organizations.

The aim of the Rational Religionists was nothing less than the total reformation of society. Their programme included wealth for all, enlightened and non-coercive government, full employment, and universal education. The change to this state of society was to be accomplished peacefully, by a radical modification of public opinion. In this operation a high place was assigned to 'infant and other schools'.[41] The magnitude of the task might have daunted any other man than Owen, but armed with his own views of human nature and society, Owen convinced himself and his followers that the millennium was capable of realization. Education played an even more important part in the schemes of the Rational Religionists than it had done in those of the Co-operators; the universal community could only be brought about if young people were educated from an early age to become rational beings.[42]

The Rational Religionists were organized very much like a modern political party, with a central board of directors, chosen annually at

---

[39] J. F. C. Harrison, *Learning and Living, 1790–1960* (London, 1961), p. 110.

[40] *Union*, vol. 9, no. 1, 1 Dec. 1842.

[41] *The Constitution and Laws of the Universal Community Society of Rational Religionists* (London, 1839), p. 17.

[42] 'Report of the Leeds Congress of Rational Religionists', *New Moral World*, vol. i (N.S.), no. 3, 18 July 1840.

Congress, together with officers, district boards, and travelling missionaries. Members paid dues of 1½*d.* a week, and at one period at the beginning of the 1840s the movement had sixty-five branches in England and Scotland, with over three thousand members. It employed eighteen full-time missionaries and lecturers, and established Halls of Science in many of the larger towns.[43] This solid organizational framework made it much easier to establish stable and effective schools.

The 1840 Congress resolved that the branches of the Society should immediately set up day and Sunday schools, to teach, in addition to 'the usual routine' of education, facts and general science.[44] During the next three or four years enormous efforts were made by the branches to carry this resolution into effect. The difficulties facing them were very great, as an editorial in *New Moral World* pointed out in 1841. Branches had to contend with prejudices among their fellow-workers, stimulated as they were by 'teachers of sectarian dogmas', with a lack of suitable and conveniently situated schoolrooms, and with a deficiency of suitable schoolmasters.[45] A further difficulty concerned the fees. Fees of up to 4*d.* a week were insufficient to defray expenses in some schools,[46] and as an anxious correspondent wrote to the *New Moral World*, it was impossible for craftsmen earning a mere twenty or twenty-five shillings a week to pay the shilling or more that some schools charged.[47] But the chief difficulty was to find suitably qualified members of the Society to act as teachers. 'It would be much more easy', declared Robert Owen at the 1842 Congress, 'to find a dozen men suitable for the office of prime minister than one qualified to instruct children.'[48]

Despite all difficulties, however, a number of schools attached to branches were set up, and by 1842 there were nine day schools and twelve Sunday schools in operation.[49] These varied greatly in size and quality, but all attempted a wide curriculum, with attention to science teaching and the deliberate avoidance of religious instruction. A correspondent in the *New Moral World* stressed this important aspect

[43] Mary Hennell, *An Outline of the Various Social Systems and Communities Which Have Been Founded on the Principle of Co-operation* (London, 1844), p. 173.
[44] 'Report of the Leeds Congress', *loc. cit.*
[45] *New Moral World*, vol ii (N.S.), no. 23, 6 June 1841.
[46] Ibid., vol. ii (N.S.), no. 21, 22 May 1841.
[47] Ibid., vol. ii (N.S.), no. 5, 30 Jan. 1841.
[48] Ibid., vol. iii (N.S.), no. 47, 21 May 1842.   [49] Ibid.

of their work ; a young man who taught in a branch Sunday school was, he wrote, 'effectually superseding the baneful institutions of the priesthood'.[50]   The priesthood, not unnaturally, were in full cry against the 'infidel schools', as they had been against the Co-operative schools in the 1830s.   In Manchester a day school, 'free from the influence of the lash or sectarianism', attached to the Hall of Science flourished for several years from 1841 onwards,[51] and the Rev. W. J. Kidd founded a committee to oppose it, distributed tracts from door to door warning parents against its 'horrible and disgusting doctrines', and opened a rival Christian Institute as a counter-attraction.[52]   Kidd also managed to prosecute Robert Buchanan, one of the Hall of Science lecturers, on a charge of refusing to take the oaths of supremacy required of Dissenting ministers.[53]

What peculiar features did these institutions possess that could arouse such opposition on the part of the clergy ?   The aims and organizations of a Rational School can be studied in detail in the prospectus of the Liverpool school, which was printed in full in E. T. Craig's newspaper, *Star in the East*.[54]   The first meeting of the Liverpool Rational School Society took place on 21 July 1839, and its resolutions clearly indicated the Owenite strategy of attempting to found an alternative educational system for the working class.   The opening statement of the prospectus began with the proposition that the great mass of the people were brought up in 'a lamentable state of ignorance' and this ignorance was the source of 'intemperance, vice and crime'. Existing schools for the poor, however, merely inculcated 'mysterious and unintelligible dogmas, creeds, and catechisms of faith', and since it was obvious that neither the Government nor 'the priesthood' would provide a superior system (the reference was to the recent abandonment by Parliament of plans for an unsectarian normal school or training college), the people must 'unite, and determine to educate themselves'.   After adopting this fighting statement the meeting then resolved to form the Society for the purpose of providing as many schools as were required and urged the setting-up of similar schools

[50] *New Moral World,* vol. vii, no. 83, 23 May 1840.

[51] Ibid., vol. ii (N.S.), no. 16, 17 Apr. 1841 ;   no. 23, 6 June 1841.

[52] A. Black, 'Owenite Education, 1838–1851, with Particular Reference to the Manchester Hall of Science', unpublished dissertation, University of Manchester (1953), pp. 35, 40–41.

[53] R. Buchanan, *A Concise History of Modern Priestcraft* (Manchester, 1840), p. 146.

[54] *Star in the East,* 17 Aug. 1839.

subjects were to be taught by means of 'practical experiments, object teaching, familiar conversation and oral instruction'. A similar adventurousness in curriculum and method characterized other Rational Schools. The Huddersfield school examined its pupils in 'general objects, the atmosphere, geography and astronomy, Cuvierian division of the animal kingdom, osteology, arithmetic and geometry'.[56] In April 1841 the social missionary Alexander Campbell reported that, in the Manchester school, reading was being taught from the works of Robert Owen, the phrenologist George Combe, and John Minter Morgan the Owenite utopian.[57]

One of the most interesting aspects of these schools was the number that had adopted the Pestalozzian method of teaching. The Ashton Sunday school in Lancashire and the Hyde day school adopted it,[58] as did the school at Yarmouth, which was conducted 'on the principles of object teaching, united with the best portions of the Pestalozzian system'.[59] George James Holyoake, later to become the elder statesman of the Co-operative movement, during his short stay as teacher at the Sheffield branch school, adopted as his method 'the idea of Pestalozzi as developed by Dr. Mayo at Cheam'.[60] According to Holyoake, one reason for the adoption of Pestalozzi's method by the Owenite schools was that they were 'tangible, practicable and of immediate application'.[61] On the other hand, the fact that it was considered an advanced and progressive method probably also had its appeal. However, a clear distinction was made between Pestalozzian methods and 'object teaching', despite their close identification brought about by the widespread popularity of the Mayos' work on object lessons. Object teaching in Owenite schools apparently was derived from the experience of the New Lanark schools, in which 'objects' normally meant botanical and geological specimens, maps, globes, and models. The importance accorded to these objects in the Rational Schools sprang from the Owenite insistence that knowledge of the natural world was one of the means by which the mind could be freed from the preconceptions of existing society. Objects were fragments of

[56] *New Moral World,* vol. iv (N.S.), no. 21, 19 Nov. 1842.
[57] Ibid., vol. ii (N.S.), no. 16, 17 Apr. 1841. For an example of a Rational School see illustration above, facing p. 49.
[58] Ibid., vol. iii (N.S.), no. 23, 4 Dec. 1841 ; no. 16, 16 Oct. 1841.
[59] Ibid., vol. i (N.S.), no. 2, 11 July 1840.
[60] Letter to the *Sheffield Iris,* reprinted in *New Moral World,* vol. iii (N.S.), no. 2, 10 July 1841.   [61] Ibid.

the world of nature, and children's appreciation of them came through the senses, whereas books and teachers were a source of preconceptions. Hence the insistence of Owenite educationalists on placing 'facts' before children, on letting children make up their own minds, and hence also the distrust of textbooks and the importance placed on the interrogative method of teaching, based on knowledge gained by individual inquiry.

Some insight into the aims and methods of Owenite education is provided by the activities of John Ellis, one of the most capable and successful of the travelling schoolmasters of the early 1840s.[62] In September 1841 Ellis took charge of the day and evening schools of the Hyde branch in Cheshire and by the end of the year the day school had 110 pupils, and Ellis was trying to conduct it on Pestalozzian lines. The school was co-educational, for Ellis did not believe in relegating girls to sewing and knitting ; in fact, he thought they should have preferential treatment in order to redress the usual bias against educating them. He would, he claimed, try to give an all-round physical, moral, and intellectual education, but would also suit the instruction to the capacity of the child. He would not teach words without ideas, nor present ideas that did not convey facts. His aim was to arouse 'the perceptive and reflective faculties' of children, 'to unbuild, to raise the superstructure of the mind'.

These theories were extremely advanced in the 1840s, and very few schoolmasters would have thought of conducting a working-class school of over a hundred children on these lines. Ellis's curriculum was also much in advance of the time, putting the emphasis on science and cutting out religious instruction. He included, besides the three R's, 'elements of the most popular and useful sciences and a general knowledge of natural phenomena'. He appealed to the parents to donate fossils and mineralogical specimens to the school in order to build up a museum for object teaching. If any criticism is made of Ellis it must be that he was too ambitious, for the children could hardly have gained much more than a smattering of the sciences, and there is no evidence that he carried out any experiments. He also included a good deal of moral teaching, of a vaguely Owenite character — 'universal governmental principles' and 'universalism', as well as 'moral

---

[62] This account is based on reports in the *New Moral World*, vol. iii (N.S.), no. 16, 16 Oct. 1841 ; no. 26, 25 Dec. 1841 ; no. 35, 26 Feb. 1842 ; no. 39, 26 Mar. 1842 ; no. 41, 9 Apr. 1842.

truths' from the Bible, the Koran, and Confucius — but he emphasized that he would be careful 'not to teach any kind of religion, whether constructed by Confucius or Jesus Christ'.

As was to be expected, the school came in for opposition from the churches, and in order to counteract this, Ellis held a monthly public examination, which attracted a good deal of favourable notice in the district and was a kind of rationalist progress report. He invited the parents, provided tea, and interspersed the proceedings with singing and a magic-lantern show. The Christmas examination of 1841 was an oral one, in which the pupils were questioned on the properties and qualities of objects, human physiology, natural history, and geography. The following examination covered geography, geometry, the derivation of words, and astronomy. On the walls was set up a large drawing of the solar system ; on the latter 'the pupils described the distances of each planet from the sun, their revolutions, circumferences, and the relation they bear one to another, in a manner which astonished even the thinking portion of the audience'.

Ellis was not only a 'practical schoolmaster', as he described himself, but also a writer of textbooks. He wrote three — *Songs for Children, The Human Body Described*, and *Lessons on Objects* ; the last named of these was an official textbook for use in Owenite schools, together with *Chambers's Educational Course*.[63] Ellis's book on anatomy was written in simple language ; in fact, much of it was based on exercises on oral lessons written by children themselves. The book was divided into twenty-six lessons, each dealing with a different aspect of the subject — the skin, the muscular system, the bones, and so on. Each lesson consisted of a dozen or so short and simple statements :

The trunk is divided into the spine, the chest, the loins and the .pelvis[64]

Moral precepts on health, diet, or clothing were often inserted in the appropriate lesson :

Though I am young, I have a strong desire to be good and happy.[65]

Though I learn to calculate accurately, write correctly, draw neatly, sing sweetly, dance gracefully, speak fluently and read admirably, if I do not preserve my health these acquirements will be of little use.[66]

---

[63] *New Moral World,* vol. iii (N.S.), no. 47, 21 May 1842.

[64] J. Ellis, *The Human Body Described for the Instruction of the Young of Both Sexes* (London, 1856), p. 6. See also illustration above, facing p. 64.

[65] Ibid., p. 1.   [66] Ibid., p. 2.

Apparently these precepts were meant to be learned by heart and repeated to the teacher. In addition, there were five sets of exercises, with accompanying plates. The answers to these could presumably be written down.

Much of Ellis's teaching could have degenerated into mechanical questioning and answering, and he seems to have been aware of this, for he was careful to point out that his examinations were not 'as with scholars generally, a mechanical, parrot-like mode of proceeding', but 'a sifting of the acquirements of their knowledge'. Probably much depended on the aims, the energy, and the ability of the teacher ; what seems to have been a successful method with Ellis could have become a cramming routine with a less enlightened teacher.

It is unfortunate that Ellis's progressive experiment lasted no longer than a school year, but the closure of the school was due to desperate economic conditions in the town, not to internal failure. In April 1842 Ellis wrote despairingly to the *New Moral World*: 'Hyde is in ruins, misery is depicted on every countenance . . . the people are going to America by sixty or more per week. . . .' Many of his best scholars emigrated and when his chief monitor left 'there was scarcely a dry cheek in the school'. This boy, who had come to Ellis from a day school in the town, had made extraordinary progress, especially in scientific studies ; apart from a general knowledge of astronomy and other subjects, he had lectured to his fellow pupils on geography, human physiology, the nature and qualities of objects, and natural history. Ellis was much affected by the break-up of his school, and it seemed to have strengthened his determination to bring about a new order of society.

Most of the schools mentioned appear to have closed for one reason or another by about 1843 ; their decline paralleled that of the organization of the Rational Religionists, which failed to survive the break-up of the Queenwood experiment in 1845. During the three or four years of their heyday, however, they had provided a kind of education far in advance of anything hitherto given to working-class children. Their special claim to distinction was that they were the only popular educational institutions of the nineteenth century that were specifically designed to produce a change in society by changing the character of the knowledge given to the individuals composing it, and through their influencing the society itself.

These schools exemplified the struggle between two differing concepts of working-class education, which has persisted from the Mechanics' Institutes to the Workers' Educational Association and beyond — whether education should consist of 'knowledge', or whether it should be based on working-class ideology and social and economic factors. Though the Owenites took the latter position, they were not merely ideologists. Their position, as Ellis put it, was rather that the education he gave (which contained little positive Owenite propaganda) would influence not only body and mind but character, creating an aversion from 'irrational amusements' and 'ignorant company', developing the reason, and creating a desire for a rational system of society.[67] Whatever weaknesses may exist in this line of argument, it was at least one that was based on an analysis of social responsibility and social structure and it was very much in advance of the current view that the three R's and the Bible, taught relentlessly and by rote, were properly the staple educational food of working-class children.

III

Robert Pemberton and Others

The last of the world-makers who followed in the footsteps of Robert Owen was one Robert Pemberton. He announced his scheme as that of the 'Happy Colony', and he fixed upon New Zealand as the place where it was to be founded. The New World, as he conceived it, was to be circular. More mechanical and horticultural than any other projector, he avoided altogether parallelogrammatic devices. He declared his system was deduced from the discovery of the true attributes of the human mind. He had the merit of being solicitous both about education and the arts, and spent much money in publishing books which were never read, and in devising diagrams which were never examined.[68]

George Jacob Holyoake's ironical description of Pemberton contains more than a grain of truth. His educational schemes were a utopian *reductio ad absurdum* of Owenite educational policy, the last of a genre that included the theories of John Minter Morgan and James Silk Buckingham. As the working-class disciples of Owen had taken from the master's principles their scientific and rational aspects,

---

[67] *New Moral World*, vol. iii (N.S.), no. 16, 16 Oct. 1841.
[68] G. J. Holyoake, *The History of Co-operation* (London, 2nd ed., 2 vols., 1906), ii, pp. 545-6.

so did the middle-class Owenites speculate upon the grand educational designs that might exist in their ideal colonies and commonwealths. Pemberton, however, deserves notice not only for his splendid visions, but also as a minor pioneer of language theory and teaching.

Robert Pemberton was born in 1787 and grew up in London as the adopted son of a Mrs. Southbrook. Blessed with a private income, he married in 1824 and spent his time travelling on the Continent.[69] Returning to England, he spent his time writing educational treatises until in 1854, at the age of sixty-seven, he came across the works of Robert Owen and was immediately converted. 'I am perusing your works with intense interest,' he wrote to Owen, 'and I shall read them over and over again as long as I exist . . . by what I have already read of your philosophy I at once perceive that you are the father of the true philosophy of the human mind. . . .'[70] Three weeks later, with characteristic immodesty, he informed Owen that 'I find we are in perfect harmony and agreement in all the principal points of our investigation'.[71] He was rewarded by being greeted by Owen as 'a welcome co-adjutor'.

Pemberton's own investigations had been summed up in his first work, *The Attributes of the Soul from the Cradle*, published in 1849. His views, rooted in the social philosophy of the Enlightenment, contained echoes of the theories of Rousseau, Pestalozzi, and Owen himself. He stressed the importance of the environment in education, of natural methods of teaching, of the primacy of the senses in perception, the significance of the years of infancy, and distrust of formal teaching from books.[72]

The work that Pemberton considered to be most in harmony with the Owenite vision was *The Happy Colony*, published in 1854. Inspired by More's *Utopia*,[73] it was dedicated to 'the Workmen of Great Britain' and envisaged the founding of a classless society in New Zealand, financed by shilling subscriptions from working men. Its chief feature was an Elysian Academy, at which young people would spend the first twenty-one years of their life, acquiring, as part of an encyclopaedic education, no less than eight languages, which

[69] R. C. B. Pemberton, *Pemberton Pedigrees* (Bedford, 1923), Chart 40.
[70] Pemberton to Owen, 2 Oct. 1854 (Owen correspondence).
[71] Pemberton to Owen, 21 Oct. 1854.
[72] R. Pemberton, *The Attributes of the Soul from the Cradle* (London, 1849), *passim*.
[73] Pemberton to Owen, 21 Oct. 1854.

would fit them for free communication with the countries of the world.[74]

Having caught the interest of Owen, Pemberton soon became immersed in the millennial plans that occupied the last years of Owen's life. Pemberton was also in correspondence with John Minter Morgan, who had written to express his admiration for *The Attributes of the Soul*, and enclosed a copy of his own *Christian Commonwealth*,[75] a similar utopian scheme, which, unlike those of Owen and Pemberton, had received the support of the Church.[76] Pemberton also came to know Thomas Atkins, a civil engineer and disciple of Owen and another author of utopian plans for education, and in *An Address to the Bishops and Clergy* Pemberton linked Robert Owen, himself, and Thomas Atkins together as educational visionaries, whose labours in the mental kingdom would go far beyond the achievements of science.[77]

The high point of Pemberton's public endeavours to convert the people to a higher conception of education was achieved at a meeting at St. Martin's Hall on 1 January 1855. This was convened by Robert Owen as an advertisement for his long-promised millennium, which would be inaugurated on 14 May of that year by an aggregate meeting in London of delegates from all governments, countries, religious sects, parties, and classes. The revolution would be brought about by peaceful means and with the consent of mankind, and it was the object of the meeting to discover and develop the actual means. A London newspaper described the proceedings as 'a host of visionary and impracticable schemes connected with political, social, educational and religious reforms'.[78] Owen and Pemberton appeared on the platform together and the latter actually read Owen's speech, in which Owen praised Pemberton's ideas on education as 'true, beautiful, and with himself perfectly original', though they had both come to the same fundamental conclusions. Pemberton in his turn praised Owen as 'a good and divine agent' employed by Providence 'for bringing about the perfection and happiness of man' and whose system was too

[74] R. Pemberton, *The Happy Colony* (London, 1854), *passim* ; *An Address to the People, on the Necessity of Popular Education, in Conjunction with Emigration as a Remedy for All our Social Evils* (London, 1859), pp. 4–5, 9.

[75] Pemberton to Owen, 21 Oct. 1854.

[76] W. H. G. Armytage, *Heavens Below* (London, 1961), pp. 209 ff.

[77] R. Pemberton, *An Address to the Bishops and Clergy of All Denominations* (London, 1855), pp. 13–15.

[78] *Lloyd's Weekly London Newspaper*, 7 Jan. 1855.

beautiful for 'the uneducated priesthood and the uneducated gambling commercial world'.[79]

Pemberton gave an outline of his educational views and explained the details of his 'projected new city', the capital of the Happy Colony, a large drawing of which hung at the back of the platform. It consisted of a series of concentric circles which contained dwelling-houses, parks, gardens, and orchards. In the inner circle, in grounds covering fifty acres, was situated the Academy, which was made up of four colleges with conservatories, workshops, swimming-pools, and riding-schools near by. On the ground geographical and astronomical maps were laid out and circular groves embodied the Muses, history, and pathology (see illustration facing p. 65).

After Pemberton had demonstrated his particular scheme a letter was read from James Silk Buckingham, former M.P. for Sheffield (1832–7), seafarer, traveller, editor, and social reformer. A drop scene showing his model town was presented, a project similar to that of Pemberton except that it consisted of concentric squares rather than circles. Thomas Atkins then told the meeting about his model town, the chief feature of which was a model school 'for scientific, visual and practical education'. It consisted of a circular area, 60 feet in diameter, from which diverged, at the points of the compass, four corridors 150 feet long, 30 feet wide, and 30 feet high. The corridors forming the two arms of the cross were thus 360 feet long, the equivalent of the number of degrees from the earth's poles. Each corridor would contain specimens of the animal, vegetable, and mineral kingdoms, classified according to the latitudes in which they were found. In addition, the model school would have an industrial department which would include a farm, garden, workshop, laboratory, and factory.[80]

Visions are necessary to reformers, and few had been more influential than those of Owen's early communitarian schemes. But to exercise power such projects had to be capable of realization. The painted drop scenes of the millenarians of 1855 represented nothing more than the hopes of those who had despaired of changing the existing educational system and were seeking a short cut to progress. They were too involved, too far beyond anything remotely possible

[79] *Robert Owen's Address, Delivered at the Meeting in St. Martin's Hall, Long Acre, London, on the 1st January, 1855* (London, 1855), p. 21.

[80] Ibid., pp. 26–28 ; cf. also 'Prospectus of the Industrial and Provident Moral, Scientific, and Educational Association (Proposed by Thomas Atkins, Esq., C.E. Oxford)' (Owen correspondence).

at the time, despite Pemberton's brave hope of getting the British workman to finance his projects. Perhaps Pemberton sensed this, for within a few years, although still an admirer of Owen, he was beginning to doubt the possibilities of bringing about the ideal society by means of meetings, petitions, and propaganda, and thought Owen was 'out of his depth' in trying to create societies by philanthropic means.[81]

Pemberton turned once more to exploring the importance of sound and speech in education. In early works he had stressed the importance of the sense of hearing and the role of speech (allied to the reading of special cards) in the learning of such diverse subjects as grammar or anatomy.[82] Now, basing himself on the observation that all children learned a language naturally in the first three years of their life, he maintained that all knowledge could be brought under the heading of language, and that the ideal form of the natural method would be continuous oral teaching by relays of teachers, so that an unbroken stream of sound might be kept up, interspersed with music and poetry.[83] In order to put these ideas into practice, Pemberton opened the Infant Euphonic Institution at his residence, 33 Euston Square. Sometimes called the Philosophical Model Infant School, it has been suggested that this was an ordinary day school,[84] but it is clear that it was really a demonstration school for intending teachers of his methods. At the opening ceremony on 22 August 1857, Pemberton stated that the object of the school was to exhibit 'the true system of education' that he had outlined in his various works. He then introduced his son Robert Markham Pemberton who read a paper entitled 'The Educational Question', written by his father.[85] Pemberton began by referring to the recent conference on education presided over by Prince Albert, at which various criticisms of the current educational system had been made. He took this as corroboration of his own views on the deficiencies of the school system, and advocated that the New Model School must be founded on natural lines ; all the pupils would receive

---

[81] R. Pemberton, *The Science of Mind Formation* (London, 1858), pp. 72–73.

[82] Cf. R. Pemberton, *The Natural Method of Teaching the Elements of Grammar, for the Nursery and Infant Schools* (London, 1851) ; *The Natural Method of Teaching the Technical Language of Anatomy, for the Nursery and Infant Schools* (London, 1852).

[83] R. Pemberton, *To the Right Honourable Earl Granville* (London, 1857), p. 6 ; *The Infant Drama* (London, 1857), *passim* ; *The Science of Mind Formation*, pp. 113–14.

[84] Armytage, p. 222 n.

[85] [R. Pemberton], *Report of the Proceedings of the Inauguration of Mr. Pemberton's New Philosophical Model Infant School* (London, 1857), pp. 8–17, on which the following account is based.

equal benefit, no task-work would be given, and rewards and punishments abolished. The first stage of the proposed new education would consist of the acquisition of words, which would be learned by the children at the rate of some thousand a day, followed by grammar taught on the Pembertonian method. Poetry and literature, which would demonstrate the correct harmony of the language, would be conveyed to the children by the teacher reading daily extracts from the poems of Homer, Petrarch, Milton, and other authors, ancient and modern. The infant would hear music from the time of his birth : 'the sounds of music vibrate delectable sensations on the whole nervous system and through its electric power it animates and vigorates both mind and body'. Pemberton had invented the Nursery Chromatic Barrel Organ expressly for this purpose and a small model for the nursery and a larger one for schools were then exhibited. The next stage of the system was the learning of languages, firstly the child's own native language, then foreign languages by sound alone.

After the reading of this paper some music was performed on the harmonium by a Mr. C. H. Osborne and much practical work was demonstrated. Robert Pemberton concluded the proceedings by emphasizing that what the audience had just seen was the true method of teaching infants, that sound was the principal agent of this method, and that by this natural system of teaching carried out in the different branches of knowledge, a perfect education would be attained. The school was then announced to be opened. The demonstration would be repeated every Wednesday afternoon and the public would be admitted by ticket.

Pemberton's experiments in language teaching, although intellectually arbitrary, were as concrete and workable as his previous utopian schemes had been visionary and impracticable, though both were interconnected and sprang from the same philosophical soil.

IV

The followers of Owen in educational experiments of the 1830s were working men trying to provide for themselves and their children a schooling and an outlook on life that would have an influence on other schools and arouse a working-class response to education for a changing society. The professional teaching skill, the organization of the schools, the necessary money, and the innovating zeal did not last, and this radical educational experiment, the only one started and maintained by working-class groups, died within ten years. Other ventures for poorer children were the Rational Religionists, maintained by an ethical zeal and a well-conceived organization, and these carried forward in the 1840s Owen's strategy of founding an alternative educational system to the elementary schools of the Anglican and Free Church societies. But the organization of the religious bodies was stronger and rationalist socialism was a minority movement.

Utopians sprang from Owenism as from unorthodox religious groups, and Robert Pemberton's scheme for the 'Happy Colony' in New Zealand was like a number of other ideal schemes, some of which reached no further than written prospectuses and preliminary meetings. The 1850s and 1860s were the decades of the great Commissions, which evaluated the whole educational provision of the country, and by that time the energy of working-class innovation was spent.

6. The Hills and Hazelwood School [1]

I

I met in London several members of a very remarkable family, possessing, I think more practical ability, administrative and deliberative, than I have ever since found united in any one household ; a family deserving well of their country, and every member of which has since made his mark, in one department or other ; the Hills, formerly of Hazelwood, Birmingham.[2]

The justness of Robert Dale Owen's assessment of Thomas Wright Hill and his five sons becomes clear when we consider their careers. Matthew Davenport became Recorder of Birmingham and M.P. for Hull ; Rowland is known to history as the originator of the Penny Post ; Arthur was a well-known educationalist who became principal of Bruce Castle School ; Frederic became Inspector of Prisons and

[1] C. G. Hey's M.A. thesis, 'The History of Hazelwood School, Birmingham, and its Influence on Educational Developments in the Nineteenth Century', Wales (1954) has provided a valuable survey of the subject. This chapter, however, differs somewhat from Hey in both treatment and conclusions.

[2] R. D. Owen, *Threading My Way* (London, 1874), pp. 307-8.

secretary to the Postmaster-General; and Edwin was a prominent inventor who became a high official in the Post Office. The first three sons, however, have another claim to fame as the founders of one of the famous progressive schools of the nineteenth century, Hazelwood, and its extension, Bruce Castle, which Thomas de Quincey considered 'the most original experiment in Education which in this country at least has been attempted since . . . the Edgeworths'.[3]

Hazelwood was the successor to Hill Top, a school that Thomas Wright Hill had founded in Birmingham at the beginning of the nineteenth century. Hill had settled in late eighteenth-century Birmingham, which he found fruitful soil for his scientific and educational interests. After a strict and puritanical upbringing and a good education at Kidderminster Grammar School, he had become successively a brass-founder, a charity-school teacher, a partner in a leather firm, and a works superintendent at Kidderminster. He opened Hill Top School in 1803, having bought it cheaply from his friend Thomas Clark, who left teaching to make his fortune manufacturing cotton machinery.[4] An enthusiastic educationalist and a man of wide if indiscriminate learning and enlightened ideas, Thomas Wright Hill was described by a former pupil, William Lucas Sargant, as 'tender hearted, intelligent and reflective: imbued with the liberalism which is now predominant: of moderate scholastic attainments . . . but resolute in making his boys understand whatever he taught them'.[5] He was, however, somewhat unpractical in the ordinary concerns of life, found sustained effort difficult, and was often in debt. Hill Top, though it had some unorthodox features — science lectures, shorthand, elocution and a wide programme of reading in contemporary authors — did not begin to introduce anything really revolutionary until the elder sons began to take a hand in the running of the school somewhere around 1816.[6]

The five brothers were educated mainly at Hill Top, and even in their childhood and youth they showed a love of detailed organization, classification, and constitution-making which was to be a prominent

[3] [T. de Quincey], 'Plans for the Instruction of Boys in Large Numbers', *London Magazine*, vol. ix (1824), p. 410.
[4] J. L. Dobson, 'The Hill Family and Educational Change in the Nineteenth Century. I: Thomas Wright Hill and the School at Hill Top, Birmingham', *Durham Research Review*, no. 10 (Sept. 1959), pp. 261–3.
[5] W. L. Sargant, *Essays of a Birmingham Manufacturer* (London, 4 vols., 1869–72), ii, pp. 186–7.   [6] Dobson, pp. 265–6.

feature of their work at Hazelwood. Rowland Hill organized a successful dramatic society at Hill Top and drew up a detailed constitution
for it; Arthur wrote plays; Matthew Davenport began 'A Description and Laws of Juvenile Games'.[7] Before they were out of their
teens the young Hills had helped in the teaching at Hill Top and held
a variety of outside jobs. Rowland Hill, for instance, was for some
years a part-time official in the Birmingham Assay Office.

When the brothers reached manhood, they took an increasing share
in the direction of Hill Top School. Edwin started to train as an
engineer and Matthew Davenport to study law, though he continued
to take a close interest in education. Rowland Hill, however, began to
establish at Hill Top those features that were fully worked out at
Hazelwood. In 1816 a Court of Justice was set up, followed by the
establishment of a jury system which took the place of corporal punishment, formally abolished in 1818. A system of marks was introduced for rewards, and rank (by this was meant assessment of character
and ability) was made the basis of election to a committee by which
the pupils governed the school.[8]

Hill Top was really a trial ground, a pilot experiment for a new type
of school. In July 1819 the whole institution moved to Hazelwood
in Edgbaston, occupying a building that had been specially designed
by Rowland Hill, with a large schoolroom seating 250, a stage at one
end, numerous classrooms, and a museum. In 1820 it was partly
rebuilt and extended following a disastrous fire. The reconstructed
school had several novel features: a built-in heating and ventilation
system, an observation platform on the roof for astronomical observation and surveying operations, in addition to studies, a library, a
reference library, a gymnasium, and a swimming-bath (a drawing is
reproduced facing p. 128). It was after these extensions and recon-
structions at Hazelwood that the school acquired its characteristic
features: complete self-government by the boys, a mark system of
reward and punishment of great complexity, a minutely ordered timetable, and attention to useful rather than classical knowledge in the
curriculum.

Hazelwood was a school very much in the radical and utilitarian
tradition. Thomas Wright Hill, as a friend of Joseph Priestley, was
greatly influenced by the example of the eighteenth-century Dissenting

[7] R. and F. Davenport-Hill, *The Recorder of Birmingham : A Memoir of Matthew Davenport Hill* (London, 1878), p. 7; C. Hill (ed.), *Frederic Hill* (London, 1894), pp. 23, 33.   [8] Dobson, p. 266.

Academies with their emphasis on producing the cultured, self-reliant man of affairs. The most striking point about Hazelwood, however, was its resemblance to the Chrestomathic proposals of Jeremy Bentham, though the Hills denied that they had seen Bentham's treatise when they published the first edition of their book describing the Hazelwood system, *Public Education*.[9] Bentham's suggestions that utility and facility should decide the attention given to various subjects, his emphasis on the importance of science and technology, his belief that the prime purpose of knowledge was to enable a person to earn a future livelihood, his stress on the principles of 'comparative proficiency', 'place capturing', 'uninterrupted action', 'distraction-prevention', the exclusion of religion, and the practice of pupil self-government,[10] all find an echo in the arrangements at Hazelwood. It is immaterial whether or not the Hills took these ideas from Bentham's writings, though there is a strong presumption that they did. Such views were a part of the climate of middle-class radical thought in the immediate post-Napoleonic period. The systems of Bell and Lancaster to whom Bentham admitted a debt, also had an influence on the arrangements of Hazelwood School.

The radical intelligentsia at this period were greatly concerned to improve the education of the middle class. The attempt of the Benthamites to found a Chrestomathic School in London, the writings of James Mill, the criticisms of existing education and proposals for reform in the *Quarterly Journal of Education*, are all evidence of a desire to break away from the classical public school and university towards a more practical and utilitarian form of education.[11] Hazelwood School and its later extension at Bruce Castle can best be understood in this context, for it gathered together the varied yearnings of the middle class for an education of their own and developed them coherently to a highly idiosyncratic conclusion.

II

Most of our knowledge of the system of education pursued at Hazelwood comes from *Public Education*, first published anonymously in

9 *Public Education : Plans for the Government and Liberal Instruction of Boys, in Large Numbers ; as Practised at Hazelwood School* (London, 2nd ed., 1825), p. 185 n.

10 J. Bentham, *Chrestomathia*, in J. Bowring (ed.), *The Works of Jeremy Bentham* (Edinburgh, 11 vols., 1838–43), viii, pp. 46 ff.

11 Cf. B. Simon, *Studies in the History of Education, 1780–1870* (London, 1960), pp. 72 ff.

1819, with a revised and extended second edition in 1825. Much of it was composed by Matthew Davenport Hill with the assistance of Arthur Hill, but the credit for the details of the system are largely due to Rowland. *Public Education* was published partly as a justification for Hazelwood, partly as an advertisement for it. Though written in a plain and undemonstrative style, which hardly does justice to the exciting innovations in its pages, it was an epoch-making book. It showed a wide acquaintance with leading educators both living and dead, and every aspect of the system was given extremely careful thought and thorough consideration.

The general object of the school was simple; it was to produce 'men of business'.[12] 'Business' was not understood in the narrow commercial or industrial sense, but seen as the capacity for practical administration in any walk of life. Arthur's son Birkbeck Hill told the Schools Inquiry Commission of 1868 that the main concern of Bruce Castle School was with 'the upper stratum of the middle classes'.[13] The schools produced, in fact, the kind of administrators and commercial intelligentsia that the Hill brothers, themselves products of the system, so well exemplified.

At Hazelwood and Bruce Castle the guiding principle of leadership was not fundamentally different from that in force at Arnold's Rugby: 'He who is to command, should first learn to obey.' Though Hazelwood boys were trained to be the directors, as the Hills termed it, they were also given experience as subordinates or instruments who executed the orders. Directors, the Hills believed, should have ascendancy over the minds of others, be able to estimate the qualities of those around them, be acquainted with the principle of the division of labour, but above all have a practical acquaintance with the science of evidence.[14] The operations of the school court provided ample opportunity for boys to familiarize themselves with the latter. The duties of the instrument were defined as 'punctual, intelligent, unhesitating obedience', which the arrangements of the school were also in part designed to cultivate. Other, more positive, virtues were not forgotten:

> The object which we have kept in view, in forming our system of government and instruction, is to render our pupils, in the highest

[12] *Public Education*, pp. 315 ff.
[13] *Report of the Schools Inquiry Commission*, P.P. (1867–8), xxviii, p. 839.
[14] *Public Education*, pp. 324 ff.

degree, virtuous and intelligent men ; and at the same time so to modify the education of each, as to enable him to pass with honour, success and happiness, through that path in life into which he will probably be thrown.[15]

The nineteen principles on which the school was run further exemplified how the philosophical basis of the school affected its organization. The attention given to each subject in the curriculum was measured, in true Benthamite fashion, by 'its effect on the welfare and happiness of the individual pursuing it, and of society at large', and each child was to concentrate upon those studies 'for which nature had best qualified him'.[16] There was emphasis on a thorough grounding in the elements, together with individual work, constant revision, and reasonable hope of reward so that the pupil could advance steadily in each subject with 'moderate exertion'.[17] 'This plan', says Arthur Hill, in a language more descriptive of a factory than a school, 'has all the advantages which a master and workman both obtain, in the man's being employed in *piece-work* instead of *day-work*.' [18]

The division of the school day was based on the Benthamite principle of 'the regular and systematic disposal of time' ;[19] it began at 6 a.m., and during the hours that elapsed till the senior boys retired at 9 p.m., not a minute was wasted. All the mechanical tasks of moving from lesson to lesson or place to place, of calling the roll, and so on, were turned to positive account, in that the high degree of organization and system, and the habits of punctuality and order that they invoked, were held by the Hills to be an essential part of the kind of character-training they aimed at. As de Quincey remarked in a review of *Public Education*, a school organized on this system 'burns its own smoke'.[20]

Between 6 a.m. and 7 a.m. the school was aroused and preparations were made for the tasks of the day.[21] Just before 6 a.m. a bugler sounded reveille ; at 6 a.m. the bell rang, and the boys left their beds at the word of command, dressed themselves, and arranged themselves in each room in a certain order preparatory to marching downstairs. The boys in each dormitory were under the command of a prefect

[15] [A. Hill], *Sketch of the System of Education, Moral and Intellectual, in Practice at the Schools of Bruce Castle, Tottenham, and Hazelwood, Near Birmingham* (London, 1833), p. 1.   [16] Ibid., p. 3.   [17] Ibid., pp. 3 ff.
[18] Ibid., p. 5.   [19] Ibid., p. 7.   [20] [de Quincey], p. 413.
[21] This account is based upon *Public Education*, pp. 153 ff.

and divided into divisions under sub-prefects. At 6.10 a.m. the bell rang again, the divisions were given the command 'March', and each proceeded down the stairs in regular order to the music of the band. When they reached the schoolroom they stood, in order of march, in ten parallel lines, and the boys' shoes, collected in baskets the previous evening, were distributed.

Then, at five-minute intervals from 6.15 a.m., the boys went to the wash-house in three groups, depending partly on their rank and partly on their age, the smaller boys being washed by servants. On leaving the wash-house each boy was given a slice of bread.

At 6.35 a.m. the boys were mustered for prayers. Since great importance was placed upon the time-saving methods employed at these gatherings, and since the whole process was a complex essay in logistics, the procedure of the muster is here given in some detail.

After being summoned by a bell to the main schoolroom, the boys formed up in rows of ten, or 'decads'. Twenty seconds after the bell ceased, the band struck up and the doors were closed. Twenty seconds later a teacher exhibited a card with the word PLACE on it, after which no boy could join his rank. The tune then ceased and if a rank was then incomplete a teller raised his hand, and the absentees were called out and recorded by the Registrar. The roll was then checked by the tellers calling out the number of those present, each adding their number to the previous one until the last number was received. The Registrar added this to the number of absentees, and if the process had been correctly carried out, the total equalled the number on the school roll. Then the time taken to conduct the operation was announced by a boy, the word 'Form' called out, and the pupils rearranged themselves into classes and prepared for prayer-reading or for marching away. The Hills claimed that the average time occupied between the ending of the tune and the calling of the order to 'Form' was forty-two seconds, and that it had, on occasion, been reduced to twenty-five seconds.

After this muster, prayers were read. 'Great care is taken', wrote the Hills diplomatically, 'that they shall contain those expressions of devotion only, in which every denomination of Christians may join with perfect sincerity.' [22]

Between 6.45 a.m. and 7 a.m. a monitor visited the bedrooms to check on those who might still have been in bed on account of illness

[22] *Public Education*, p. 156.

or indisposition, and a rally on the drum was sounded to warn all officers and others engaged on duties that the general muster for the start of lessons was about to take place.

Immediately after the muster the boys formed into classes appropriate to the subject on the timetable. The first lesson of the day lasted half an hour, and at 7.35 a.m., at a signal on the drum, the three highest boys in each class (with the exception of one or two of the highest classes) received small rewards and were allowed to depart.

The procedure for dispersal to the next lesson was as rigorous as before and was repeated at all changes of class. After ringing the bell at 7.30 a.m. the monitor waited for one minute, then struck the drum and waited twenty seconds; the door was then closed. He then struck twenty-five strokes on the drum, each at the interval of one second, during which time all the school was expected to join their next class at the parallel lines; when this was done each group marched away to its respective class, which lasted until 8.50 a.m.

Then two ceremonies took place. Some of the younger boys, and others described as having 'not acquired a character for neatness', went into a room where they were individually examined as to personal appearance. The rest formed into ranks in alphabetical order, and the lost property of the previous day was distributed, for each item of which a small fine was paid to the class prefects. In addition, fines levied the previous day were paid, rewards paid to those who submitted evidence of voluntary labour, and stationery given out. The Troverer, who was in charge of the Trovery, a bookcase with doors of open wire-work in which unclaimed lost property was placed, also distributed, on payment of a fine, such property as could be recognized and claimed.

At 9.10 a.m. the bell rang for breakfast, and the boys marched into the breakfast-room to the music of the band. Breakfast lasted half an hour, but defaulters were allowed twenty-five minutes only, after which time they had to go to work. At 9.30 a.m. the end of breakfast was signalled, and boys were free to re-enter the main schoolroom if they wished. At 9.45 a.m. there was another general muster, after which the boys dispersed to their respective classes in the usual way. Between 9.45 a.m. and 1 p.m. there were four periods of varying length, with time allowed for repetition under boy monitors in some of them, according to the subject.

At 1 p.m. there was a muster for dinner, which lasted for an hour, with twenty minutes only allowed for defaulters. Afternoon school began at 2 p.m., with lessons at hourly intervals until 5 p.m., when refreshments were taken. The boys were then free till 5.45 p.m., with the exception of 'a few boys who have acquired a habit of stooping'; these underwent remedial exercises, which mainly consisted of lying down in a prescribed manner, during which they were read to by another boy, for which office he drew a salary of marks.

At 5.45 p.m. there was a muster for evening school, attended by the boarders only. This session lasted only three-quarters of an hour, the main occupation of the boys being the preparation of the following day's lessons. At 6.30 p.m. ablutions were carried out in the same manner as in the morning. The Library was also open at this time for the exchange of books. At 7 p.m. there was a muster for supper, with the usual minimum period for defaulters. At 7.35 p.m. followed prayers. The younger boys marched to bed at 8 p.m., the older at 9 p.m. In the dormitory they arranged themselves in the order in which they marched down in the morning and exchanged their shoes for slippers, and the former were collected in wickerwork baskets to be dried, if necessary. Sometimes, for the senior boys, the hours between 8 p.m. and 9 p.m. were occupied by a voluntary lecture or singing lessons.

This strictly controlled regimen was probably less fearsome in practice than it sounds in cold print. The Hills, by adding touches of ceremony — such as the fifteen-piece band, which performed twelve times a day — gave it some solemnity and glamour. 'Many of the boys here are very odd and amusing', wrote a new boy to his mother. 'Do you know Mamma there is a band here, and the boys play in it; we have a different tune almost every muster; amongst others I heard my favourite Tyrolese song, which Louisa plays on the piano.' [23]

The Hills' insistence on punctuality was based on the belief that efficiency in the affairs of life depended on the exact disposition of time, and the knowledge that the only way to ensure approximate punctuality in later life was to insist upon absolute punctuality at school. The focal point of timekeeping at Hazelwood lay in the office of Monitor. The duties of the office were ringing the bell at stated times and attendance upon boys at various tasks. The Monitor's duties were set out on a card near the clock, and he had to ring the bell and make other signals no less than sixty times during the day.

[23] *Hazelwood Magazine*, vol. vi, no. 3 (Apr. 1828), p. 46.

If the bell was rung at the wrong time, or some other duty not carried out on the dot, the Monitor was fined heavily, the fine increasing with every minute of error. At the end of the day if he carried out his duties perfectly, he was rewarded with transferable marks, which increased with every consecutive perfect day. But an error of even a single second was punished by a fine. To make the system work, the Hills found that they had to do two things — 'to induce an almost superstitious punctuality on the part of the monitor', and to increase the duties to the maximum; 'the same boy', they observed, 'who had complained of the difficulty of being punctual when he had to ring the bell only ten times in the day, found his duty comparatively easy when his memory was taxed to a fourfold amount.'[24] The Hills found that after a large number of boys had acted as Monitor, a sense of punctuality was diffused throughout the school, and nominal and real hours of attendance became exactly the same. But occasionally there were lapses. The Hills remembered with amusement the look of utter astonishment on the face of a new member of the staff when he was informed that he was one minute late for assembly.[25] There was even one authentic case of a boy who scalded his foot with boiling water immediately before a muster, but who hurried into the hall at the exact time despite intense pain.[26]

The same approach was applied to the other twin bugbears of school life — attendance and silence. It was held that regular attendance, particularly at the first muster of each term, was beneficial to a boy's character and was therefore rewarded. Again, the boys entered into the spirit of the thing, and cases were known of boys walking twenty miles a day to be at the first muster on time.

It was easier to preserve perfect silence, the Hills maintained, than to make approximations for particular purposes; in other words it was impossible to maintain for any length of time a medium between silence and noisiness. When the boys were engaged in work or private study in the main schoolroom, and at mealtimes, the duty of preserving silence fell upon a boy called a Silentiary, who wore slippers for silence and a hat to distinguish him from other boys. The Silentiary was paid a salary out of a fund made up from two sources — a tax on talkative boys and a subsidy paid by older pupils. The latter was justified on the grounds that it was in the interests of the older and therefore more influential boys to render the labour of the Silentiary

[24] *Public Education*, p. 186.   [25] Ibid., p. 316.   [26] Ibid., p. 91.

as light as possible, as his salary rose in proportion to the difficulties of his office.[27]

Delegation of responsibility to the pupils in this manner was an integral part of the Hazelwood system. The complex arrangements for pupils' self-government, however, were not merely an elaborate game that would give the pupils a taste of legislative and executive procedure, but a carefully designed scheme to inculcate a particular morality that would animate the functioning of the whole school :

> by the establishment of a system of legislation and jurisprudence, wherein the power of the master is bounded by general rules, and the duties of the scholar accurately defined, and where the boys themselves are called upon to examine and decide upon the conduct of their fellows, we have provided a course of instruction in the great code of morality, which is likely to produce far more powerful and lasting effects than any quantity of mere precept.[28]

The foundation of moral sentiment they defined as 'the power which brings the wishes and opinions of the individual into unison with those of society'.[29] In other words, there were to be no conflicting loyalties. The good of the school should be put before any personal or group aim, and the minds of the pupils directed outwards to the real merits of each other. The 'natural warfare' between masters and boys, which seemed so normal to Tom Brown and was almost universal in schools of this type, was to be replaced by co-operation.

A detailed account of the government of Hazelwood, and its system of rewards and punishments, is given in chapter 14 of *Public Education*. In outline the arrangements consisted of a School Committee, the supreme law-making body, and an elected jury Court, presided over by a judge, which tried major offences against school discipline. Minor offences were dealt with by a Magistrate, assisted by elected officials. A number of Executive Officers, some of whose duties we have already described, assisted in the running of the school. Corporal punishment, public disgrace, and minor impositions were abolished, and their place was taken by a system in which misdemeanours were punished by the loss of marks, a token coinage that could be earned by good performance in academic work and school administration. Nearly all punishments were in the form of fines from the boy's personal stock of marks. Only in rare cases was solitary confinement

[27] *Public Education,* pp. 68–69.   [28] Ibid., p. 175.   [29] Ibid., p. 183.

imposed or boys deprived of their free time. Marks contributed to rank, which was a measure of the pupil's general standing in the school, and made up on a weekly and aggregate system. As the assessment of school work was made at intervals and varied from subject to subject, all boys had a chance to gain rank. A later innovation was the introduction of Circles and Guardians, the latter being senior boys who took charge of a circle or group of ten junior boys, and were responsible for their welfare, conduct, and general adaptation to the school routine. This idea was taken direct from the practice of Fellenberg's Institution, on the advice of Robert Dale Owen, a former pupil there.[30]

III

The academic aspect of Hazelwood School was in some degree more conventional than the organizational side. Nevertheless, there was a seriously thought-out procedure concerning curriculum and method that foreshadowed a great deal of what was considered progressive much later in the century. The Hills never hesitated to take over and adapt the latest and most advanced teaching methods of their own day. In fact, they claimed little credit themselves for their methods, but stated they were merely an improvement on various techniques that had been current for years. The Hill brothers were familiar with the work of most of the leading educators of their time, and gave particular notice to the Edgeworths and Bell and Lancaster, but whatever they learned from others they transformed and improved and welded into a single working system.

The academic aim was so to dispose the available time and to provide the greatest motivation for learning as to allow each boy to work to his maximum efficiency. The Hills realized that the full employment of time, which was the second great aim of the school next to the inculcation of morality, could not be enforced but had to be realized by giving the pupils the opportunity to employ their time to the best advantage. This was ensured by means of punctuality, division into classes (by no means common in the 1820s), a complete bar on idleness, and clearly defined goals and objectives.

The next step was to provide the necessary motivation for academic study. Here the Hills inverted the usual practice in schools, and relegated fear of punishment and hope of reward to the bottom of the

[30] Ibid., pp. 370 ff.

scale as motives to study, on the grounds that they were not only degrading but also inefficient. They did not completely abolish rewards and punishments in the academic sphere, but kept them to the minimum. Punishment was to be certain in its effect, and rewards were to be various, light, and adapted to the disposition of the pupil. Even emulation was to be utilized, provided its exercise was made 'gentle and temperate'.[31]

The Hills argued that the two most powerful stimuli to academic work were love of employment and love of knowledge, and of these the latter was undoubtedly the more powerful and permanent. Love of industry could not solely be relied upon without some worth-while purpose or activity, and the Hills attached a great deal of importance to generating a love of knowledge in their pupils. Generally speaking, they directed their staff to give their pupils a perspective to relate the part to the whole, to stress the utility of the subject under consideration, and to relate the studies as closely as possible to life outside the school. To this end, they felt it was important that the planning and presentation of knowledge should be clear, vivid, and accurate, and easily apprehended by the senses. Hence their stress on first-hand experiences and practical illustration and their lavish use of apparatus, models, maps, and documents.

Nevertheless, they also realized that it was essential to give each boy a personal stake in mastering a subject, and they believed that one of the best methods was to give each boy an experience of success. No rational person, they argued, would continue exertions that met only with disappointment and failure ; therefore, every pupil should have an opportunity, continuously throughout his school life, of tasting the sweets of achievement. Given differences of preference and ability, this was best done by ranking the school frequently according to subject, so that each boy had an opportunity to do well in something. Thus the pupils were sometimes graded according to mathematical ability, sometimes according to classical attainments, manual work, or perhaps conduct and behaviour. Experience of success, they found, became generalized and spread from subject to subject :

Thus each boy, in his turn, attains rank and consideration in that branch of study wherein nature fitted him to excel, and where comparatively moderate efforts will ensure success. If this were all, if our plan merely served to carry each boy onwards in the path which

[31] *Public Education,* p. 190.

nature had pointed out for him, we should consider a valuable point to have been gained; inasmuch as we hold single excellence in higher estimation than various mediocrity. But the cause continues to operate. The confidence that exertion will be followed by success, being established in his mind, will cheer him on in other departments of education.[32]

Although the Hills were not alone in putting boys into 'sets' based on ability in individual subjects rather than placing them in classes according to age (a similar system was operated by Arnold at Rugby for classics, French, and English),[33] they were certainly the first to base the organization of a whole school on this system. The school was divided into departments of study, each containing a number of classes. A boy's assignment to a class depended upon his proficiency in a particular subject. Thus a boy might be in the highest class for Latin but in the second class for arithmetic, and so on. A dozen or so of the youngest boys formed a separate class and were taught by specialist masters in turn.[34]

There were the usual features of weekly or fortnightly examinations, half-yearly exhibitions, and various methods of grouping individuals in merit order by a ladder system, but two aspects of the methods employed were unusual — the use from time to time of boy teachers on the Bell system, with each boy in the upper half acting as teacher to one in the lower, and the extensive use made of private study. The latter was a facility much used by the senior boys in the eighth class, and usually they worked on a subject or subjects bearing on their future careers.

Another important feature of the system was the practice of voluntary labour. This was introduced to enable those duller boys who excelled at hard work to obtain parity with their more brilliant fellows, for voluntary labour was paid in personal marks that contributed to rank. In this way boys could, by working the printing-press, producing the school magazine, making models, doing etchings and paintings, studying music, modelling in clay, constructing machines, composing verses, and similar tasks, contribute to their own position in the school as well as enjoying themselves at a hobby, and the able boys had benefit from this as well as the others. Among the most inventive

---

[32] Ibid., pp. 209–10.
[33] 'Rugby School', *Quarterly Journal of Education*, vol. vii, no. xiv (1834), pp. 234 ff.
[34] *Public Education*, p. 95.

were Follett Osler, later a well-known public man in Birmingham, and William Bowman, who attained a national reputation as an ophthalmic surgeon. A model of Hazelwood School built by the latter still exists in Birmingham.[35]

Another unusual out-of-class activity was the encouragement given to the boys to follow political events, and the Hills' own Radical views played a part here (in 1819 Matthew Davenport Hill defended Major Cartwright on charges of sedition,[36] and was active with Rowland in the Reform agitation of 1832). In 1824 a Hazelwood Greek Committee was formed which raised £60 in aid of the Greek struggle for independence.[37] The boys also followed closely the fortunes of republican revolutionaries in South America and in August 1827 listened to Arthur Hill's 'excellent speech concerning the affairs of South America'.[38]

The Hazelwood curriculum was a wide one, with a commercial bias. The subjects offered were : English, spelling, elocution, parsing, penmanship, shorthand, geography, history, mathematics (including arithmetic, algebra, geometry, trigonometry, and mensuration), French, Latin, Greek, gymnastics, drawing, and science. The teaching, however, varied, and a former pupil, William Sargant, recalled that the arithmetic teaching was 'amazing', the classics tuition 'defective', and that 'a good deal of time was wasted on shorthand'.[39]

In many subjects a well thought-out method, sometimes an adaptation of the latest theory, sometimes an original idea of the Hills, was used. In penmanship, to which the Hills attached great importance for its use in business and commerce, they devised a method of their own, in which the boys practised to the playing of notes on a scale. Use of the school printing-press was found, as David Williams had discovered, to be a useful means of improving spelling. Elocution (a particular study of Thomas Wright Hill) was much practised, and demonstrated extensively at the half-yearly exhibitions. Sargant wrote that 'the broad midland -i was severely repressed. The dropping of an -h was one of the seven deadly sins ; and the punishment for it would have moved the holy ire of St. Augustine : who complained that among his teachers, more stress was laid on pronouncing this

---

[35] J. Burdon-Sanderson and J. W. Hulke, *The Collected Papers of Sir W. Bowman* (London, 2 vols., 1892), i, p. xiii.   [36] C. Hill, p. 46.
[37] *Hazelwood Magazine*, vol. ii, no. 6 (Aug. 1824), p. 40.
[38] Ibid., vol. v, no. 7 (Sept. 1827), p. 97.
[39] Sargant, ii, p. 189.

important letter, than on the observance of GOD's eternal laws'.[40] Geography was taught on the concentric method, beginning with a study of Hazelwood School, followed by studies of the district, the country, Europe, and the world, together with some astronomy. The eighth class was taught geography entirely in French. History was taught conventionally enough with regard to content, but there was a lavish use of maps, charts, and illustrations. The younger boys, for instance, used Mrs. Trimmer's prints, mounted on cards and arranged chronologically.[41]

Mathematics was a subject in which Thomas Wright Hill and Rowland Hill were particularly interested, and great pains were taken to make the subject interesting and comprehensible. The pupils did a great deal of basic number work by means of the practical manipulation of marbles and counters, with a step-by-step progression and attention to concrete problems. In trigonometry, a good deal of practical surveying was done in the surrounding districts, for which special excursions were arranged. Much was made of the practice of mental arithmetic (for which there was a special set) and of 'mixed arithmetic', whereby boys solved problems by their own methods in the shortest possible time — which was intended by the Hills to approximate to what would later be the situation in after-school life.[42]

The introduction of gymnastics and physical exercise into the curriculum was unusual for the period. In this the Hills admitted their debt to the Rev. Lant Carpenter, the Unitarian divine, whose *Principles of Education : Intellectual, Moral and Physical* had been published in 1820. In addition to cricket and Rugby, the boys had one hour per day of running, leaping, wrestling, vaulting, and spear-throwing, and there was also swimming in the school's own pool. An Athletics Committee gave prizes at the end of each session, but these were small and athletics and games were not allowed to take a superior place in the life of the school.[43]

In language teaching the Hills were undoubtedly pioneers. In their day, language teaching was a centre of great controversy and all sorts of systems abounded. But in the public schools and academies the classical language was usually taught by the rote-learning of grammatical rules in Latin, and the English language was considered to consist mainly of grammar. The Hills were strongly attracted to the

[40] Ibid., p. 188.   [41] *Public Education*, pp. 105 ff.
[42] Ibid., pp. 111 ff.   [43] Ibid., pp. 133–5.

'natural' methods of language teaching associated with the names of Hamilton and Dufief and the Elliptical method of Dr. Gilchrist, successfully practised by Samuel Wilderspin.[44]   Language teaching at Hazelwood had two guiding principles — that language is primarily for the transmission of meaning, and that language was not taught by means of grammar, but grammar by means of familiarity with the language.

The Hills had noticed that Welsh children became bilingual at an early age with no apparent difficulty, and this 'life-situation', they felt, was of key importance.   They believed that the nearest approach to a life-situation was in the enactment of drama, which accounted for the classical dramas presented every half year at the exhibitions.   In teaching languages the Hills also used a great deal of analytical and extemporaneous construing of classical texts, in which the basic aim was to get as much of the meaning of the passage as possible with the minimum of recourse to grammatical rules.   In extemporaneous construing, each boy indicated the amount that he thought he could translate successfully.   If he succeeded, he was rewarded ; if he failed he was fined 'as a tax upon his presumption'.   Double translations were also often used.   Private preparation of texts was done nightly and construing at the first lesson in the morning.[45]

The classical languages were included in the curriculum largely because the Hills considered that they formed the basis of modern culture.   The English language itself, however, they regarded less and less as a 'subject' than as a means of communicating ideas, whose use underlay much of the organization and day-to-day work of the school. To the Hills, all teachers were teachers of English and much of the English work of the school was, therefore, incidental to voluntary labour, court and jury work, dramatic performances, the production of the magazine, and so on.

In formal lessons the method used was an extension of that of N. G. Dufief, a Frenchman who had sought political refuge in America and who had published a book on the natural method of learning English entitled *Nature Displayed in Her Mode of Teaching Language to Man*, which appeared in twelve English editions between 1818 and 1831.[46] Dufief had advocated using the phrase as a starting-point for language-

---

[44] *Public Education,* p. 110 ;   for Wilderspin cf. below, Chap. 14.

[45] Ibid., pp. 124 ff., 220 ff.

[46] Edith Philips, *Louis Hue-Girardin and Nicholas Gouin Dufief* (Baltimore, Md., 1926), pp. 57 ff.

learning, but the Hills went further and made the sentence the point of departure. They also used, as we have seen, Dr. Gilchrist's method, in which the child filled in blanks left in sentences. Both Dufief's and Gilchrist's systems, and the Hills' adaptations, were based on attention to meaning rather than on adherence to formal grammar, which was treated incidentally as the need arose. Above all, they followed Maria Edgeworth's advice that in all forms of self-expression, but particularly in written work, there must be genuine motivation.

The greatest curricular innovation of the Hills was undoubtedly the science course, which they introduced at Hazelwood and Bruce Castle in 1829. It has had little notice, possibly because no account of it appears in *Public Education*, which was published before the science studies began. The interest of the Hill brothers in science came from their father, who had been a member of the Birmingham Philosophical Society, a keen lecturer on scientific subjects, and a friend of Joseph Priestley. Thomas Wright Hill had given science lessons to the pupils at Hill Top as early as 1807, and had imbued his sons with an interest in science and a respect for the scientific attitude.

In 1829 the Hills engaged a brilliant young scientist, Edward Wedlake Brayley, the eldest son of the topographer and archaeologist of that name. After an early interest in topography, the younger Brayley had turned his attention to science, editing scientific journals, teaching and writing on a wide range of scientific subjects, and making a special study of meteors, on which he became an authority. After he had been teaching at Hazelwood and Bruce Castle for a year, the Hills, feeling that the experiment possibly needed more support and publicity among the parents, asked Brayley to give a public lecture at Hazelwood that would make clear the aims and scope of the scientific teaching. The lecture, given on 26 October 1830, was well attended, and the text was afterwards published as a pamphlet.[47]

Brayley's main aim was to demonstrate the utility of a knowledge of science as an integral part of a liberal education and to convince the parents that whatever their sons' future employment might be, a knowledge of science would be a positive advantage. Brayley's standpoint was essentially Baconian; he defined civilization as the stage in human development in which nature is known and controlled by man for the welfare and happiness of mankind. A knowledge of

[47] E. W. Brayley, *The Utility of the Knowledge of Nature Considered* (London, 1831) on which this account is based.

science, he argued, expands the intellectual faculties ; it preserves the mind from the inroads of superstition ; and it is a means of improving the arts and manufactures. But he appeared to be running his argument hard when he instanced the uses of science in preventing people taking poison in mistake, as an aid to the discovery of minerals on landed estates, or its value as a means of investigation in the history, languages, and arts of classical antiquity.

Whatever doubt there might be about some of the arguments Brayley produced in favour of science teaching, there could be none about the range of subjects offered. The complete course, in the order in which it was taught, was as follows :

Chemistry, Inorganic and Organic	*Natural Philosophy* (contd.)
Heat	Meteorology
Electricity	General Principles of
Electrochemistry	Botany
Natural Philosophy	General Principles of
Light ; Optics	Zoology
Acoustics	*Physical Geography*
Pneumatics	
Hydrostatics	*Magnetism*
Mechanics	Electromagnetism
Mineralogy	Thermomagnetism
Geology	*Astronomy*

This outline was an ideal to be aimed at, for at the time of the lecture only the first two sections had been completed and little of the rest had even been 'prepared for tuition'. The course was given to the whole school, with some exceptions — presumably the youngest boys not placed in classes and possibly a few foreigners with insufficient grasp of the language.

Two methods were employed — lectures to the whole school and class instruction to groups of six to twenty in a specially prepared laboratory. At Bruce Castle, Brayley taught five classes a day (in a six-day week) and also gave five lectures of one hour each per week to the school. He adds that 'uniformly more' was done at Hazelwood. In addition to this basic eleven hours a week, those boys who, for instance, intended to take up the medical profession did considerably more science voluntarily.

The lectures were given by Brayley from prepared notes, on various subjects chosen from the syllabus — chemistry, geology, the invertebrates, meteorites, and so on. Fairly simple illustrative experiments, prepared by interested boys, were carried out. Apparatus included a thermometer, hygrometer, cryophorus, steam engine, and galvanic battery, and every effort was made to illustrate the lectures with objects, specimens, and drawings. The lessons on the invertebrates, for instance, were illustrated by 'transparencies representing the animals, or parts of them, on a highly magnified scale'.[48] 'No school in the world', wrote an enthusiastic ex-pupil, 'probably, at that time contained such an array of costly models, instruments, apparatus and books as Hazelwood possessed.' [49] The last ten minutes of the lecture were given over to questions from the boys, which they handed up to the lecturer on slips of paper.

For the younger boys Brayley read from a textbook, amplifying where necessary. The subject might be a reconsideration of the previous day's lecture, with explanations and additions based on the boys' queries given in such a way as to bring out some important generalization. Sometimes the boys read through Maria Edgeworth's *Harry and Lucy* and its sequels, with oral comments by Brayley. The lesson always included an experiment. The elder boys used more specialized textbooks, including those written by Sir Humphry Davy, Dr. Arnott, Michael Faraday, and others. Faraday's *Chemical Manipulation* was read by the boys 'with great delight', and much used by them as a guide to experiments.[50] The usual method was for the boys to study the textbooks silently, applying to the master only when they needed help. Examinations in science were both written and oral, and counted towards rank, and in classwork care was taken to keep the standard high by continual revision for those who found the course difficult.

Hazelwood and Bruce Castle have a just claim to be considered the pioneers of the teaching of science as a subject in the nineteenth century. Only Mill Hill, one of the newer foundations, whose curriculum was not bound by ancient statute or tradition, and Bootham, a Quaker school in York founded in 1828, can be said to have preceded it, but the natural and experimental philosophy taught at Mill Hill in 1821 and Bootham in 1828 could not compare with the Hills' ambitious efforts. It was not until 1859 that Rugby built a science laboratory

[48] Brayley, *The Utility of the Knowledge of Nature Considered*, p. 84.
[49] E. Edwards, *Sir Rowland Hill, K.C.B., A Biographical and Historical Sketch* (London, 1879), p. 40.   [50] Brayley, p. 111 n.

and lecture-room, and this was an isolated effort. The Schools Inquiry Commission Report of 1868 noted that science was taught only in a handful of the 128 schools examined and that for all practical purposes was excluded from the education of the upper classes in England.[51]

The Hills' scientific course failed because of the opposition of the boys' parents. Despite Brayley's final plea for science at the end of his pamphlet and his personal brilliance as a teacher, they were unconvinced that science had a useful place in commercial and general education. Brayley argued that even given the relatively small amount of time a boy spent at school, science would be a worth-while subject, more useful to those entering a business or commercial career than the study of dead languages. Substitution of science for the classics in the curriculum could not be made, however, without the parents' express instructions which, of course, never came, and the science course was discontinued, greatly to the disappointment of Rowland Hill, who gave up teaching very soon afterwards. At Mill Hill and Bootham, however, the more modest offerings were maintained and developed.

IV

Bruce Castle School was a branch of the parent school started in the summer of 1827 at Tottenham, North London. It was opened mainly because Hazelwood was not attracting pupils in the numbers for which the Hills had hoped; London, it was felt, would provide better opportunities for expansion than the Midlands. Hazelwood continued to exist side by side with Bruce Castle for six years and did not close until 1833.[52] Bruce Castle had a junior school for boys from four to nine that had many features in common with the infant school, and the influence of Robert Owen was noticeable.

Initially Rowland Hill took charge of Bruce Castle, but in 1833 Arthur Hill took over the leadership which he retained until 1868, when his son, George Birkbeck Hill, who had taught there for ten

[51] D. M. Turner, *A History of Science Teaching in England* (London, 1927), pp. 89–91.

[52] J. L. Dobson, 'Bruce Castle School at Tottenham and the Hills' Part in the Work of the Society for the Diffusion of Useful Knowledge', *Durham Research Review*, no. 12 (Sept. 1961), p. 74.

years, succeeded him. George Birkbeck Hill, described by his daughter as having 'a certain fineness of feature and delicacy of hand, so often seen in those who withdraw from the active battle of life into a world of quiet thought and scholarship',[53] preferred the peace of the library to the bustle of public life (he became an authority on Johnson) and would have left the school in the early 1860s but for the strength of the family tradition.[54]

Under his rule as headmaster, the standard of scholarship was raised, but less attention was given to the detailed working of the original Hazelwood system, and from the evidence available it appears that Bruce Castle, during the years of Birkbeck Hill's stewardship, moved nearer to the usages of the average private boarding-school.

The main information about Bruce Castle School in its later years comes from the evidence that George Birkbeck Hill gave to the Schools Inquiry Commission in 1866.[55] It is clear from his testimony that though the main structure of the Hazelwood system was still intact, including marks and rank, the role and activities of the Guardians was given much greater weight and Hill compared them to public-school prefects. Guardians were chosen by a process of indirect election at the beginning of each term. Apart from his general pre-fectorial role, each Guardian had ten boys under his special care and management, and lots were drawn as to which Guardian should have first choice of wards. Each week the Guardians and their Circles were interviewed by Hill, their school record examined and commented upon, and a report drawn up.

The masters' conference, which had existed at Hazelwood, had somewhat more extensive duties at Bruce Castle. Whereas in the original school its weekly meetings were mainly concerned with purely pedagogical matters,[56] at Bruce Castle the conference interested itself in the management of the school and the superintendence of the boys' moral status. At the weekly meeting a sort of character account for each boy was made up in which dishonesty or mischievousness meant a loss of marks. After the weekly report had been completed in this way a larger or smaller sum of money, according to the general be-haviour of the school, was placed at the disposal of the Guardians and

[53] Lucy Crump, *Letters of George Birkbeck Hill* (London, 1906), p. 110.
[54] Ibid., p. 97.
[55] *Schools Inquiry Commission*, pp. 838–49, on which this account is based.
[56] *Public Education*, pp. 8–9.

an hour's holiday given or withheld on every alternate Wednesday or Saturday. The general effect of the upgrading of the Guardians' responsibility and the widening of the scope of the masters' weekly meetings was to tilt the balance of democracy away from the boys themselves towards the staff.

The Guardians, who at the date of Hill's evidence numbered seven in a school of nearly eighty boys, maintained their authority mainly by means of personal influence. They were not allowed to use violence and their only power of punishment was their control over the granting of holidays. The Circles operated by means of the pressure of communal approval or disapproval. A black sheep would have to be very black, maintained Hill, in order to affect the good name of the whole of the Circle, for the other members kept a close watch over his conduct and endeavoured to keep him out of scrapes. Corporal punishment was still forbidden in the school; the only punishments were deprivation of playtime or keeping a boy in school, or sending an offender on a four-mile walk in the country in charge of a trustworthy Guardian. In extreme cases, when all other means had failed, Hill had recourse to expulsion.

On the academic side there was also a move to more traditional processes. The number of subjects was reduced, classes were made larger, the opportunities for promotion from one class to another increased, a greater degree of specialization introduced, and formal examinations instituted. Languages increased in importance (Hill himself taught Latin and French and a Pole taught German), but the teaching of the natural sciences was abandoned. Hill claimed that as long as the teaching had been a kind of popular lecture with several experiments the boys liked it very much, but as soon as the technical terms of chemistry were taught, they lost much of their relish for it. What may have been a stronger reason was Hill's own dislike of the subject. 'If I had any taste that way,' he admitted, 'I have no doubt that I could lead my boys to be interested in it, but as I have very little taste that way I cannot.' [57]

Birkbeck Hill's fastidious humanism contrasted strongly with his grandfather's scientific enthusiasms. The former's position, in fact, reflected not only a slackening of the pristine Hazelwood impetus, but also the different social and educational climate of the mid-Victorian years.

[57] *Schools Inquiry Commission*, p. 847.

V

In 1877 Birkbeck Hill gave up the headship of Bruce Castle School because of ill-health, relinquishing the building to the Rev. William Almack, who continued to run the school until its final closure in 1891.[58] The connection of the Hill family with Hazelwood and Bruce Castle had lasted for fifty-eight years and the two schools had the longest life of any progressive foundation of the nineteenth century.

In its early days at least, Hazelwood had lived in a blaze of publicity. The system was given extensive notice in the leading reviews, from the *Westminster* to *Blackwood's*, from the *Edinburgh Review* to the *London Magazine*. Charles Dickens was a great admirer of Bruce Castle,[59] and as 'Gable College' it was written up in *Household Words* in the early 1850s.[60] Hazelwood was also the only English progressive school to inspire a Continental counterpart. In 1830 Hillska Skolan, directly inspired by Hazelwood, was opened in Stockholm, Sweden, with the assistance of Edward Lewin, a former pupil of the Hills, and remained in being for sixteen years.

What attracted attention to the Hazelwood system was its modernity, its sense of being not only up to date but ahead of its time. It represented a conscious departure from Renaissance and Enlightenment educational ideals, and seems 'modern' in a way that even the most advanced of previous schools do not. Despite some borrowings from the experience of previous generations, Hazelwood was permeated with the ideas of utility, progress, order, the rational organization of resources, and the immanence of the cash nexus. These were in essence the values of the new industrial age that was replacing or modifying the old order. Hazelwood had few formal links with Benthamism in its early days despite the fact that by 1822 the Hill brothers had presented Bentham with a copy of *Public Education* and established links with him sufficiently close to endure for several years. Nevertheless, one feels that Hazelwood was permeated from the very beginning with the utilitarian spirit, even in the smallest particulars.

It was the proliferating detail and complexity of its organization that made Hazelwood virtually inimitable. No British school, it would

[58] Dobson (1961), p. 79.

[59] P. A. W. Collins, 'Bruce Castle : A School Dickens Admired', *Dickensian*, vol. ii, no. 316 (Sept. 1955), pp. 174–81.

[60] 'Gable College', *Household Words*, no. 101, 28 Feb. 1852, pp. 546–50.

appear, attempted to copy its regime; nevertheless, some aspects of Hazelwood were among the first examples of what later became widespread practices in middle-class schools, for instance the introduction of sport and gymnastics, the imaginative use of natural methods of language teaching, and the comprehensive if short-lived science course. Individual work as a recognized part of the school curriculum, though it had been to some extent anticipated by David Williams, received wide currency from the Hazelwood example. Emphasis on science and modern languages, as we show later, became a mark of the demand for middle-class education in the 1850s and 1860s, and in setting out to educate the middle classes the Hill brothers took note in their schools of the educational expectations of the new men, the industrialists and professional intelligentsia of the mid-Victorian age. Eminent old boys included, in addition to Sargant, who inherited an ordnance factory, Follett Osler, F.R.S., a glass manufacturer; J. D. Goodman, another gunmaker; T. H. Ryland, a screw manufacturer; Sir William Bowman, the celebrated ophthalmic surgeon; William Scholefield, an exporter and M.P. for Birmingham from 1847 to 1867; Toulmin Smith, the lawyer and geologist; and Henry Villiers, Bishop of Carlisle.

Where the public schools stressed etiquette, manners, 'good form', the mystique of the gentleman, Hazelwood supported the virtues of utility, efficiency, individual initiative and rational self-reliance. Where public schools encouraged the amateur, the ideal of the leisured gentleman who did things for their own sake and not for economic motives and who tacitly accepted wealth as the means to the enjoyment of the good life, Hazelwood rewarded individual initiative with pecuniary gain and made clear that lack of application or irrational action would involve financial loss. Money, even though the coin was imitation, was literally the measure of virtue and progress at Hazelwood. The public school lived in an atmosphere that implied that social and political relations were bounded by an unwritten code of tradition and ethical restraints, whereas the life of a Hazelwood boy was bounded by a proliferation of explicit and printed laws, rules, and regulations, numbered and codified and operated throughout his waking hours.[61] The whole school organization, in fact, rested on the un-British foundation of a written constitution.

Brilliant in conception and logical in execution as it was, Hazelwood

[61] Cf. R. and F. Hill (eds.), *Laws of Hazelwood School* (London, 1827).

had in it much of the Chrestomathic plan, with its minute instructions and grotesquely titled principles for the regulation of all aspects of school life. In the school too was some of the soulless regime to which James Mill submitted his son. As the Hazelwood system worked out in practice it appears at times to be the very opposite of the libertarian Rousseauist spirit that had inspired an earlier generation of educators. Its achievement was not without cost to the individual boy, as William Sargant perceived:

> By juries and committees, by marks, and by appeals to a sense of honour, discipline was maintained. But this was done, I think, at too great a sacrifice: the thoughtlessness, the spring, the elation of childhood were taken from us; we were premature men . . . the school was in truth a moral hotbed, which forced us into a precocious imitation of maturity. . . .[62]

On occasion, however, the pupils reacted against the system to behave very much like boys. Marks were borrowed and sometimes stolen, and Sargant remembered one occasion when a quantity of counterfeit marks circulated in the school, introduced by the son of a manufacturer whose die-sinker was made to imitate the genuine Hazelwood coinage.[63]

Hazelwood's values were on the whole suited to the social class of the boys it attracted, and the quality of the schoolwork was sufficiently high to ensure for it a steady flow of pupils. The celebrated 'system' endured not only because of its singularity but also because it re-inforced the ethic of the school and stimulated the academic achieve-ment of the pupils. The Hills themselves had little doubt of their suc-cess and they concluded *Public Education* with the assertion that they had created the Edgeworths' 'Utopian idea of a school', in which the pupils 'improve . . . in the social virtues, without learning party spirit; and though they love their companions, they do not, therefore, combine together to treat their instructors as pedagogues and tyrants'.[64] If Bentham's influence was to be found at Hazelwood, so too were traces of the spirit of Rousseau and Pestalozzi, but mediated through the mind and skill of the remarkable succession of the Hill family.

[62] Sargant, ii, p. 191.   [63] Ibid., p. 190.
[64] Cited in *Public Education*, p. 356.

7. King's Somborne School

It is difficult to categorize King's Somborne School, the creation of the Rev. Richard Dawes, Dean of Hereford. Opened in 1842 as a village school in rural Hampshire, it was influenced by none of the domestic or Continental educational theories described elsewhere in this book, nor was it overtly a response to particular economic or social conditions. King's Somborne was simply an attempt at educational progress made by an original man in conditions that were daunting in the extreme. It was the first rural school seriously to attempt to raise educational standards above the acquisition of mere literacy, and the first to make a breach in the custom that different classes of the community should be educated in separate schools. These achievements of Dawes were effected in the face of an almost total initial opposition to education by the local farmers. That Dawes overcame this and other difficulties was almost entirely due to the quality of the education he provided at the school, to the freshness and originality of his methods, and to the way in which he was able to integrate learning with the life of the local community.

Although Dawes took easily to the role of rural clergyman and schoolmaster, he was, for twenty years of his life, a Cambridge don, and might have remained so had he not been unexpectedly passed over for the Mastership of his college. Dawes was born in Yorkshire in 1793, received his early education at Mr. Gough's school near Kendal, and entered Trinity College, Cambridge, in 1813. Passing out Fourth Wrangler in 1817, he became Fellow, Mathematical Tutor, and Bursar of Downing College and was ordained the following year.[1] 'In Dawes's time', wrote the historian of the College, 'the Downing Combination Room acquired a social and convivial celebrity second to that of no other college in the University.'[2] William Whewell, the scientist and mathematician, later Master of Trinity College, and George Peacock, later Dean of Ely, were also members, and through them Dawes became associated with Babbage, Herschel, and others who were beginning to raise the standards of Cambridge

[1] W. C. Henry, *A Biographical Notice of the Late Rev. Richard Dawes, M.A., Dean of Hereford* (London, 1867), pp. 5–6.
[2] H. W. Pettit Stevens, *Downing College* (London, 1899), p. 168.

and to introduce the analytical methods of Continental mathematicians to England.[3]

Dawes might have continued a pleasant and useful existence at Cambridge for the rest of his life but for the incident over the Mastership. In 1836 the office fell vacant and Dawes was a natural candidate. But 'a small external body of high-placed ecclesiastics', including the Archbishops of Canterbury and York and the Masters of St. John's and Clare, with whom the Mastership was in gift, recalled that Dawes, with characteristic independence, had once voted for the admission of Dissenters to the University. Dawes lost the election, the Master of Clare protesting that 'if Mr. Dawes had been his own brother he could not have given him his support'.[4]

All prospect of advancement in the University having ceased, Dawes married and took the College living of Tadlow with East Hatley, and in the following year Sir John Mill, a former pupil, gave him the Rectory of King's Somborne in Hampshire.[5]

Thus Dawes found himself, at the age of forty-four, in one of the most backward rural districts in the country. King's Somborne was a parish of some 7,500 acres, lying in the Test Valley, with a population of 1,125.[6] Three factors in particular seemed insuperable barriers to any kind of educational advance — the poverty of the labourers, the lack of any educational tradition, and the hostility of the farmers to the acquisition of the merest literacy by their tenants.

The land was in the hands of five or six farmers, and the labourers existed on wages of between 6s. and 9s. a week, and in order to avoid starvation drew heavily on the poor-rate, the annual average amount of which in the seven years ending in 1835 was £1,600.[7] The teachers were often barely literate and had usually failed at other callings, and their low pay reflected their low standards : 'It is but little they pay me, but then it is but little I teaches 'em', admitted one honest old dame to an Inspector.[8] Even in the best of the village schools, the three R's and a great deal of religious instruction, taught mechanically,

---

[3] *Dictionary of National Biography, sub* William Whewell.
[4] Henry, p. 10.   [5] Stevens, p. 170.
[6] Rev. H. Moseley, 'Report for the Year 1847 on Schools Inspected in the Southern District', *Minutes of the Committee of Council on Education, 1847–8*, P.P. (1847–8), p. 180.   [7] Ibid., p. 172.
[8] R. Dawes, *Suggestive Hints towards Improved Secular Instruction, Making it Bear on Practical Life* (London, 6th ed., 1853), p. xv.

was the rule.[9] Dawes quickly discovered the farmers' view of education :

> One wants to know if it will make a boy plough a straighter furrow ;
> another quaintly asks, if it will make his turnips grow (he knows
> hard work will) : and I actually know a case where the farmers of
> a parish turned against the clergyman's plan, because he proposed
> teaching geography, saying, 'they would not have the labourer's
> toes treading on their heels'.[10]

If the labourer was educated, it was held, he would not work ; it
would invert the order of society by raising the labourer above his
place ; it would interfere with the workings of Divine Providence,
for the labouring classes were never intended to know anything but
the Bible ; it was impossible because labourers were born with
inferior intellect.[11] All dismally familiar prejudices, rooted deep in
rural Hampshire as elsewhere.

Dawes, however (whom George Eliot described as 'the first true
specimen of a man in the shape of a clergyman that I ever met with'),[12]
was equipped with the ability and personality to overcome prejudices
and difficulties. In Matthew Arnold's opinion, he had 'an energy in
promoting education, and a genius for organising schools, quite rare
and exceptional'.[13] Dawes's wide cultural and educational interests
marked him off from the typical Evangelical of the period and the
doctrinal aspects of religion played little part in his life. Science,
education, and administration were his main concerns, and his social
outlook was hard-headed rather than pietistic. He had no illusions
that acquaintance with the Scriptures necessarily resulted in improved
morals,[14] and he was willing to allow that the heavy drinking and wild
amusements of the totally uneducated might be due more to bad circumstances than to original sin.[15] Moreover, he was not above en-

---

[9] Rev. R. A. Gordon, *Observations on Village-School Education, With Suggestions for
its Improvement* (Oxford, 1850), *passim*.

[10] R. Dawes, *Hints on an Improved and Self-Paying System of National Education,
Suggested from the Working of the Village School of King's Somborne, in Hampshire* (London, 5th ed., 1855), p. 3.

[11] R. Dawes, *Observations on the Working of the Government Scheme of Education and
on School Inspection* (London, 1849), pp. 46–49.   [12] Cited in Stevens, p. 172.

[13] Matthew Arnold, 'General Report for the Year 1853', *Minutes of the Committee
of Council on Education, 1853–4*, P.P. (1854), lii, p. 725.

[14] Dawes, *Suggestive Hints*, p. xiii.

[15] R. Dawes to Rev. J. Allen, *Minutes of the Committee of Council on Education, 1843–4*
P.P. (1845), xxxv, p. 306.

joining his fellow clerics to pay more attention to improving education and to spend less time preaching charity sermons.[16]

Dawes made a similarly realistic assessment of the educational possibilities of his district. He believed that in order to establish a school under the prevailing conditions, three things were necessary : a high standard of education ; the co-operation of the farmers and the labourers in sending their children to the same school ; and in order to make it seem a thing of value, the schooling itself should not be free or even cheap.

The quality of the education given was always the first consideration. 'The task I set myself,' wrote Dawes, 'was to make the schools so good that the parents might see that there was no question about the fact that their children were the better for attending them, and that the knowledge they were acquiring was in their (the parents') estimation interesting and valuable.' [17] The 'comprehensive' basis of the school was perhaps its most interesting feature. Dawes felt that this measure would not only encourage social cohesion in the countryside but also assist the finances of the school. Fees, and the length of time spent by a child at school, were adjusted to the class of the parent. Labourers paid 2*d*. a week for the first child and 1*d*. for the others. Farmers and tradesmen paid 6*s*. a quarter if they lived in the parish and 10*s*. if they lived outside.[18] In addition it was expected that the children in the second group would remain at school a longer time. This would constitute the sole benefit they gained over the labourer's children, for both would receive the same education in the school. The appeal to the farmers and tradesmen was on the score of cheapness because for £2 a year or less their children would receive an education hardly inferior to that of a boarding-school that might charge twenty times that amount.

The capital expenditure on the school was provided by grants from the Committee of Council on Education, the National Society, the Diocesan Board at Winchester, and a contribution from Dawes himself.[19] It was provided with a master and mistress, a married couple, at a salary of £70 a year, together with a house and garden. In course of time a second master was added (a former pupil of the school,

---

[16] Dawes, *Suggestive Hints*, p. xxii.
[17] R. Dawes, *Schools and Other Similar Institutions for the Industrial Classes* (London, 1853), p. 11.　　[18] Dawes, *Hints on National Education*, p. 8.
[19] Dawes, *Schools for the Industrial Classes*, p. 4.

aged seventeen), four paid monitors, and after 1847 pupil-teachers were engaged.[20] In the early years, however, both Dawes and his wife taught in the classroom.[21]

At the opening of the school in October 1842 there were 38 children present. By 1850 this had grown to 219 children. Apart from the 52 children in the junior school, 55 pupils were the children of farmers and tradesmen and 112 children of labourers. In the same period the fees had risen from £49 11s. 10d. to £133 3s. 1d., and the income from the sale of books from £7 5s. 5d. to £41 1s. 8d.[22]

There was much contention about school fees in the nineteenth century. Towards the end of the century, when education increasingly came to be seen as a social service, the demand for free schooling became an essential corollary, but in the conditions of his parish in the 1840s, Dawes took the view that free education would not appeal to the labourer, but would be seen as merely another aspect of the benevolence that consistently regarded the labourer as a pauper fit only for charity.[23] For the same reasons Dawes refused to provide school books free, and insisted that parents buy them for their children.

Dawes immediately distinguished the teaching given in his school from the monitorial instruction in the three R's that was common in all but a few of the British and National village schools of the time. He sought to make the children think and reason rather than to master facts, and he modified the usual curriculum in order to bring it closer to everyday life and in particular to include a good deal of science. Above all he realized that children learned most rapidly and effectively when solving problems that related directly to their own experience. He made this explicit in one of his books :

> The great aim of the schoolmaster ought to be to make the children observant and reflective ; to make them think and reason about the objects around them — the animal world, the vegetable world ; to instruct them in the school of surrounding nature, and to bring their minds to bear upon the every-day work of life.
>
> When the master or the teacher can do this, the life of the school-boy becomes a life of discovery and of pleasure.[24]

---

[20] Ibid., p. 7 ; *Hints on National Education*, p. 14.

[21] R. Dawes, *Effective Primary Instruction* (London, 1857), pp. 7–8 ; Stevens, p. 17.

[22] Dawes, *Hints on National Education*, pp. 9–10.

[23] Ibid., pp. 5–7.   [24] Dawes, *Effective Primary Instruction*, p. 7.

Hazelwood School. Note the platform for astronomical observations

Bruce Castle school

Rowland Hill

Arthur Hill

For the children of King's Somborne, school life rapidly became both exciting and pleasurable. The whole of nature became their textbook. They roamed the fields to collect information, to discover on which side of their bodies sheep lay down, and to examine the differences in the teeth of various animals ; they worked out the velocity of the wind by watching the shadows of clouds race across the sunlit meadows and the speed of sound by watching a distant woodman fell a tree and noting the lapse of time between the blow of his axe and the sound reaching their ears. They calculated the water pressure on the fish in local streams and found out the principles of the pop-guns they were accustomed to make from elder trees.[25]

In the classroom the same methods of observation and experiment were used, but apart from the inclusion of the sciences, the formal curriculum was not particularly wide. 'Few subjects well taught, rather than many ill-taught,' maintained Dawes, 'ought to be the maxim of the schoolmaster.'[26] He emphasized problem-solving and the relation of the most abstract subject to everyday life wherever this was possible. Dawes once asked a class of children of different ages who was the eldest, but instead of directing and controlling the lesson himself, he let them reason out the answer among themselves and noted the questions they asked each other. The children found the exercise difficult, but, observed Dawes, 'simple things of this kind may be made most instructive lessons, by showing them how one question suggests another, and making them proceed, step by step, in a logical manner, until they arrive at an exact answer'.[27]

This concern with method was carried into the formal subjects of the curriculum by devising learning situations related to the children's own experience. Grammar, for instance, was taught almost entirely by reading, nouns were presented by relating them to objects that children could see around them and all changes of number and gender were treated similarly.[28] Every grammatical problem was associated with their daily life and the crafts of the village : 'The importance of making the instruction turn a good deal upon their own occupations and domestic consumption, can scarcely be overrated.'[29] However,

[25] Dawes, *Suggestive Hints*, pp. 5–8, 73 ff.
[26] Dawes, *Effective Primary Instruction*, p. 12.   [27] Ibid.
[28] Dawes, *Suggestive Hints*, pp. 8–9.
[29] Ibid., p. 14.

the children also read a good deal of poetry, including Cowper, Scott, Mrs. Hemans, and others.

Geography was taught with the aid of maps, a magnetic compass, and a globe, in addition to several models of the local features and landscape. The children were made familiar with neighbouring towns and villages and the geography of the local parish, relating their knowledge to maps and gradually extending it to the whole of England. They also studied the commercial and economic life of the country and opportunities were taken to illuminate their reading by following up geographical allusions and emphasizing the connections between different countries.[30]

History was linked to local history and much use was made of local remains. The children learned that one of John of Gaunt's houses used to stand on the site of the school, and they could see for themselves the remains of the Roman road from Winton to Sarum, which ran through the parish. Invasions, and the manners and customs of the invaders, were related to local lore and Dawes sought to make history into the story of the people of England and their way of life, 'instead of making it a dry detail of the chronological order of reigns, which in itself would not be instructive, endeavouring to give an interest to it, by speaking of those things in past ages which bore upon their daily occupations, and showing how they may improve the future by reflecting on the past'.[31] A typical question from a history examination shows Dawes's approach :

> John of Gaunt used to live where this school stands. Do you think he had tea and coffee with sugar for breakfast ? — give your reasons for thinking he had or had not.[32]

'The great art in teaching children', wrote Dawes, 'is not in talking only, but in practically illustrating what is taught',[33] and he made full use of the opportunities that the sciences offered in carrying this out. The number of experiments and demonstrations in his *Suggestive Hints towards Improved Secular Instruction* and his booklet on *The Teaching of Common Things* would have kept a teacher going for years and would provide interesting lessons even today.

The sciences formed a large part of the curriculum and covered a very wide field. There were lessons in arithmetic, geometry, mechanics,

---

[30] Dawes, *Suggestive Hints*, pp. 27–36.
[31] Ibid., pp. 39–40.   [32] Ibid., p. 27.   [33] Ibid., p. 83.

physics, astronomy, chemistry, natural history, geology, and statistics. All of these were taught in a practical manner and, wherever possible, in relation to the crafts and commerce of the district. In geometry and natural history it was simple. Mechanics began with an examination of the theory of local activities such as raising water from a well, turning a grindstone, digging with a spade, cutting down a tree. Physics, or natural philosophy as it was then called, consisted of experiments with air-pumps, bellows, barometers, thermometers, and electrical machines. Elementary statistics also had a practical leaning, and was based on an examination of the census figures ; from these the consumption per head of population was worked out, and combined with other commercial and manufacturing statistics.[34]

The idea of teaching science to village children, Dawes observed, was 'by many looked upon as visionary, by some as useless, and by others even as mischievous'.[35] One of the ways in which Dawes was able to gain acceptance for it was by linking chemistry to agriculture. The science of agriculture was beginning to excite attention in England in the 1840s. Dawes was friendly with the staff of the neighbouring Queenwood Agricultural College, particularly with Tyndall and Frankland, then young lecturers there. The latter gave a course of six lectures on agricultural chemistry at King's Somborne School in 1847, which aroused great interest in the neighbourhood, many of the local farmers attending as well as the pupils.[36] There was in fact a good deal of useful exchange between the school and the college ; the principal visited the school from time to time, and two of the most promising boys worked in the college chemistry laboratory for two days a week.[37]

Unlike some earlier educational innovators, Dawes was a believer in school books and paid a great deal of attention to their selection, for the most part using the books published by the Irish National Board, partly on account of their cheapness. This was an important factor, because as the pupils bought all their own books, the outlay on these was an important part of the school economy. Apart from Dawes's belief that the children and parents would place greater value on volumes that they had purchased themselves, the possession of books enabled the pupils to do lessons at home in the evening — a

[34] Ibid., pp. 37–142 *passim* ; W. H. Brookfield, 'General Report for the Year 1850', *Minutes of the Committee of Council, 1850–1*, P.P. (1851), xliv (2), p. 384. Cf. also N. Ball, 'Richard Dawes and the Teaching of Common Things', *Educational Review*, vol. 17, no. 1 (Nov. 1964), pp. 59–68. [35] Dawes, *Suggestive Hints*, p. xi. [36] Ibid., p. x. [37] Dawes, *Schools for the Industrial Classes*, p. 12.

form of homework unprecedented in an elementary school of that date. The school also had a large lending library which was well patronized ; in 1845, for instance, 540 books were borrowed.[38] The perusal of books and maps also interested many parents and gave them, in Dawes's words, 'new sources of happiness and of social comfort . . . to which they have hitherto been strangers'. There was at least one case of a father giving up drink because of a new-found interest in his children's homework.[39] One mother said to Dawes :

> You cannot think, Sir, how pleasantly we spend our evenings now, compared with what we used to do ; the girls reading and getting their lessons done while I am sewing, and their father working with them ; and he is so disappointed, Sir, if the evening task is above him, so that he cannot help in it.[40]

King's Somborne School received a great deal of attention from the Inspectors, no doubt because it was educationally so far in advance of other schools of its type. The most detailed report was made by the Rev. Henry Moseley, one of the most perceptive of the early Inspectors. He pointed out that in school hygiene, reading, spelling, width of curriculum, attendance, and length of time spent at school, King's Somborne excelled all other schools of its type. The average attendance was 89 per cent, compared with the 66 per cent of other schools ; 32 per cent of the pupils remained at school after the age of eleven years, compared with 23 per cent at other schools. As in the case of all successful and happy schools, the appearance and demeanour of the children spoke for itself. Every girl had a hairbrush and comb, and regular washing and brushing of the teeth was the rule.[41] Inspectors noticed that the children looked intelligent, modest, and purposeful.[42] Significantly, the children created their own voluntary circles. A dozen of the older boys organized a voluntary chemistry class which met on Saturday mornings,[43] and many of the pupils kept journals in which observations on natural history at different seasons of the year were kept. Moseley also discovered that the width of the curriculum had a very beneficial effect on the children's powers of reading, for at one of his examinations 40 per cent of the children read with

[38] Dawes, *Hints on National Education*, p. 35.
[39] Dawes to Allen, *Minutes of the Committee of Council, 1843–4*, p. 307.
[40] Dawes, *Hints on National Education*, p. 37.
[41] Moseley, p. 173.   [42] Ibid., Brookfield, p. 385.
[43] Dawes, *Schools for the Industrial Classes*, p. 12.

'tolerable ease and correctness', whereas at other schools the percentage was under 17, despite the fact that at these schools scarcely anything but reading was taught.[44]

The demonstration of this proposition alone would have ensured Dawes's place as an innovator, for it gave implicit support to the contention that the policy hitherto pursued by religious and charitable bodies was educationally unsuccessful. Dawes himself was convinced of this, and condemned the narrow aims and religious bias of the National Society, becoming one of the leaders of the progressive wing of the Society in opposition to the policies of the conservative Archdeacon Denison, whom he described as 'struggling in a direction so contrary to the feelings of the age . . .'. Dawes was a strong supporter of Kay-Shuttleworth and his efforts for state education, the policy of the Committee of Council, and the work of the Inspectors.[45] He condemned the labours of the National Society as 'a national deception, retarding the cause of education rather than advancing it', and described the instruction given in many of their schools as 'absolutely valueless'.[46]

If the National Schools suffered in comparison with Dawes's standards of education, neither could they match his social attitudes. Though in making King's Somborne a comprehensive school for the rural lower and middle classes he admittedly aimed at connecting 'these lower adjoining and important links in the social chain',[47] Dawes had little of the Hannah More–Mrs. Trimmer brand of philanthropy in his make-up. Moseley, for example, considered that one of the secrets of the success of King's Somborne lay in the abandonment of the idea that the poor were the natural objects of charity and the unquestioning recipients of 'a fragment of our own education', and the acceptance of Dawes's 'abundant faith in the affection of a labouring man for his children' and his adoption of education suitable to their wants.[48] W. H. Brookfield, another Inspector, pointed out that the curriculum at King's Somborne, though connected with an agricultural labourer's probable future tasks, was not rigidly adjusted to these employments in a 'spirit of caste', but was wide enough to give them a general education qualifying them, if necessary, for other

[44] Moseley, p. 175.

[45] Dawes, *Observations on the Government Scheme*, pp. 5–9, 32.

[46] R. Dawes, *Remarks Occasioned by the Present Crusade against the Educational Plans of the Committee of Council on Education* (London, 1850), pp. 4–11.

[47] Dawes, *Hints on National Education*, p. 5.   [48] Moseley, p. 180.

employments.[49] Thus Dawes's experiment was, in Moseley's words, one of the earliest vindications of the principle that 'education is not a privilege to be graduated according to men's social condition, but the right of all'.[50]

Dawes left King's Somborne in 1850 to become Dean of Hereford, on the recommendation of Lord John Russell (though he was passed over for the see of Carlisle by Palmerston in 1856). He remained there until his death in 1867, repairing the cathedral, speaking at educational and scientific meetings, visiting his friends Professors Frankland and Tyndall in London, and campaigning for the reform of educational charities and the opening of the lower ranks of the Civil Service to elementary school children by competitive examination.[51] His educational policy in King's Somborne was, however, continued on much the same lines by his successor Charles Nicoll,[52] and perhaps the greatest tribute to the success of the school was the decision of the farmers and ratepayers, five years after Dawes left the parish, to levy on themselves a 6*d.* rate, plus subscriptions, in order to build an extension to the school.[53] Taking into account the prevailing attitude to education of farmers in general, this was an unprecedented decision. Dawes's example was also followed by others and some half-dozen similar schools were in operation in Hampshire in the early 1850s, with others in Norfolk, Suffolk, and elsewhere.[54] Unfortunately the inspiration of most of them seems to have died out before the end of the following decade ; R. R. W. Lingen, the secretary to the Committee of Council on Education, in his evidence to the Select Committee on Scientific Instruction in 1868, claimed that he knew of only one inspected school of the elementary type in which a scientific education was being given, and that was the Blue Coat School at Hereford, also founded by Dawes when Dean of that city.[55]

Thus although Dawes's work at King's Somborne continued to strike a chord here and there (his work was known by Thring of Uppingham,[56] and William Johnson, an Eton master, better known as

---

[49] Brookfield, p. 383.   [50] Moseley, p. 181.

[51] Henry, *passim* ; *Dictionary of National Biography* : *Gentleman's Magazine*, May 1867, pp. 674–5.   [52] Dawes, *Schools for the Industrial Classes*, pp. 8–10.

[53] Dawes, *Effective Primary Instruction*, pp. 38–40.

[54] Dawes, *Schools for the Industrial Classes*, pp. 16 ff.

[55] *Report from the Select Committee on Scientific Instruction, Minutes of Evidence*, P.P. (1867–8), xv, p. 39.

[56] E. Thring, *Theory and Practice of Teaching* (London, 2nd ed., 1885), p. 98.

William Johnson Cory the poet, claimed that the directions in Dawes's *Suggestive Hints* were 'obeyed faithfully in my pupil room'),[57] it was not taken up on any serious scale and failed to inaugurate a new era of educational progress in the countryside. This must be attributed partly to Dawes's own independent and liberal views, which twice cost him preferment and made him the scourge of the right wing of the National Society and highly suspect with an establishment that regarded religious instruction as the core of all education. As we have seen before, opposition to the Church of England in the educational field, in the first half of the nineteenth century at least, placed grave handicaps upon enlightened educational ideas and methods. The failure to inaugurate a movement to spread Dawes's theory and practice was also partly due to the fact that the very high standards reached at King's Somborne during Dawes's stewardship were extremely difficult for the average clergyman or schoolmaster of the time to attain. Dawes combined a first-rate scientific mind with a genius for making difficult concepts both simple and interesting, and few, if any, men of this calibre were to be found in rural villages in the mid-nineteenth century, or indeed at any other time.

[57] W. Johnson, 'On the Education of the Reasoning Faculties', in F. W. Farrar (ed.), *Essays on a Liberal Education* (London, 1867), pp. 322 ff.

Section Three

CONTINENTAL INFLUENCES

8. Pestalozzi, Fellenberg, and English Education

THE schools started by Robert Owen and his followers, together with Hazelwood and King's Somborne, can be regarded as largely native products, responses to the conditions in town and country occasioned by the massive changes to an industrialized England. Dawes and the Hills did not draw heavily on the Continental thinkers, although Owen had more of a debt to them. Indeed, Continental theories of education did not easily take root in nineteenth-century England. They were either ignored, adopted piecemeal, or so modified to suit English conditions that much of the original spirit was lost. However, this did not happen to the theories of Pestalozzi and Fellenberg. On the Continent, their educational principles had given a new impetus to the educational systems of Switzerland, the Low Countries, the German states, and other West European countries. The Napoleonic Wars had impeded the free flow of ideas between Britain and the Continent, but the resumption of Continental travel after 1815 revealed the originality of Pestalozzi's institutions at Yverdon and Fellenberg's at Hofwyl to the inquiring British educationalist, and because it was possible to see their ideas in action, Pestalozzi and Fellenberg were the two Continental reformers whose theories made the greatest impact on post-war British education.

Robert Owen and Andrew Bell were the best-known of the early visitors, though neither was greatly influenced by the schemes that he examined. Henry Brougham was a much more energetic champion of both Pestalozzi and Fellenberg, publicizing their theories in the press, in Parliament, and elsewhere. Others followed his example, and for about twenty years from 1815 there were many attempts to publicize and act upon the schemes of the two Continental masters. This chapter will attempt to trace the most important and influential of these, but before this is done it is necessary to give some account of the life and activities of both Pestalozzi and Fellenberg.

Pestalozzi : His Work and Influence

In England Pestalozzi is often thought of as a brilliant but eccentric schoolmaster, unpractical in all the ordinary concerns of life, who invented object lessons and new ways of teaching arithmetic. From the first it was Pestalozzi's method rather than his social and philosophical outlook that interested English educationalists, although he was throughout his life a philosopher and man of affairs, deeply concerned with political, social, and educational conditions in Europe. He cared little for conventional prestige, however, and like his predecessor, Rousseau, and his successor, Froebel, lived a restless, unsettled life, trying several different occupations and rarely holding a post for more than a few years.

Pestalozzi was born in Zürich in 1746 of Italian lineage, a man thirty-four years younger than Rousseau and twenty-five years older than Robert Owen.[1] His father died when he was five years old and he was brought up by his mother and a family maidservant. His early schooling largely consisted of being forced to learn passages by heart and thus, early in life, he gained a distaste for orthodox educational methods and a belief that some other way of instructing children must be possible, probably at best related to the ways shown in a mother's upbringing of her child.

Pestalozzi went through elementary and grammar school and on to college and in 1769, at the age of twenty-three, he married Anna Schultess. In his late teens and early twenties he had become involved in the Helvetic Society, a group of young men inspired by the writings of the French Enlightenment, especially those of Montesquieu and Rousseau. The object of the Society was to work a renewal in the country's morals on the ideals of asceticism, public duty, and 'natural life', and inspired by Rousseau, Pestalozzi repudiated both the Law

---

[1] This account of Pestalozzi's life is based upon K. Silber, *Pestalozzi : The Man and His Work* (London, 1960), *passim*.

and the Church for which he had been educated and turned to nature and the countryside. Like his almost exact contemporary in England, Thomas Day, who was born in 1748, Pestalozzi wished to lead the life of a countryman, cultivating the land and serving the poor. Though he belonged to an upper-class Zürich family, he gave up the possibility of advancement in Church or State to live among the people. 'I suffered as the people suffered,' he wrote, 'and the people showed themselves to me as they were, and as they showed themselves to no one else.' [2]

In 1767, at the age of twenty-one, he went to learn farming methods at Tschiffelli's experimental farm at Kirchberg in the canton of Berne, but his early ventures were disastrous. He impulsively took up madder-farming at Birr, which failed within a year, and an industrial school that he opened at Neuhof in 1774 failed in five years. Depressed, with a sense of failure and openly accused of incompetence — 'You poor wretch,' scoffed an observer, 'you are less able than the meanest day labourer to help yourself, and do you fancy you can help the people?' [3] — he turned to writing, attempting to write for the poor in a manner they would understand. He worked on philosophical and fictional themes, including *Leonard and Gertrude*, a novel of village life, didactic in tone and reforming in purpose, *The Evening Hours of a Hermit*, and contributions to the *Swiss Journal*. In 1799 there came a turning-point when he took charge of a group of war orphans at Stanz, living as one of them and sharing their burdens. In his teaching he alternated manual work with the three R's, and strove to win over his pupils by kindness and love. After about six months, however, the progress of the war caused the abandonment of the project, and at the end of the year he started teaching at the infant school at Burgdorf. Encouraged by the progress that the children made, Pestalozzi opened an Institute of Education in Burgdorf Castle. In 1804 this community was transferred to Münchenbuchsee and a year later he settled at Yverdon.

During all these years of writing and teaching, Pestalozzi was consumed by two aims — the idea of social amelioration, which was the prime motive of all his work, and the desire to discover the key to the educative process. He believed that the methods then current in Europe, with their verbalism and catechizing, their learning of words

---

[2] J. H. Pestalozzi, *How Gertrude Teaches Her Children*, trans. L. E. Holland and F. C. Turner (London, 1894), p. 11.   [3] Ibid.

and religious formulae, were ruining the natural impulses of young people. What was wanted was an educational content and method based upon the psychological processes of children :

> The mass of our public schools not only give us nothing, but, on the contrary, they quench all that in us which humanity has without schools, that which every savage possesses, to a degree of which we can form no conception.[4]

Minor reforms, he believed, were useless : 'the public school coach throughout all Europe must not only be driven better, it must be turned round and put on quite a new road.'[5] This new road was to be the way of nature — the development of the inner powers of the child :

> the aim of all instruction is, and can be, nothing but the development of human nature, by the harmonious cultivation of its powers and talents and the promotion of manliness of life.[6]

Pestalozzi's sympathy for the peasantry and his own remembrance of his mother's care convinced him that the clue to educational progress was to be found in those processes of learning exemplified by the peasant mother and her child. His teaching experience had convinced him that a beginning must be made by the reduction of a subject to its simplest elements which should then be presented in an orderly form proceeding from the simple to the more complex.

To a child, the world seemed 'a sea of confused sense impressions, flowing into one another'.[7] The human mind, however, received and worked up these sense impressions into definite ideas. Pestalozzi believed that if the subject-matter of instruction could be broken down into its elements and arranged in the proper sequence according to 'the original, unchangeable form of the development of mind', then education would become a science based upon clear-cut and definable laws.

Pestalozzi worked out the principles of his method in his book *How Gertrude Teaches Her Children*, published in 1801, which ranks with *Émile* as one of the most significant books in the whole history of education. The book had little direct connection with either Gertrude or her children, but was a series of twelve letters to his friend Gessner, in which he developed his psychological and educational theories.

---

[4] Ibid., p. 153.   [5] Ibid.   [6] Ibid., pp. 156–7.   [7] Ibid., p. 85.

Pestalozzi's starting-point was that all knowledge derived from sense impressions. He believed that a person's mind, when presented with a mass of confused objects, would attempt to discover three things :

1. How many, and what kinds of objects are before him.
2. Their appearance, form, or outline.
3. Their names ; how he may represent each of them by a sound or word.[8]

These three qualities, Pestalozzi believed, could be discovered in all objects and thus he propounded his theory that all elementary instruction took place according to the threefold principle of counting, measuring, and naming, or as he expressed it, by means of the three concepts of Number, Form, and Language.

The fundamental power that underlay the operations of the mind relevant to the formation of concepts Pestalozzi called *Anschauung*, which may be translated as intuition or psychic energy. This ability of the human mind to form what Pestalozzi called 'distinct notions' from the first 'obscure impressions' by stages of 'definite impressions' and 'clear images', he believed existed in every human being, but it needed to be fostered and cultivated. In short, as Silber defines it, 'his power of *Anschauung*, must be raised from the lowest (unconscious) to its highest (conscious) level'.[9] In this way, Pestalozzi argued, the art of teaching would go hand in hand with the fundamental operations of the human mind.

Reading, writing, and arithmetic could be analysed and broken down into a series of operations, the learning of which could then proceed according to definite laws in harmony with 'natural' mental activity. In reading, for instance, words were broken down into separate sounds, which were repeated by the children ; from there they proceeded to letters and then to words describing simple objects. In writing, the structure of the letters was related to the straight line and the square ; these were imitated by drawing, then related to one another to form letters. Arithmetic was taught first of all by allowing the child to add and subtract with small pieces of cardboard on which were printed letters of the alphabet. Number was taught by the division of squares into rectangles of equal dimension and the further division of each rectangle into ten small squares.[10]

---

[8] Pestalozzi, p. 87.
[9] Silber, p. 139.   [10] Pestalozzi, pp. 90 ff.

The teaching of the three R's and other subjects on these lines formed the basis of Pestalozzi's method, which was refined and extended by his numerous assistants at Yverdon and entered the classrooms of Europe. Unfortunately, it was to Yverdon after 1810 in the later period of Pestalozzi's life, when quarrels with his assistants and disputes with others had reduced the effectiveness of the instruction there, that many of the European visitors came and received their impressions of Pestalozzian method. This was true in the case of Charles Mayo, the most celebrated English disciple of Pestalozzi. Mayo and others accepted the more general aspects of Pestalozzi's teachings — the stimulation of the child's self-activity, the development of his physical, intellectual, and moral growth, the fostering of knowledge through the training of the senses, and, in all teaching, progression from the simple to the complex. In themselves these were valuable developments and, although not completely original, where they were applied they stimulated British educational practice. But the implications of what Pestalozzi understood by *Anschauung* were virtually ignored.

The Educational Ideas of Fellenberg

In 1804, when Pestalozzi moved to Münchenbuchsee, he found himself neighbour to a like-minded educational theorist, Philipp Emanuel von Fellenberg, who had adopted and put into practice many of Pestalozzi's own principles on his estate at Hofwyl. Pestalozzi, impressed by Fellenberg's business sense and love of order, agreed to a merger of the two institutions, an arrangement that would allow him time to pursue his own theories. The venture, however, was not a success. Although the views of both were ultimately based on nature, their temperaments and methods were different. Fellenberg's 'adherence to convention where Pestalozzi was utterly spontaneous, his stress on class distinctions in contrast to Pestalozzi's conviction of men's equality, his disciplinarianism as opposed to Pestalozzi's belief in freedom for the children' [11] — all these made the venture a failure and the two educators ultimately returned to their own ways.

Fellenberg was born in Berne in 1771 of a patrician family.[12] His

[11] Silber, p. 152.

[12] This account of Fellenberg's life and work is based upon E. M. Gray, 'The Educational Work of Emanuel von Fellenberg (1771–1844)', unpublished M.A. thesis, University of Belfast (1952).

father was a progressive, a follower of Rousseau and an advocate of educational reform on the lines of Pestalozzi. In his youth Fellenberg was a supporter of the American patriots, Washington, Franklin, and Jefferson, and was sympathetic to the early ideals of the French Revolution. He travelled throughout Europe and visited Paris in 1794, where he became convinced that any political change must be preceded by a spiritual change, which could only be achieved by education. He was also interested in the ideas of the German philosophers, Kant and Fichte, and hoped for a fusion of the enlightened political and social ideas of revolutionary France and the idealistic philosophy of the Germans. A further visit to France, however, disillusioned him and he sought to solve the problems of society in his own way. He was distressed by the neglect of religion and morals, the selfishness and avarice of the Swiss aristocracy, and by the ignorance and torpor of the people. Only a spiritual change within human beings, based upon a simpler and purer way of life, would prevent social upheaval, and this way of life must centre upon an agricultural community where people could pursue an unsophisticated, pastoral, and religious existence. From such a community in his native canton of Berne ripples of regeneration would, he hoped, spread across Europe and the world.

Fellenberg was essentially an agriculturalist and throughout his life upheld the integral relationship between agriculture and education. On his estate at Hofwyl he founded a number of establishments in which he attempted to realize his aspirations. In the first forty years of the nineteenth century, five different institutions were founded: the Scientific Educational Institution for the Higher Social Classes (1806), the Poor School (1810), a girls' school (1823), an intermediate school (1830), and a nursery school (1831). The Institute and the Poor School were by far the most celebrated and, in their different ways, affected education throughout Western Europe, not least in Britain. The organization of these two schools exemplified Fellenberg's fundamental doctrine that apart from a minimum of elementary mental training, the range and content of education provided in any society should vary from class to class. Education for the higher social classes, for instance, should enable them to become honest, rational, and scientific agriculturalists, conscious of their duty to society and determined to improve social conditions. The peasantry, on the other hand, apart from basic moral and religious training, needed an education that would reconcile them to a life of simplicity, economy, and self-discipline. Denied any large portion of the world's goods, they were to be trained to the enjoyment of their own simple and undemanding existence and their education, therefore, was to be adapted to the peasants' daily tasks and so designed that they would not need to seek satisfaction outside these.

The Institute for the Higher Classes attracted pupils from all over Europe and from as far afield as the Americas. It had about a hundred pupils, nearly all from wealthy or aristocratic families, for whom were provided no less than thirty highly qualified teachers. The compulsory lessons were minimal but of a high quality, and a great deal of initiative was allowed to the pupils, though they were expected to utilize every hour of a long day. The curriculum was practically unlimited, ranging from languages and literature to science and philosophy, and it included a wide range of agricultural pursuits. Theories of the self-activity of the pupils, derived from Pestalozzi and Herbart, influenced the learning of natural history, geography, history, and other subjects. In addition there were numerous social and cultural activities — a choir, an orchestra, a band, gymnastics, games, military exercises, walks, swimming, riding, rowing, dancing, skating, and fencing.[13] Student self-government was also encouraged and the Institute had a students' union with its own council and offices.

The scope, equipment, and facilities of the Institute were such as had never been seen in Europe before. It had in it elements of the public school, the university, and the military academy, and it instilled manly virtues in a manner that was almost a caricature of the methods and ideals of the English public school. Robert Dale Owen, Robert Owen's son, who was a pupil there, related how he and his brother, walking in the country with an older German pupil, retreated in fear from a fierce dog which the German beat off with a stick :

'Look here !' said he, 'this will never do. Remember if you ever show the white feather, you're done for with us. I give you fair warning.'
All we could plead was that we had no canes. 'Yes, that was my fault. You shall have a good Ziegenhainer apiece, just as soon as

---

13 The best contemporary account of the Institution is the discursive but informative *Letters from Hofwyl, by a Parent, on the Educational Institutions of de Fellenberg* (London, 1842). This contains a reproduction of the timetable and a detailed analysis of the curriculum.

we get back. But, anyhow, you ought to have stood your ground, and kicked the brute, if you could not do better.'

I thanked him, adding, 'You'll see that this is the last time any-body will have to find fault on that score.' (And I kept my word.)

'All right ! I think you'll do. I'm glad I had a chance to warn you before the other fellows came. Raw young ones always need drilling.' [14]

The Poor School at which vagrant children were trained to agri-cultural labour by a teacher of genius and transparent goodness named Jacob Wehrli, was, on the other hand, restricted in scope and curricu-lum. Eleven hours each day in summer and nine in winter were spent in agricultural and craft labour, and only an hour or two a day on the three R's, history and geography, drawing, and music. As far as possible, the formal education was merged with, or made a function of, the agricultural work, as Wehrli, who lived and worked with the children, believed that an education based on agriculture was a unified process, which at all times helped to form the morality suitable for the peasant's station in life.[15]

It is evident that Fellenberg's educational theory was primarily a social one in which the full development of the individual was related to his probable future role in society. With very few exceptions, a child's social position, not his individual talents, determined the education he should receive. Robert Dale Owen's verdict aptly summed up Fellenberg's educational credo :

> The one great idea of his life appears to have been, not (as Madame Roland and the Girondists thought possible) to fuse, in the crucible of equality, what are called the upper and lower classes, but to seize the extremes of society, and carefully to educate them both ; the one to be intelligent, cultivated workers ; the other to be wise and considerate legislators, enlightened and philanthropic leaders of civilisation. I believe he imagined that there would be rich and poor to the end of the world ; and he restricted his endeavours to making the rich friends of the poor, and the poor worthy of such friendship. To carry out this last he considered agriculture, when intelligently followed as a calling, to be an essential aid.[16]

[14] R. D. Owen, *Threading My Way* (London, 1874), p. 123.
[15] Eventually the Poor School became a semi-Normal School, in which a number of boys were trained for posts as teachers in rural schools. See Rev. M. C. Wood-bridge, 'Sketches of Hofwyl', in *Letters from Hofwyl*, Appendix, pp. 324–5.
[16] Owen, p. 135.

T. Craig

Rev. Richard Dawes

ward Pelham Brenton

Dr. Charles Mayo

Cheam School in Dr. Mayo's time

Battersea Normal College

Fellenberg's educational views were really more in accord with the spirit of the Congress of Vienna than with that of the French Revolution. Some observers saw in the methods pursued at Hofwyl a safeguard against post-war social revolution; but they also noted that Fellenberg had made some valuable contributions to educational practice in combining manual labour and intellectual work, particularly in the Poor School.[17] It was Wehrli's activities in the Poor School that impressed Lady Byron and Kay-Shuttleworth and led to the introduction of agricultural labour into the syllabuses of Ealing Grove School and Battersea Normal College.

It was, in fact, the practices of the Poor School that attracted the attention of educators in England in the first thirty years of the century, a time when the education of the poor was the most important question of educational policy. As early as 1813 an account of Hofwyl had appeared in William Allen's journal, the *Philanthropist*, and eight years later Robert Owen's *Economist* drew attention to the similarities between Owen's system and that of Fellenberg.[18] These articles created little stir, and it was not until the indefatigable Brougham began to publicize Fellenberg's activities in press and Parliament that Hofwyl began seriously to impinge upon the educational consciousness of England.[19] In 1820 translations were published of two of the many reports upon Hofwyl, those of Capo D'Istria and Count Louis de Villevielle, previously reviewed by Brougham in the *Edinburgh Review*. Brougham had written hopefully:

At a time indeed when all men's minds were turned towards the great questions connected with the characters and support of the Poor, with Universal Education and the Poor Laws, there is nothing more natural than that the first intimation of Mr. Fellenberg's plans should powerfully interest the thinking part of the community.[20]

Little practical result followed for several years, but during the 1830s, with the growth of interest in agricultural schools in Britain, Fellenberg

[17] Cf. J. Attersoll, *Translation of the Reports of M. le Comte de Capo D'Istria and M. Rengger upon the Principles and Progress of the Establishment of M. de Fellenberg at Hofwyl, Switzerland* (London, 1820), pp. 22–23, 35; Count Louis de Villevielle, *The Establishment of M. Emmanuel de Fellenberg at Hofwyl* (London, 1820), pp. 23, 24–25.
[18] 'A Remarkable Institution for Education at Berne in Switzerland', *Philanthropist*, vol. iii, nos. 9 and 10 (1813); *Economist*, no. 9, 24 Mar. 1821.
[19] Cf., e.g., *Parl. Deb.*, xli (16 Dec. 1819), 1197–8.
[20] H. Brougham, 'Mr. Fellenberg's Establishment at Hofwyl', *Edinburgh Review*, no. xli (Dec. 1818). Cf. also 'Establishments at Hofwyl', ibid., no. lxiv (Oct. 1819).

attracted a large circle of eminent correspondents, including Lady Byron, the poet's widow, Shelley's second wife Mary, Sir Walter Scott, Louisa Barwell, the children's authoress and writer of the anonymously published *Letters from Hofwyl*, and B. F. Duppa, the lawyer who became secretary of the Central Society of Education and later acted as Fellenberg's agent in Britain, popularizing his theories and suggesting a scale of charges for English pupils at Hofwyl.[21]

Through the medium of these correspondents Fellenberg made known his educational views. He admired Britain as the strongest and most civilized nation in the world, though he was horrified by such concomitants of industrialism as child labour and juvenile delinquency. He developed a grandiose concept of Britain as the leading power in a world-wide Christian-humane Empire, in which his own schemes of moral and educational regeneration would come to fruition. He hoped to use his contact with Lady Byron to win over the young Queen Victoria to his ideal and actually drafted a letter to the Queen herself, urging her to take the initiative in a civilizing mission to the world. It is not known, however, whether the letter ever reached the Queen or what her reaction to it was if it did.[22] Fellenberg's real impact on Britain was made in the sphere of agricultural education. His influence in this field is described in detail in later chapters.

Pestalozzianism in Britain

Pestalozzi's earliest disciples in Britain, with the exception of Elizabeth Hamilton mentioned earlier, were those who had taught at or paid extended visits to Yverdon. Among them was John H. Synge, grandfather of the playwright John Millington Synge, who founded a school at Roundwood, Co. Wicklow, on his return from Yverdon at the end of the Napoleonic Wars, and later published translations of Pestalozzi's works.[23] Another Irishman, Dr. Charles Orpen, unsuccessfully tried to form a committee to raise funds to publicize Pestalozzi's ideas in 1819.[24] Among the people he tried to interest was James Pierrepoint Greaves, a former businessman ruined by the Napoleonic Wars. Greaves devoted himself to educational and philosophical pursuits,

[21] K. Guggisberg, *Philipp Emanuel von Fellenberg und sein Erziehungstaat* (Bern, 2 vols., 1953), ii, pp. 469, 471–3, 478.   [22] Ibid., pp. 464, 468, 475–6.
[23] Silber, pp. 289 ff.   [24] Ibid., pp. 293–4.

which included some four years at Yverdon from 1818 to 1822, teaching English. He was a disciple of Pestalozzi himself, and a great number of letters from the master to his followers were published in translation in 1827 as *Letters on Early Education*, a book that did much to make Pestalozzi's ideas well known in this country.[25]

If some educationalists confined themselves mainly to publicizing Pestalozzi's ideas, others attempted to put them into practice by organizing and running schools on Pestalozzian lines; one of the most interesting of these flourished in South Lambeth in the middle 1820s and was described in an anonymous pamphlet published in 1826.[26] The author of the pamphlet (presumably the head of the school) had lived for several months at Yverdon, where like Greaves he had come into close contact with Pestalozzi himself.

Instruction in the school was divided into three parts, physical, moral, and intellectual, according to the true Pestalozzian canon. Games and gymnastic exercises, therefore, played a larger part in school life than in most private academies. Games in which there were winners and losers were forbidden, however, and gymnastics, which included military evolutions, the use of fire-arms, and fencing, were superintended by the principal himself with as much punctiliousness as lessons in the classroom. Excursions were also made into the country, as was proper for a Pestalozzian school.

Reading, writing, and arithmetic were taught according to the methods of the master, and the curriculum was very much wider than that of the average private academy, including natural history, logic, rhetoric, mythology and English literature. The number of languages offered was remarkable — French, German, Spanish, Italian, Russian, Latin, Greek, Hindustani, and Persian. In addition there were the usual extra subjects — music, drawing, dancing, and book-keeping. A further unusual feature of the school was that moral instruction, which formed the third section of the curriculum, was completely separated from religion; the latter, claimed the principal, often merely disguised prejudice, sectarianism, 'unqualified faith in dogmas', and a wish to instil into children's minds that of which neither teachers nor pupils could give any rational account. The author of the pamphlet called in Pestalozzi as witness to the ideal that

[25] Ibid., pp. 295 ff.
[26] *A Short Account of the System Pursued in the Pestalozzian Academy, South Lambeth* (London, 1826), from which this account is taken.

the basis of morality lay in the inward feeling, which gave rise to
ethical duties and social virtues :

> The performance of all the social duties, and this from a love of
> doing that which is right and pleasing to the Great Author of all,
> is the religion taught and practised in this establishment.[27]

As in many unorthodox schools, this academy had a system of rank
and reward, though no justification for this, of course, was to be found
in Pestalozzi's theories. In fact, the ranking system was Lancasterian
in inspiration, though tickets or marks were not awarded, on the
grounds that they gave an advantage to the talented. Instead, a daily
record of the performance of each boy was kept by the master and
every Saturday each pupil was required to give a written account of
the addition that he felt had been made to his stock of knowledge
during the week, and on the basis of this he was ranked in a list. On
this reckoning a boy was eligible for an Order of Merit, of which
there were three classes. The highest was called the Grand Cross of
the Order of Merit, on which was inscribed 'Truth, Order, Industry,
Courteousness'. To obtain this award a boy must have had a trouble-
free record throughout the year and at least one order of a lower
class. If any of the virtues inscribed on the Order were violated it
was immediately forfeited. Similarly, the other two Orders were available at a somewhat less exacting standard. In general, however,
failure to obtain one of the Orders was considered as a form of punishment. A certain amount of coercion was in fact applied to ensure
completion of academic work.

Another unusual institution whose methods and ethics were directly
influenced by Pestalozzi was Alcott House, founded in 1838 at Ham
Common, Surrey, and conducted by H. G. Wright and his sister. It
was named after Bronson Alcott and influenced by his Temple School
in Boston, Massachusetts. Alcott described Wright as having

> more genius for education than any man I have seen; and not of
> children alone, but he possesses the rare art of teaching men and
> women. That I have dreamed and stammered and preached and
> prayed about so long, is in him clear and definite.[28]

Although a correspondent in Robert Owen's *New Moral World*, in
describing Alcott House, declared that 'the mantle of Pestalozzi has

[27] *A Short Account . . . . South Lambeth,* p. 47.
[28] Cited in W. H. G. Armytage, *Heavens Below* (London, 1961), p. 176.

fallen on the shoulders of its master',[29] the ideas of the Swiss educationalist were more in evidence in the relationship between Wright and his pupils and the harmony between physical, intellectual, and moral aspects of the syllabus than in any particular adherence to Pestalozzian method. Wright's ideas were a peculiar amalgam of Pestalozzianism, transcendentalism, and Owenism. He addressed the Co-operative Congresses of 1840 and 1841 and the Congress of Rational Religionists in 1841 on education. In an account of the school that he wrote in 1840, Wright enunciated the basis of the educational principles : 'the essence which is to be educated is inestimably more important than the science to be taught.'[30] Wright also believed that the primal duty of the educator was 'entire self-surrender to love' and that only in this way could the children be reached by the teacher. The children were dressed in the simplest possible way and their food was of the plainest nature, consisting mainly of brown bread made with natural flour, for Wright was an intense believer in vegetarian principles and the children did gardening with the aim of making the school self-supporting in food. Examples of Wright's methods of teaching were quoted in *New Moral World* in 1840 and 1841, and while he is clearly indebted to Pestalozzi both for subject-matter and method of attack, he is very much a brilliant individualist.

An infant school was added to Alcott House in 1842. 'The proposed end', wrote Wright, 'is the culture of the best affections, a healthy and beautiful development of body, joined with such mind-exercise as is appropriate to the age of infancy.'[31] Alcott House came to an end in October 1842, when Wright, with Charles Lane, emigrated to Concord, Massachusetts, and Alcott House was reorganized as the First Concordium, which lasted till 1848 by which time both Wright and Lane had returned to Ham Common from America.[32]

The most important English disciple of Pestalozzi was, however, Dr. Charles Mayo. He was born in London in 1792 and educated at Merchant Taylors School and St. John's College, Oxford, graduating in law, taking his bachelor's degree in 1817 and his doctor's degree in 1822. He was originally intended for the Bar, but had to give this up because of deafness, but this handicap did not prevent him from

[29] *New Moral World*, vol. vii, no. 86, 13 June 1840.
[30] H. G. Wright and Miss Wright, *Retrospective Sketch of an Educative Attempt at Alcott House, Ham Common, Near Richmond, Surrey* (London, 1840), p. 4.
[31] *New Moral World*, vol. iii (N.S.), no. 27, 1 Jan. 1842.
[32] Armytage, p. 178.

becoming headmaster of the Grammar School at Bridgnorth in Shropshire on graduation in 1817, and he was ordained shortly afterwards. Mayo first heard of Pestalozzi through Synge and he resigned his headmastership in July 1819 to spend three years at Yverdon, where Pestalozzi had set up a 'colonie britannique'.[33]

Mayo was kindly received by Pestalozzi himself, then seventy-six years old, and Mayo described him as grey-haired and hollow-eyed, with a care-worn countenance and bent figure, but still young in heart and full of hope and confidence, ever ready to show kindness to children or to give all his money or even the silver buckles off his shoes to a casual beggar.[34] Mayo was impressed, as most visitors were, with his simplicity and force of character. 'Pestalozzi once known is never forgotten', declared Mayo, and felt proud to have known him as a friend.[35]

Mayo taught English and classics at Yverdon, supervised the English boys there, and was shown the details of the methods pursued by Jacob Heussi, one of the most able assistants. Mayo left Yverdon with a testimonial from Pestalozzi himself in his pocket that emphasized Mayo's excellent work at Yverdon and the firm grasp he had gained of the principles and methods used there.[36] After an attempt to organize a committee to popularize Pestalozzi's ideas in Britain, which once again failed, Mayo turned to what was to be his life-work, the setting-up of a school on Pestalozzian principles, which he believed was the best way now open to him to assist in spreading the master's teaching. This school is described at greater length in Chapter 10 below.

One of the most enduring aspects of the Mayos' work — apart from their efforts to bring Pestalozzian ideas into the infant school through the Home and Colonial Infant School Society set up in 1836 — was their elaboration of the object lesson. Of all methods deriving from Pestalozzi, this had by far the greatest and most lasting effect on British education, and illustrates how easily one aspect of a complex and coherent system could come to stand for the whole. The object lesson, from its introduction by the Mayos, became an important part of the elementary curriculum from 1829 until the end of the century. The significant point is that Mayo, when he arrived at Yverdon in 1819, found that object-teaching had been abandoned because the

---

[33] Silber, p. 298.   [34] Ibid., pp. 322–3.
[35] Ibid., pp. 325–6.   [36] Ibid., p. 299.

teachers thought that such lessons were bound to be miscellaneous and disconnected when based upon the random examination of whatever objects came to hand.[37]   He felt, however, that object-teaching might be revived in an improved form if a planned selection of groups of objects were made and the teaching of their qualities planned in a progressive way.   His views on the subject were eventually put into practice in Elizabeth Mayo's book *Lessons on Objects*, first published in 1829.   It proved enormously popular and reached its sixteenth edition thirty years later.

The plan of the book was simple.   It had five sections, each containing descriptions of a graded series of objects that the child might see every day.   The first series, for instance, included glass, indiarubber, leather, loaf-sugar, a piece of gum arabic, and so on.   The children were supposed to discover the qualities of the objects by visual examination assisted by questions from the teacher.   Lesson XI for instance, was as follows :

Bread

Ideas to be developed by this lesson, edible, wholesome, nutritious.

Qualities of Bread

It is porous.
absorbent.
opaque.
solid.
wholesome.
It is nutritious.
edible.
The crum is yellowish white.
soft when new.
moist.
The crust is hard.
brittle.
brown.
Use. — To nourish.[38]

The four succeeding sections of the book were planned to stimulate the child's ability to arrange and classify, improve the use of reason and judgement, and finally to facilitate his means of written expression. The book was welcomed as a great step forward in child education

[37] E. Mayo, *Lessons on Objects* (London, 6th ed., 1837), pp. ix–x.
[38] Ibid., pp. 16–17.

and as the first elementary school book devoted to the explanation of things as opposed to the traditional methods of teaching words in what was essentially 'a dead language'.[39]   Later critics, however, maintained that Mayo's object-teaching was merely a mechanical method of putting large words into children's mouths and making them repeat them without real understanding of their meaning.[40]

Mayo defended the system by stressing that it was important to remember the principles involved and that the real evil was the effect upon the children of their ignorance of the surrounding world and the consequent poverty of their perceptions and their language.[41]   Elizabeth Mayo had pointed out that persistent faults of teachers using the method were to tell the children too much and to use terms before the pupils felt the need for them.[42]   As with many well-defined methods of teaching, a great deal depended on the ability of the teacher.   When object-teaching became widespread it was almost bound to degenerate into the very verbalism that the Mayos hoped to overcome.   Its persistence as a teaching method throughout the nineteenth century was no doubt due to the ease with which it could be used, although if it were not linked to the rest of Pestalozzi's system its value was greatly diminished.   In the hands of a good teacher who was also a Pestalozzian, object-teaching had certain merits.   Here is a description, by one of his pupils, of an object lesson conducted by Charles Reiner, Mayo's assistant at Cheam School :

> Suppose Glass was the object.   He would ask the class what he held in his hand and then write their answer — 'Glass' — on the slate.   Then he would pass the piece round and ask who could tell him anything about it.
> A hand would be held up.   'Well, what do you say ?'
> 'You could break it.'   Appeal to the class generally — 'Is that right ?'
> 'Yes.'
> 'When you can break something, what do you say it is ?'   Probably no child could answer this question.   He would then point out certain substances which can not be broken and some that can, the class being encouraged to mention as many of each as they could, and then the word 'Brittle' would be given.   'Objects that are

---

[39] *Quarterly Journal of Education*, vol. i, no. 1 (1831), pp. 151–61.
[40] E. Mayo, *Lessons on Objects* (London, 16th ed., 1859), p. xiii.   [41] Ibid.
[42] E. Mayo, *Model Lessons for Infant School Teachers and Nursery Governesses* (London, 1838), pp. iv–v ; *Religious Instruction* (London, 1845), p. iii.

easily broken are called brittle' would be repeated several times by the class and then the word would be drawn out in the same way and the class appealed to for assent or dissent. This pupil remembers the quality Transparent was drawn out in the same way, as 'you can see through it' and the knowledge of the difference between 'Transparent' and 'Translucent' dates from that lesson. When all the qualities had been chalked up, they were read over by the class, the slate was cleaned and each child wrote out as much of the lesson as he could.[43]

Later in the century, the object lesson became domesticated. It settled down into descriptions of homely artefacts like tables, chairs, letters, and pins, neatly ordered into groups with their attendant qualities, and best illustrated in Miss Ross's *How to Train Young Eyes and Ears*, which went through twelve editions between 1863 and 1891.[44] The attraction of the object lesson for teachers seemed to lie in its concreteness and vividness, but few, if any, among the thousands who practised it could have known of the complex philosophy and high ideals that lay behind its origin, nor of the fact that it was eventually abandoned by its creator.

One other English educationalist who was influenced by the Pestalozzian method remains to be noticed — Sir James Kay-Shuttleworth. His efforts, when secretary to the Committee of Council on Education, to introduce a modified form not only of Pestalozzi's practice but also of Fellenberg's ethic into the mainstream of English education, were on a sufficiently large scale to deserve detailed treatment and they will be dealt with in Chapter 11 below.

The writings and public activities of Elizabeth Hamilton, Synge, Orpen, Higgins, Greaves, and others ; the institutions at Ham Common, Ealing Grove, South Lambeth, Cheam, and elsewhere that incorporated a greater or lesser amount of the Pestalozzian doctrine ; Kay-Shuttleworth's introduction of Pestalozzian principles into Government-sponsored textbooks ; all these helped to modify the rigidity of early-nineteenth-century elementary education. Between the 1820s and the 1850s the influence of the Swiss educator, though diffuse and uneven, played a major part in the transformation of classroom teaching. Whatever criticisms might today be made of

[43] Anonymous MS. entitled 'An Account of Cheam School in the Rev. Dr. Mayo's Time' (by courtesy of Dr. K. Silber).
[44] Mary Anne Ross, *How to Train Young Eyes and Ears, Being a Manual of Object Lessons for Parents and Teachers* (Edinburgh, 1863).

those elementary schools of the 1850s that taught drawing and writing, gave phonic reading instruction, based their arithmetic on Pestalozzian methods, and introduced object lessons, there can be no doubt that they were a great advance on the literacy-by-rote-learning methods that characterized the Bell and Lancaster schools of the 1810s and 1820s.

9. Lady Byron, E. T. Craig, and Ealing Grove School

I

LADY BYRON's school, established at Ealing in 1834, owed its inspiration to the doctrines and practices of Fellenberg to a greater extent than any of the agricultural schools that are described in Chapter 12 below. But though it embodied the main principle of the Hofwyl Poor School — the alternation of mental work with labour in the fields — it also added several variations and refinements introduced by its first principal, E. T. Craig, the Co-operator and Owenite.

The school owed its foundation to the beneficence of Lady Byron and her interest in social and philanthropic works, to which she had turned in the later 1820s when recovering from the effects of the separation from her husband and his subsequent death at Missolonghi in 1824. Lady Byron's first interest was the Co-operative movement, to which she brought the over-zealous idealism of the aristocratic reformer and the advantages of a lady of means. She aided it with gifts, loans to Co-operative societies, and propaganda on behalf of its principles.[1] She was not, however, a follower of Robert Owen, had no faith in his environmental theories, and after meeting him saw in his character little beyond 'vanity and presumption'.[2] Goodwill and mutual aid were the tendencies she hoped to foster, and Dr. King, the Brighton Co-operator and tutor to her daughter Ada, and similar

---

[1] W. H. Brown, *Brighton's Co-operative Advance* (Manchester, n.d.), pp. 57–58.
[2] Ibid., p. 59.

men of 'rational piety', were, she believed, the best antidotes to the more militant political tendencies of the movement.[3]

Her dissatisfaction with the Co-operative artisans ('The Societies look too exclusively to objects of *sense*', she complained in 1829)[4] caused her to revise her opinions respecting human character : 'With regard to Adults, I expect less than I did from good *influences*. . . . The best we can do for them is to place them in circumstances favorable to the excitement of whatever right and kind feelings they possess.'[5] This, she considered, might best be done with juveniles rather than adults. Arriving at Ealing in 1831, she toyed with 'a co-operative plan of education' under which children would be taught, besides the three R's, baking, churning, and simple cookery. In this way she hoped to bring together 'the class out of which the children would be taken, and the class to which my family belongs . . .'.[6] The regeneration of the poor by means of rural employments and association with the higher culture had inspired Fellenberg and was later to evoke a similar enthusiasm in Kay-Shuttleworth. It was to Fellenberg that Lady Byron turned for confirmation and elaboration of her educational ideal. She had visited Hofwyl in 1828 in order to place two young cousins there,[7] and now that she had the founding of a school in mind, Fellenberg became her infallible guide, and according to Kay-Shuttleworth's biographer Frank Smith, 'the final authority in any matter of dispute'.[8]

---

[3] E. C. Mayne, *The Life and Letters of Anne Isabella, Lady Noel Byron* (London, 1929), p. 329.   [4] Ibid.   [5] Ibid., pp. 329–30.
[6] Ibid., p. 323.   [7] Ibid., p. 330.
[8] F. Smith, *The Life and Work of Sir James Kay-Shuttleworth* (London, 1923), p. 52. Her admiration for Fellenberg even expressed itself in verse in a sonnet composed in 1839 :

To de Fellenberg — the Schoolmaster

Patrician ! but whose lineage fades from mind,
When thy life's nobler volume is unroll'd ;
When thou art known the friend of human kind,
Truth's latent gems devoted to unfold
And draw from Nature's mines the purest gold :
The mountains — witnesses of ages past
Remember not their shadows to have cast
Over a Patriot so sublimely bold !
Tho' not a war-note startled vale or lake,
The heroic spirit of the land to wake,
Thou, — once by dreamers of material glory fix'd,
Wert rous'd by Childhood's holier appeal ;
And with thy Saviour's glowing love inspir'd
Dids't for 'these little ones' prove all a
Martyr's zeal !

In many ways their background and outlook were similar. Both were patricians, both viewed the developments of the French Revolution with horror (Lady Byron condemned the Directory as 'a band of robbers' who ravaged 'with fire and sword'),[9] both saw the solution to contemporary social problems in a form of education that would give a prominent place to the moral improvement of its charges. It is worth while looking more closely at Lady Byron's theory of education, for with changes in form and emphasis it embodied much of the thinking of B. F. Duppa, secretary of the Central Society for Education, Kay-Shuttleworth, and others who wished to give dignity and intellectual content to agricultural labour and the preparation for it.

Lady Byron's educational principles were basically social and strongly affected by the unsettled state of society ; this she traced to the French Revolution, an upheaval that appeared to her to have unleashed all that was vicious in human nature. This emphasis on moral catastrophe rather than on economic or social conditions as leading to popular discontents was characteristic. 'The moral depravity of men in their social relations', she argued, was responsible for 'the tumults of the age.' [10] She looked in vain, however, to existing schools for the reformation of character or morals, concerned as they were with the mere technical aspects of instruction. Education needed a new direction over and above that of producing readers or mathematicians.

> There is a growing conviction that the great antidote to vice and crime, and therefore to political disturbances, is to be found in an improved moral education in the mass of the people.[11]

The improved moral education would have rural labour as its core. To Fellenberg went the honour of first perceiving 'the bearing which the pursuits of agriculture might have upon the morals of mankind',[12] and Lady Byron hoped for an English Fellenberg. In default of this, however, there was work for her to do on the lines laid down by the master, and in this spirit she opened Ealing Grove School in 1834.

II

Though the school was founded and financed by Lady Byron, the initial organization and day-to-day running of it was in the hands of

[9] Lady Noel Byron, 'History of Industrial Schools', in Mayne, App. iv, p. 479.
[10] [Lady Noel Byron], *What Fellenberg Has Done for Education* (London, 1839), p. xi.   [11] Ibid., p. xxxiii.   [12] Ibid., p. 24.

E. T. Craig. A thoughtful and original educationalist, Craig left the stamp of his ideas on the organization of the school and strongly influenced its general orientation.

Craig has had less than justice done to him in accounts of Ealing Grove School; few writers mention his name or his contribution. H. M. Pollard, in *Pioneers of Popular Education*, describes the first principal as having been dismissed after six months as being 'totally incapable' of coping with either the difficult children or the rough pioneer work.[13] Actually Craig, despite the initial turbulence of some of the boys,[14] organized the school efficiently enough to win the praise of the discerning American W. C. Woodbridge, editor of the *Annals of Education* and author of the first and best account of Ealing Grove, and left the school not because of inefficiency but as the result of a curious exercise of Lady Byron's charity.

Edward Thomas Craig, born in Manchester in 1804, had a long lifetime of varied activities and enthusiasms. He was at different times a fustian-cutter, editor, teacher, land steward, journalist, post-office clerk, and ventilating engineer.[15] His intellectual interests ranged from Owenism, phrenology, and mesmerism to the advocacy of longevity through physical exercise, clean air, and vegetarianism. Apprenticed early in life as a fustian-cutter, he had, when young, witnessed the Peterloo massacre and watched Luddites marched to their execution in Lancaster. As a young man he studied geometry and mathematics at the Manchester Mechanics' Institute and educated himself by reading volumes of fiction, poetry, and travel and the works of Locke, Dugald Stewart, Helvétius, and Volney. He also picked up MacNab's account of New Lanark, which led him to develop an appreciation of the Owenite doctrine. He never became identified with millenarianism or rational religion, however, but took from Owen's theories ideas on the education of children and an interest in the formation of rural communities. Craig also concerned himself, as we have seen, with the working-class school in Salford. He became a keen Co-operator and founded an Owenite society in Manchester and took over the editorship of the *Lancashire and Yorkshire Co-operator* in 1831. With the decline of Co-operation in Manchester in the early

[13] H. M. Pollard, *Pioneers of Popular Education, 1760–1850* (London, 1956), p. 204.
[14] Mayne, p. 330.
[15] This account of Craig's life is based upon R. G. Garnett, 'E. T. Craig: Communitarian, Educator, Phrenologist', *The Vocational Aspect of Secondary and Further Education*, vol. xv, no. 31 (1963), pp. 135–50.

1830s, Craig left England and took a post as superintendent of the agricultural colony at Ralahine in Ireland, founded by the wealthy Owenite J. S. Vandeleur. It was here that Craig was able to organize some remarkably effective and original educational experiments, the results of which he later introduced into Ealing Grove School.

At Ralahine, in addition to his duties connected with the agricultural co-operative, Craig organized two schools, an infant school for children up to five years of age, and a school for children from five to eighteen years.[16] The infant school, modelled on Owen's at New Lanark, was essentially a crèche for the younger children of the colonists, and was supervised for a time by Mrs. Craig. It was open twelve hours a day from 6 a.m. and the children were occupied with simple mental tasks and amusements and their only punishment was to be kept from school. 'These interesting beings', wrote an observer, 'often surprise their parents and astonish visitors by their little fund of facts, their knowledge of sensible objects, and gymnastic amusements.' [17]

It was the senior school, however, rather than the infant school, to which Craig gave most of his attention. The hours were not long — the children spent one and a half hours on intellectual work and the same amount of time on agricultural labour in the fields. The duration of lessons, in accordance with a strongly held principle of Craig's, varied with the age of the child. Children from five to seven years had fifteen minutes, followed by a break, those from seven to ten years twenty minutes, those from ten to twelve years twenty-five minutes, and older children between fifteen and eighteen years half an hour. Craig taught writing, grammar, simple accounting, geography, music, and drawing, and carried out experiments with air-pumps, chemical apparatus, an orrery, and a terrestrial globe, which the local Catholics believed were dealings with the Devil and the black art, particularly as the Bible was not used in the school. Craig's curriculum reflected both his own interests and the working-class Owenite's faith in useful and scientific knowledge. He also introduced some of the latest teaching methods : drawing was made the first step in learning to write (derived from Pestalozzi), and Jacotot's method of teaching English was adapted to the needs of the children.

---

[16] This account of the Ralahine schools is based upon W. Pare, *Co-operative Agriculture* (London, 1870), pp. 88 ff., 100 ff. ; E. T. Craig, *The Irish Land and Labour Question, Illustrated in the History of Ralahine and Co-operative Farming* (London, 1882), pp. 126 ff.   [17] *Crisis*, vol. ii, no. 27, 13 July 1833, p. 214.

Craig's views on the importance of labour in education seemed, however, to have been his own, and to have owed nothing to Fellenberg. They arose from a working-class faith in the importance of labour and a dissatisfaction with the kind of instruction being given in contemporary British and National Schools. In his opinion these establishments prepared children for clerical tasks only. 'The boys intended for the carpenter's shop, the mason's mallet or the draughts-man's pencil,' he wrote later, 'are all prepared alike for the office of copying clerks ; and the exercise of their muscles and their mechanical faculties neglected as if they were of no prospective use to them.' [18] The educational system, he argued, needed a reassessment of the im-portance of the work of the wealth-producer ; labour should be viewed 'not as a disgrace, but as the honourable means of health and independ-ence'.[19] Long sedentary exercises and task-work, requiring the stimu-lus of place-taking and prizes, were not only unhealthy and unsuitable but also unnecessary, and Craig claimed that he had shown at Ralahine that although the children spent only half of their school day at in-tellectual work, their progress in this sphere was at least equal to that of children who did twice as much.[20] This he ascribed to the varied and agreeable nature of their training in the fields, where in addition to learning rural crafts such as gardening, agriculture, and mensuration, they showed an improvement in 'health, discipline, industry, love of work, mental quickness in perception and mechanical executive skill'.[21] It confirmed and underlined the findings of the philanthropists, des-cribed in Chapter 12, who were at the very same time organizing agricultural schools in England, though Craig's work had roots in the Owenite rather than the philanthropic tradition. Craig's discoveries harmonized well with the practical aims of Lady Byron, and he was an appropriate choice as the principal of her school, but his own inde-pendent and important discoveries deserve recognition on their merits.

When his duties at Ralahine ended with the bankruptcy of the sponsor, J. S. Vandeleur, Craig accepted Lady Byron's offer to take charge of Ealing Grove School. Before doing so, however, on an allowance of £30 from Lady Byron he made a tour of industrial schools in Holland and Switzerland, attended the 1834 teachers' course at Hofwyl, and left for England with Fellenberg's good wishes for his success.[22]

---

[18] *Co-operative News*, 5 Oct. 1878.   [19] Ibid.   [20] Pare, p. 98.
        [21] Ibid.   -   [22] Craig, pp. 196–200.

III

Ealing in the early 1830s was a picturesque town of some 8,000 inhabitants, linked by stage-coach to central London. The school building was a plain, three-storeyed mansion standing in its own grounds
near the site of the present Ealing Green.[23] From this gaunt and
unprepossessing building, standing in six acres of untilled ground, the
thirty-year-old Craig and his wife began, in 1834, one of the most
interesting experiments in nineteenth-century education. The establishment was to be a combination of day and boarding-school, and a
prospectus was issued setting out its main features :

Ealing Grove School, Conducted by Mr. Craig

Children will be admitted either as Boarders or Day Scholars.

Boarders must be 12 years of age, or upwards. They must come
first on trial for a month, and if approved, will be educated either
for village teachers, or for some other useful and respectable situations in life.

Charge £14 per annum. The Parents to furnish clothing.

Day Scholars must be 6 years of age, or upwards. They will be
required to pay 2d. a week, to attend from 9 to 4 in winter, every
week-day, and to bring their dinners with them.

The boys of both classes (boarders and day scholars), who are
strong enough to work in the garden, will go out twice a day to do
so. Care will be taken not to expose them to bad weather, nor to
task them beyond their strength. When employed in tilling that
part of the land, of which the produce goes to the support of the
establishment, they will receive fair wages :—but a separate piece
of land will be allotted to such of the Boarders or Day Scholars, as
may be able to cultivate it on their account, and whose conduct shall
render them deserving of that advantage. They will have to pay
a low rent, *punctually*, once a month. The quantity allotted to each
will not exceed 1–16 of an acre. The Tenant may either take the
produce to his Family, or sell it to the School.

The Scriptures will be inculcated as the rule of life, and precepts
selected from them will be committed to memory : the master will
also make it one of the principal objects of his management to imbue
the children with the spirit of the gospel, in their behaviour towards
each other, and in their performance of the school duties. Besides
the instruction in Reading, Writing, Arithmetic, &c. commonly

[23] E. Jackson, *Annals of Ealing* (London, 1898), pp. 155–6, 214.

afforded in schools for the industrious classes, lessons will be given in Drawing, Carpentry, and some other useful arts, to any boys who may have a turn for them. The best behaved scholars will be admitted in the Evening for that purpose.

It will be perceived from these Rules, that the object of the School is to combine useful instruction with useful employment, so as to fill up the whole of the children's time, profitably and cheerfully; and while teaching them good habits, to prevent their forming bad ones.[24]

The social composition of the school was clearly mixed, although E. C. Mayne, the biographer of Lady Byron, described its pupils as coming from the 'vagrant class',[25] and A. D. Bache, the American educationalist, after a visit there, placed the children as belonging to 'the English peasantry'.[26] According to Woodbridge, however, who went into the question more thoroughly, the reason for taking boarders and charging fees was to remove from people's minds the stigma of a charity school, and thus allow 'respectable parents' to send their children there. Benevolent individuals were also encouraged to sponsor and to provide for the attendance of poor pupils, presumably both vagrant and peasant.[27]

The schoolroom occupied the ground floor of the building and this room also did duty as a dining-room, by the conversion of the desks into tables. The first floor was the dormitory, and also contained a carpenter's shop and modelling-room. The regime was Spartan; boarders (who in 1835 numbered fifteen out of a total of seventy-five scholars) rose at 6 or 6.30 a.m., according to the season, and retired at 8 p.m. They had an hour's extra study, and were made responsible for all the domestic chores of the school. Woodbridge found the boys' diet 'exceedingly plain': porridge in the morning, pudding and fruit at noon, and 'slight repast' in the evening.[28]

The curriculum and teaching method were eclectic and consciously progressive, with borrowings from Fellenberg, Pestalozzi, Owen, and others, and every attempt was made to get away from the rigidity and mechanical methods of the monitorial school. Number and form were taught with the aid of objects, drawing was stressed as an aid to

---

[24] [W. C. Woodbridge], 'Manual Labor School for the Working Classes, at Ealing in England', *American Annals of Education and Instruction*, vol. vi (Jan. 1836), pp. 76–77.   [25] Mayne, p. 330.
[26] A. D. Bache, *Report on Education in Europe* (Philadelphia, 1839), p. 316.
[27] [Woodbridge], p. 77.   [28] Ibid., pp. 77, 79–80.

perception, and much time was given, in the best Owenite tradition, to gymnastic exercises and singing. Apparatus was widely used — maps, globes, diagrams, and engravings of objects in geography, models of farms and buildings (some of which were made by Craig) for drawing classes, a collection of raw materials and manufactured objects, and an arithmeticon — a musical scale made of bars of wood, deriving from Wilderspin.[29]

In respect of organization and discipline, there was also some experiment. Corporal punishment was abolished, and the superintendence of the work of the school was put in the hands of a committee appointed monthly by the pupils themselves ; among their duties was the keeping of an account of each boy's labour and the recording of the state of the weather. Two of the instruments of discipline were inventions of Craig himself — the Charactrograph and the Classometer. The former was a set of cubical blocks arranged in several columns on a frame, and turning on a wire passed through them. Each had a number corresponding to that of a boy, and the four visible faces were coloured white, red, blue, and black (sometimes yellow), indicating respectively freedom from reproach, excellence of conduct, a minor fault, and a serious offence. Craig later described the virtues of the Charactrograph in uncharacteristically extravagant language :

> This apparatus completely supersedes the necessity of corporeal [*sic*] correction, and powerfully stimulates the pupil to moral and intellectual exertion and rectitude of conduct, by appealing to those faculties of the mind which are the best instruments in the hands of a judicious teacher for the rational development of the superior faculties.[30]

Every morning the machine was prominently displayed and each boy began with white. Changes were recorded daily, and at the end of each week each boy's status was entered in a book called a Classometer, and the blocks rearranged in merit order accordingly.[31] The Charactrograph and Classometer were very similar to Owen's Silent Monitor and Books of Character, which he used as 'a check upon inferior conduct' in his factory at New Lanark.[32] After Craig's departure, according to Kay-Shuttleworth, the blocks were abandoned and each child wore a coloured counter round his neck to indicate the

[29] [Woodbridge], pp. 80–81.   [30] *Star in the East*, 29 Dec. 1838.
[31] [Woodbridge], p. 81.
[32] R. Owen, *The Life of Robert Owen* (London, 2 vols., 1857), i, pp. 80–81.

state of his conduct.[33] Woodbridge criticized the competitive spirit associated with the Charactrograph as inconsistent with the aim of moral excellence, for only one pupil could be at the top of the scale, though several might deserve to be, and the leading pupil might be there because of the defects of others, rather than because of his own

Craig's Charactrograph

positive excellence ; he suggested that all who had done well should receive a mark of approbation, based on specific rules, which would tend to unite pupils rather than separate them by competition.[34] Kay-Shuttleworth, however, praised the system because it made moral conduct rather than intellectual proficiency the chief ground of

[33] Evidence of J. P. Kay, in *Report from the Select Committee on the Education of the Poorer Classes in England and Wales*, P.P. (1838), vii, pp. 18–19. James Phillips Kay added his wife's name to his own on his marriage in 1842. Hereafter the name Kay-Shuttleworth will be used in the text.   [34] [Woodbridge], p. 82.

distinction in the school,[35] and Craig defended his invention on the grounds that each pupil was admonished or approved without reference to any other, and himself made the standard of comparison between his past and present conduct, without public criticism by the master.[36]

Craig's Charactrograph
(detail)

Moral ideals were positively inculcated by means of lessons in Christianity.   Lady Byron believed that mere Bible reading had little influence on a child's conduct, and she was against confining religious

[35] Kay, p. 18.   [36] *Co-operative News*, 12 Oct. 1878.

instruction to the tenets of one particular church or sect, so the aim was the formation of character by instruction in the Christian virtues, a course that led, Woodbridge hinted, to some difficulties with the Established Church.[37]

The agricultural side of the school is best described by Craig himself:

> The land was divided into small gardens, one-sixteenth of an acre in size, which was let to deserving boys above seven years of age as a privilege, on the payments of $1\frac{1}{2}d.$, per month. Tools were provided, and the boys eagerly cultivated their little gardens, rearing flowers, fruits or vegetables at discretion, which they could sell to the Institution or carry home to their friends in the village. When working for me, I paid the boys $\frac{1}{4}d.$, per hour in labour notes. The boys kept little account books, in which all receipts and payments were duly entered by themselves, and thereby acquired habits of order, thrift, forethought, industry, and prudence, learning through mistakes and gaining by experience, which mere school lessons could not impart.[38]

By this means the pupils worked a system not unlike that of the medieval villein — part of the time for the estate and the rest for themselves — and Craig found that it gave several striking results. The most energetic and troublesome boys became the most enthusiastic gardeners. A visitor, Joanna Baillie, noticed that the boys, after finishing their lessons, 'got up at the sound of a little bell, and ran eagerly each to his spade or mattock, and worked away at levelling ground and other works so sturdily, and, in proportion, as effectively as men, but far happier'.[39] Some of the boys, in fact, were in the habit of climbing over the fences long before school began in order to tend their crops.[40] Thus Craig's experience at Ralahine was confirmed; garden work stimulated the mental faculties and the boys made greater progress in their studies than those who sat all day at their desks.[41] Part of the reason for this, of course, was that the manual work involved ancillary disciplines such as measuring, simple geometry, and the keeping of accounts, to whose beneficial effects Craig had drawn attention. B. F. Duppa reproduced some of the juvenile accounts for the year 1836, and they are eloquent of the attention to detail that the school insisted upon. During the seven months February to September

[37] [Woodbridge], pp. 83–84.   [38] Craig, p. 202.
[39] Cited in Jackson, p. 215.   [40] Craig, p. 202.
[41] [Woodbridge], p. 80.

George Kirby, aged fourteen, paid out 4*s.* 1*d.* for plants, seeds, and rent (which amounted to 1½*d.* a month). There is a balancing entry for income showing the produce sold (there seemed to be large quantities of scarlet runners) and the amount of labour for which payment was made. During these months George Kirby had a credit account of £1 0*s.* 11¾*d.* A similar account for William Boler, aged thirteen, showed his total earnings and profit as £1 2*s.* 6½*d.*[42]

The labour-note system Craig brought from Ralahine, where the tickets ranged in value from the equivalent of one week's labour to that of one-sixteenth of a day.[43] An Ealing labour-note is reproduced in an issue of the *Star in the East*, a newspaper that Craig edited in Wisbech after he had left Lady Byron's service. On one side of the note was printed some seasonal gardening instructions :

January Quarter

Dig and delve the ground. In frosty weather wheel manure to those beds which may want it. Gooseberry, currant and rasberry [*sic*] cuttings may be planted.

On the other side was an uplifting motto :

Sloth, like rust, consumes faster than labour wears ; while the used spade is always clean.[44]

No opportunity was lost to elevate manual work in the curriculum above merely digging the ground and in fact Craig, a thoughtful and well-read man, based his practice on a well worked-out theory of education founded on the creation of opportunities that allowed each individual pupil to develop his own peculiar faculties in the most appropriate way. Popular education, Craig believed, spent far too much time developing the memory, and he thought the curriculum gave little scope for the exercise of 'the reasoning, judicial or mechanical faculties', which could best be developed by an intelligent teacher setting his pupils to work in the garden or workshop, rather than by the intensive study of the three R's : 'A boy who might fail at figures might yet display great ingenuity in practical geometry when making a box or rabbit hutch, or when profitably planting his garden.' [45]

Underlying this was the belief that children were unique individuals

[42] B. F. Duppa, 'Industrial Schools for the Peasantry', in Central Society for Education, *First Publication* (London, 1837), pp. 182–3.

[43] *Crisis*, vol. ii, no. 27, 13 July 1833.   [44] *Star in the East*, 15 Dec. 1838.

[45] *Co-operative News*, 19 Oct. 1878.

who needed to be treated and educated in accordance with their personalities. Though innate functions were, according to Craig, 'nature's handiwork', temper and disposition were 'the result of heritage' and each pupil had 'special aptitudes, in various degrees of activity, for distinct pursuits'.[46] Craig treated each child as an individual, without reference to the skill or conduct of others, and condemned the treatment of pupils as one undifferentiated mass :

> To put boys of varied degrees of capacity in one department, and reward the first and punish the last, is evidence of a profound misapprehension of the nature of the human mind. It is like putting a Shetland pony to race with a thoroughbred horse, and then thrashing the little one for not winning.[47]

Craig's ideas have a more sophisticated and modern ring than those of the agricultural philanthropists described in Chapter 12 or of Lady Byron herself. It is unfortunate that his stay at Ealing Grove was too short to do more than initiate his ideas and practices. He was justifiably proud of the testimonials he received from parents on their sons' progress at the school. In each case improvement in character was reported. 'All his comfort appears to be going to school,' wrote one father, 'either for the books or his garden that you have let him have. For a child, I must say you have improved his mind for industry, as at all leisure times he likes to be doing something. . . .'[48]

Not only the parents had a high opinion of the school. During Craig's time it became 'a show place for the aristocracy',[49] and the number of visitors became so great that special rules had to be prominently displayed :

> Visitors are requested not to interrupt the master, when teaching, by making any observations.
> Not to put questions to the children, without previously mentioning their intention to him.
> Not to make remarks at any time, respecting the abilities or dispositions of the children, *in their hearing*.
> Not to give them money, or any other presents.[50]

Craig continued as principal until Christmas 1835,[51] and the occasion of his departure was curious, and indirectly attributable to his own

---

[46] Ibid.   [47] Ibid.   [48] Ibid., 12 Oct. 1878.
[49] *Memoir of E. T. Craig* (? Manchester, ? 1885), p. 10.
[50] [Woodbridge], p. 82.   [51] Duppa, p. 178.

success. According to the anonymous *Memoir* of Craig, the boys attending the village school were deserting it for Ealing Grove in such numbers as to jeopardize the position of the master, Mr. Atlee, who was 'crippled in one hand, and often used the cane with the other', and was a nephew of the parish clerk. Atlee wrote to Lady Byron, complaining that the industrial school had ruined his own school, and Lady Byron, 'with the usual waywardness of her charity', put Atlee in Craig's position.[52] As a result, many of the children left Ealing Grove.[53] Atlee, however, though forced to abandon the cane and pick up Craig's methods from the young assistants, eventually made a success of the position, though Bache thought the system was not in full operation according to the original idea even in the late 1830s.[54]

When Seymour Tremenheere, one of Kay-Shuttleworth's Inspectors, visited Ealing Grove in 1842, however, he found the school in much a better organized state than any previous visitor had done. It was divided into four classes, with ages ranging from under nine years in the fourth class to thirteen years in the first or highest class, and operated a well-organized pupil-teacher system. He was impressed by the cheerful and relaxed atmosphere, the plentiful supply of apparatus, the well-stocked school library, and the enlightened teaching methods. Some changes had been made, however, according to the timetable that Tremenheere reproduced. Gardening was confined to the two higher classes and occupied only one hour in the afternoon. Religious instruction did not appear in the curriculum but was given on Sundays only, being replaced by the reading of secular prose passages 'selected with a view to some moral or useful object'.[55]

The latest teaching methods were still apparent ; writing was taught by Mulhäuser's Writing Boards, arithmetic with the aid of Pestalozzian arithmetic boards, and singing was conducted on the Wilhem method.[56] The word 'Pestalozzi' in the timetable presumably meant an object lesson. Tremenheere was also impressed by the whole approach — 'careful and systematic, requiring individual mental exertion, and calculated generally to expand the faculties'. With regard to reading,

[52] *Memoir*, pp. 10–11. Craig wrote, on another occasion, of Lady Byron's 'wayward peculiarities' and 'the variable phases of her ladyship's character' : *American Socialist*, vol. ii, 13 Dec. 1877.   [53] Duppa, p. 179.   [54] Bache, p. 316.

[55] S. Tremenheere, 'Report on Schools of Industry', *Minutes of the Committee of Council on Education, 1842–3*, P.P. (1843), xl, p. 141.

[56] For details of these methods see below, Chap. 11.

even in the lowest class the boys had to understand the meaning of the words and sentences they read. In the highest class the boys were required to give the meaning of the sentence in their own words ; the etymology of every compound word ; derivatives from the same root ; various meanings of the same word ; its mode of use in different sentences ; and so on.[57] It may sound deadly today, but the curriculum of this class was in fact very wide, and well beyond the comparatively meagre fare provided in the average British and National School of the period.

Although it was essentially an attempt in educational terms to face up to the turbulent social problem of the early 1830s, Ealing Grove School, which continued in existence till 1852, differed from all the other agricultural schools of its day in that it blended two separate traditions — the working-class Owenism from which Craig had sprung, and the patrician ethic of Fellenberg, in which Lady Byron ardently believed. Craig viewed agricultural labour technically, assessing its value to the individual in educational terms, but Lady Byron saw it largely as a moral agency. In practice this fusion of purpose produced something far more original and stable than the simpler and more short-lived institutions that we shall examine in a later chapter.

10. Dr. Charles Mayo and Cheam School 1826–46

ON his return from Yverdon Dr. Charles Mayo had opened, at Epsom in August 1822, a school for the sons of the upper classes. Run on Pestalozzian lines, it made the alternation of school work with periods of play one of its main features.[1] Mayo moved to Cheam in the autumn of 1826, taking it over from the Rev. J. Wilding, who had been William Gilpin's curate. Assisted by his sister Elizabeth (who remained at Cheam until 1834), Mayo made the school the most famous of all Pestalozzian institutions in England.

---

[57] Tremenheere, p. 142.
[1] C. C.-W. Shepheard-Walwyn, *Henry and Margaret Jane Shepheard* (London, 1882), p. 6.

In bringing Pestalozzi's theories to this country, however, Mayo made certain adaptations. In his preface to *Lessons on Objects* he pointed out that he had preserved the idea but adapted the form to circumstances.[2] In this he had the backing of Pestalozzi himself who had great faith in what he took to be the English combination of exalted sentiments and practical good sense, and told Mayo, on the latter's departure from Yverdon, that he believed it would be in England that his views would be fully realized. 'Examine my method,' he urged Mayo, 'adopt what you find to be good and reject what you cannot approve.'[3]

Mayo's analysis of Pestalozzi's teachings was given to the public in a speech made at the Royal Institution in 1828 and published as a *Memoir of Pestalozzi*. He emphasized Pestalozzi's theory of the harmonious development of the moral, intellectual and physical features of the child, and his view that education was a process of progressive development in accordance with the child's own nature and ordered psychological principles. He contrasted this with current methods of teaching in England, the soulless presentation of facts, founded on 'abstract scientific considerations of the knowledge to be conveyed', and the placing of theoretical elements of the sciences before children without regard to the latter's stage of development. Mayo, as might be expected, also admired the religious and moral tone that pervaded Pestalozzi's teachings; he believed that Pestalozzi displayed the true temper and spirit of Christianity whereas other modes of instruction conveyed merely the doctrines.[4]

Mayo had absorbed the more general principles of the Pestalozzian teaching, and was not greatly concerned with the complex psychological processes that were the essence of Pestalozzi's theory. 'In every branch of study,' he told his audience at the Royal Institution, 'the *point de départ* is sought in the actual experience of the child; and from that point where he intellectually is, he is progressively led to the point where the instructor wishes him to be.'[5] This expressed much of what Mayo tried to do at Cheam.

From all accounts Dr. Mayo seems to have been well fitted for his role as headmaster, but there were contrasting elements in his character

---

[2] E. Mayo, *Lessons on Objects* (London, 2nd ed., 1831), p. vi.

[3] Cited in K. Silber, *Pestalozzi : The Man and His Work* (London, 1960), p. 234.

[4] C. Mayo, *Memoir of Pestalozzi* (London, 1828), *passim*. Cf. also C. Mayo, 'A Lecture on the Life of Pestalozzi', in *Pestalozzi and His Principles* (London, 3rd ed., 1873), pp. 1–66. [5] C. Mayo, *Memoir of Pestalozzi*, p. 26.

too. On the one hand he had what his biographer described as 'a sincere and all-absorbing yet somewhat simple piety, which was tinged with the principles of the Evangelical revival . . .'.[6] The application of these sincerely held but rather narrow religious beliefs resulted in a moral earnestness that was not quite in tune with the outlook of young schoolboys. For instance, the boys were not allowed to play or talk when they had gone to bed, and this rule was enforced by asking each boy the following morning 'Did you speak or play in your room last night ?' This, alleged Dean Fremantle, a former pupil at Cheam, 'was a mere incentive to lying'.[7] Hugh Childers, another former pupil, later to be Chancellor of the Exchequer and Home Secretary in Gladstone's administrations of the 1880s, claimed that informing and spying were almost universal, a practice he blamed on Mayo's Evangelical principles, which were not, in his opinion, 'the manly type that prevails now', and he compared Mayo's method of discipline — in which the boys were urged to watch the conduct of their companions and report it to the master — with Dr. Arnold's system at Rugby, where discipline was built upon appeals to the boys' honour. The principle of school life at Cheam, lamented Childers, was that the boys were all made to feel that they were desperately wicked.[8]

On the other hand, the very earnestness and sincerity of Dr. Mayo impressed some of his pupils, particularly those of similar religious persuasion. Dean Fremantle, even at the end of his life, clearly remembered two of the doctor's sermons, one upon the death of Dr. Arnold, the other on the occasion of the running away of a Hindu boy, whom Dr. Mayo had befriended, but who had betrayed the trust in him, and in respect of whom Dr. Mayo urged 'the Christian feelings of trustfulness and forgiveness to prevail'.[9]

In suitable company Mayo was an excellent conversationalist with a lively sense of humour. It was the practice for him and Mrs. Mayo to have meals with his senior pupils and any visitors who happened to be present. Tea was taken in the parlour and here conversation would range over many fields, including the politics of the day. The older pupils were encouraged to express their opinions, and many of them

[6] C. H. Mayo, *A Genealogical Account of the Mayo and Elton Families* (London, 2nd ed., 1908), p. 267.

[7] W. H. Fremantle, *Recollections of Dean Fremantle* (London, 1921), p. 10.

[8] S. Childers, *The Life and Correspondence of the Right Hon. Hugh C. E. Childers* (London, 2 vols., 1901), i, p. 8.   [9] Fremantle, pp. 11–12.

recalled later the charm of Dr. Mayo's conversation and his amusing anecdotes.[10]

Cheam School was, in fact, run very much like any other private boarding-school, but it also had some of the features of a public school. About half the boys left at the age of thirteen or fourteen to go to public schools, whereas the rest stayed on until seventeen or eighteen years of age, some of them to prepare for the university. Acording to Childers, this system had a somewhat unsettling effect on school life.[11]

The school day began at 6 a.m., breakfast was at 8 a.m., and lessons started an hour later. In line with Pestalozzi's emphasis on physical education, ten minutes was allowed for play at the end of each lesson and an hour was given to play from 12.45 p.m. to 1.45 p.m. and between 3 and 4 p.m. After tea at 6 p.m. lessons were prepared for the following day until 7.45 p.m., when prayers were said in the large schoolroom. The boys assembled in double rows and Dr. and Mrs. Mayo, accompanied by their children and the day's visitors, walked between them to the end of the hall. A hymn was sung with Mrs. Mayo accompanying on a seraphine or small reed organ. Dr. Mayo then gave a short address and said an extempore prayer, after which the day was over and the younger boys retired to bed.[12]

Mayo himself took charge of all the subjects in the school with the exception of modern languages, the sciences, and mathematics, which were the province of his brilliant assistant Charles Reiner, and from reminiscences of his pupils it is possible to get a glimpse of Mayo's teaching methods. In questioning, the rule was that the question should never suggest the answer. In all subjects Mayo sought to cultivate the powers of observation of his pupils, particularly in the study of nature and natural forms. He also liked to give impromptu lessons whenever possible; one pupil remembered him opening the first page of *Rasselas* and copying out two or three sentences with wide spaces between the lines. The pupils were then asked to parse each sentence, and this very humdrum improvisation on unexpected material proved for one child at least a lesson in parsing that was never forgotten.[13]

The mainstay of the school after Dr. Mayo was undoubtedly Charles

[10] Anonymous MS. entitled 'An Account of Cheam School in the Rev. Dr. Mayo's Time' (by courtesy of Dr. K. Silber). Hereafter 'An Account'.
[11] Childers, pp. 7–8. [12] 'An Account'. [13] Ibid.

Reiner. All accounts agree that he was a brilliant teacher, and Dean Fremantle wrote :

> He was without exception the best teacher I have known, both for his knowledge and his method and his discipline. He never set a punishment and was rarely disobeyed. A nation ruled as he ruled us would have few rebellious subjects.[14]

Another pupil wrote that his power of teaching was superb, and even Childers, over-sensitive to the claims of birth and breeding, thought that Reiner was the only assistant of any merit. The rest he dismissed as 'underbred and ill-informed'.[15]

Charles Reiner was a young German, a former assistant to Pestalozzi, who had been forced to leave his native land because of his radical political views.[16] His original intention had been to emigrate to America, but having met Dr. Mayo at Yverdon he decided, when he arrived in England, to remain there and teach at Mayo's school, and he continued to teach at Cheam for about three years after Mayo's death in 1846. He then left Cheam to live in London where he took on private pupils, among them the children of Queen Victoria, and also gave lessons at the Home and Colonial School Society's Training College. He eventually retired from tutoring and spent his last years at Reigate.[17] Reiner wrote two books, *Lessons on Number* and *Lessons on Form*, and in his preface to the former Dr. Mayo explained that Reiner's object was not 'to explain processes, but to unfold principles. The pupil is not taught to comprehend a rule, but to dispense with it, or form it for himself.'[18]

A pupil who began mathematics lessons with Reiner at the age of eight recalled that he gave his pupils 'a personal acquaintance' with numbers. 'Twelve was an individual who was made up of two sixes or three fours or four threes. It was as if the number was seen dissected.' This made fractions so easy to understand that the same child remembered telling one of his friends that there was a whole world below 1, which they had thought was the beginning of everything. The same pupil remembered that geometry lessons were 'very exciting'. Reiner taught the boys to solve Euclidean problems by their own efforts, using the accumulated knowledge of previous problems.

14 Fremantle, pp. 10–11.   15 Childers, p.8.
16 Fremantle, p. 10.   17 'An Account'.
18 [C. Reiner], *Lessons on Number* (London, 1831), p. viii.

The boy who accomplished this first was then asked to demonstrate the solution on the board in front of the class. Afterwards Reiner would read out the solution in Euclid's own words and the class would write it on their slates.[19] Childers attributed his own precocious mastery of mathematics entirely to Reiner. At the age of nine Childers wrote to his mother that he was learning :

> Addition, subtraction, multiplication, division (long division), reducing numbers to an improper fraction, reducing to least common denominator, reducing lowest terms ; addition, subtraction, multiplication, division of fractions ; reducing a decimal to a fraction, a fraction to a decimal ; addition and subtraction of decimals.[20]

Mayo obviously considered the mathematical side of the school as of equal importance with the classical. He looked upon arithmetical studies as an excellent mental discipline and regarded them as an avenue of success for those who might find classics and geometry beyond their powers :

> many an intellect that has not power enough for geometry, not refinement enough for language, finds them a department of study on which it may labour with the invigorating consciousness of success.[21]

Under Reiner this success was achieved by many pupils. His contribution can best be assessed, however, if his methods are compared with the kind of mathematical teaching that was general in the 1830s and 1840s. Mayo considered that 'the reproach that we are a nation of shopkeepers might seem to have originated in the spirit of our arithmetical studies' ; the average textbook degraded arithmetic to the level of 'a mere shop-boy's assistant, the *vade mecum* of the counter, and the desk'.[22] The chief fault of existing textbooks was their neglect of principles and reliance on mechanical dexterity, which failed to exercise the mental power of the pupil. Perhaps Mayo had in mind that best-seller among early Victorian mathematics textbooks, Crossley and Martin's *The Intellectual Calculator, or Manual of Practical Arithmetic*, published in 1833. By 1844 this had reached its thirty-fourth edition and it continued to appear in an average of two editions each year throughout the following decades, until in 1865 it had reached the astonishing total of seventy-seven editions.

The book certainly justified Mayo's description, for the sub-title

---

[19] 'An Account'.   [20] Childers, pp. 8–9.
[21] [Reiner], pp. v–vi.   [22] Ibid., p. vi.

promised 'A much larger number of business questions on each elementary rule', and claimed to embrace 'all the Arithmetical Requisites of the School, the Counting House, or the Shop'. It was, in fact, the parent of all the books that ever set hypothetical exercises on problems quite divorced from the child's knowledge and interest.[23]

If Reiner made a complete break with the arithmetical world of Crossley and Martin, he was no less successful in acquainting pupils with a wide range of the sciences. This aspect of Cheam School has rarely been noticed, but for many of the pupils it was one of its greatest attractions. Reiner also gave instruction in physical geography, chemistry and mechanics [24] and Fremantle mentions lessons in astronomy, zoology, and botany,[25] but it is probable that these were given irregularly under the general heading of science and did not form separate courses. Chemistry, however, had a prominent place in the curriculum, owing to Reiner's admiration for the work of Michael Faraday.[26] Chemistry was taken to an advanced level and many of the pupils were keenly disappointed when they had to give it up on entering university. At least one course of lectures on electricity is recorded, given by an outside lecturer, Professor Schonbein, in 1841,[27] and the scientific curriculum inspired some of the pupils to experiment at home. The brilliant Hugh Childers, during his holidays at his grandmother's home, constructed a model of Vesuvius that could be made to pour forth smoke, and roll imitation lava down its sides. Childers also conducted experiments with an electric battery, an airpump, and other apparatus.[28]

The mathematical and science side was thus an important part of the school. Hermann Krüsi, in his biography of Pestalozzi, considered that the popularity of the school was in great part due to Reiner's teaching of these subjects. According to Krüsi, Mayo taught Latin and Greek merely in order to meet 'the requirements of the English curriculum of fashionable learning', and this done, he devoted a great deal of time to what Krüsi called, with unconscious irony, 'real knowledge'.[29] In fact it is in the sphere of 'real knowledge' that the

[23] J. T. Crossley and W. Martin, *The Intellectual Calculator, or Manual of Practical Arithmetic* (London, 1833). A typical problem : 'A tradesman borrowed £1000 and paid in the following manner : at Christmas £56.10.6., at Lady Day £102.10.9¼., at Midsummer £587.10.11½. What had he to pay to make up the amount borrowed ?' (p. 23).   [24] 'An Account'.   [25] Fremantle, p. 10.
[26] Childers, p. 9.   [27] Ibid.   [28] Ibid., pp. 9–10.
[29] H. Krüsi, *Pestalozzi : His Life, Work and Influence* (Cincinnati, 1875), p. 223.

progressive nature of Cheam School can be seen as much as in its attempts to follow Pestalozzi's methods. The teaching of science, however, was too advanced a step for contemporary educational opinion. Even a knowledge of the properties of molluscs, Mayo pointed out in the preface to Elizabeth's *Lessons on Shells*, was regarded with suspicion by 'staunch anti-reformers in education', who claimed that whatever shortened the time devoted to the classics weakened 'the nerve-sinews of the mind' and debased the love of the ancient world by adulterating it with 'the barbarous ornaments of modern science'. Mayo's answer was that a little study of natural history could not harm the learning of the classics, and in fact the 'judicious introduction' of these branches of education into schools might even kindle the powers of scientific discovery.[30]

The curriculum at Cheam kept a nice balance between the claims of the innovators and the staunch anti-reformers ; it included the classics, mathematics, French, German, English, history, the sciences, and religious instruction, with cricket, football, and fives for recreation. Childers claimed that the boys were not taught English or modern history 'according to the ideas of those days' [31] (that is, the 1830s and 1840s), but his recollection is obviously at fault. In 1835 Mayo published anonymously a textbook entitled *Analysis of History, Ancient and Modern*, for use in the school. As a guide to historical study it is unremarkable, with periodization usually made at the beginning and end of reigns or at the dates of treaties.[32]

Religious teaching occupied a prominent place in the curriculum. In addition to long sermons in the schoolroom and in church on Sundays, the highest class studied the Greek Testament, and there was Bible reading without note or comment for the whole school once a week.[33] The boys were encouraged to undertake extra-curricular activities, and a flourishing school magazine produced some interesting work. Vere Henry, Lord Hobart, for instance, penned the following Byronic fragment at the age of fourteen :

Hannibal on his Recall from Italy

Adieu ! regretted, yet detested name,
One long adieu to Italy and fame !

[30] E. Mayo, *Lessons on Shells* (London, 1832), pp. vii–x.
[31] Childers, p. 9.
[32] [C. Mayo], *Analysis of History, Ancient and Modern* (London, 1835), *passim*.
[33] Childers, p. 10.

Adieu, ye shores, to enemy warrior dear,
My glory's cradle and my glory's bier,
And must I leave thee ! thou whose realms alone
My panting spirit burns to call its own ;
Which e'en my childhood saw with longing eyes,
And more than longing, marked them for its prize.[34]

Mental exercises were accompanied by physical gymnastics, which were a feature of Cheam School from the beginning, taken direct from Yverdon. 'I should never consider a school complete in its arrangements', Mayo wrote, 'where no provision was made for gymnastic exercises.' [35]

There is some evidence that towards the end of his life Mayo's powers began to fail and that this affected the running of the school. Childers wrote that when he went to the school in 1836 Mayo was getting too old and 'saw too much through his wife's spectacles'.[36] Mayo would be only forty-four in 1836, but possibly ill-health had reduced his vitality. Childers also alleges that Mayo began more and more to distrust the boys ; by the time he had reached the age of fourteen Childers found that the older boys' privilege of taking long walks unaccompanied by a master (a relic of Gilpin's day) had virtually been discontinued.[37] Even Fremantle, the Stanley of Cheam, felt 'a closeness about the system not suited to boys as they grew up', and was glad to find himself in the more liberal atmosphere of Eton, for which he left when twelve years old.[38] Even so, Mayo personally inspired an affection in many of the pupils, and bearing in mind the earnest religious atmosphere, we find that they retained an affection for the school throughout their lives, a circumstance that Childers chose to see as 'a little remarkable'.[39] Another old pupil remarked that when Mayo's successor took over, many of the scholars began to evince an ardent interest in the sea, 'but whether as a suitable profession for life, or only as an escape from the rule of the new master, is not clear'.[40]

Mayo took from Pestalozzi the more obvious and superficial aspects of his theory — the religious and moral tone, the need for progression,

[34] Vere Henry, Lord Hobart, *Essays and Miscellaneous Writings* (London, 2 vols., 1885), i, p. 5.   [35] C. H. Mayo, p. 269.   [36] Childers, p. 8.
[37] Ibid., p. 11.   [38] Fremantle, p. 11.   [39] Childers, pp. 10–11.
[40] Lieut.-Gen. Sir William F. Butler, *The Life of Sir George Pomeroy-Colley* (London, 1899), p. 7.

E.I.—N

development, and harmony, and the importance of a balance between moral, intellectual, and physical education. But Cheam was not a Pestalozzian school in any strict sense; it was an attempt to unite broad Pestalozzian principles with the practices of an Anglican public school. This gave the teaching methods more vitality than those in common use in similar schools, for Mayo had a genuine concern that existing teaching was too abstract, too mechanical, and had little relation to the world of children. It is difficult to say how far improved methods based on Pestalozzi's work gave Cheam its reputation for brilliance. Mayo was fortunate in having a highly intelligent group of pupils who rivalled in later life the eminence of those turned out by Gilpin in the eighteenth century. In addition to Fremantle and Childers they included Lord Hobart (1818–75), a Governor of Madras; Samuel Waldegrave (1817–69), later Bishop of Carlisle; Sir James Fergusson, Governor of South Australia; and many others eminent in academic, public, and military life.[41] Cheam was so popular in Mayo's time that in order to enter it was necessary for boys' names to be put down several years before starting at the school or even immediately following their birth. Parents were so anxious to obtain admission for their sons that on one occasion a false statement was made as to age and the boy concerned forced to keep up the deception for years.[42]

Much of the merit of the school came from Reiner's teaching of science. A subtler Pestalozzian and more brilliant teacher than Mayo, he gave to the school an unusual and unremarked distinction — that of an excellent institution for the teaching of science. Though the name and fame of Pestalozzi gave Cheam a certain esoteric attraction, its more enduring strength lay in its pioneering work in the sciences.

Here, then, is a school that is near the borderline of the progressive, innovating group and the more imaginative wing of orthodoxy. However, in the thirties and forties of the last century the features described above were a great deal more original than they would have appeared in the second half of the century.

[41] C. H. Mayo, p. 266 n.   [42] Ibid., p. 267.

11. Kay-Shuttleworth and the Continental Reformers

I

SIR JAMES KAY-SHUTTLEWORTH'S reputation began in his own lifetime when W. E. Forster, introducing the 1870 Education Bill, referred to him as 'a man to whom probably more than any other we owe national education in England'.[1] Historians of education have endorsed this verdict, and Kay-Shuttleworth's position as a founding father is still virtually unshaken today. Consideration of his work as an educational statesman has tended to draw attention from his great interest in the theories and methods of Continental reformers, particularly those of Fellenberg and Pestalozzi, and his attempts to introduce Pestalozzian teaching methods into the inspected elementary schools of England has only recently begun to be appreciated.[2]

Kay-Shuttleworth, almost alone among English educational administrators, had both a distaste for the traditional and the insular and a desire to experiment, which led him to inquire into the most up-to-date Continental theories and approaches. This is noticeable in several of the administrative reforms that he initiated during his ten years as secretary of the Committee of Council on Education. The appointment of Inspectors in 1839 was inspired by European practice, and his belief in the feasibility of a widespread system of pupil-teachers owed much to what he had seen in Holland and elsewhere.[3] Both the educational ventures in which he had a controlling interest, the Norwood School of Industry and Battersea Normal College, breathed the spirit of Pestalozzi and Fellenberg. 'The principles on which it was founded', wrote his friend Carleton Tufnell, 'were those we had learned from inspecting the institutions set on foot by Pestalozzi and Fellenberg, and by a careful study of their doctrines. . . .'[4]

[1] *Parl. Deb.*, 3rd ser., cxcix (17 Feb. 1870), 447.
[2] Cf. H. M. Pollard, *Pioneers of Popular Education, 1760–1850* (London, 1956), p. 214 ff.
[3] Cf. W. H. G. Armytage, *Four Hundred Years of English Education* (Cambridge, 1964), p. 115.
[4] E. C. Tufnell, 'Sir James Kay-Shuttleworth', *Journal of Education*, N.S., vol. ii (1877), p. 308.

These, taken with other schemes such as his sponsorship of Pestalozzian textbooks and the training of teachers in Continental methods
of vocal music, amount to a significant attack on English educational
tradition, policies, and methods. What effect did they have on the
working of the system, on evaluations of the educational process, on
day-to-day work in the classroom? These questions can best be
answered by an examination of Kay-Shuttleworth's own experiences as
an educator, the setting in which he worked, the criticisms he received,
and above all by an analysis of what exactly he meant when he talked
of Pestalozzian and 'synthetic' methods.

Kay-Shuttleworth came to education relatively late in life, and his
experiences were rooted in the narrow world of the Poor Law and the
provision for pauper children. Charged with carrying out the provisions of the Poor Law Amendment Act of 1834, as Assistant Commissioner of the Central Poor Law Board in the counties of Norfolk
and Suffolk, he found in 1835 several thousand children 'herded with
the adult paupers' in the workhouses of the Board. The pauper child
'might be an orphan, a bastard, the child of a convict, or deserted by his
parents, or dependent because the surviving parent could not provide
for him'.[5] In the ill-equipped and inadequate workhouse schools
these children were taught 'by the least objectionable pauper inmates'.[6]

The necessity of providing a reasonable standard of education for
these children began to concern Kay-Shuttleworth, and the lines on
which his ideas developed came from his estimate of the effects of
pauperism in society. His experiences as a young physician in Manchester during the late 1820s and early 1830s had given him a wide
knowledge of first- and second-generation urban workers of the industrial North, whose characteristics he tended to take as a scale for
the measure of the contemporary working man. The Lancashire
cotton operatives, he felt, were 'a race full of rare qualities — hardy,
broken to toil, full of loyalty to the traditions of family and place',[7]
and he compared them favourably with the East Anglian agricultural
labourer, who had 'a shambling gait, a depressed expression, little
activity or energy' and whose strength and vitality 'were far less than
what I had been accustomed to observe in the operatives of the north'.[8]

[5] B. C. Bloomfield (ed.), *The Autobiography of Sir James Kay-Shuttleworth*, University
of London Institute of Education, Education Libraries Bulletin, Supplement 7
(London, 1964), p. 27 (hereafter *Autobiography*).   [6] Ibid.

[7] J. Kay-Shuttleworth, *Four Periods of Public Education* (London, 1862), pp. 100–1.
[8] *Autobiography*, p. 22.

He had early decided that education was one of the best antidotes to pauperism,[9] and he determined to raise the quality and quantity of instruction for pauper children. He had no illusions as to the difficulties of the task or about the opposition he might encounter. Many of the Poor Law Guardians, he noticed, asked the question 'what had the hedger and ditcher, the team-driver, the shepherd, the hind, the ploughman . . . to do with letters, except to read incendiary prints against masters, bastilles and the oppression of the New Poor Law ?' [10] The climate of thought of the early 1830s that had given rise to the Agricultural Schools still lingered in the rural districts, and Kay-Shuttleworth's response to the problem of pauper schooling was not free from the attitudes that had surrounded the School of Industry, the Agricultural School, and the Reformatory. Among the labouring class, he felt, no habit 'is more essential to virtuous conduct than that of steady and persevering labour'.[11] 'Instructed by religion,' he felt, 'the labourer knows how in daily toil he fulfils the duties and satisfies the moral and natural necessities of his existence.' [12] On the other hand, 'the peculiarities of the character and condition' of the pauper children 'demand the use of appropriate means for their improvements',[13] and in his view these were not to be found in the monitorial system, whose 'embarrassments and shortcomings' he had noticed even before his transfer to East Anglia.[14]

In 1837, in search of the 'appropriate means', Kay-Shuttleworth visited Scotland, then a centre of educational experiment and reform, where he inspected Wood's sessional school in Edinburgh and the model schools of the Glasgow Normal Seminary. 'This visit to Scotland', wrote Carleton Tufnell, 'had the effect of making us wish to go deeper into the question of education and to investigate the methods of preparing teachers in foreign parts.' [15] Accordingly, two visits were made to Holland in 1838. The outcome of these inquiries was the hastily composed *Report on the Training of Pauper Children*, written in Norwich in 1838, a collection of educational curios. The recommendations of the Report, though specifically made for pauper schools, obviously had a wider application. Classrooms, suggested Kay-Shuttleworth, should be well stocked with blackboards, maps,

9 J. P. Kay, 'Report on the Training of Pauper Children', *Fourth Annual Report of the Poor Law Commissioners for England and Wales*, P.P. (1838), xxviii, p. 140 ; *Autobiography*, p. 57.   10 *Autobiography*, pp. 28–29.

11 Kay-Shuttleworth, *Four Periods*, p. 298.   12 Ibid., p. 299.

13 Ibid., p. 297.   14 *Autobiography*, p. 51.   15 Tufnell, p. 308.

drawings and objects, and fitted up on the plan used in Dutch schools, with all the children facing the teacher. The Continental simultaneous system or the teaching of children in classes of reasonable size (which necessitated the use of pupil-teachers) should replace the monitorial arrangements. The 'natural method' of teaching a curriculum embracing the three R's, geography, religious instruction, with the addition of vocal music as taught in Dutch and German schools, was advised.[16] In his enthusiasm Kay-Shuttleworth recommended two distinct methods of reading : Wood's 'explanatory and interrogative system', which combined reading with the acquisition of useful knowledge, and the Labarre system, a modification of Pestalozzi's method, which had been introduced into Dutch schools by Prinse.[17] The general mode of instruction, he felt, should be 'the methods of Pestalozzi, as reduced to practice by Mr. Prinse in the schools of Holland'.[18]

These recommendations, based on flexible methods of teaching children in classes, were, in effect, an indictment of the monitorial system. By the late 1830s, as Kay-Shuttleworth knew, strong criticism was being voiced of the poor standards of reading, writing, and arithmetic achieved under the rote-learning monitorial process, and concern was being expressed at the prevalence of bribery and corruption among the monitors ; the great majority of pupils taught in this way, a critic declared, made little or no progress.[19] and the report of one of Kay-Shuttleworth's own Inspectors in the early 1840s merely confirmed this diagnosis.[20]

Kay-Shuttleworth's early efforts at practical reform, however, were not directed towards elementary schools. When he was transferred to the Metropolitan Poor Law district in early 1839 the challenge of the plight of pauper children stimulated him to supervise the reorganization of the Norwood School of Industry on lines suggested by him in his Norwich Report. The new headmaster, Walter Macleod, praised by Kay-Shuttleworth for his 'intelligence, earnestness and skill',[21] had also visited Holland, and the methods used in the Normal School at Haarlem were his model.[22]

---

[16] Kay, p. 152.   [17] Ibid., p. 153.   [18] Ibid., p. 152.

[19] 'Schools for the Industrious Classes', in Central Society of Education, *Second Publication* (London, 1838), pp. 357–68 *passim*.

[20] The Rev. F. C. Cook examined some 270 monitors in 37 London schools. 17 read 'with ease and expression' ; 16 had some degree of skill with the higher rules of arithmetic ; 61 could write 'with ease and skill' : Rev. F. C. Cook, 'Report on Schools in the Eastern District', *Minutes of the Committee of Council on Education, 1843–4*, P.P. (1845), xxxv, Appendix, pp. 94–100.

[21] *Autobiography*, p. 57.   [22] Kay, p. 153 n.

Instruction included object lessons, geography, and English taught on Wood's methods. The pupils were split up into classes of about forty, divided from each other by green baize curtains that could be raised or lowered by means of ropes. [23] This arrangement was the forerunner of the classroom, which with solid walls later became universal. Outside the classrooms the children drilled around a naval mast set up in the playground, enjoyed frequent gymnastic lessons, had gunnery instruction, and worked at carpentry, smithying, and cobbling in addition to tending gardens.[24] Unlike the practice of all previous industrial schools, however, the academic work was based upon the Pestalozzian or 'synthetical' method, which presupposed that 'the teacher leads the children from the known to the unknown by such gradual steps as to require no effort of analysis on their part . . .'.[25]

The great problem that faced Kay-Shuttleworth was to find teachers who could understand and practise such Continental innovations in schools of the Norwood type. Macleod was a lucky discovery, and further teachers of his stamp were difficult to find. They could only be produced in numbers by training and the next logical step was to set up a Normal College for the purpose. His appointment as secretary of the Committee of Council on Education seemed to Kay-Shuttleworth a heaven-sent opportunity to inaugurate a college under Government auspices, but when he found that religious rivalries made this impossible, Kay-Shuttleworth set about founding his own. Characteristically, before doing so, he paid a further visit to the Continent, going to Holland, Prussia, Saxony, France, and Switzerland. He was particularly interested in the Normal Schools at Versailles and Dijon, and the School of the Christian Brothers in Paris. He visited Père Girard and Fellenberg, but was most impressed by Wehrli's Normal School at Kreutzlingen in the canton of Thurgovia, which he believed could form a model for restoring the virtues of the English plebeian, and he devoted over four pages of his first report on the Training School at Battersea to a description of Wehrli's school. What struck him most was the fact that the school made a point of educating the heart and feelings as well as cultivating the intellect.[26]

In February 1840 Battersea College was opened in a large manor-house on the banks of the Thames. The students were made up

---

[23] J. P. Kay 'The Training of Pauper Children', in J. P. Kay and E. C. Tufnell, *Reports on the Training of Pauper Children* (London, 1839), p. 4.   [24] Ibid., pp. 9 ff.
[25] Ibid., p. 6.   [26] Kay-Shuttleworth, *Four Periods*, pp. 300 ff.

of apprentice teachers, who had come from the School of Industry at Norwood, assistant teachers from the Schools of Industry for Pauper Children, and a number of trainee teachers between twenty and thirty years of age.[27] The college was run as a household on simple, frugal lines. The school day lasted from 5.30 a.m. to 9 p.m., with work in the garden, in a manner professedly copied from Ealing Grove School, as an essential part of the regime. Most of the subjects in the curriculum were taught on the inductive method based on Pestalozzi's principles, with the simple preceding the complex, familiarity with examples preceding the rule, and the use of natural objects and illustrations coming before the use of books. Reading was taught by the phonic method as used in Germany; English language teaching, as at Norwood, was based on Wood's principles and included oral lessons on grammar and etymology, dictation and composition, followed by oral instruction in grammar again at a higher level. Only after this was a grammar book consulted. Etymology was based upon the reading of standard authors and English was considered an important subject, for Kay-Shuttleworth believed that 'a thorough acquaintance with the English language can alone make the labouring class accessible to the best influence of English civilisation'.[28] Arithmetic was taught on Pestalozzian lines, beginning with lessons on number and carrying on in graded fashion to compound fractions. Second only to the basic subjects were book-keeping and elementary mechanics, the importance of both being seen in relationship to Britain's growing industrial power, Drawing and the art of design, and geography with an industrial and commercial emphasis, were also included because of their connection with industrial processes and production. Here again the techniques were derived from methods used in Swiss and German schools. At the end of the course, lectures were given on the theory and art of teaching, similarly derived from Continental sources.

Perhaps the most interesting innovation was the introduction of vocal music. The singing lessons were superintended by John Hullah, using a method of teaching based on that of M. Wilhem of Paris. Hullah's singing classes were a great attraction at Battersea and he

[27] This account is based on Kay Shuttleworth, *Four Periods*, pp. 310 ff.; R. W. Rich, *The Training of Teachers in England and Wales during the Nineteenth Century* (London, 1933), pp. 55 ff.; Rev. J. Allen, 'Report on the Battersea Training School and the Battersea Village School for Boys', *Minutes of the Committee of Council on Education, 1842–3* P.P. (1843), xl, pp. 12–21.

[28] Kay-Shuttleworth, *Four Periods*, p. 339.

became nationally famous when, on Kay-Shuttleworth's suggestion, these were transferred to Exeter Hall in London. Kay-Shuttleworth believed that vocal music had great educational value. 'We regard school songs', he wrote, 'as an important means of diffusing a cheerful view of the duties of a labourer's life; of diffusing joy and honest pride over English industry.' [29]

The object of Battersea was to turn out teachers who would devote themselves to the task of improving the mental, moral, and physical condition of the poorest and most demoralized section of the population. To achieve this the college wished to develop in the students a sense of dedication and service, and the regime was deliberately made rigorous and austere so that they might be in tune with the actual teaching conditions that they would find in the schools after graduation. Battersea went too far in this direction and the segregated, semi-monastic life, inspired by the seminaries of the Christian Brothers that had so impressed Kay-Shuttleworth, isolated the college from the world into a narrow puritanism.

Kay-Shuttleworth lost control of Battersea over the religious issue. Despite his attempts to meet their objections, influential members of the Church and the Conservative Party regarded the college with suspicion, partly because it did not explicitly refuse admission to Dissenters. With this opposition in the background, Kay-Shuttleworth was unable to persuade the Government to cover the deficit in the costs of running the college, and failed to raise the necessary subscriptions from any other source. In the end Battersea was handed over to the Anglican educational organization, the National Society, which preserved the curriculum more or less intact, except for additional religious instruction and Church history.[30] Other colleges, inspired by Battersea, were set up and the work of Kay-Shuttleworth was not entirely lost. The training of teachers in England was thus begun on lines that owed something, at least, to the genius of Pestalozzi.

II

In the early 1840s Kay-Shuttleworth, with Battersea out of his hands and his interest in Norwood relinquished, turned from the practical

[29] Ibid., p. 354.
[30] Rev. H. Moseley, 'Report on the Battersea Training School and the Battersea Village School for Boys', *Minutes of the Committee of Council on Education, 1845*, P.P. (1846), xxxii, pp. 244–57 *passim*.

application of Continental theories to their theoretical elaboration. He sponsored the organization of a series of textbooks published under the auspices of the Committee of Council on Education, which gave detailed instructions for the teaching, on Continental lines, of some important subjects in the curriculum, and he inspired a highly successful series of demonstrations in music and other subjects for teachers in Exeter Hall. During this period he was also clarifying and refining his own ideas on teaching methods, for he was coming to believe that the repetitious presentation of all subjects in the curriculum in the manner inherent in the arrangements of the monitorial system must be replaced by a thorough analysis of the way in which each particular subject might be presented to a class by a teacher in order that every child could derive the maximum benefit from it. His views were crystallized in a speech on what he called the constructive method which he made in July 1842 for the purpose of presenting to the public the principles underlying the series of classes then taking place in Exeter Hall.[31]

Speaking as a 'self-styled disinterested promoter of elementary education', he rejected the method of teaching by memory work under the authority of the teacher and came out strongly for a revaluation of the traditional view of the child and the methods pursued in schools. Teachers and educators should, he said, view children as rational creatures whose minds needed exercising. The moral discipline of a school, he emphasized, was inseparably connected with rational methods of instruction and the need for obviously imposed authority would disappear if reason and affection were called upon by the teacher.

In the teaching of reading, the most rational way of proceeding was, he suggested, by the phonic method, in which the teacher analysed the words into separate sounds and then by construction or synthesis taught the child to unite these into words. In this way the simplest elements were first brought to the attention of the child and gradually built up into the more complex. This method, claimed Kay-Shuttleworth, was superior both to the normal method used in English schools of teaching children the sounds of the individual letters of the alphabet, then one-syllable words, and so on, and also to Jacotot's method, widely used on the Continent, of teaching children whole words at once.

[31] J. P. Kay-Shuttleworth, 'The Constructive Method of Teaching', *Saturday Magazine*, vol. 21, no. 647, Supplement (July 1842), pp. 41–48, on which the following account is based.

The method of writing recommended was that popularized by Mulhäuser of Geneva, and it depended on a careful analysis of the forms of letters that entered into written characters, commencing with the simplest and proceeding in series to the more difficult, combining the elementary forms of letters in their comparative simplicity, and gradually writing words that contained the forms of previous letters. Drawing was dealt with in a similar manner and Kay-Shuttleworth considered this subject to be of great use to all classes in a commercial country and of immediate importance to the working class in bettering their conditions of life. It had two aspects — the elevation of taste and the depiction of form. The former was lacking in England, especially among artisans, but was best left to the Schools of Design. The drawing of form, however, was the province of the elementary school, and Kay-Shuttleworth advocated Dupuis's system, which he had seen demonstrated in Paris in 1839, and which consisted of models of linear figures and solid objects. By means of a wire, these could be arranged in different degrees of perspective, thus giving pupils practice in drawing increasingly complex forms.

This lecture reveals Kay-Shuttleworth basing his constructive method on some of Pestalozzi's more general principles — the analysis of objects into their simplest elements and their presentation in a series from the simple to the complex. He appeared to believe that this more or less comprehended the Pestalozzian method, which, in a footnote appended to the printed lecture, he defined as a method 'of ascending from the simple to the general through a clearly analysed series, in which every step of the progress is distinctly marked . . .'.[32] In relation to the purpose of Pestalozzi's methodological teachings, Kay-Shuttleworth's simplifications appeared jejune, and they were not backed by any appreciation of Pestalozzi's philosophical position, but the significance of Kay-Shuttleworth's recommendations was in relation to what he hoped they would replace. So strongly did he feel that the repetitive methods used in inspected schools in England were outmoded and damaging that within two years of his assumption of office he issued a Minute that made the following of the constructive method official Government policy.

The Minute was chiefly remarkable for making it clear that a different attitude to both pupils and teaching process was to be the foundation of the new proposals. After the familiar exposition of 'the elements

[32] Ibid., p. 47 n.

of the Pestalozzian method', the child was defined as 'a rational creature, whose memory may be most successfully cultivated when employed in subordination to the reasoning faculty'. His moral sense could only be cultivated by inspiring him with a love of truth : 'the first step to this result is to satisfy the intelligence on every point which can be rendered clear. The means to this end are the arrangement of the facts presented to the mind of the child in such order that each new truth may naturally succeed, and be supported by those which have preceded it. . . .'[33]   In order that teachers might be in no doubt as to what was wanted, a number of teaching manuals were prepared under the imprint of the Committee of Council.

Mulhäuser's manual of writing took the pupil in some detail through the three main stages of analysis of letters into their simplest forms ; classification of these into order from the simple to the complex ; and synthesis of the elementary forms into letters of the alphabet.[34]   The phonic reading-book explained at length the method already outlined.[35] The arithmetic book, 'after the method of Pestalozzi', was probably the best of the manuals, a straightforward series of exercises on the Pestalozzian Board of Units divided into a hundred squares, further subdivided by horizontal and vertical lines, and the Board of Compound Fractions in which squares were subdivided into smaller squares representing fractions.[36]   The most controversial of the volumes was John Hullah's *Wilhem's Method of Teaching Singing*.   The method advocated and used by Hullah, whose work has already been mentioned, came in for such extremes of praise and criticism, and surprisingly enough raised such important points of principle concerning popular education in general and Kay-Shuttleworth's whole line of strategy in reforming English education in particular, that the episode of Hullah and the Exeter Hall singing classes deserves some attention.

In 1839 John Hullah, an obscure music-teacher, conceived the idea of forming a school for popular instruction in vocal music, and was led to investigate Wilhem's method as practised in Paris.   Through

[33] 'Minute on Constructive Methods of Teaching Reading, Writing and Vocal Music, Published by Direction of the Committee of Council on Education', *Minutes of the Committee of Council on Education, 1840–1*, P.P. (1841), xx, pp. 18–23.
[34] *A Manual of Writing : Founded on Mulhäuser's Method of Teaching Writing, and Adapted to English Use* (London, 1842), pp. 13–14 and *passim*.
[35] *The First Phonic Reading Book* (London, 1843), *passim*.   Cf. also *The Second Phonic Reading Book* (London, 1844).
[36] *Exercises in Arithmetic for Elementary Schools.   After the Method of Pestalozzi* (London, 1844), *passim*.

the interest of Henry Reeve, the registrar of the Privy Council, Hullah was brought into contact with Kay-Shuttleworth, who was greatly interested in Hullah's scheme and secured his services, as we have seen, for classes at Battersea.   In August 1840 Kay-Shuttleworth and Hullah visited Paris to investigate the Wilhem method in more detail and in December of that year a conference of schoolmasters was held at Kay-Shuttleworth's house, at which Hullah urged the formation of public singing classes for teachers.[37]   A prospectus was issued and the support of Lord Wharnecliffe, the Lord President of the Council, and various bishops and lords was secured.   On 1 February 1841 the classes commenced, with Hullah in charge, a hundred schoolmasters in attendance, and a group of Battersea boys for demonstration purposes.   During the year various other classes were formed, including one for schoolmistresses.   In the spring they were opened to the public and in December advanced classes were started.   In addition, Hullah took a number of Battersea boys on successful demonstrations throughout the provinces.[38]   The preface to Hullah's manual described the aims that the Committee of Council felt should inform the teaching of vocal music to the masses :

> Amusements which wean the people from vicious indulgences are in themselves a great advantage : they contribute indirectly to the increase of domestic comfort, and promote the contentment of the artisan. Next in importance are those which, like the athletic games, tend to develop the national strength and energy ; but the most important are such as diffuse sentiments by which the honour and prosperity of the country may be promoted. . . . The songs of any people may be regarded as important means of forming an industrious, brave, loyal, and religious working class.[39]

The singing classes of Exeter Hall, as they were popularly known, were a curious manifestation of popular interest in education. They outgrew their original object of providing intensive short courses for teachers, though this aspect remained the core of the experiment.   In 1842–3 classes in drawing, writing, and arithmetic were added, based on the principles popularized by the Committee of Council, until in 1843 no less than 2,300 pupils were enrolled in the school.[40]   The fees

[37] F. Hullah, *Life of John Hullah, LL.D.* (London, 1886), pp. 25–26.

[38] F. Smith, *The Life and Work of Sir James Kay-Shuttleworth* (London, 1923), pp. 128–9.

[39] J. Hullah, *Wilhem's Method of Teaching Singing* (London, 1841), p. 4.

[40] Smith, p. 128.

charged were moderate; schoolmasters and mistresses paid 15*s*. for sixty lessons, mechanics and others paid 8*s*. or 10*s*., but the well-to-do were charged 30*s*. for the course.[41]   The classes appealed to both the middle and working classes, though the latter by far predominated. In 1842 the first workmen's singing class, to mark their appreciation of Hullah's efforts, presented him with a music stand in the shape of an angel, gilded and bearing a palm branch, which had been made entirely by members of the group (see illustration facing p. 208).[42]   In addition, the classes were much patronized by the nobility.   At one meeting the Duchess of Sutherland, Lord Wharncliffe, and Lord Howard were present and in the course of the evening the Duke of Wellington appeared.   'The singing was suspended', wrote a con- temporary journalist, 'and all the assembly — both singers and auditors — rose with one unanimous impulse, and cheered the noble Duke with the most enthusiastic fervour and energy.'   The programme for the evening, we are told, included a madrigal, the Hundredth Psalm, and the Austrian hymn 'God Save the Emperor'.[43]

The classes, particularly the singing classes, clearly possessed enor- mous appeal and seemed to have universal support.   They had been enthusiastically taken up by teachers who introduced the Hullah method into hundreds of classrooms as an exciting new project, and by artisans and others as a means of popular culture.   Lord Lansdowne, the Lord President of the Council, had backed the classes because he elt they furnished neutral ground upon which conflicting educational parties might agree.[44]   Wharncliffe, his successor in the 1841 Peel administration, hoped they would keep people out of taverns.[45]   Kay- Shuttleworth honestly believed that the Hullah system, because it re- presented the latest in Continental methods, must be the best way of teaching the most civilizing of subjects.   Hullah himself made the most of a semi-governmental post from which rivals were automatically ex- cluded.   Everybody, it appeared, was satisfied, yet within a couple of years of their commencement the classes met with criticism, scorn, and opposition and in 1843 were eventually forced to leave Exeter Hall and continue in a much reduced fashion elsewhere.   What had happened ?

[41] *Parl. Deb.*, 3rd ser., lxv (12 July 1842), 8.
[42] *Illustrated London News*, vol. i, no. 28, 19 Nov. 1842, pp. 437–8.
[43] Ibid., vol. i, no. 5, 11 June 1842, p. 69.
[44] C. C. F. Greville, *A Journal of the Reign of Queen Victoria, from 1837 to 1852*, pt. ii (London, 3 vols., 1885), i, p. 372 n.
[45] *Parl. Deb.*, 3rd ser., lxv (12 July 1842), 8.

The opponents of the Hullah system, mainly the independent and radical press, were not beguiled by its popularity, and after scrutinizing the method carefully, produced three main criticisms : the system was technically unsound, it created a monopoly, and it hindered the efforts at musical culture made by other bodies and individuals. Hullah's method, sometimes called the 'fixed Do' method, was based upon the introduction of a new musical notation, related to what was later called tonic sol-fa, in place of the commonly used key notation. The Hullah plan was attacked as confusing and unnecessarily difficult, and it was felt that pupils and instructors using it would be able to understand nothing beyond the contents of their own manuals. The teaching itself involved complicated hand movements ; as each pupil repeated notes in the ascending scale he raised his right arm and opened and closed his fingers at stated intervals, a process that when performed by large groups was, according to the *Illustrated London News*, 'not a little grotesque'.[46] The hand, in fact, was an essential feature of the system, for the five fingers represented the five lines in music and the spaces between them corresponded to musical spaces in Hullah's notation. The pupils kept their left hands open at waist level while the right hands moved swiftly in four predetermined directions before finishing with a clap in their left palms. Similar hand-movements can be seen in the illustration facing p. 208. The semi-breve, minim, and crotchet were taught by repeating these words aloud, the last shorn of a syllable. 'The monotonous cry of "crotch", "crotch" *ad libitum*', exclaimed the *Illustrated London News*, 'carries the imagination to a village duck pond.' [47]

This sort of criticism did not need to be taken too seriously, nor did the *Spectator*'s condemnation of Hullah's manual as 'needlessly diffuse' [48] or the *Inquirer*'s dismissal of it as 'a spurious abortion'.[49] The *Illustrated London News* was on firmer ground when it compared the Hullah pupils to those who excelled at public examinations in mathematics under the eye of a master, but were utterly unfit for any job involving mathematical calculation. They could do much together but little for themselves :

> The railroad system of tuition is always suspicious, and but throws hundreds of conceited smatterers upon a land where too many are already found. All such schemes, however successful in appearance,

[46] *Illustrated London News*, 11 June 1842, p. 77.   [47] Ibid.
[48] *Spectator*, 10 July 1841.   [49] *Inquirer*, 19 Nov. 1842.

are amazingly like the notable one of building a tower without mortar.[50]

The critics were particularly annoyed, however, that Hullah's work should receive the status of what appeared to be a state monopoly. The *Inquirer* flatly stated that 'the authority of the Council of Education, the influence of rank and wealth, the countenance of lords and princes' was the system's sole claim to merit, but more important than this, the exclusive authority to teach singing given to Hullah by the Government excluded the talents of those teachers and musicians who had long laboured at the musical education of the people, including John Curwen whose tonic sol-fa was more flexible than Hullah's. 'Their reward has been neglect', wrote the *Inquirer*, 'and their efforts have been thwarted, instead of encouraged, by those very crowds who now throng in silks and satins to Mr. Hullah's exhibitions at Exeter Hall.' [51]

It was this conviction that the Government was actually holding up the musical development of the masses by a monopoly that informed the view of W. E. Hickson, the most cogent critic of the Hullah scheme. Hickson, a former colleague of Kay-Shuttleworth as a collector of statistics for the Poor Law Commissioners,[52] was a man of diverse enthusiasms and original views. A former boot and shoe manufacturer, he retired at thirty-seven to buy and edit the radical *Westminster Review*. A composer of merit, he was also a fervent educationalist, with a strong admiration for the school systems of Holland and the German states.[53] He had served on the Royal Commission on Hand Loom Weavers, signing a separate report which advocated the repeal of the Corn Laws and the improvement of popular education.[54] Forgotten today, he was described in the *Dictionary of National Biography* as 'one of the pioneers of national education, and in particular of popular musical culture'.

Hickson, in the first place, repudiated the claim that Hullah's manual was an example of the synthetic method, for it contained too many technical terms in the first lessons and introduced difficult concepts at too early a stage ; above all, it revived the discarded method of

[50] *Illustrated London News*, 11 June 1842, p. 77.
[51] *Inquirer*, 24 Sept. 1842.   [52] Kay, p. 141.
[53] *Dictionary of National Biography* ; W. E. Hickson, *Dutch and German Schools* (London, 1840), *passim*.
[54] *Copy of Report by Mr. Hickson, on the Condition of the Handloom Weavers*, P.P. (1840), xxiv.

teaching children to sing from imaginary notes placed on or between the fingers.[55]   A more effective method, thought Hickson, was to begin with melodies :

> The first step in musical education is to make the ear familiar with melodies ; the second is to teach the voice to sing them ; and when this is accomplished, and not before, we may proceed to the rules of the science.[56]

Methods such as this had been pursued by the Society for the General Encouragement of Vocal Music.   The patronage of Hullah and the publication of his book at Government expense, complained Hickson somewhat bitterly, drew attention, subscribers, and support from this organization, which had been encouraging vocal music in schools,[57] and from others who had been doing similar work.   Hickson recommended Turner's *Manual for Teaching Singing in Schools* and Forde's *The Art of Singing at Sight*.   He also praised the efforts of Edward Taylor, the Gresham Professor of Music (also commended by the *Illustrated London News*), who twenty years earlier had taught his own method of sight-singing to two hundred Norwich weavers, who performed Spohr's oratorio *The Crucifixion* to the entire satisfaction of the composer.[58]   Teachers of vocal music were thus not lacking.   The Government's task, insisted Hickson,

> is not to find new methods for bad teachers, but good teachers, with full liberty to adapt any method which may appear to them the readiest means of obtaining a given end.[59]

If textbooks were required, a Committee of school inspectors could be set up to do the necessary research and writing.

The importance of Hickson's criticism was that he placed the question of music teaching in the setting of Government policy on education as a whole.   The problem as he saw it was not only one of how music should be taught, but whether the steps taken were in accordance with those by which every branch of education might be improved. If these steps were in the wrong direction they were worse than no

[55] 'H.' [i.e. W. E. Hickson], 'Music and the Committee of Council for Education', *Westminster Review*, vol. xxxvii (Jan. 1842), pp. 15 ff.

[56] [W. E. Hickson], *The Singing Master* (London, 1836), p. 6.

[57] [Hickson], *Westminster Review*, pp. 4–5.

[58] Ibid., pp. 1–2 ; *Illustrated London News*, 11 June 1842, p. 76.

[59] [Hickson], *Westminster Review*, p. 6.

advance at all. 'The question is,' he continued, 'what should be the spirit of the whole educational policy of the government?' He had little doubt of his own answer: build more schools, increase the pay of teachers from the local rates, and set up a greater number of training colleges with special emphasis on educational theory.[60]

Hickson was implicitly suggesting that the policy for which Kay-Shuttleworth had responsibility, of concentrating on the improvement of method to the relative neglect of buildings and teachers, was retrograde and wrong.

The criticisms we have just outlined apparently had little effect on the popularity of the classes at Exeter Hall, which were faced with more mundane difficulties. As the groups grew larger the question of finance became a problem. The whole of Exeter Hall was engaged for the classes, and the best teachers secured, but the running expenses were not being met by fees and donations, nor were special subscription concerts able permanently to bridge the gap. In 1842 a petition from 1,600 people attending the classes was presented to Parliament, asking the Government to support the classes financially.[61] Lord Wharncliffe presented the petition in the Lords, his support being given, as we have seen, on social rather than educational grounds.

At this point the singing classes became entangled with the question of the annual grant for education, then running at the rate of £30,000 a year. During 1842 the question as to whether the grant should be augmented to include provision for the singing classes was debated in both the House of Lords and the House of Commons, with the Radicals in the Commons pressing for increased expenditure on education, including that for the classes, and the Conservative Government stonewalling on the issue.[62] Inevitably, the religious question was raised. In July 1842 the Bishop of London declared that the classes were in effect a species of Normal School, and since no religious instruction was given there they would inevitably lead to the formation of a Normal School on undenominational lines supported by the Government.[63] Though Lord Wharncliffe, for the Government,

---

[60] [Hickson], *Westminster Review*, pp. 6, 42.

[61] 'Memorial to the Committee of Council on Education, and Likewise Petition to Parliament, from the Members of the Singing School for Schoolmasters and Schoolmistresses at Exeter Hall', *Minutes of the Committee on Education, 1841–2*, P.P. (1842), xxxiii, pp. 50–53.

[62] *Parl. Deb.*, 3rd ser., lxv (12 July 1842), 18–19; (15 July 1842), 185–96.

[63] Ibid. (25 July 1842), 569–71.

shrugged off this allegation, the damage had been done, and henceforward the classes existed under a cloud, with a section of the Committee of the Anglican National Society adding weight to the opposition.[64] In August 1842 the Government finally announced that no grant would be made in support of the Exeter Hall classes.[65]

Kay-Shuttleworth temporized. He suggested that Lord Wharnecliffe should decide upon the future of the classes himself instead of entering into a full-scale public debate with the Church and the National Society, but Lord Wharnecliffe replied that unless the classes could be self-supporting and make fewer calls upon the time and labour of his staff, he was unwilling for them to continue.[66] This marked the end of the Exeter Hall experiment, but in 1843 the classes were continued on a small scale at St. Martin's Lane, with the financial backing of Kay-Shuttleworth himself.[67]

III

Kay-Shuttleworth's idea of what constituted Pestalozzianism was extremely vague. His tours of Europe were made ten years or more after Pestalozzi's death and the schemes that attracted his attention were second- or third-hand, and the adoption in England of the schemes of Prinse, Labarre, Wilhem, Dupuis, Mulhäuser, and others did little to counteract this impression. Nevertheless, the educational ideas of these men were unorthodox and innovations in themselves.

This synthetic or constructive method was not solely intended to foster the growth of the individual child, despite the new approach to children in the Minute of 1841, but was seen as part of a social policy on education that differed little from that of the philanthropists of the Industrial and Agricultural Schools in whose ambit Kay-Shuttleworth's own educational ideas had been formed. As to the general acceptance of the new methods themselves in the English elementary schoolroom, the phonic method of reading took the strongest root. The Pestalozzian spirit behind the teaching of arithmetic, however, did not oust the Crossley-and-Martin approach mentioned in Chapter 10 above, nor did the handwriting methods of Mulhäuser become universal. The Hullah method of singing lived and died with its creator and none of the Committee of Council manuals, significantly

[64] Smith, p. 130.   [65] *Parl. Deb.*, 3rd ser., lxv (9 Aug. 1842), 1178.
[66] Smith, pp. 130–1.   [67] Ibid., p. 131.

enough, went into a second edition. To the extent, however, that simplification, order, and step-by-step teaching in many schools influenced classroom methods in the basic subjects, there was a net gain.

But could more have been done? An article in the *Westminster Review* in 1851 (almost certainly written by Hickson) was emphatic that Kay-Shuttleworth faltered here as he did in other aspects of his policy. In the presentation of new methods of instruction, the article alleged, care was taken to introduce those that were associated with men 'in no way compromised by liberal opinions', and that no one who had distinguished himself as an educational reformer was allowed a share in the work. In this way the Scottish reformers Combe and Simpson were excluded, and Sir Thomas Wyse (who wanted a national system of free compulsory education and whose book *Education Reform* was a manual of up-to-date Continental practice) and John Lalor, a noted Pestalozzian and winner of the Central Society of Education's prize essay on education, were not consulted. Real reform and radical reformers, it was implied, were thus ignored, and derivative schemes were offered instead.[68]

The substance of Hickson's criticism in this and earlier articles was that the educational establishment had not only lost an opportunity to introduce the pure gospel of reform into the educational system, but that what was done frustrated further effort. Furthermore, the Committee of Council's policy neglected the more fundamental aims of increasing the numbers and improving the quality of teachers and of building enough schools in which they might teach.

At this distance of time we may be able to see Kay-Shuttleworth and his work in a more balanced perspective. The other innovators considered in this volume were either actively interested theorists or philanthropists like Rousseau or Edgeworth or Lady Byron, or else they were practitioners who valued the unorthodox, like Williams, the Hill brothers, Fellenberg, Wehrli, Mayo, or Buchanan. Only one is an administrator, Kay-Shuttleworth, the secretary of the Committee of Council on Education. Trained as a physician, knowing at first hand the lives of the poor in the city and the country, he was not a professional politician, nor was he a professional educator, but he held the chief administrative responsibility from 1839 to 1848 when the

[68] [W. E. Hickson], 'Educational Movements', *Westminster and Foreign Quarterly Review*, vol. liv (Jan. 1851), pp. 402 ff.

debate between Church and State in education was tense and the extension of secular education backed by national funds was in a critical position. Hickson and others say that Kay-Shuttleworth was timid in his reforms, tending to compromise before the consequences of a firm stand were fully tested, but they were not trying to effect a whole national policy as he was.

In the late 1830s and early 1840s, the time of the Corn Law, prices were high in a period of industrial depression, upheaval, and unemployment ; rioting was reported as freely as the appalling conditions of the poor in the textile mills and the coal and iron mines ; the pitiable lot of children in all branches of industry and manufacture was made public in report after report. Chartism was militant early in the period and the beginning of urban trades unions appears later. During the nine years when Kay-Shuttleworth was secretary of the Committee of Council on Education the economy climbed painfully to some stability and the Government marked time on educational legislation.[69] Many believed, as did Graham, the Home Secretary, that to provide more education was to unsettle the masses still further and that what they needed was something much stronger.[70]

Kay-Shuttleworth was a tactician and an innovator. He transformed the monitors into pupil-teachers and introduced the Queen's Scholarships for the training of promising young students. He started a training college, he developed the Inspectorate 'as a means not of exercising control, but of affording assistance'. He introduced as directly as he could experimental methods of teaching. In all of these things he was influenced by the innovations he saw in Scotland, Holland, France, and parts of Germany. He negotiated with the Church, and he tried to accelerate and increase national financial support, but 1838–48 were lean years for the economy and for education within the economy. When his health broke down in 1848 he retired from his post, and when the Revised Code was approved in 1862 Kay-Shuttleworth denounced it as the negation of the humane and mildly experimental regime for which he strove in all his educational ventures. He did not welcome universal free education and his views on education for the masses were patriarchal ; he believed that administration, like politics, was the art of the possible. For him what was liberal was feasible as a national policy : what was radical was tactically unwise.

[69] Cf. Greville, ii, p. 212.   [70] Smith, p. 140.

Section Four

SOME GENERAL THEMES

12. Labour and Education, 1780–1850

I

ONE of the curiosities of the British educational scene during the past two hundred years has been the relatively recent date at which manual subjects have become part of the secondary curriculum. Woodwork, metalwork, and handicrafts have established their position as subjects in the curriculum largely during the twentieth century. During the classical period of the Industrial Revolution, the teaching in all types of school was strongly academic. In only a few special or experimental schools did the curriculum include manual work, and not all of these recognized the significance for the educational process of the connection between academic discipline and manual labour.

In the later eighteenth century Continental educationalists had stressed the value of manual arts in education. Rousseau, in *Émile*, considered that manual labour was the pursuit that came nearest to a state of nature.[1] He would have children learn a trade and gave it the same importance as the more traditional subjects. 'He must work like a peasant and think like a philosopher,' he wrote of Émile, 'if he is not to be as idle as a savage. The great secret of education is to use exercise of mind and body as relaxation one to the other.'[2] This recognition that work with the hands could be an important aid to mental education was developed by Pestalozzi, Fellenberg, Basedow, and other Continental educationalists.[3] Fellenberg's agricultural estate

[1] J.-J. Rousseau, *Émile*, trans. Barbara Foxley (London, 1961), pp. 151, 158.
[2] Ibid., p. 165.
[3] C. A. Bennett, *History of Manual and Industrial Education up to 1870* (Peoria, Ill., 1926), pp. 82–86.

at Hofwyl took the principle to a high level, as we have seen in Chapter 8. Thousands of visitors to Hofwyl carried the ideas away into almost every country in Europe, where they became the subjects of discussion and experiment within various national cultures.

In Britain in the later eighteenth century there were two types of school in which manual labour formed an important part of the curriculum — schools of industry and certain Quaker schools. Neither, however, owed anything to Continental models. Nor was there any connection between them, each springing from quite different circumstances and educational assumptions. In neither case, however, were the implications of the significance of manual work fully faced. At the Quaker schools of Ackworth, Sidcot, and Wigton, at the turn of the century, the boys carried out a variety of domestic tasks and worked on the land attached to the school and in the school gardens. At Ackworth, in 1819, it is recorded that the boys undertook seasonal work in hay-making, potato-picking, apple-picking, and similar tasks.[4] In the intermediate schools of the Society of Friends, including those mentioned above, the domestic chores and work on the land became less as the nineteenth century progressed, and it was only in the labouring schools for children of the 'disowned' that work on the land became part of the school day.[5] In no case, however, did the schools of the Society succeed in effecting an educational synthesis of manual and intellectual work. The reasons for the introduction of labour were in all cases social or economic, never educational.[6]

Schools of industry date back to the seventeenth century, but found a new lease of life in the early period of the Industrial Revolution, taking in the unemployed children of the non-manufacturing districts. The establishment of the schools was left to voluntary effort and from 1796 onwards was largely the province of the Society for Bettering the Condition of the Poor. Information on these schools can be found in Sir Thomas Bernard's *Of the Education of the Poor*. He draws attention to a school of the Rev. William Gilpin of Boldre, the Mendip schools of the More sisters, the Kendal schools of Dr. Briggs, and others at Oakham, Lewisham, Bamburgh, Fincham, Birmingham, and Cheltenham. In these schools a variety of tasks was carried out: spinning, knitting, weaving, gardening, farming, cooking, and the making of clothes, gloves, stockings, hats, infants' shoes and socks,

---

[4] W. A. C. Stewart, *Quakers and Education* (London, 1953), p. 167.
[5] Ibid., pp. 167–8.   [6] Ibid., p. 170.

and similar articles.[7] In all the cases the manual work was the chief feature of the school and occupied most of the day; reading and religious instruction, and occasionally a little writing and arithmetic, occupied the rest of the time.

Industrial schools were first and foremost working schools, and the labour of the children contributed to the upkeep of the establishment. The children themselves earned a few shillings a week each. These schools were successful in only a small number of cases, however, and were difficult to organize mainly because of the lack of supplies of suitable raw materials and the right kind of market. It was estimated that in 1803 only 20,336 children were receiving instruction in schools of this kind.[8] The work itself was supposed to give the children 'habits of industry', the great social panacea of the Evangelicals and reformers of the period. To this extent the introduction of labour was an attempt to influence the character of the children, because Satan had work for idle hands.

It was assumed that the habits of skill and industry were transferable and, once obtained, could be put to use on a variety of crafts. Samuel Parr, the educationalist and divine, writing in 1786, stressed that schools of industry were not narrowly vocational: 'the habits of diligence . . . may be easily transferred to other employments more difficult and more profitable, to which they will be hereafter advanced.'[9] As Margaret Jones says, in her history of the charity-school movement, manual skill, in the juvenile industrial world, 'played the part usually attributed to the classics in the world of learning'.[10]

If some thinking had been done on the subject the influence of labour on the child's character might have been followed up and extended, but industrial schools were intended for the poor, and the lower strata of the poor at that, and few, if any, were willing to believe that this section of the population deserved anything but the barest literacy. The education they received in industrial schools was designed to fit the children for their place in society, by the inculcation of the habits of 'order, cleanliness and application'.[11] If we wish to discover the conscious application of labour to education with a view to something

---

[7] [Sir Thomas Bernard], *Of the Education of the Poor : Being the First Part of a Digest of the Reports of the Society for Bettering the Condition of the Poor* (London, 1809), *passim*.

[8] M. G. Jones, *The Charity School Movement* (Cambridge, 1938), p. 158.

[9] S. Parr, *A Discourse on Education* (London, 1786), p. 50.

[10] Jones, p. 89.   [11] [Bernard], p. 205.

more than the teaching of social humility we must turn to experiments in a different type of school.

Schools in which the manual labour of young children formed an important part of the curriculum fell into two main classes : those, other than pure industrial schools, in which technical skills such as printing were practised, and those that incorporated the agricultural arts into their curriculum. During the early part of the nineteenth century, few of the former were in evidence. In fact, only two important examples of the introduction of technical subjects into elementary schools can be found : the Printing School in Whitechapel and the Experimental School of Industry in Westminster.

The agricultural schools were more numerous, and belonged, as we have seen in Chapters 8 and 9, almost entirely to the early 1830s, in most cases being a response to the agricultural distress and rioting of that period. In both industrial and agricultural types of school, however, there was, on the whole, a recognition of the value of manual labour not only in the development of a more balanced individual and the formation of a more favourable response to the rest of the curriculum, but also as an aid to the learning of the academic subjects.

II

The first two schools that we shall consider were both conducted to some extent on a modification of the monitorial system introduced by Dr. Bell. In each school the introduction of manual work was expressly designed to modify the rigidity of the system and to increase the pupils' interest in the work of the school. The earlier of these schools was the Printing School, Gower's Walk, Whitechapel, which attained a considerable degree of fame in the first part of the nineteenth century. It had been built in 1808 by William Davis, a London businessman, for boys and girls from eight to fourteen years of age. The boys worked at printing for up to three hours a day, the rest of the time being spent on ordinary lessons taught on the monitorial system. About a third of the boys were constantly employed on printing under the guidance of a superintendent, and they carried out commissions for the neighbourhood.[12]

According to the evidence of William Davis himself before the

[12] *Report from the Select Committee on the State of Education*, P.P. (1834), ix, pp. 211–212.

Select Committee on Education of 1834, the introduction of a technical subject into the curriculum made the school much more acceptable both to the children and to the parents, and helped the children to learn the more formal subjects. The school had not entirely broken away from the old industrial-school outlook, and the printing was still looked upon as a training in generalized skill leading to good qualities of character; according to Davis, very few boys became printers when they left school. This, he thought, did not matter because they had, during their school career, 'attained the habit of diligence'.[13]

The most interesting account of the school was given by Frederic Hill, brother of Rowland and Matthew Davenport Hill, who paid a visit there in July 1835. Hill was much impressed and saw nothing that was not worthy of praise, and he considered the printing class, consisting of some sixty boys, to be the focal point of the school. Boys joined this group by reaching a certain standard of competence in the three R's, and as the printing work was very popular this gave an added incentive to classroom studies. The printing class was divided into three groups of twenty each, only one of which was at work in the printing shop at any one time. Hill found the standard of work high and on the day of his visit the boys were printing the Reports of the National Society. Payments from customers of these jobs covered the costs of tuition and the general expenses of the school and left a surplus to be divided among the boys, amounting on an average to £100. Half of this was given immediately in the form of pocket money and the rest set aside to form a fund to meet the expenses of their outfit and the apprentices' premium when they left school. The boys also received an accrued share of the interest from the Savings Bank in which money was from time to time invested.[14]

Hill found that the school had several educational advantages. The boys were 'refreshed and relieved by an alternation of manual and mental labour',[15] and they became 'thriving men and successful members of society' when they left school.[16] There was, in fact, a waiting-list of applicants for admission to the school and departing pupils were much in demand as apprentices.[17] Thus according to Hill, and he was a sagacious educationalist with much experience of different types of school, the inclusion of printing in the curriculum

---

[13] *Report from the Select Committee on the State of Education*, P.P. (1834), ix, p. 214.
[14] F. Hill, *National Education : Its Present State and Prospects* (London, 1836), pp. 20–23.   [15] Ibid., p. 21.   [16] Ibid., p. 24.   [17] Ibid., p. 20.

had a beneficial effect upon both the school work in general and the attitude of the pupils. Here was an early version of what is nowadays called a sandwich course.

Some seven years later, however, the school appears to have declined from the standards observed by Hill. According to W. B. Hodgson, the phrenologist and associate of William Ellis, who visited the school in September 1841, he found that the teacher on the boys' side was flippant in his general manner towards the boys, who were in consequence rather disorderly both in the classroom and in the printing-shop. Hodgson, a progressive educationalist to his finger-tips, was appalled by the rigidity of the monitorial system, the emphasis on religious teaching, and the fact that the children did not learn geography or grammar.[18] On the other hand he found that the printing work was of a high standard (the boys were printing the parish accounts at the time of his visit), that the exercise books were 'very good', and that the boys read 'pretty well, in the usual hum-drum way'.[19] It was the lack of both freedom and purpose that disappointed Hodgson. He was, however, 'highly delighted' with the 'superior order and neatness' of the girls' side of the school, and felt instinctive confidence in the 'kindness and integrity of their teacher, a very pleasing woman with a fine head'.[20]

Gower's Walk Printing School represented a half-way house between the conventions of a school of industry and a new conception of labour as an ingredient in the curriculum in its own right. This idea was carried a stage further in the Experimental School of Industry in Westminster. This was a National School superintended by Mrs. Hippisley Tuckfield, who in the 1830s experimented with the application of industry to education. She believed that many children were admitted into National Schools at too early an age, before they were ready for the discipline, and that many children also stayed too long in infant schools. She therefore planned a school for children between the ages of five and ten years, in which the imperfections of monitorial teaching might be softened by increased attention to the individual child, and in which 'little families' would replace the large and impersonal 'system' of the monitorial school.[21]

The main features of Mrs. Tuckfield's school were that it was

[18] J. M. D. Meiklejohn, *Life and Letters of William Ballantyne Hodgson* (Edinburgh, 1883), pp. 252-3. [19] Ibid., p. 252. [20] Ibid.
[21] Mrs. H. Tuckfield, 'The Experimental School of Industry, Tufton Street, Westminster', *Educational Magazine*, vol. ii, N.S. (1840), pp. 84-89.

co-educational for children from five to ten, that the teacher was a qualified woman (Mrs. Tuckfield believed that it was possible to employ
'one excellent female teacher' at the same salary as 'an ill-qualified
master'), and that manual or industrial employment was introduced
into the curriculum.

The employments that Mrs. Tuckfield had in mind were of a rather
rudimentary kind — knitting, needlework, netting, straw-plaiting, and
chalk-writing. Chalk-writing on a blackboard was, of course, somewhat of an innovation in an age when writing on slates was almost universal, and she considered it as a form of manual employment that not
only taught the children writing but was something they could do with
relative freedom from supervision. Mrs. Tuckfield believed that manual employments helped to 'tranquillise and humanise the character',
and that the introduction of an interesting and purposeful occupation
brought about some degree of order and silence in the school without
any need to resort to the authoritarian discipline and slavish fear
common in the monitorial schools. She laid great emphasis on individual attention to the children, and the literary side of their education,
she believed, should be approached gradually according to the individual needs of the child, and for this it was necessary to have adult
teachers rather than monitors, especially with the younger children.
Her whole educational outlook was opposed to the cheap mass-
production of the monitorial school; it was better, she believed, to
educate forty children properly than 1,500 superficially.

Mrs. Tuckfield was an example of an individual educationalist
working towards new methods pragmatically and in isolation. She
was quite clear, however, about the importance of her work and the
need for its wider application :

> But the advantage I have principally in view is a constant alternation
> of manual and intellectual labour, a point which, I think by no means
> meets with the attention it deserves. It should never be lost sight
> of in any stage of education. But especially before a child has
> reached its tenth year, all excitement of the brain should be avoided ;
> and yet, from five to ten, it is peculiarly necessary to subdue the will,
> and tranquillise the passions, by introducing habits of fixed occupa-
> tion. Linear drawing and good writing may both be considered as man-
> ual labour, and are particularly fit occupations for young children.[22]

[22] Mrs. H. Tuckfield, *Letters to a Clergyman, on the Best Means of Employing Funds
for the Religious and Moral Education of the Lower Orders* (London, 1840), p. 15.

III

The other outstanding example of the application of labour to education occurred in what was essentially a reformatory school, the Brenton Asylum, Hackney, and tends to bear out the thesis that several of the innovations in educational practice that we can broadly call progressive were carried out with children in need of special care and attention. Brenton Asylum, opened in the early 1830s, was a school that prepared vagrant children for emigration, and was founded by a remarkable naval officer, Captain Edward Pelham Brenton, one of the originals whom the Services from time to time throw up. Outwardly, Brenton's career had been a normal one for his day and age. Born in 1774, he had entered the Navy when very young and served in action throughout the Napoleonic Wars in command of various ships, leaving active service at the end of the war in 1815.[23] During his service, however, he had been disturbed by the drunkenness and cruelty that were a part of the life of naval ratings at that time, and later he campaigned against impressment and flogging.

Brenton had a dogged desire to penetrate to the truth of a situation irrespective of the weight of prevailing opinion. In an age when imprisonment, corporal punishment, and hanging were widely practised as deterrents for even minor crimes, he stood for the view that the prison system fostered rather than prevented crime : 'the felons of 1834 are the neglected children of 1814', he wrote. 'Thus even-handed justice treads quickly on the heels of our guilty omission.'[24] In an age in which Malthus's theories were widely accepted, Brenton thundered magnificently against the 'absurd nonsense of over-population' :

I have often listened with horror to the hateful objection set forth by some political economist, viz., 'that the poor if made comfortable, would increase too fast ! ! !' Dare any man publicly avow this cruel, this selfish, this murderous and atheistical proposition, I will tell him that he is confuted by common sense, common experience, and well known facts ; but were it true as it is false, have not the poor as good a right to live as the rich ? Is the order of nature to be

[23] Vice-Admiral Sir Jahleel Brenton, *Memoir of Captain Edward Pelham Brenton* (London, 1842), pp. 2–35 *passim*.
[24] E. P. Brenton, *Observations on the Training and Education of Children in Great Britain* (London, 1834), p. xii.

counteracted for the pleasure of the few and the destruction of the many ? [25]

Above all, Brenton was convinced that the educational system was defective and often inhuman and tolerated practices, such as flogging and the fagging system, that were a denial of education.[26] Even gross social differences, he believed, were often due to educational deficiencies :

> When we see a man calmly meeting death, or enduring the severest punishments known to our civil or martial laws, we ought to reflect, with deep humility, that a good education was only wanting to make that man superior to his judges.[27]

As might be expected from a man of such unorthodox opinions, Brenton ran his Asylum on lines quite different from those we have seen in the industrial or working schools considered earlier. The object of the Asylum was not only to teach the boys industrious habits and fit them for their station in life, but to effect a total reformation of their character. The methods Brenton employed have some affinity to those used in Lady Byron's school and in the Hills' school at Hazelwood, though there is no evidence that Brenton initially was familiar with either of them.

Brenton admitted to the Asylum only the most deprived class of boys — street boys, workhouse boys, those from other reformatories, orphans, and boys from families in reduced circumstances.[28] He insisted that during their stay the boys should be entirely under the care of the master ; there should be no interference by the parents, if any were alive or interested, nor were the boys to be allowed out in the evening. This seclusion was an important feature of the establishment, for even limited freedom, said Brenton, 'would be the ruin of them . . . they must be totally separated from their former haunts'. In this way he was able to devote the full resources of his method to the rehabilitation of the boys without interference. The object of the

---

[25] J. Brenton, *Memoir, op. cit.,* p. 76.

[26] E. P. Brenton, *The Bible and Spade* (London, 1837), pp. 17, 40.

[27] E. P. Brenton, *Observations*, p. xv.

[28] The following account is based upon the evidence of Brenton himself to the Select Committee on the State of Education, P.P. (1834), ix, pp. 201–7 (hereafter *Select Committee*) ; the evidence of William Wright to the same Committee, ibid., pp. 208–11 ; and a small book by Charles Forss, Second Master at Brenton Asylum, *Practical Remarks upon the Education of the Working Classes* (London, 1835).

institution was to give the boys 'a strictly moral, religious and indus-trious education and training'.

The chief features of the Asylum were the combination of intellectual and manual work, the classification and ranking of the pupils, and the strict division of time during the whole of the day. The daily timetable was as follows :

5.45 a.m.	rise, at the blowing of a whistle.
6.15 a.m.	whistle for assembly : register called, inspection by monitors.
6.45–8 a.m.	lessons.
8 a.m.	inspection.
8.15 a.m.	breakfast — file in, no talking.
8.45 a.m.	leave breakfast room.
9. a.m.	assemble with spades and pick axes for work in fields.
12 noon	end of work in fields.
2 p.m.	more work in fields.
5 p.m.	end of work in fields.
6.30–8 p.m.	lessons ; address by master.
8.30 p.m.	retire to hammocks.[29]

The boys thus had six hours of manual work a day and two and three-quarter hours of intellectual instruction. The manual work was divided into domestic duties such as washing and mending their own clothes, maintenance work on the premises, the cooking of the food, and work on the land. Each boy had one-tenth of an acre of land on which he grew crops such as flax, potatoes, and turnips ; in 1834 the produce of the land was valued at £77.[30] The school curriculum included, in addition to the three R's, geography, geometry, algebra, and astronomy, together with religious instruction and singing. Brenton claimed that after six months of this regime boys were enabled to read and write and enjoy books like *Robinson Crusoe*.[31] According to William Wright, the master of the school, the boys learned more rapidly when their day was divided between industry and mental work than they did when fully engaged on the school curriculum. He found that the combination of manual and intellectual labour gave them greater powers of attention and greater vigour of body and mind. Wright also pointed out that this process was aided by a positive

[29] Forss, pp. 16–19.   [30] Ibid., pp. 37–38.
[31] E. P. Brenton, *Select Committee*, p. 207.

attitude on the part of the master ; the boys learned faster when familiar explanations of difficult points were given and when reasons for learning were made clear and the lessons were entertaining, and that smaller classes and constant and personal interest in the boys also helped a great deal. As soon as the confidence of a boy was gained, he believed, almost anything might be done with him.[32]

The treatment of the boys was facilitated by their classification into three classes, A, B, and C, based on an assessment of their moral character. Class A, the first in order of merit, was divided into two divisions ; the boys in division I could read and write, had good moral habits, and could be placed in a situation or apprenticeship at the first available opportunity, while those in division II were morally on a level with the first group but lacked their acquirements. Class B included boys who were assessed as endeavouring to do right, but whose faults sprang from carelessness. Class C, the lowest group, consisted of boys who were both difficult to handle and who seemed determined to do wrong. The membership of a class determined the extent of a boy's privileges. From Class A were drawn the school office-holders, which included the cook and his mate, who supervised the meals, the porter, whose job was cleaning and waiting at meals, and the schoolboy, who cleaned and took care of the bedrooms, schoolrooms, and library. In addition Class A boys were allowed to hold some of the school keys, to accompany the master to town, to have access to the library, and to serve on the school jury. Class C boys, on the other hand, had no privileges whatever and sat at the bottom of the table at meals. A journal of conduct was kept for every half-day by the master ; if the conduct of a boy improved he rose in rank ; if it deteriorated he was demoted to a lower class. All boys on entering were placed at the bottom of Class B. In the schoolroom boys were graded according to achievement into sets in the various subjects.[33]

This system of classification and promotion took the place of corporal punishment as a disciplinary measure. It operated in an atmosphere of trust and kindness, and youths could be made to do almost anything by kind treatment, Forss pointed out, provided there was also justice and impartiality. Brenton summed it up :

Our system is mildness, constant inspection, constant labour or amusement, constant innocent occupation ; I may say we never

[32] Wright, ibid., pp. 209–10.   [33] Forss, pp. 20–22.

Hullah conducting his pupils at Exeter Hall

The presentation of a music stand to Hullah by members of the first workman's singing class

Lord Lovelace's Agricultural School at Ockham. The buildings were designed in the Swiss manner after the example of Fellenberg

The Agricultural School at Willingdon

punish, except with solitary confinement for a few hours or privation of animal food.[34]

Solitary confinement with bread and water was, indeed, the only punishment in the school; it never lasted more than a few hours and appears never to have been inflicted vindictively, but, as far as the masters were concerned, with a view to helping a boy to reflect on the impropriety of his conduct when undergoing the punishment.

Brenton was an enlightened pioneer of the rehabilitation of the submerged tenth of the child population, in an age when neglect was universal and brutality common. His greatest contribution was to demonstrate the value of labour in the educational process and the effect of a steady trust, but his work was also important in the history of reform institutions in particular. Later reformatory schools made farm labour an important aspect of the rehabilitation process.[35]

IV

Unlike the schools of industry we have examined, agricultural schools were pre-eminently the product of the early 1830s, and in most cases were a response to the situation created by the agricultural riots that swept the southern counties at the beginning of the decade. A number of middle-class commentators established that the areas of deepest unrest were those with the highest illiteracy. Frederic Hill, in his book *National Education*, cited evidence in support of the case [36] and Edwin Chadwick argued that the most dangerous rioters came from among the most ignorant and ill-educated of the labouring classes. A committee of the British and Foreign School Society, having inquired into the state of education in the disturbed districts, concluded that 'the ignorance of the peasantry' was 'a necessary link in the chain' of causes that led to 'the incendiary fires'.[37] Radicals such as Sir Thomas Wyse and J. H. Roebuck made similar points, and said that education could help to change this dangerous state of affairs.[38]

Thus a strong body of opinion developed in favour of civilizing the agricultural labourer by providing special schools in the country districts, making labour an important feature of the curriculum. The

[34] E. P. Brenton, *Select Committee*, p. 201.
[35] See below, pp. 217–18. [36] Hill, pp. 265 ff. [37] Ibid., p. 265.
[38] T. Wyse, *Education Reform* (London, 1836), p. 425; *Parl. Deb.*, 3rd ser., xx (30 July 1833), 143.

assumptions behind these schools had their beginnings in the eight-eenth-century philanthropic ethic associated with schools for the poor. To William Davis, the founder of the Gower's Walk Printing School, labour in general had three characteristics : it was conducive to health, it was favourable to virtue and inimical to vice, and above all it was a source of national wealth.[39] Agricultural labour, however, in the view of the philanthropists, had a special function :

> Agricultural occupations seem altogether unobjectionable ; and they are generally acknowledged to be admirably adapted, under the direction of a pious instructor, to be the means of leading the minds of the young to contemplate the wisdom and goodness of the Creator in all his works. . . .[40]

The moral–religious aspect of rural industry was considered most important. British and National Schools gave intellectual instruction only and this was not enough to meet the special needs of the country-side and to enable the agricultural labourer to get his moral bearings. The case was cogently argued by B. F. Duppa, secretary of the Central Society for Education. Duppa wanted for the rural districts an educa-tion that would create a harmony between the individual and his position in life.[41] He had first put this proposition forward in his book *The Education of the Peasantry in England* published in 1834, in which he argued the necessity for schools that would cultivate the child's intellect to some extent but add to literary instruction something more, 'to give a steadiness to its influence, and render it applicable to the actual position of the individual in society'.[42]

In his writings Duppa mentioned several schools, and accounts of others can be found in the pages of the *Labourer's Friend Magazine*, in the writings of philanthropists, and in reports of the Inspectors of the Privy Council. One of the most celebrated was Mrs. Gilbert's Self-Supporting School of Industry, founded in 1840 at Willingdon, Sussex. Twenty children from four to thirteen years spent three hours daily on the land and three hours in the classroom, learning the three R's and religion. The land was cultivated on the Belgian system,

---

[39] W. Davis, *Hints to Philanthropists* (London, 1821), pp. 1–2.
[40] J. Hull, *The Philanthropic Repertory* (London, 1835), p. 20.
[41] B. F. Duppa, 'Industrial Schools for the Peasantry', in Central Society of Education, *First Publication* (London, 1837), pp. 172–7.
[42] B. F. Duppa, *The Education of the Peasantry in England* (London, 1834), p. 2.

with stall-fed cattle and spade husbandry.[43]   An earlier institution, founded in 1832, was Smith's Allotments for Scholars at Southam, Warwickshire, the basic object of which was to keep the boys off the streets.   The institution was attached to a National School and the boys rented one-twelfth of an acre of land on which they grew flowers, vegetables, and herbs for their own use or for sale.   The education provided was minimal, consisting of little more than a lending library, and Smith's aim was to humanize the children by providing them with moderately skilled and interesting horticultural employment.[44]   Other institutions in which schooling alternated with work on the land were Lord Chichester's at Brighton, founded in 1832, the Rev. Pearson's school at Chelmsford, and the Agricultural School at East Dean, Jevington.[45]

Among the more famous and ambitious agricultural schools was one run by the Rev. W. L. Rham at Winkfield near Windsor, Lord Lovelace's school at Ockham in Surrey, James Cropper's school near Liverpool, and William Allen's school at Lindfield, Sussex.   Enough information exists about each of these schools to form a clear idea of their activity and purpose and to draw conclusions about the role of agriculture in education.   In some of these schools there were also some interesting experiments in educational methods.

The Reverend W. L. Rham opened his school in April 1835, the building consisting of a house for the master and mistress, two schoolrooms, a workshop, and auxiliary buildings.   The building was situated on a hill near the church, commanding a view of the richly wooded country of Windsor Forest.   The school, which stood in the centre of a two-acre field, cost £500 to build and Rham's main object was to make the school a happy and pleasant place for the children.   He had noticed that children in common day schools were weary by the end of the day, and this boredom they associated with every kind of instruction, an attitude that persisted after they had left school.   By dividing the school day between classroom and agricultural labour, Rham hoped to make the school a pleasant and attractive place.[46]

[43] [J. Nowell], *On Self-Supporting Schools of Industry and Mental Discipline* (Huddersfield, 1844), *passim* ;   *Minutes of the Committee of Council on Education, 1841–2*, P.P. (1842), xxxiii, p. 273.
[44] *Labourer's Friend Magazine*, no. lxxx, N.S. (Nov. 1837), pp. 164–5 ;   Duppa, *First Publication*, pp. 193–5.
[45] Duppa, *The Education of the Peasantry*, pp. 7–9 ;   *First Publication*, pp. 192–3 ; *Minutes of the Committee of Council, 1841–2*, p. 273.
[46] *Minutes of the Committee of Council, 1841–2*, p. 272 ;   *Labourer's Friend Magazine*, no. lxix, N.S. (Dec. 1836), p. 230.

The school day began at 8.30 in the morning and lasted until 5 p.m. for the girls and 6 p.m. for the boys. In winter the day ended at 3.30 p.m. for the girls and at 4 p.m. for the boys. One hour was allowed for dinner, and four hours of the day were employed in academic work. At first this consisted of reading, writing, and arithmetic, but Rham intended to introduce the theory of agriculture at a later date. Four hours of the day were also devoted to work in the fields, and here the children had various agricultural and horticultural processes explained to them, and the best boys had a small plot of their own to cultivate at their leisure ; Rham found that during the summer months there was always a considerable number of boys at work on their own plots at six o'clock in the morning. In the workshop they learned the making of baskets and nets. The garden produce, over and above what was used by the master and given away to the children, realized, in a typical year, over £20.[47]

The master was a retired sergeant of the Guards, not a little proud of having been at the battle of Waterloo, and under the direction of Rham he became an expert horticulturalist. He had a good relationship with the children, many of whom stayed at school from the age of seven till the age of thirteen. An Inspector noticed that the children were happy and of good appearance and Rham found that the children learned their lessons somewhat faster than those at other schools, despite the fact that only half their day was spent on mental work.[48]

The school at Ockham, founded by Lord Lovelace (a kinsman of Lady Byron), contained several unusual and interesting features. The school hours were from 9 a.m. until 11.30 a.m., and from 2 p.m. to 4 p.m. The rest of the day, until 5 p.m., with the exception of an hour for dinner, was spent in the garden or workshop. The boys were required to spend one hour a day working in the nursery or in the fields, under the direction of the teacher, and the remainder of the time they spent out of doors cultivating their own allotments or amusing themselves in any manner they chose (see illustration facing p. 209).[49]

Three and a half acres of land were set aside for agricultural work and two acres of this were devoted to a small experimental forest where curious specimens of forest trees were grown, in order to discover varieties that would best be suited to English conditions. The master

---

[47] *Labourer's Friend Magazine*, no. lxxvi, N.S. (July 1837), pp. 95–96.
[48] Ibid., no. lxix (Dec. 1836) ; no. lxxvi (July 1837).
[49] *Minutes of the Committee of Council, 1841–2*, p. 272.

had been trained in Scotland and had considerable skill in chemistry and other matters. The school was, for those days, well supplied with equipment and visual aids, for in addition to chemical apparatus and a printing-press on which the boys printed their own regulations, there was an organ, a pair of globes, a magic lantern, and around the walls some busts and a barometer. On the schoolroom ceiling there was a sketch of the solar system, and some of the tables in the room were marked out as chess-boards. The boys kept their own notebooks and they also made good use of the extensive school library.[50] The school was not only much more academically ambitious than Rham's, but seemed to allow the boys more freedom and initiative. It was, in fact, in its curriculum and appointment, far superior to the average British or National School of the period.

A school on more orthodox lines than Lord Lovelace's was set up by James Cropper at Fernhead near Liverpool.[51] Cropper, a Quaker, was born in 1773, and became a successful merchant shipper in Liverpool. He had first conceived of an agricultural school as early as 1807, but his work for the anti-slavery movement and his business commitments forced him to shelve the matter until the early 1830s. It is significant that he saw his early plan for a school as an expression of his religious views, but when he came to set up the school he also regarded the education of the poor as a means of keeping them happy and contented with their station in life and damping down their restlessness and desire for change, which he felt was 'the prevailing evil of the age'. In 1833 Cropper visited Germany and Switzerland in order to familiarize himself with systems of agricultural education in those countries, and was particularly impressed with the arrangements of the agricultural school at Cara near Geneva.

Cropper opened his school at Fernhead, between Liverpool and Warrington, on 1 August 1834. On the foundation stone was the inscription: 'From and after the 1 August, 1834, slavery in the British Dominions shall forever cease . . . on that day the foundation of this school was laid.' Attached to the school was six acres of land for cultivation by spade husbandry by the boys, with an additional dozen acres to be worked by agricultural labourers on a

[50] Ibid.
[51] K. Charlton, 'James Cropper (1773–1840) and Agricultural Improvement in the Early Nineteenth Century', *Transactions of the Historic Society of Lancashire and Cheshire*, vol. 112 (1960), pp. 65–78, on which this account is based.

profit-sharing basis, with the promise that their boys could attend the school.

After several initial difficulties concerning the finding of a suitably qualified master, and after the expulsion of a number of unruly boys, the school settled down. The boys were paid for their work in the fields, and two-thirds of what was earned went towards the running of the school, the remaining third being divided among the boys according to the work done. Profits, which in 1838 amounted to the sum of £60, were shared between master and boys in proportion of one to two. In the following year Cropper introduced the principle of the boys renting land and taking the subsequent profit (which amounted to about £3 a year each), in order to give them an interest in the prosperity of their particular plot. Work in the fields occupied two-thirds of the children's day and the remaining third was spent in the schoolroom acquiring knowledge of the three R's, geography, geometry, grammar, and natural history, together with religious instruction. Cropper found, as Rham and others had done, that 'their requirements would bear comparison with most other boys whose whole time has been employed in the common routine of education in either National or British schools'. Thus, although Cropper's school was not the most imaginative of the agricultural schools of the period, it had once again demonstrated that the mixing of agricultural labour and mental activity appeared to benefit the quality of education offered.

The most celebrated agricultural school, apart from Lady Byron's at Ealing, was William Allen's at Lindfield near Haywards Heath in Sussex.[52] Allen, in fact, founded two schools there, a day school for local children in 1825 and a boarding-school for the children of Quakers ten years later. The Lindfield Day School was a palpable missionary effort. The site had been deliberately chosen by Allen after a search throughout the country to find a district in which the peasantry were in the worst possible state of ignorance, and here Allen built 'commodious school rooms' for boys, girls, and infants, together with a reading-room and library. The early curriculum was rather narrow and consisted of the three R's, needlework for the girls, and 'other branches of useful knowledge', and the teaching method was based 'upon the liberal principles of the British and Foreign School Societies'.

Despite his good intentions, Allen met with opposition from all

---

[52] This account is based upon *Lindfield Reporter*, no. 2 (Feb. 1835), p. 18 ; ibid., no. 13 (Jan. 1836), pp. 201–2 ; Hill, pp. 46–50.

classes. Most of the wealthy inhabitants of the neighbourhood tried to thwart him, and the peasantry, suspicious of his motives, believed that the building was being set up for the express purpose of kidnapping their children ; a high palisade was to be built around the school, the children to be collected inside, the gates closed, and the entire number shipped off to some distant land. It was not surprising that Allen had difficulty in getting scholars to attend when the building was finished. Once the school got under way, however, local prejudices broke down and the attendance began to increase.

The school was visited in July 1831 by that indefatigable investigator, Frederic Hill, who found that there were no less than three hundred children on the books, that is every child whose parents lived within a distance of three miles. As in many rural schools, however, difficulties in communications and the call made on children for work on the land cut the regular attendance down to about half that number. The school day was divided into five hours of ordinary school work and three of manual labour. The former was run on routine lines, but the manual work offered a great deal of interest and diversity. Some of the children were employed as shoemakers, others as tailors, and there was opportunity for basket-making, weaving, printing, gardening, and farming. Hill found that the children liked the manual classes much better than the ordinary school work, a conclusion that he did not find surprising because of the lack of originality in the classroom teaching.

When the children first arrived at school they were set to straw-plaiting, which was the first craft to be taught. The crafts were graded in order of complexity, with printing as the highest ; the children were encouraged to take up more than one and they often left school expert in three or four. Those who worked on the farm had one-eighth of an acre each to look after and had to do their own digging, sowing, manuring, and reaping, producing oats, turnips, mangel-wurzels, potatoes, and cabbages. Each child was allowed half the produce of his plot for himself, the other half being paid for the use of the land, farming implements, and the like. Hill believed that a child who concentrated on farming at the school would have learned much that would have been of use to him for any size of farm ; he would also have acquired 'habits of industry, intelligent observation, and forethought'.

The boarding-school for Quaker children that Allen built in 1835 was designed to take the children of more affluent parents than the local peasantry. The fees were £10 a year and the number of boys was restricted to twelve, each of whom was given a small apartment containing a bed, chair, and table, and allotted a small garden of twenty-six rods, two of which could be cultivated in any way a boy pleased, providing the remainder was divided between potatoes and corn. The value of the produce of the latter was given to the boys as pocket-money, after expenses for seed and manure had been deducted. The average yearly amount received by the boys was 17s., for which they laboured five hours a day on the land and also carried out domestic tasks, such as bed-making, pot-cleaning, and assistance with the cooking. A boy's time was roughly equally divided between school work, meals and recreation, and work on the land, with a period of religious education in addition each day. The staff consisted of a principal super-intendent who was the schoolmaster in charge of the academic side, and a superintendent for labour, who always accompanied the boys to work and whose wife superintended the cooking and household con-cerns. There was also an agricultural labourer who assisted the boys in the fields.

The academic side of the school provided not only subjects in instruction — the three R's, English grammar, geography, the use of globes, and land-measuring — but also opportunities for self-analysis by the boys. Each boy kept a diary in which he entered the time spent on each of the following subjects, which were arranged in vertical columns :

> Private religious reading
> Arithmetic
> English grammar
> Natural history
> Natural philosophy
> Geography.

A conduct book was also kept, and at the end of every month there was a moral accounting. A summary of the boys' diaries was made and the progress of each boy noted, reference being made to entries, if any, opposite his name in the conduct book.

V

Agricultural schools were pre-eminently the product of the 1830s. They came into being as part of an attempt to civilize the agricultural labourer, who was, in the eyes of the farmers and landowners, always ready to rise in revolt or at least to seek some form of improvement. In some cases the schools were inspired by the example of Fellenberg's Poor School, but in most cases they were a well-intentioned attempt by a clergyman or a philanthropist to improve the conditions and calm the turbulence of the agricultural labourer by attending to the moral health and practical skill in country pursuits of his children.

Essentially the schools were seeking to preserve the existing social structure, and proud of the fact that they disproved the widely held belief that, to quote a contemporary writer, 'the acquisition of the mechanical knowledge of reading, writing, and arithmetic, tends to make those who acquire it [reach] above their station in life . . . choosing rather to live by their wits than by their hands'.[53] Technically the schools made no advance on previous agricultural methods, relying mainly on spade husbandry, and showing little concern for the introduction of machinery or the application of science to the land. It was not until the end of the 1830s that improved ploughing and drainage and the introduction of fertilizers occurred on any large scale. Schools in which agriculture was part of the curriculum began then to give way to institutions in which agricultural science was taught.[54]

In almost all the schools we have described, whether industrial, agricultural, or reformatory, the inclusion of manual labour in the curriculum not only helped children to respond more positively to school life, but also improved their performance in the schoolroom so that it was often better than that of children whose entire school life was devoted to the classroom subjects. The founders of the schools did not realize sufficiently the significance of this discovery. With the exception of Kay-Shuttleworth and some Quakers, the point was not taken by educationalists. The idea of the value of practical work had to wait until the 1890s and until this century before the significance that Rousseau saw could be worked out. In the first half of the nineteenth century agricultural labour established itself almost entirely in reformatory schools, where it was used as an aid to moral

[53] Hull, p. 19.

[54] C. Daubeny, M.D., F.R.S., 'On the Public Institutions for the Advancement of Agricultural Science', *Journal of the Royal Agricultural Society*, vol. iii (1842), pp. 364–386 ; *Chambers's Edinburgh Journal*, no. 271, 8 Apr. 1837, p. 84.

discipline, and the most famous school of this kind was the Philanthropic Farm School at Redhill in Surrey.[55]

The failure to draw the full lessons from the agricultural schools was partly due to the fact that they had originated in a social rather than in an educational context, and partly because few were interested in the intellectual education of the poor. Short-range aims of vocational training and containment in the class structure dominated the approach of nearly all the philanthropists, and even Duppa's writings were more concerned with social than educational theory. Except for garden-keeping and similar crafts, which were still to be found in some twenty or so rural schools in the 1840s,[56] manual labour by the middle of the nineteenth century had failed to establish itself in the elementary or secondary curriculum. The Revised Code of 1862 made any further experiment unlikely, at least for a number of years. Voluntary schools and later the Board Schools had to rediscover and reintroduce manual work into the curriculum as craft subjects under later Codes.

Perhaps the most that can be said on the theme of labour in schools in the nineteenth century is that in the first half a few pioneers tried to work out a relevant vocational training, whether in town or in the country. It arose out of and was designed to meet the needs of those who worked with their hands, whether in trades, crafts, or agriculture, and stayed within the bounds of the social structure. The implications of practical work, its relationship with traditional crafts, with developing technology, with the whole school curriculum, and with a nation's culture, were not seen then, except in flashes by such men as Owen and much later by Ruskin and Morris. In schools they were explored again by Cecil Reddie at Abbotsholme in the 1890s and by many others since then. These implications are still being discovered and considered today.

[55] H. Barnard, *Reformatory Education* (Hartford, Conn., 1857), pp. 296–7, 314 ; J. Fletcher, *The Farm School System of the Continent and Its Applicability to the Preventive and Reformatory Education of Pauper and Criminal Children in England and Wales* (London, 1852), pp. 39–41.

[56] *Extracts from the Reports of Her Majesty's Inspectors of Schools* (London, 1852), pp. 104–17.

13. Rewards and Punishments, 1780–1850

I

EDWARD HOLMES, in his philippic against the British educational system *What Is and What Might Be*, published in 1911, ascribed the practice of disciplining children by means of punishment or the threat of punishment to the fundamental theological belief that the nature of man and his impulses was wholly evil. 'The God of popular theology', he wrote, 'has been engaged for more than thirty centuries in educating his child, man. His system of education has been based on complete distrust of Man's nature. . . .'[1] If the position has somewhat improved during the course of the twentieth century, this has been due not only to the decline of this kind of retributive religious faith and the developed knowledge of child psychology, but also to the increase in the power and the widening of the horizons of underprivileged sections of society, the growth of a belief in social equality, and a more critical attitude to traditional authorities.[2]

In the period we are considering in this chapter — the later eighteenth century and the first half of the nineteenth — two of the suggested preconditions for the acceptance of corporal punishment as normal were in operation : a theological conception of the fallen nature of man and the depressed condition of the masses. There is abundant evidence that flogging and brutality were rife in nearly all types of school from the public school to the common day school. The tradition of Dr. Johnson's Mr. Hunter, who 'beat a boy equally for not knowing a thing, as for neglecting to know it',[3] continued throughout the eighteenth century and well into the nineteenth. Samuel Wilderspin remembered that his schooling, in the 1790s, was chiefly concerned with caning and how the master and mistress became 'objects of terror'.[4] George Combe and Samuel Morley, also to appear later in these pages, recorded similar experiences. Combe at the turn of the century was caned by a master who never stopped

[1] E. Holmes, *What is and What Might Be* (London, 1911), p. 42.

[2] K. G. Collier, 'Changing Attitudes to Authority and their Implications for the Educator', *Researches and Studies*, University of Leeds Institute of Education, no. 15 (Jan. 1957), pp. 78–89.

[3] James Boswell, *The Life of Samuel Johnson, LL.D.* (London, 2 vols., 1791), i, p. 13.   [4] S. Wilderspin, *The Infant System* (London, 8th ed., 1852), p. 4.

until 'he was fairly out of breath and could beat no more'.[5]   Morley
some thirty years later was fastened to five other boys, their heads
placed under the master's desk, and all simultaneously flogged with a
postilion whip.[6]   The attitude of the zealously religious parent of the
early nineteenth century may be gauged from Mrs. Sherwood's story
The History of the Fairchild Family, which went through five editions
between 1818 and 1822.   The youngest child, a boy of six, was flogged
with a horsewhip, put on bread and water, and sent to Coventry for
refusing to learn Latin.   On another occasion the three children, after
a childish quarrel, were punished by being forced to look upon the
corpse of a murderer, who had killed his brother in a quarrel, hanging
in chains from a gibbet.[7]   In 1838 Kay-Shuttleworth declared that education in day schools was generally felt to be best promoted by coercion
and that the feeling among all classes in England was that 'the best
way to make boys learn was to whip them well'.[8]

Flogging was justified on the grounds that (as Arnold maintained)
boys were naturally inferior to adults, or that children differed from
grown-ups in that they lacked a sense of conscience and could only
be affected and therefore controlled by means of the infliction of pain ;
it was easier to inhibit a child by fear of the consequences of an act
than to appeal to his conscience.   The main reason for regarding the
period under consideration as the golden age of flogging, a mid-
Victorian educationalist argued, was the influence of the Napoleonic
Wars ; the war atmosphere and the prevalence of flogging in the Army
and Navy encouraged similar brutalities in the schools.[9]   It is in and
around this 'classical period' of corporal punishment in education,
however, that we find the first attempts to provide a substitute.   The
reaction against flogging gave rise to several experiments in school
organization based upon humane and rational forms of discipline.

Opposition to corporal punishment among educationalists might
spring from a variety of reasons : a view of child nature that saw the
child as essentially good and in no need of coercion, a generalized

[5] C. Gibbon, *Life of George Combe* (London, 2 vols., 1878), i, p. 18.
[6] H. S. Solly, *Life of Henry Morley, LL.D.* (London, 1898), p. 17.
[7] Mrs. Sherwood, *The History of the Fairchild Family* (London, 3 pts., 1818–47), i, pp. 55–60, 265 ff.
[8] *Report from the Select Committee on the Education of the Poorer Classes*, P.P. (1838), vii, pp. 3, 4.
[9] Rev. A. F. Thomson, *The English Schoolroom, or Thoughts on Private Tuition, Practical and Suggestive* (London, 1865), pp. 176–7.

opposition to force and violence on social or religious grounds, a belief that teaching with the aid of punishment was educationally inefficient and harmful, or a mixture of all three.

The question was, what to be put in its place ? The common alternative was to replace corporal punishment and coercion by schemes that made the occupation of a high position in the eyes of the school dependent on good behaviour. Direct punishment of all kinds was reduced to a minimum and often consisted of solitary confinement or similar deprivation of liberty. Complicated systems of merit and rank, the award of medals, tokens, and tickets, the inscription of names in books of honour were worked out. Sometimes the children were made directly responsible for judging each other by means of school juries. Some of these experiments, in particular that in use at Hazelwood School, were of a complexity that almost defies description.

The earliest of these schemes predate the Napoleonic War period and arose from attempts to cope with the wild-running children of the towns and cities of the early Industrial Revolution. The effects of the growth of industry, the disruption of the old pastoral relationships, and the increase in urban population were leading to vagrancy and crime and causing philanthropists to think hard about new measures and methods to meet the case.

One of the earliest philanthropists to devise new methods of discipline was Robert Raikes, known to history as the founder of Sunday schools. Raikes began his public career as a prison reformer attempting to alleviate the lot of prisoners, particularly debtors, in the Gloucester jails by the distribution of books and other articles. Here he learned the connections between ignorance and crime, and the futility of punishing the effect without removing the cause.[10] Raikes reflected that the ignorance and depravity of the inmates of the prisons which he knew so well were largely due to the harsh treatment and lack of education during their childhood. If the children could be caught early enough, he argued, removed from their environment even temporarily, and harsh treatment replaced by tangible rewards for good conduct, delinquency could be very much reduced.[11]

Soon after he had opened his first Sunday school in 1780 jointly with the Rev. Thomas Stock, Raikes began to reward his pupils and to 'excite emulation' in them by the occasional distribution of prizes

---

[10] A. Gregory, *Robert Raikes : Journalist and Philanthropist* (London, 1877), pp. 27–35.   [11] Ibid., pp. 48, 56.

such as books, combs, shoes, or other articles of apparel to the most diligent.[12]   It was not until the later 1780s, however, that he first introduced a ticket system of awards.   An account of this was written by an old pupil, Mrs. Summerill, in 1880.   She had been one of Raikes's later pupils and had attended his funeral (which took place in 1811) while still at Sunday school.   According to her account, the Bible and the catechism formed the substance of the education, and tickets were given for proficiency.   When a certain number of tickets had been collected they could be exchanged for a prayer-book.[13]   A similar system was in operation in 1810 at College Lane Sunday School, Northampton, where between 50 and 150 tickets were distributed every Sunday.   'Value of the tickets, four to one penny', we are laconically told.[14]   Raikes had inaugurated a system of material rewards because he was forced to recognize the impossibility of re-habilitating children who were used to kicks and blows by inflicting more of the same punishment in school.

A similar line of reasoning was used by the Philanthropic Society, a body formed in 1788 to rescue the children of the vagrant and criminal poor.   These children, the Society argued, had entered the school of vice at an early age and their condition was the consequence of a state of society not in their power to change.   Even if taught the three R's and a handicraft, they would retain the vices of their infancy unless powerful correctives were brought to bear, for punishment had little or no effect on them.   Their character could only be improved by 'strong, vigorous and systematic education in morals'.[15]   The feature of this education would be a system of rewards for excellence based on the principle of emulation.

The Society provided schools of industry for the rehabilitation of its delinquent charges and, in its own frank words, attempted 'to unite the spirit of charity with the principles of trade, and to erect a temple to philanthropy on the foundation of virtuous industry'.[16] The children lived in several houses, called Schools of Morals, at Cambridge Heath, on the Hackney Road, under the general supervision of a Chaplain Superintendent.   In each house, besides the children, a

---

[12] Gregory, p. 123.

[13] *Gloucester Journal*, 3 July 1880, cited in P. M. Eastman (ed.), *Robert Raikes and Northamptonshire Sunday Schools* (London, 1880), pp. 14–15.

[14] Eastman, p. 22.

[15] *The Second Report and Address of the Philanthropic Society* (London, 1789), p. 47.

[16] *First Report of the Philanthropic Society* (London, n.d. but 1789), p. 23.

skilled tradesman such as a carpenter, a bricklayer, a shoemaker, or a tailor lived on the premises and taught the children his trade.[17] The whole organization foreshadowed so many of the basic principles of all subsequent systems of emulation that it is worth while looking at it in some detail.

The master or mistress of each house kept a Day Book, into which was entered a daily report on the children's conduct.[18] It was found that an entry of a fault into the book had a salutary effect on the children, particularly those who would have despised or disregarded a flogging. Entries from the Day Books of the several houses were collected into a common book and a debit and credit account of each pupil's faults and virtues made up. Every Sunday evening between 6 p.m. and 8 p.m. an officer called the Regulator presided at a muster of all the children. He explained to the children the nature of their misdemeanours and good conduct in relation to the happiness and misery of the community. Then he distributed the rewards and punishments. Those who had no faults recorded against them for the previous week were given a ticket of good behaviour. The children were taught to consider these tickers as 'treasure', and were diligent in accumulating them. Those guilty of slight faults were punished by the deprivation of one or more tickets at the weekly muster. This system of ticket distribution was professedly copied from that of Robert Raikes. Faults of a more serious kind, or frequent repetitions of slighter faults, were punished by the offenders having to wear 'badges of disgrace', which were worn until a certain period of good behaviour purchased their removal. Chastisements were rare, but when they did occur the punishment took place solemnly in public.

In addition to this weekly moral stock-taking, there was an annual 'day of account and retribution'. The weekly registers were made up and 'badges of honour' distributed for consistent merit; these were to be worn 'as a constant incitement to others to attain a similar recompense'. Unspecified penalties for 'accumulated crimes' were also administered.

In addition to the periodical distribution of awards, the pupils had a daily reminder of the vices and virtues that they should cultivate or disdain. The virtues, painted in golden letters on a white ground,

---

[17] *An Address to the Public from the Philanthropic Society* (London, 1790), pp. 7, 15.
[18] The following account is taken from the first and second *Reports of the Philanthropic Society*.

were hung on the classroom wall, flanked by the vices, painted in red
letters on black :

Industry	Idleness
Speaking truth	Lying
Honesty	Dishonesty
Piety	Impiety
Obedience	Disobedience
Good Temper	Ill Temper
Kindness	Cruelty
Decent Language	Immoral Language
Gratitude	Ingratitude
Contentment	Discontent.[19]

The choice and order of the virtues are sufficient indication of the
kind of behaviour expected from the pupils.

The Philanthropic Society's system of tangible reward was based
on the theory that it was 'natural' for virtue to be rewarded :

Reward, agreeably to the order of nature, is the consequence of
merit, and the proper motive by which virtue ought to be recommended and enforced.[20]

Children, the Society argued, needed more tangible reward than an
aura of virtue when a meritorious act was performed ; the infant mind
needed 'sensible evidences' of esteem. Therefore, badges of distinction of rank were to be preferred to money or anything that was soon
consumed, because the effect was more lasting. Thus were three
principles established : virtuous actions should be rewarded ; the
reward should be tangible ; the reward should be lasting. These
became the standard justifications for systems of material reward. A
fourth was often added : rewards and penalties should be cumulative,
to enable a profit-and-loss account of vice and virtue to be built up.

The widely popular Sunday school movement and the well-reported
activities of the Philanthropic Society did more than establish the
norms of the ticket and rank systems of discipline. They also popularized it and demonstrated its feasibility. It received its most widespread dissemination, however, during the early part of the nineteenth
century, when, with variations of detail and emphasis, it was taken up
by two educationalists who were in all other respects anything but

[19] *Second Report*, p. 41.   [20] Ibid., p. 32.

Hazelwood coinage

Joseph Lancaster's silver monitors' badges

Reformed delinquents showing specimens of printing at the Philanthropic Society's School of Industry. This illustration probably dates from the 1840's

Ronge's Kindergarten. Children playing a game called 'The Pigeon House'

progressive in the terms of reference of this study — Andrew Bell and Joseph Lancaster.

II

The innovations of the Philanthropic Society began one year before Dr. Andrew Bell took charge of his famous asylum at Madras in southern India. Bell and Lancaster are known to history as the popularizers of the monitorial system, the scheme whereby children were instructed by other children called monitors. Though Bell and Lancaster's methods differed in detail, both had the basic idea of making children teach other children the three R's. This was indisputably an innovation and certainly an ingenious method of making up for the lack of teachers, but it left a legacy of rote-learning and narrowness of curriculum, and a belief that the education of the masses ought to be as cheap as possible dogged English elementary education throughout the century.

Nevertheless, there were some aspects of Bell and Lancaster's systems, little regarded by educational historians, that tended to modify some of the bleakness of the actual monitorial method, and which were taken up and improved by other innovators, notably the Hill brothers of Hazelwood School. Dr. Andrew Bell aimed at giving a minimum amount of education to the greatest possible number of poor children in the most effective manner in the shortest possible time. He was not interested in a varied curriculum, the wide diffusion of general knowledge, or any improvement in method beyond his own. He condemned 'Utopian schemes, for the universal diffusion of general knowledge', which would 'confound that distinction of ranks and classes of society, on which the general welfare hinges . . .'.[21] On the other hand, he was equally against the prevailing methods of corporal punishment used in the schools, which, in the context of the period, showed an enlightenment rare among his contemporaries.

Bell's curious mixture of narrowness, benevolence, and self-satisfaction can be grasped from his own description of his system :

The system, with its concatenation of Occasional Usher and Sub-Usher, its Teachers and Assistants, Tutors and Pupils, Registers of Daily Tasks, Black-book, and Jury of Peers — being a series of

---

[21] A. Bell, *An Analysis of the Experiment in Education, Made at Egmore, near Madras* (London, 1807), p. 90.

consecutive regulations, linked together in the closest union, and forming a digested theory, composed of laws derived from observation, confirmed by experience, and founded on acknowledged principles of humanity, I regard as completed in all its parts, and requiring no addition.[22]

The key to Bell's disciplinary scheme was not that it was one for the detection, conviction, and correction of the offender (although the machinery for this existed), but that the unified nature of his plan and close interconnection of teachers, monitors, and pupils established 'habits of industry, morality and religion, tending to form good scholars, good men and good Christians'.[23]

Bell's maxim was that praise, encouragement, and favour should be tried before disapproval, shame, and disgrace. The authority of the master, however, was not abrogated and was to be maintained in one form or another.

The machinery for maintaining authority was very similar to that of the Philanthropic Society. It consisted of a register of the daily tasks performed and of the award of tickets for good work, with a weekly distribution of prizes for those with the greatest number of tickets. A register of daily offences, or Black Book, was also kept and the misdemeanours recorded here were tried at weekly sittings of a jury of twelve or more boys especially selected for the purpose.[24] This could decide on the form of punishment that the offence merited — either confinement in school, or in very extreme cases, solitary confinement in the 'black hole'.

Bell had introduced the register of offences and a rudimentary form of the jury system in the Madras Asylum in 1790.[25] The Asylum was a charity school for the orphan children of British soldiers, many of them coloured. Bell, when in 1789 he took charge of this as chaplain to the forces, was faced with a problem similar to that of Raikes and the Philanthropic Society, for the boys had developed corrupt practices encouraged by their mothers, and in school were 'stubborn, perverse and obstinate ; much given to lying, and addicted to trick and duplicity'.[26] His introduction of new methods of correction was

---

[22] Bell, *An Analysis*, pp. 44–45.   [23] Ibid., pp. 13–14.   [24] Ibid., p. 2.
[25] A. Bell, *An Experiment in Education, Made at the Male Asylum of Madras* (London, 1797), p. 27.
[26] A. Bell, *An Experiment in Education, Made at the Male Asylum at Egmore, near Madras* (London, 1805), p. 24.

a recognition of the futility of corporal punishment in these circumstance.

There is a description of the jury at work in the Central School of the National Society at Westminster by Lord Colchester, who on a visit to the school in 1812 saw the Black Book opened and a record of a boy having destroyed another boy's hat read out:

> A jury of best boys out of each class was immediately empanelled, a witness was called, who proved that he saw the thing done; the culprit denied it, but the jury, one after another, all said they believed the charge to be true. The culprit could not bring any witness to disprove the fact, nor any one good boy to give him a character. The jury were then required seriatim to say what his punishment should be, — one said 'to be expelled', another 'to be well beaten'; but Dr. Bell told him that 'there were no rods in that school, he did not lay out his money in that way; that the punishments were confinement in school, or in the black hole, or to be expelled'. The vote was then given for the black hole; others said it should be for one hour, for two hours, a night, two days, a week, etc. The majority being for one night in the black hole he was sentenced accordingly; but his behaviour then grew so outrageous that he was by common cry expelled and turned out of the school.[27]

Bell was careful to leave the decision as far as possible in the boys' hands, and he only intervened when he thought that the formality of the trial and the sentence were insufficient as a deterrent.[28] With this one exception the boys themselves operated the disciplinary side of the school. Bell believed that by involving pupils in tasks and decisions that gave them practical experience of order and government, he fostered in them the qualities of punctuality, diligence, impartiality, justice, and concern for the welfare of others.[29] A similar line of reasoning was to be used by the Hill brothers at Hazelwood School.

Lancaster's system, though in principle similar to that of Bell, involved the use of one monitor in charge of a group of ten or more pupils, whereas Bell had each boy in the top half of a class teach his opposite number in the lower half. Lancaster's theory of reward and punishment rested on a very different basis from that of Bell. Whereas

---

[27] Charles, Lord Colchester (ed.), *The Diary and Correspondence of Charles Abbot, Lord Colchester* (London, 3 vols., 1861), ii, pp. 393–4. The visit was made on 27 June 1812.   [28] Bell, *An Experiment* (1797), p. 27.
[29] Bell, *An Analysis*, pp. 14–15.

Bell saw his disciplinary and reward schemes as the means of stimulating positive values in the school community, Lancaster had a curious notion that rewards were a measure of a pupil's elevation to the ranks of the elect, or nobility as he termed it. He believed that even one or two boys of 'superior merit' could influence the whole school by their example and therefore deserved to be rewarded by prizes of silver medals, pens, or valuable books. In accounts of his expenditure are found items such as 'Five thousand toys — £16. 16. 0.'; 'Twenty Five French Half-Crowns, engraved "A Reward for Merit", £4. 17. 6.'; 'Eight silver pens, 3s. each — £1. 4. 0d'.[30] He established an Order of Merit, whose members were distinguished by a silver medal suspended from their necks by a plated chain, and the condition of admittance to this order was a proficiency in studies, consistent help to others, or endeavours to check vice. Lancaster looked upon membership of this order as evidence of a 'natural' nobility, a beneficial distinction that existed in all groups and societies. At the same time he saw the hope of reward as the motive force of society, and one that animated all members of it. Thus emulation, which produced a top layer of nobility, was also a stimulus for those of average ability.[31]

Lancaster had numerous schemes of rewards, with special application to various subjects. At the end of a reading lesson, for instance, the top boy received a leather ticket inscribed 'Merit in Reading', plus a picture pasted on pasteboard suspended upon his breast; he could exchange the picture for another, which became his own. Tickets numbered 1 to 5 for good performance in writing could be exchanged for money on the following scale:

> No. 1, 3 times, receives $\frac{1}{4}d$.
> No. 2, 6 times, receives 1d.
> No. 3, 8 times, receives 2d.
> No. 4, 9 times, receives 3d.
> No. 5, 12 times, receives 6d.

In addition there were badges for proficiency in arithmetic labelled 'Prize Book', 'Prize Cup and Ball', 'Prize Kite', etc. If a boy retained the ticket three or four successive times, he obtained the prize lettered on the ticket. If a monitor won a ticket lettered 'Commendable Monitor' six times, he could choose any prize he liked.[32]

[30] J. Lancaster, *Improvements in Education, as it Respects the Industrious Classes of the Community* (London, 3rd ed., 1805), pp. 13–16 *passim*.
[31] Ibid., pp. 93–96.   [32] Ibid., pp. 91–97.

Unlike Bell, Lancaster believed in the salutary effect of public disgrace or shaming as an alternative to corporal punishment, an idea he doubtless derived from his association with the Quakers, who practised it widely in their schools although without the severity that Lancaster used.[33] Idling and talking were incompatible with lessons, claimed Lancaster, and therefore some punishment was necessary. If a monitor saw a boy misbehaving, the latter was handed a card on which was printed 'I have seen this boy talking', or 'I have seen this boy idle'. The card then had to be presented to the head of the school, from whom he received an admonishment. But if admonition failed and the boy repeated the offence, then he was liable for a series of penalties almost diabolical in their ingenuity and discomfort. These punishments included tying a log of wood weighing up to 6 lb. round the defaulter's neck or shackling a boy's legs with wooden shackles up to a foot long, and forcing him to walk around the room till tired out. Sometimes up to six boys would be yoked together and paraded round the school, walking backwards. Other children might publicly chastise the boy, decorating him in a ludicrous fashion, and parading him round the school, crying out his fault. If a boy came to school with dirty hands and face, a girl was appointed to wash his face in sight of the whole school. But these punishments were relatively mild compared to some that Lancaster had up his sleeve. A bad offender would be put in a sack or a basket and suspended from the roof of the school. 'This punishment', Lancaster remarked, 'is one of the most terrible that can be inflicted on boys of sense and abilities.'[34]

Lancaster considered that the most effective punishment of all was confinement after school hours. As he pointed out, it was attended by one unpleasant circumstance — it needed the presence of the master also. 'This inconvenience may be avoided', he advised, 'by tying them to the desks in such a manner that they cannot untie themselves.' Alternatively, offenders could be tied up in a blanket and left to sleep at night on the schoolroom floor.[35]

Whether or not these public chastisements did more harm to a child's mind than a rod would have done to his body cannot be assessed. Certainly, they raised in a very sharp form the question of what kind of punishment should be substituted for the rod. Lancaster hardly made a good case for public contempt as a substitute. The forfeiture

[33] W. A. C. Stewart, *Quakers and Education* (London, 1953), p. 208.
[34] Lancaster, pp. 100–3.   [35] Ibid., pp. 103–114.

of reward, which was no part of his system, still seemed a feasible
method if one accepted as he did the principles of systems of emulation.
Coleridge, friend of Southey, the biographer of Bell, raged against
the public disgrace practised in Lancaster's schools, calling it 'soul-
benumbing ignominy, this unholy and heart-hardening burlesque on
the last fearful infliction of outraged law'.[36]

It is possible that Lancaster's elaborate punishments were instituted
as much for their publicity value as for their disciplinary effect.[37] In
the end Lancaster himself abandoned them, and in his best-known
school at Borough Road a simple system of merit tickets, which could
be lost for bad behaviour, was put into force.[38] This system of giving
tickets or prizes for good conduct, the tickets being exchangeable for
books, penknives, or other rewards, remained in existence in British
Schools until the middle 1830s.[39] By this time, however, the award
schemes in both British and National Schools were breaking down, and
corporal punishment taking their place. As early as the middle 1820s
Robert Dale Owen had noticed that one of the teachers at Dr. Bell's
model school at Westminster had given a boy such a blow on the head
for a minor grammatical mistake that he had staggered and fallen to
the ground.[40] Frederic Hill, some ten years later, believed that there
were very few British or National Schools from which corporal
punishment was wholly excluded.[41]

III

The system of pupil self-government and rewards and punishments at
Hazelwood School, which we have briefly noticed in Chapter 6, was
undoubtedly the most elaborate and sophisticated development of its
kind in the nineteenth century. It is clear that it also owed a great
deal to previous developments, and was at the peak of a trend that
covered the whole era dealt with in this chapter. Its connection with
the jury, rank, and ticket schemes of Bell and Lancaster is close, and

---

[36] S. T. Coleridge, *Biographia Literaria* (London, 2 vols., 1817), ii, p. 60 n.

[37] D. Salmon (ed.), *The Practical Parts of Lancaster's 'Improvements' and Bell's
'Experiment'* (Cambridge, 1932), pp. 104–5.

[38] *Report from the Select Committee on the Education of the Lower Orders in the Metro-
polis*, P.P. (1816), iv, pp. 182–3.

[39] *Report from the Select Committee on the State of Education*, P.P. (1834), ix, p. 25.

[40] R. D. Owen, *Threading My Way* (London, 1874), p. 249.

[41] F. Hill, *National Education : Its Present State and Prospects* (London, 1836), p. 73.

the Hill brothers admitted themselves that 'we act in concurrence with them in many parts of our system'.[42]

There was, however, a half-way house between the arrangements of Bell and Lancaster already described, and the fully developed Hazel-wood scheme. The link was provided by the Barrington School, a superior Bell school in Bishop Auckland, Co. Durham. It was widely publicized by Sir Thomas Bernard, the philanthropist and moving spirit of the Society for Bettering the Condition of the Poor, in his book *The Barrington School* published in 1812. There is no direct evidence that the Hill brothers had read this book, but the similarities of their methods with those of Barrington are so close that Bernard's book can hardly be excluded from the many works on education that the Hills claimed to have read.

The Barrington School was founded in 1810 by Shute Barrington, Bishop of Durham, with moneys accruing from the Bishop's share of the turnover of the Weardale lead mines. Dr. Bell himself and Sir Thomas Bernard took a great interest in the school. In its size, organization, and equipment it was undoubtedly one of the best of the schools founded on the Bell system, and its disciplinary methods in its early years went beyond those already ascribed to Bell.[43]

The system was based upon the award of tickets for good academic work. Every day two tickets were given to the scholar who most distinguished himself that day in his class for conduct and proficiency in spelling and reading ; one ticket was given to the next most meritorious scholar in each class. In addition, two tickets were given every day to the pupil most improved in writing and one ticket each to the next two. These tickets were exchanged every Friday for money at the rate of six tickets for one penny.[44]

In conjunction with this, a register of individual proficiency was kept, which had some of the features of the Hazelwood rank system. Every evening after lessons the boys of each class were brought before the master and he marked a figure 1 opposite the name of the boy at the head of the class, and so on in order down the list. At the end of the week the boy with the smallest total was considered first in rank

[42] *Public Education : Plans for the Government and Liberal Instruction of Boys, in Large Numbers ; as Practised at Hazelwood School* (London, 2nd ed., 1825), p. 217.

[43] M. Richley, *History and Characteristics of Bishop Auckland* (Bishop Auckland, 1872), p. 124 ; J. L. Dobson, 'The Barrington School at Bishop Auckland', *Durham Research Review*, vol. i, no. 5 (Sept. 1954), pp. 34–46.

[44] Sir Thomas Bernard, *The Barrington School* (London, 1812), p. 184.

and was rewarded with six tickets (or whatever other reward was decided by the school). These tickets were worth one-twelfth of a
penny each, or half the value of the other tickets. Those who were
absent without leave at these musters were given the highest number
(e.g. eight out of a total of eight) ; those who were sick were given
the middle number (e.g. four out of eight).[45] Idle pupils were thus
prevented from obtaining high rank merely by intermittent intellectual
brilliance. An example of the weekly rank table for a class of eight
boys in 1809 is given below : [46]

Form of the Register for ascertaining individual Proficiency.
John Stokes, Teacher ; James Merry, Assistant

Oct. 2. 1809						Weekly Total	Rank	Tickets due
Third Class	Mon.	Tues.	Wed.	Thurs.	Fri.			
Adam, George	1	1	2	1	2	7	1	5
Bean, Philip	3	5	s4	2	1	15	2	4
Clark, John	5	7	6	4	3	25	5	1
Dunn, Thomas	7	6	7	6	s4	30	6	
Eyles, Peter	8	2	8	7	6	31	7	
Todd, John	4	3	3	3	5	18	3	3
Venn, William	6	a8	5	a8	7	34	8	
Wells, Henry	2	4	1	5	8	20	4	2

A register of daily tasks was also kept, applying to every pupil.
Offences were recorded in a Black Book, and a weekly trial of offenders
held, judged by a jury of boys. Charges were made, evidence given,
and speeches for the defence delivered, a process that Bernard considered to be Dr. Bell's contribution 'to the preservation of our free
constitution'.[47] A certain number of offices were filled by the boys,
similar to those instituted at Hazelwood. A monitor and a deputy-
monitor were appointed every day by a master to take charge of the
schoolroom during 'extra hours', keeping it open for those scholars
who wished to do voluntary study or those whose punishment by the
jury consisted of confinement there. In addition, the monitor had
duties of ringing the school bell at stated times and of keeping a roll
of absentees.[48]

[45] Bernard, pp. 58–60.

[46] Ibid., p. 190.   [47] Ibid., p. 163.   [48] Ibid., pp. 174–6.

When we turn to the Hazelwood system we see a basically similar scheme improved and extended to every aspect of school life.[49]   At Hazelwood very nearly the whole running of the school was placed in the hands of the boys.   Self-government was the principle of the discipline, as self-education was an important feature of the academic side.   All the traditional forms of corporal punishment were, of course, abandoned, including the shaming practised by the Quakers and by Joseph Lancaster, which was considered an affront to the dignity of the boys.

The government of the school was based on English constitutional practice and those liberties of the individual, stemming from 1688, which were specially prized in the Radical tradition.   The separation of the legislature and the judiciary was a prominent feature of the school.   The government of the school consisted of four main elements : the School Committee, the Jury Court, the office of Magistrate, and the Executive Officers.

The Committee was the sovereign, law-making body of the school and consisted of fifteen boys (out of a school population of some 120), chosen on the first Monday of every month, and those elected had usually shown excellence in every aspect of school work.   The Committee met in open session once a week in the large schoolroom.   It chose officers who included the Chairman and Secretary, the Judge and Magistrate, and the Prosecutor-General and the Defender-General. The Committee enacted all penal laws and dispensed privileges which consisted of exemption from such laws ; it fixed fines, appointed school officers, conferred rank on pupils, managed the school funds, including a benevolent fund for local, national, and international charities.   All decisions of the Committee had the force of law, subject to endorsement by the principal.   From 1817 to 1825, however, the latter never found it necessary to withhold assent to a single resolution.   The constitution of the school was codified in 1827 (in eleven chapters), and this was known as the *Laws of Hazelwood School.*

The Court of Justice, presided over by the Judge, consisted of certain officers and an elected Jury, which met when a defendant elected to stand trial.   The Jury consisted of six boys chosen by lot ; it met every Wednesday afternoon and functioned as a court for trying the more serious of the offences of the school, which included truancy, lying, disobedience, and dishonesty, and levied fines where the

---

[49] The following account is based on *Public Education*, pp. 8–66.

defendant was found guilty. Cases in dispute were sent to the Committee, which acted as a Court of Appeal, but this was a rare occurrence.

The Magistrate, who was in charge of 'a small but vigorous police', was charged with the detection of all offences committed in school and with a decision of all petty cases of dispute. The Executive Officers were in charge of the prefects and the silentiaries, who were responsible for seeing that silence was maintained.

In conjunction with this extensive system of institutions and officers went an extremely elaborate scheme of rewards and punishments. The Hill brothers, of course, believed that rewards and punishments, however necessary, were evil, and that it was desirable to reduce them both in weight and number. Arthur Hill pointed out that the objects generally aimed at by the use of punishment were 'promotion of industry, respect, order and morality'.[50] Those who disagreed with the use of punishment should, however, seek other means of bringing about these desirable objects and of making them permanent. The key to this was to offer to the pupils durable motives for attention to school work. Hill suggested that these might be 'love of employment, desire to please, sense of duty, desire of the benefits dependent on knowledge, force of example and emulation'.[51] The Hills believed that their system offered the boys in their school these motives.

The rewards in Hazelwood School consisted of the acquisition of rank and privileges, transferable and personal marks, prizes, and holidays. Punishments consisted of the loss of any or all of these.

The basis of the system was the distribution of coins known as transferable marks. These could be gained for excellence in class, for filling certain offices, and for various kinds of voluntary labour, which was paid at fixed rates beginning at forty marks an hour at ten years of age. It was the ambition of every boy to possess the greatest number of marks. The table of coinage was as follows :

Prime	.	.	.	.	.	1 mark
Triad	.	.	.	.	.	3 marks
Pentad	.	.	.	.	.	5 marks
Decad	.	.	.	.	.	10 marks
Demi-cent	.	.	.	.	50 marks
Cent	.	.	.	.	.	100 marks

[50] A. Hill, 'On Rewards and Punishments', *Journal of the Society of Arts*, vol. ii (1854), p. 671.   [51] Ibid.

Quingent . . . . 500 marks
Chiliad . . . . . 1000 marks

Some examples of these coins are reproduced facing p. 224.

Large silver coins called personal marks were given for superior work, such as original essays, high-quality translations, striking drawings, and so on. Personal marks could purchase additional holidays, which were obtainable by no other means, and they could also procure high places in aggregate rank.

The attainment of rank was perhaps the most important part of the exercise of rewards and punishment at Hazelwood. There were three possible kinds of rank : moral, weekly, and aggregate. Moral rank was obtainable mainly by careful observance of the school laws. A boy's moral or personal rank also depended upon the prompt payment of fines and solvency with regard to Hazelwood coinage. The grades, in ascending order of merit, were as follows :

1. *Ward* : these were new entrants, or those convicted in court.
2. *Frank* : this group was allowed four holidays a year, credit in settling fines, and a superior playground.
3. *Veteran Frank* : a rank reached after one year's Frankship ; these boys were allowed exemption from bounds and other restrictions.
4. *Autarch* : this elevated status was reached by election only, and boys in this category paid no fines. Usually the group was limited to two or three boys.

Weekly rank was obtained by diligent attention to school work and a rise in position in class. Each subject of study was taken weekly in turn to determine rank. For instance, in one week the rank of each pupil might depend on his progress in Greek, in the following week in geometry, in the third week in Latin, and so on. Those boys whose rank in academic merit surpassed that in the personal rank table were suitably rewarded. As a variation, rank was determined twice each half-year by the boy's record of conduct. This system allowed each boy to excel in his own subject and gave as many as possible a taste of success, and was one of the outstandingly successful innovations introduced into Hazelwood.

At stated intervals, each boy's weekly rank position in the school was totalled and points deducted for any voluntary work of outstanding merit that he might have done. The boy with the lowest rank total was then considered to be first in aggregate rank. High aggregate rank carried a number of privileges including the position of a boy's seat at meals, and the ten highest were allowed free choice of employment on one afternoon each week.

At the end of the session, prizes were awarded to the first five boys in aggregate rank. The prize-winners in 1824 were typical :

> John Jones chose a copy of Southey's 'Roderick the last of the Goths', valued at 26s. William Sargant had reserved the prize which he had obtained at Christmas to join the one he gained at Midsummer : he chose a copy of 'Marmion' and 'Rokeby', valued at 18s. John Williams chose a Telescope, valued at 10s. 6d. Henry Beckett a copy of the 'Eastern Tales', valued at 7s. William Watson 'Milton's Poetical Works', valued at 4s. 6d.[52]

These prize-winners, and the Judge and Magistrate, were known as Students, and entitled to special privileges, such as the use of a private room and exemption from certain offices.

The whole system, from marks to rank, interlocked and allowed the maximum amount of pupil participation. No boy, however untalented, could fail to benefit from some aspect of the system, and it was impossible for the most brilliant permanently to take all the limelight or gain all the prizes. The scheme also aimed at developing mathematical skill, initiative, self-reliance, and administrative experience, and punishments were nearly always loss of marks or loss of rank, deprivations that lowered a boy in the estimation of his fellows more surely than a flogging. On rare occasions boys were kept in by the masters, and only if they then refused to work were they imprisoned in a closet ; they could, however, appeal to the Committee against this decision if they wished. Undoubtedly the system was complex and based on competition and the profit motive without much appeal to group co-operation. But it offered clear, stage-by-stage objectives and compared with caning or flogging it was humane.

IV

The mark system practised at Hazelwood and Bruce Castle was widely known and respected as a considerate method of disciplining large numbers of children. Perhaps the best indication of its success was the way in which the principle of the scheme was adapted and used in

---

[52] *Hazelwood Magazine*, vol. i, no. 10 (Aug. 1823), p. 6.

institutions outside the middle-class educational world, such as prisons, reformatories, and factory schools.

One of the most interesting applications of the mark system was made by the prison reformer, Captain Alexander Maconochie, sailor, geographer, scholar, and sometime prison governor of a notorious convict settlement at Norfolk Island in the Pacific.[53] After his return from there in 1845, Maconochie enjoyed 'close personal intercourse' with Matthew Davenport Hill,[54] who was so impressed with him that he included a long article on his reforming activities in his volume entitled *Our Exemplars*.[55] According to George Birkbeck Hill, the principal of Bruce Castle, Maconochie 'confessedly took his system from ours'.[56]

At Norfolk Island Maconochie had successfully introduced a scheme whereby prison sentences were to be measured not by time but by tasks, which were paid for by marks. These were also awarded for good conduct and forfeited for misbehaviour. The length of a prisoner's sentence thus depended on the number of marks that he could amass. Punishment was made, in Maconochie's words, 'primarily a school of hardy reform', in which a prisoner was morally and physically strengthened by 'properly stimulated exertion and self-restraint'.[57] On his return to England Maconochie amplified and popularized his scheme in a number of pamphlets that created great controversy at the time and inspired the liberal reorganization of the Irish penal system.

A somewhat unlikely imitator of Maconochie's method was Charles Dickens, also a friend of the Captain's, who used a modified form of the mark system in Urania Cottage, the Home for Homeless Women that he helped to run with Miss Burdett-Coutts at Shepherd's Bush. The Home was a reformatory for prostitutes, petty thieves, and destitute vagrants, whom Dickens hoped to reform by means of a combination of domestic tasks and a little education. Every day each girl was awarded up to four marks for the attainment of certain virtues — truthfulness, industry, order, cleanliness, and so on. The marks,

[53] J. V. Bury, *Alexander Maconochie of Norfolk Island* (Melbourne, 1958), *passim*.
[54] R. and F. Davenport-Hill, *The Recorder of Birmingham : A Memoir of Matthew Davenport Hill* (London, 1878), p. 185.
[55] M. D. Hill (ed.), *Our Exemplars, Poor and Rich* (London, 1861), pp. 213 ff.
[56] *Report of the Schools Inquiry Commission*, P.P. (1867–8), xxviii (4), p. 846.
[57] Captain Maconochie, *Secondary Punishment : The Mark System* (London, 1848), p. 3.

which could be lost for bad behaviour, were redeemable for cash when the girls left the Home.[58]

Both these applications of the mark system were simplified in comparison with that in use at Hazelwood. The scheme in use at the factory schools of Wentworth Blackett Beaumont, M.P., at Weardale, however, more nearly resembled that of the Hill brothers, and showed the use to which it could be put in very different circumstances. The schools were run by Beaumont on his lead-mining estate, said to be the largest in the world at the time, in Weardale, comprising seven buildings expressly for the use of the children of miners. The Weardale miners in the 1840s and 1850s were noted for their zeal in promoting education for their families. In 1847, for instance, they formed the Weardale Miners' Improvement Society, with the object 'to promote the Welfare, Peace, and Happiness of the Inhabitants of this Mining Dale'. Members took a vow of total abstinence until the age of thirty and met weekly to hold classes in literary and other subjects.[59] The miners also subscribed £400 for the erection of one of the schools in Weardale.

The general direction and management of the schools was vested in Mr. Beaumont as patron, but the actual running of each institution was carried out by a committee of six visitors, elected annually, four of whom were miners or other workmen, the remaining two being the owners' business agents. The task of these committees was to ensure that the schools were conducted according to the regulations.[60]

These regulations were clear and comprehensive, covering details of religious and moral training, times of attendance, fees, curriculum, and so on, and they included a description of the working of the ticket system. The curriculum consisted of reading, writing, arithmetic, English grammar, geography, natural history, mensuration, drawing, and religious instruction. Fees were 6*d.* a month and scholars were expected to buy their books, slates, and other equipment, which were supplied at cost-price by the management.

Corporal punishment was not entirely prohibited but in practice it was found that it was never required because of the efficiency of the

---

[58] P. A. W. Collins, *Dickens and Crime* (London, 1962), pp. 94 ff., 164 ff.

[59] Pamphlet entitled *Weardale Miners' Inmprovement Society* (n.d., ? 1847).

[60] This account is based on A. F. Foster, 'Report on the State of Popular Education in . . . Durham and Cumberland', *Report of the Commissioners Appointed to Enquire into the State of Popular Education in England*, P.P. (1861), xxi (2), pp. 345–7 ; App. H, pp. 387–91.

ticket system. Daily rewards were given for punctuality and general good conduct, weekly rewards were given for attention to study, and a monthly prize was given for prompt payment of school fees. In addition to these a special reward, an 'office ticket', was given from time to time for meritorious conduct and these were retained permanently by the scholars as a testimonial. Four or more of these office tickets entitled the recipient to a Bible, which he applied for at the district mining office when he left school.

The distribution of tickets resembled a simplified form of the Hazelwood system, but it is probable that the organization of the Barrington School, which was still in operation in the district until the 1840s, also had some influence. One ticket was given every morning and afternoon to each scholar who was in the school before the bell had ceased ringing. An extra daily ticket was given for good appearance and behaviour but it was lost if reproof was given. Every Friday afternoon each pupil was given a number of tickets, not exceeding ten, for satisfactory progress in academic studies. In addition to these each pupil received ten tickets for prompt monthly payment of school fees. The greatest number of tickets a pupil could receive in a month was 110, though this was very rarely obtained. The main forfeitures were for lateness, absence, and disobedience or delinquency. As was the case at Hazelwood, an accumulation of tickets could be exchanged for ones of a higher value. At the end of the year, prizes consisting of books, mathematical instruments, pictures, maps, were given to each scholar who had obtained sixty tickets in each of six or more months of the year.

As with most other schools where a mark system had been substituted for corporal punishment, the atmosphere and achievement of the school made it outstanding enough to earn an Inspector's special report. According to A. F. Foster, the Inspector for the district, the Newhouse School in Weardale reached the highest standard in formal education, singing, and drawing. What caught Foster's attention, however, was the generally good behaviour of the pupils. 'In the Beaumont schools', he wrote, 'I witness what otherwise I should not have supposed possible — desks which had been in use for nine years without exhibiting a single cut or other mark of ill usage ; school books well kept, though carried home every day, and the ordinary copybooks without a blot.'

Foster attributed this behaviour entirely to the ticket system ; the emulation that it engendered among the children gave them an entirely new attitude to schooling. He quoted the case of an eminent visitor who, asking for a holiday for the children, was surprised to find that it was greeted with boos rather than cheers.

V

The multifarious schemes of tickets, marks, coinage, medals, rank, and so on rose and flourished, we have suggested, in the period when corporal punishment in schools was believed by many observers to be at its height. The systems substituted for the cane and the whip, based as they were on the principles of emulation, competition, and the acquisition of rank and prizes, obviously took their inspiration from the competitive capitalist ethic to which the growth of the Industrial Revolution was giving rise. The spirit of individual enterprise and the capital, wage, labour relationship were beginning to dominate society.

Lancaster, as we have seen, believed that the hope of material reward was the main motive force of any society. Patrick Colquhoun, economist, magistrate, and founder of a Bell school in Orchard Street, Westminster, urged his pupils: 'Struggle therefore to outdo each other, that you may have many prizes.' [61] Maconochie, in advocating his system, suggested that the marks were a form of wages which he considered to be 'the habitual stimulant to virtuous exertion in free life',[62] and the Hills compared some of their arrangements at Hazelwood to factory piece-work. In substituting the individual collection of redeemable merit marks by each child for corporal punishment by the teacher, the progressive educationalists of this period were reflecting the new developments in society, but it was debatable whether this was totally desirable in the school situation.

This point was raised by James Simpson, the radical Scottish educationalist, in evidence to the Select Committee on Education in 1835. Simpson believed that merit-ticket systems, though they could be used generously, were more likely to be used selfishly, and would encourage 'the propensity to accumulate property', and those who collected tickets would regard it as a mode of making money. 'Is not the disposition to accumulate one of the most valuable principles

[61] P. Colquhoun, *A New and Appropriate System of Education for the Labouring People* (London, 1806), p. 47.   [62] Maconochie, p. 5.

by which society is governed ?' asked a member of the Committee. Only if regulated by intellect and moral sentiments, argued Simpson ; in society, he pointed out, nine-tenths of the laws were directed against the grosser manifestations of the tendency to private accumulation, and he altogether deprecated the ranking system in schools as leading to selfishness and ill-will towards others. Punishment should begin and end with the individual and operate on his character only; this, however, said Simpson, was no argument for corporal punishment which in itself was degrading.[63]

Simpson's words were the voice of the future. The rewards and punishments in this chapter flourished most extensively in the first half of the nineteenth century. During the 1850s there was a large-scale operation of prize schemes for attendance in elementary schools, largely sponsored by the Church or by private philanthropy, with the main object of keeping working-class children longer at school.[64] The Revised Code of 1862, however, with its prescriptions and payment of grants to schools on a basis of the numbers in attendance from six to twelve years of age, became a formidable obstacle to projects of this kind because it narrowed down the educational aims of these schools to results. At its most developed, the system of rewards up to 1850 was applied to many aspects of school life and, as in Hazelwood and the Weardale schools, encouraged a good quality of response in the children. Payment by results after 1862 concentrated on a standard product, and thereafter rewards and punishments were directed to that end.

14. The Teaching of Young Children :
James Buchanan and Samuel Wilderspin

I

THE formal education of children under five years of age was almost totally neglected in Britain until the end of the Napoleonic Wars. It

[63] *Report from the Select Committee on Education in England and Wales*, P.P. (1835), viii, pp. 177–9.
[64] A. Hill (ed.), *Essays Upon Educational Subjects Read at the Educational Conference of June 1857* (London, 1857), pp 125–215.

E.I.—R

was not until Robert Owen had begun his experiment at New Lanark that the idea of setting up specially equipped and well-staffed schools for young children took root in this country. The need for the super-intendence and instruction of the increasing number of young children of the cities whose mothers were often working all day was inade-quately filled by dame-schools, which were little more than child-minding establishments, often kept by old men or women 'whose only qualification for this employment seems to be their unfitness for any other'.[1] Premises were usually small, unsuitable, ill-ventilated rooms, books were few, and instruction rarely extended beyond the elements of spelling, some reading, and a little sewing for the girls.[2]

The first attempt to set up an infant school outside New Lanark was made by a group of Whigs and Radicals, led by Brougham and James Mill, who, impressed by the success of Owen's experiment, opened a school in London in 1818, securing the services of James Buchanan as master. The same group started a second infant school shortly afterwards, with the redoubtable Samuel Wilderspin as master. The aim of these early schools was as much social as educational ; 'the moral discipline was the great consideration', according to Brougham.[3] They were mainly concerned to take children off the streets and away from criminal and anti-social influences. Samuel Wilderspin wrote at length of children who stole brass weights from shops, wrenched the brasswork off doors, robbed necklaces and lace caps from the well-to-do, cloth from drapers' shops, and cakes from confectioners ; juvenile prostitution and 'such scenes as human nature shudders at' he found in every city.[4] Infant schools thus arose both from a dissatisfaction with the existing educational provision for very young children and from the need to grapple with a pressing social problem.

Although the early infant schools were largely concerned with social rehabilitation, they also tended to be centres of experiment in method and organization, and the work of Buchanan and Wilderspin, for in-stance, had a significance well beyond their own establishments. Children in infant schools did not finish their schooling at the point at which their employment began, and thus were not immediately be-ing prepared for their 'station in life', the obsession of the day schools

[1] *Report from the Select Committee on the Education of the Poorer Classes*, P.P. (1838), vii, p. 105.   [2] Ibid., pp. 2–3, 26–103.
[3] *Parl. Deb.*, N.S., ii (28 June 1820), 87–88.
[4] S. Wilderspin, *On the Importance of Educating the Infant Children of the Poor* (London, 1823), pp. 141–8 *passim*.

for the industrious poor, and infants were more malleable than older children and presented new problems which many of the early teachers tried to solve in untraditional ways.

The first infant schools were all founded or conducted by persons of strong individual talent and character who were vigorous in pressing their own claims as originators of this or that system. Owen, Wilderspin, and Buchanan all advanced, or had advanced on their behalf, claims to be the founder of infant schools. Other claims were put forward, of course, for the work of Oberlin, Pestalozzi, and Fellenberg. The details of the altercations that arose are unimportant except in so far as they throw light upon the circumstances in which infant schools were founded and on the kind of institutions they were held to be.

Much of the original argument was concerned with the definition of an infant school. Owen maintained that the school in Brewer's Green was so inferior to the New Lanark original in aim and purpose as hardly to constitute a school at all : 'poor James Buchanan had to form his children into the old character of society, a little improved,' wrote Owen, 'into believers and slaves of a system, founded in falsehood and supported only by deception. . . .'[5]

Brougham, on the other hand, claimed that the school at Brewer's Green was the first of its kind in Britain, if not in the world, since those of Owen and Fellenberg, which provided the idea, were formed to serve a manufacturing or agricultural establishment and were therefore limited in application and not day schools in the normal sense.[6] In Brougham's view, therefore, the first infant school worthy of the name was the one he helped to found in 1818. Wilderspin, who opened an infant school at Spitalfields in 1820, was considered by Brougham to be merely an agent who helped to popularize and spread an institution already fully formed.

This, as might be expected, was not the view of Samuel Wilderspin himself, the City clerk turned schoolmaster. The schools at New Lanark and Brewer's Green, he claimed, were mere asylums for children and lacked any systematized plan for their instruction.[7] In later life Wilderspin was fond of describing himself in his books as the

---

[5] *New Moral World*, vol. ii, no. 64, 16 Jan. 1836, p. 94.
[6] *Report from the Select Committee on the State of Education*, P.P. (1834), ix, p. 223.
[7] *Educational Magazine* (Aug. 1835), p. 149 ; *Report from the Select Committee on Education in England and Wales*, P.P. (1835), vii, p. 16.

'Inventor of the System of Infant Training',[8] and claimed that others had taken advantage of his success ; 'as soon as the thing began to establish itself,' he exclaimed bitterly, 'then we have disciples of Pestalozzi, disciples of Mr. Owen, Frenchmen, Germans, and even nursemaids, laying claim to the system.' [9] Infant schools, in Wilderspin's eyes, were schools conducted on the lines devised by himself :

> I beg leave explicitly to state, and I defy proof to the contrary, that I was not only the *first* person to invent and develop the system, but I was the first practically to show to a disbelieving public the possibility of one man and woman managing two hundred and forty infants, for many years together, without any assistance whatever.[10]

The argument between Owen and Wilderspin on the origin of infant schools continued for many years. Owen regarded Wilderspin, more in sorrow than in anger, as technically a good teacher who lacked the 'powers of mind' to comprehend the Owenite philosophy and who was subsequently influenced by 'the so-called pious and would-be over-righteous'.[11] Wilderspin, for his part, although he recognized Owen's contribution to infant education and always paid tribute to Owen's aid in his early days at Spitalfields, became increasingly reluctant to acknowledge Owen as the founder of the infant system. The controversy came to a crisis in 1837, when the two protagonists met at Liverpool and agreed to differ on the importance of their specific roles in infant-school history. Despite this, Wilderspin claimed that during his absence in Ireland shortly afterwards, Owen or his agents were still travelling the country laying claims to the invention of the system.[12]

Owen believed that an infant school had to be founded upon the philosophical and educational theories to which he subscribed before he would give it the name. Wilderspin, on the other hand, thought that the essence of an infant school lay in the way in which the curriculum, teaching, and organization were systematized, and cared little for any general philosophical framework. On their own assumptions, each could claim to have been first in the field in Britain. Both Owen and Wilderspin, however, must give way to the claims of Johann Friedrich Oberlin, who had established an infant school at

[8] S. Wilderspin, *A System of Education for the Young* (London, 1840), title-page.
[9] Ibid., pp. 94–95.　　　[10] Ibid., p. 95.
[11] R. Owen, *The Life of Robert Owen* (London, 2 vols., 1857), i, p. 153.
[12] S. Wilderspin, *Early Discipline* (London, 3rd ed., 1840), pp. 331–2.

Ban de la Roche in Alsace in the 1770s in which young children were taught singing, natural history, simple botany, drawing and colouring, religion, morals, and speech training, together with a variety of manual tasks such as knitting, sewing, spinning, and so on.[13]

Neither Owen nor Wilderspin was aware of Oberlin's pioneering efforts when they began their schools, although Owen visited Oberlin in 1818. The line of progression in Britain was from Owen via Buchanan to Wilderspin, who in turn founded many other schools on his own system. Owen's philosophical theories, however, remained at New Lanark. If the early infant schools can be said to have had any theoretical basis at all, it was Swedenborgianism. It is a remarkable fact that three out of the four pioneers of infant schools — namely Oberlin, Buchanan, and Wilderspin — were members of the New Church, or adherents of the Swedenborgian doctrine.[14]

The New Church, based on the doctrines of Emanuel Swedenborg (1688–1772), was a messianic sect that took root in England in the later eighteenth century. Its esoteric visions of a material heaven, its doctrine of correspondence between heavenly and earthly life, its conception of man as the embodiment of the divine order had, to all appearances, little direct educational significance.[15] The Swedenborgians took a great interest in education, however, and at their first conference in England in 1789 they initiated measures for the education of children of their members in day and Sunday schools.[16]

Perhaps their habit of regarding children as spiritual beings possessing an earthly body (Buchanan often referred to children as 'angels'), their belief that education began in infancy and was a lifelong training of the soul for the reception of truth, and that education itself was based upon the cultivation of the memory of things that came within the range of the physical senses,[17] helped Swedenborgian teachers such as Buchanan and Wilderspin to reject contemporary attitudes on the

---

13 H. Holman, *Oberlin and His Educational Work* (London, n.d., ? 1904), pp. 72, 81.

14 For the influence of Swedenborg's doctrines on Oberlin, cf. J. H. Smithson, 'Visit to the Celebrated Oberlin in the Ban de la Roche Two Years Prior to his Death', *Intellectual Repository and New Jerusalem Magazine*, vol. i N.S. (1840), pp. 151–62.

15 For a description of the English Swedenborgians, cf. D. Bogue and J. Bennett, *History of Dissenters* (London, 4 vols., 1812), iv, pp. 126–45.

16 R. Hindmarsh, *Rise and Progress of the New Jerusalem Church* (London, 1861), pp. 106–7.

17 J. Deans, 'Swedenborg on Education', in F. Watson (ed.), *Encyclopaedia and Dictionary of Education* (London, 4 vols., 1922), iv, pp. 1614–15.

nature of children and the method of teaching, and strike out on new paths.

Wilderspin, although he never admitted it in print, was a lifelong adherent of the New Church. His father, Alexander Wilderspin, had been a member of one of the earliest Swedenborgian societies in England,[18] and Wilderspin was a member of the New Jerusalem Temple in Waterloo Road, to which James Buchanan also belonged.[19] It was possible that Buchanan had been introduced to Swedenborgianism, after his migration to London in 1818, by Benjamin Leigh Smith, his later employer, who certainly had connections with the New Church and as a young man had conducted an infant school on Swedenborgian principles.[20]

II

The decision to set up an infant school in London was made by a group of Whigs and Radicals associated with Brougham and James Mill, some of whom had played a prominent part in both the Royal Lancasterian Society and the Society for the Diffusion of Useful Knowledge. The project arose out of discussions that Brougham and Mill had had with Robert Owen in 1818. They were joined by the Marquis of Lansdowne, Zachary Macaulay (the historian's father), John Smith, M.P., Henry Hase (cashier of the Bank of England), Joseph Wilson of Spitalfields, Benjamin Leigh Smith, and others. Robert Owen agreed to let them have James Buchanan as the master.[21] The school was opened in 1818 in Westminster, and for the first three mornings Brougham himself, together with Lord Lansdowne, welcomed the children at the school-house door.[22] In the early days there was apparently some justification for Wilderspin's later remark that the school was merely an asylum that collected children together without any systematized plan,[23] for over the door was a large brass plate inscribed 'The Westminster Free Day Infant Asylum'.[24] According

[18] *Minutes of the First Seven Sessions of the General Conference of the New Church* (London, 1885), p. xii.

[19] *First Annual Report of the Committee of the New Jerusalem Church Free School* (London, 1823), p. 3 ; *Sixth Annual Report* (London, 1828), p. 17.

[20] Hester Burton, *Barbara Bodichon* (London, 1949), p. 2.

[21] T. Pole, *Observations Relative to Infant Schools* (Bristol, 1823), p. 8.

[22] *Parl. Deb.*, 3rd ser., lxxxviii (14 Aug. 1846), 699.

[23] *Educational Magazine, loc. cit.*

[24] [B. I. Buchanan], *Buchanan Family Records* (Cape Town, 1923), p. 5.

to Wilderspin, who was a frequent visitor, the school was held in an unfurnished room, in which there were no organized lessons or apparatus of any kind, beyond some little penny books and some inch cubes, a fact that offended his systematic soul.[25]

Brougham assured the House of Commons at the end of the school's first year of existence that 'it was going on in the most satisfactory manner',[26] but despite its success most members of the original committee lost their early zeal and drifted away. According to Benjamin's daughter Barbara Leigh Smith, later Barbara Bodichon, their lack of interest was due to Buchanan's unorthodox ways and novel teaching method : 'all the other gentlemen gave up the idea', she stated bluntly, 'when they saw the queer fish R[obert] O[wen] had sent from Lanark.' [27] The whole burden was left to be borne by Benjamin Leigh Smith, who then bought another site at Carey Street, Vincent Square, Westminster, and built a double-storey building to serve as a school and a residence for the teacher and including such amenities as a large playground and baths for the children.[28] Joseph Wilson, the only other member of the committee still interested in infant education, then founded his school at Quaker Street, Spitalfields, at which Wilderspin began his career.

Wilderspin, who seemed to regard Buchanan as kind-hearted but rather inefficient, later claimed that the success of his school caused an exodus of children from Buchanan's school, presumably the one at Vincent Square. This is not attested by Barbara Leigh Smith nor recorded in the *Buchanan Family Records*. Wilderspin further claimed, however, that the committee removed Buchanan from the school and gave it to Wilderspin to reorganize on his own plan, and that a protégé of Wilderspin's named Mote was put in Buchanan's place. Wilderspin hinted that Buchanan's removal was engineered by hostile religious factions and claimed that Buchanan had gone to Derbyshire in the interim, where he lived in wretched circumstances. He was only reinstated, claimed Wilderspin, after his own representations to the committee, who were not at first disposed to relinquish the building.[29] This enforced absence had little ultimate effect on the school, for there

[25] *Educational Magazine, loc. cit.*
[26] *Parl. Deb.*, N.S., lix (16 Dec. 1819), 1199.
[27] Barbara Bodichon to Alice Bonham Carter, 28 May 1884 ; [Buchanan], p. 25.
[28] Ibid., p. 8.
[29] *Educational Magazine, loc. cit.* ; *New Moral World*, vol. i (3rd ser.), no. 19, 7 Nov. 1840, p. 291 ; S. Wilderspin, *Early Discipline* (London, 1832), p. 74.

is abundant evidence from Barbara Leigh Smith, who attended the school in her childhood to help with the younger pupils, that it continued happily and effectively very much on the lines on which Buchanan had run the New Lanark Infant School.

The Vincent Square school had a great room quite sufficient to accommodate the whole population of a hundred children. It was fitted with a number of low benches arranged around the walls, on which were hung colourful pictures of animals, and lesson cards with geometric figures pasted on them in brightly coloured paper. There was very little other apparatus except for a ball-frame for teaching arithmetic.[30] The children came from the poorest classes around Vincent Square, and Julia Leigh Smith, Barbara's aunt, believed that the children were supplied with a midday meal, because in the afternoons they did not seem obviously hungry and were too small to go home by themselves at dinner-time. On the whole the children were poor, dirty, and wild, and she paid tribute to the way in which the Buchanans carried out their 'heroic and successful undertaking' of keeping such an unruly band of children happy and comparatively orderly.[31]

Buchanan's methods of teaching, if methods they can be called, stemmed entirely from his personality; his chief qualities were his patience and his ability to enter into the child's world. He had brought with him from Lanark his flute, which he used to the greatest effect. 'The first I remember of him', recalled Julia Leigh Smith, 'is seeing him with a hundred or more little children in the great room at Vincent Square. . . . Buchanan came forward to greet us, or I should have hardly distinguished him from some of the children, for he was very small, and had an infantile expression, one might have called it angelic, when he was leading his troop of little ones marching to the sound of his flute.'[32] The centre of the schoolroom was always cleared for marching, playing, and exercising. 'It was a scene of perpetual bustle, movement and noise,' continued Julia, 'always growing into good humour, and I think the smile was always playing on his features though it did not look fixed there. He was always alive, not mechanical, and I believe he could have quieted the whole infantry at any moment when he chose with the help of his wife and flute.'[33] Her niece relates many stories of Buchanan's extraordinary influence over the children;

[30] [Buchanan], p. 8.   [31] Ibid., p. 27.
[32] Ibid., p. 26.   [33] Ibid., pp. 26–27.

she remembered seeing 'the poor little things clustering on him like hiving bees, all trying to caress him'.[34]

Buchanan's Swedenborgian religious views were so much part of his life that he naturally brought them into his teaching of the children. According to the Swedenborgian doctrine of correspondences every substance or object had its spiritual and moral equivalent ; a stone corresponded to truth, a circle to harmony, and so on. It is not certain that Buchanan fully comprehended the entire range of the doctrine, but the more fantastic elements were certainly real to him and Barbara Leigh Smith recalls him using them in his teaching :

> He would arrange the children in a circle and make us all dance round joining hands with them. 'There!' said he, 'when the round is made is truth' (or harmony I forget which). 'Yes', said I, not attending, but taking for granted he was explaining something that could not be explained. 'Yes', replied he in a rather scornful tone. ' "Yes", says you, but don't know what I mean.'
>
> 'Well, what do you mean?' I asked.
>
> 'I mean that the circle corresponds with harmony (or truth), and then the angels come and join us.' [35]

Buchanan loved to tell the children Bible stories, which he made lively and significant. In the *Buchanan Family Records* it is related how the children loved to hear the story of Daniel in the lions' den, and how 'the space under the gallery became the den occupied by some of the older boys, who growled lustily, and how Grandpa would mount the gallery, and leaning over the railing, call "Daniel, has God kept you safe?", and Daniel would reply, "O, King, live for ever!" Daniel was always duly rescued, but the story ended there, for Grandpa did not approve of punishment, especially for children.' [36]

Buchanan did not neglect to instruct the children in the three R's, but his methods were entirely original and had nothing at all in common with the usual monitorial drill. He taught the multiplication table by a combination of words and actions, in much the same way as Wilderspin was to do later :

> Twice one are 2, thumbs up to view,
> Twice two are 4, fingers on the floor,
> Twice three are 6, fingers playing tricks,

[34] Barbara Leigh Smith to Florence Nightingale, 1 July 188? ; ibid., p. 22.
[35] Burton, pp. 6–7.   [36] [Buchanan], p. 4.

> Twice four are 8, count them now they're straight,
> Twice five are 10, all hands up again.

These rhymes and actions were composed by Buchanan himself, and when teaching grammar he used the same methods, combining elementary information with simple rhymes, a method also to be used by Wilderspin. Here is an example of his method :

> Three little words we often see
> Are articles — *a*, *an*, and *the* ;
> A noun is the name of anything,
> As *school*, or *garden*, *hoop* or *swing* ;
> Adjectives tell the kind of noun,
> As *great*, *small*, *pretty*, *white*, or *brown*,
> Instead of nouns the pronoun stands —
> John's face, *his* head, *my* arm, *your* hands ;
> Verbs tell of something being done —
> To *read*, *write*, *count*, *swing*, *jump*, or *run* ;
> How things are done the adverbs tell,
> As *slowly*, *quickly*, *ill* or *well* ;
> The prepositions stand before
> A noun, as *in* or *through* a door ;
> Conjunctions join the nouns together,
> As men *and* children, wind *or* weather ;
> An interjection shows surprise,
> As *Oh, how pretty ! Ah, how wise !*
> The whole are called nine parts of speech,
> Which reading, writing, speaking teach.[37]

Buchanan used no books or slates in his school and all his teaching was done by encouraging the children to sing, recite, and play. Since he always took part in the lessons himself, much of the children's learning was by imitation. Julia Smith noticed, however, that the children in his school gained much proficiency in reading, writing, and counting.[38]

Robert Owen's account of Westminster Infant School in his autobiography gives a different picture of Buchanan, which for many years influenced accounts of his methods. Since the publication of the *Buchanan Family Records*, however, it is possible to vindicate the character of the Buchanans and the methods they used in the school. Owen, it will be remembered, was struck with 'surprise and horror', on a visit to the school, to see Mrs. Buchanan terrifying the children

---

[37] [Buchanan], p. 5.   [38] Ibid., p. 27.

with a whip, and drew the conclusion that the Buchanans were not only cruel but inefficient.[39] Owen's words were written in his eighty-sixth year and some forty years after the event, when it might be charitable to assume that his memory for detail was somewhat impaired by his advancing years. Whatever Owen saw (and his account cannot be categorically refuted), cruelty was certainly uncharacteristic of the Buchanans, as the evidence already given shows. At least two contemporary accounts contradict Owen. Thomas Pole, in his *Observations Relative to Infant Schools*, stated plainly that no corporal punishment was ever introduced into the school.[40] Barbara Leigh Smith also defended Mrs. Buchanan's character : 'If he says she was hard, or cruel, or rough, it is quite false. She was a thrifty, bustling, managing, shrewd Scotswoman.' Miss Leigh Smith, though representing the two Buchanans as very different characters — he was 'unpractical, childlike, thriftless', she was 'the real bones of the school', never more in her element than when bathing the children — acquits both of them of severity towards their charges.[41]

Julia Smith agrees that looking after the comfort and health of the children was Mrs. Buchanan's great contribution to the school. 'One day I saw a dozen or more in the large bathroom', wrote Julia Smith. 'It must have been warm or they could not have enjoyed it as they did. It was pretty to see the little ragamuffins tumbling, splashing and kicking about, and their angel smiling over their antics.' Mrs. Buchanan did all this in addition to looking after her own young children and, according to Julia Smith, was always patient and good-humoured even when James Buchanan neglected her for 'some of his Swedenborgian inventions or phantasms or fancies'.[42]

It was part of Buchanan's character that he was unable to live the regularly ordered and planned life necessary for a schoolmaster. Although he was a kind husband and father he sometimes tired of the domestic life and would disappear altogether, returning perhaps with some copper chains 'which he asserted were gold because they had been seven times in the fire after some receipt in the Cabala'.[43] He would have strange dreams and would foretell calamity and death. At the times when he gave up the school for his dreams or wanderings, Benjamin Leigh Smith would send him to his own children at home.

[39] Owen, *Life*, p. 152.   [40] Pole, p. 51.
[41] Barbara Leigh Smith to Florence Nightingale, 1 July 188?; [Buchanan], p. 22.
[42] Ibid., p. 27.   [43] Ibid., p. 24.

There he would spend his time reading aloud to the Smith children from his three sacred sources — the Bible, the *Arabian Nights*, and Swedenborg, a circumstance that had a great effect on Barbara Leigh Smith and which she remembered for the rest of her life.[44] Buchanan's character was so simple and unaffected that he was easily tyrannized by the Smith children ; Barbara, even at the age of nine, would command him to carry her upstairs, and the children would make him read the *Arabian Nights* to them at mealtimes and refuse to allow him to eat, and unless rescued by the housekeeper he would have almost starved. Nevertheless, he still regarded the Smiths as angels. In contrast to his treatment of children, he was rather hard on adults, particularly if they disagreed with him. 'He used to lecture my father considerably,' recalled Barbara Leigh Smith, 'and he commonly stops people in the street to exhort them if he thought they were doing anything wrong.' [45]

The Westminster Infant School attracted many visitors, and besides Owen, they included Wilderspin, who obviously took good note of Buchanan's methods, and no less a person than King William IV, accompanied by his niece, the future Queen Victoria. Buchanan also trained several teachers, including Thomas Bilby who later ran a school in Chelsea, published a book on infant schools, and was involved in a dispute with Samuel Wilderspin.[46]

Buchanan was invited to open at least two other schools. About 1826 the Nightingale family (Benjamin Leigh Smith was Florence Nightingale's uncle) invited Buchanan and his wife to open a school in the small village of Crich in Derbyshire, which was described as 'ultra savage', and the local clergyman greeted them with the discouraging observation : 'You expect to do good — well, I've been here four and twenty years, and I've never done a ha'porth o' good in all that time.' With the help of Fanny Nightingale, Buchanan set up an infant school and despite all difficulties kept it going, and it was later merged into a large village school. The villagers rebelled, however, at Buchanan's attempt to teach their children grammar and geography and a deputation told him of their alarm at their children learning 'grammar, jogniffy and things of that sort, of no use nor signification whatsoever to gentle nor simple, and they would not have such things taught to their children nohow'.[47] According to the

---

[44] Barbara Leigh Smith to Florence Nightingale, 1 July 188?; [Buchanan], p. 23.
[45] Ibid., pp. 23–24.   [46] Ibid., p. 9.   [47] Ibid., pp. 28–29.

Buchanan Family Records Buchanan later opened another school in Derbyshire under an arrangement with Benjamin Leigh Smith, and stayed at the Nightingale residence at Lea Hurst while doing so.

The school at Vincent Square continued under Buchanan's direction until 1839. In that year it was visited by a representative of the London Statistical Society, whose report revealed that, twenty years after its foundation, Brewer's Green School had grown and prospered. It had 170 scholars, fairly equally divided between boys and girls, though the turnover of pupils was extensive, 300 having entered the school during the previous year. It was still privately financed (presumably by Benjamin Leigh Smith) and Buchanan apparently still relied on his own personality and inventive genius to fill the school day, for the formal curriculum remained narrow, consisting of reading, writing on slates, mental arithmetic, a small amount of sewing, and conversations on moral and religious duties. Even in the formal language of the report, which referred to conversation, individual instruction, and questioning, one can perceive that the typical Buchanan method of mixing with the children, telling them stories, and generally sharing their lives was still in operation.[48]

Despite the success of the school, Buchanan failed to gain the personal advancement to which his abilities and experience entitled him. This was partly due to his own simple and self-effacing character which precluded indulging in the kind of self-advertisement to which Owen and Wilderspin were prone. Another factor was his religious views, which, unlike Wilderspin, he made no attempt to conceal. He frankly informed the London Statistical Society, for instance, that he was a Swedenborgian,[49] and in the prevailing religious atmosphere of his day, schools conducted outside the orthodoxies of the Established Church were suspect. Brougham, Buchanan's lifelong champion, believed this was the main factor in Buchanan's failure to advance: 'the shadow of Westminster Abbey', he wrote, 'fell coldly on the dissenting teacher.'[50]

The possibility of greater opportunities abroad perhaps influenced Buchanan in his decision to emigrate to New Zealand in 1839 in order

[48] 'Appendix to the Second Report of the Statistical Society of London of the State of Education in Westminster', *Journal of the Statistical Society of London*, vol. i (1839), pp. 298–315.
[49] 'Second Report of a Committee of the Statistical Society of London, Appointed to Enquire into the State of Education in Westminster', ibid., pp. 193–215.
[50] *Westminster and Foreign Quarterly Review*, vol. liv (Jan. 1851), p. 397.

to start infant schools there, under the auspices of the New Zealand Land Company. On his way to the Antipodes, however, he disembarked at Cape Town in order to see his son, and decided to settle there, where shortly afterwards he was joined by his wife and his daughter Annie. His wife died soon after landing, however, and Buchanan then went to live in Pietermaritzburg, where he died in 1857.[51]

Buchanan's methods died with him. They were, in fact, so intimately bound up with his personality that they could hardly be passed on entire. He was a good example of what Francis Newman called a 'once-born', one of those characters who 'are not distressed by their own imperfections: yet it would be absurd to call them self-righteous ; for they hardly think of themselves at all. This childlike quality of their nature makes the opening of religion very happy to them ; for they no more shrink from God, than a child from an emperor, before whom the parent trembles.' [52]

This description fitted Buchanan perfectly. It was his character rather than his methods that impressed both his pupils and other educationalists. He inspired Wilderspin to take up teaching and twenty-five years after he had started work in London Buchanan's spirit pervaded the school of his former pupil, Barbara Leigh Smith, in Portman Hall.[53]

III

Historians of education have dealt harshly with Samuel Wilderspin. Even when his contribution to infant education has been recognized, there has been a tendency to accuse him of too great a reliance on verbalism and memory work : 'he exaggerated the importance of memory work'; [54] 'memory methods . . . marred the excellence of the rest of his approach' ; [55] 'there is no doubt that the memory was too much employed . . .'; [56] these are fairly typical comments.

---

[51] [Buchanan], pp. 9–10.

[52] Cited in William James, *The Varieties of Religious Experience* (London, 1902), p. 81.   [53] See below, Chap. 18.

[54] H. C. Barnard, *A Short History of English Education* (London, 1947), p. 72.

[55] S. J. Curtis, *History of Education in Great Britain* (London, 4th ed., 1957), p. 213.

[56] D. Salmon and W. Hindshaw, *Infant Schools, Their History and Theory* (London, 1904), p. 64.

These and other assessments of Wilderspin rely too much upon his earliest works and upon Wilderspin's own tendency to seek publicity for his schools by means of exhibitions at which chanting and verbal tricks were the main attraction.

What is the truth about Wilderspin ? To what extent can he be claimed as a pioneer of experimental education ? What was the value of his theories and methods for English education as a whole ? Closer inquiry suggests that Wilderspin's contribution to theory and practice has been underestimated and misunderstood, that he was a theorist of some stature, and an innovator in teaching method who radically altered our way of looking at very young children. In many ways, however, Wilderspin was his own worst enemy. His early works were badly written, prolix, and made few concessions to the reader, his character was combative, and he shared with Owen a dislike of giving others, or even sharing with others, credit for innovations.

Wilderspin began his work as a young and inexperienced man without any special equipment for his task. Educational theory was a relatively unexplored field and few, apart from Owen, had examined the psychology of very young children. Wilderspin rejected Owen's philosophy, though he used the Owenite experience (he had visited New Lanark soon after setting up his own school) [57] as the base on which to begin his work. His close association with Buchanan also provided him with some useful hints, and his own Swedenborgian views gave him a frame of reference essentially different from that of orthodox Christianity on which to judge the child. His main efforts were directed to founding an objective system of infant education, based on the observation of children, which would be generally valid and appreciated by educationalists of every persuasion. He achieved this after a long period of trial and error, and it is only in his later works, published in the 1840s and 1850s, that his theories can be seen in their developed form.

Samuel Wilderspin was born in Hornsey, north of London, in 1792. He was an only child and lived a somewhat isolated life without childhood companions. He found pleasure, however, in 'the beautiful fields and wild coppices about Hornsey', though his early school experiences were painful and for reasons unknown he was deprived of parental care early in life. On leaving school Wilderspin served an apprenticeship in a merchant's office and later set up in business on his

[57] *Select Committee on Education* (1835), p. 16.

own account for a short period. While working in London he began to take an interest in education and taught for a short time in a Sunday school, presumably one run by the New Church, where he took the backward class with great success.[58] It was during this period that he became acquainted with James Buchanan at the New Jerusalem Temple and visited Brewer's Green School. 'It engaged all my thoughts', he recalled, 'and I was often at this school.' [59] One day a member of the school committee, presumably Joseph Wilson, invited Wilderspin, now a married man with a young child, to help in the running of a similar school, and he immediately accepted the offer, taking over at Spitalfields Infant School, financed by Joseph Wilson, in August 1820.[60]

The district in which the school was situated was one of the poorest and most turbulent in London. One of the customs of the inhabitants was to steal an ox from Smithfield Market, drive it back to Spitalfields, and then make it wild by goading it and putting peas in its ears until it rampaged through the streets.[61] It was a common experience in his early days for Wilderspin to be pelted with filth and to be jeered at on his way to school in the morning,[62] but he was not to be daunted. In fact, he made it a practice to investigate the lives of the populace by disguising himself with a beard and old clothes, and visiting public houses and the haunts of the poor.[63] He became particularly concerned about what we would now call juvenile delinquency, and infant schools, he considered, had an important part to play in helping to combat the post-war wave of juvenile crime. 'Whatever the generality of the world may think upon the matter,' he maintained, 'I am morally certain that most of the crimes committed by infants arise from the neglect of moral cultivation.' [64]

Wilderspin's first day at school must have convinced him of the difficulties of his task. Faced with a horde of noisy and near-hysterical children in his classroom, he and his wife retreated into the living-room at the rear. In despair Wilderspin picked up his wife's cap adorned with coloured ribbon, put it on to a clothes-prop, and returned to wave it in front of the milling infants. 'All the children', he found to his amazement, '. . . were instantly silent.' Before general disorder

[58] S. Wilderspin, *The Infant System* (London, 8th ed. 1852), pp. 2–6.
[59] *New Moral World*, vol. i (3rd ser.), no. 19, 7 Nov. 1840, p. 291.
[60] *Importance of Educating the Infant Poor*, p. 7.
[61] *Select Committee on Education* (1835), pp. 19–22.   [62] Ibid., p. 18.
[63] Ibid., p. 35.   [64] *A System of Education*, p. 55.

could break out again Wilderspin started to play childish games with the infants and found it succeeded like a miracle ; twelve o'clock came before they knew where they were.[65] Wilderspin drew two important conclusions from the incident : that in any valid scheme of teaching the senses of the children must be engaged and that the teacher must be prepared, if necessary, to make contact with the child on the child's own level.

As he gained more experience as a teacher, Wilderspin was led to investigate the importance of the child's senses in the educational process. He had little to guide him at first except his own observation of children in his school, but later on, as he travelled around the countryside organizing infant schools, he was able to refine his experience and meet in discussion with other educationalists, although his views of child nature, based on the assumed 'natural' endowments of the child, remained essentially his own. They are remarkably perceptive and clear, and there seems little truth in the allegation, made in the *Report of the Consultative Committee on Infant and Nursery Schools* in 1933, that 'the philosophical basis of his system was crude and vague . . .'.[66]

The education of the child, asserted Wilderspin, should begin with the senses. 'A child as soon as it begins to observe objects,' he wrote, 'is a fit subject for education.' [67] The senses should be developed by allowing the children to examine the size, weight, colour, and other properties of objects. The child's spirit of inquiry and natural curiosity should then be directed in a balanced and harmonious manner. Wilderspin specifically condemned the exercise of memory and the storing of the child's mind with information as 'much better adapted to parrots than children'.[68] The duty of an infant-school teacher was to set children examining, comparing, and judging in relation to their own level of development, and Wilderspin's fundamental principle was 'let the children think for themselves'.[69] It follows that he was opposed to the verbalism that dominated English education at the time. 'It therefore cannot be too strongly insisted on, and too frequently repeated,' he wrote, 'that one of its most fundamental principles, as regards the unfolding, properly and easily, of the intellectual

---

[65] *New Moral World, loc. cit.*, p. 291.

[66] Board of Education, *Report of the Consultative Committee on Infant and Nursery Schools* (1933), p. 7.   [67] *Select Committee on Education* (1835), p. 14.

[68] S. Wilderspin, *The Infant System* (London, 6th ed., 1834), p. 28 ; ibid. (8th ed., 1852), pp. 16, 82, 84–85, 86.   [69] Ibid. (8th ed., 1852), p. 83.

faculties, is to communicate *notions* and *ideas* rather than words and sounds, or at least to let them be done together.'[70]   In the actual teaching situation Wilderspin liked to abandon the formal restraints of set hours and locations, combating listlessness and apathy by deliberately changing the mood or the scene and utilizing 'a hundred devices to keep up the spirits and vitality of the pupils'.[71]   This is reminiscent of the writings of several educationalists we have already encountered.   Starting from very different premises, Wilderspin reached a position that has some similarities not only with the theories of Edgeworth, Williams, and others, but also with those of Pestalozzi.

On the basis of this estimation of the nature of the child, Wilderspin built up his conception of the infant school.   He attempted to fashion an entirely new institution, different from both the dame-schools, in which 'ignorant and inactive old women', failed to awaken the infants' capacities for 'extensive mental development', and from the National and British Schools, which 'deaden the faculties of the children, by obliging them to commit to memory the observation of others, few of which they comprehend . . .'.[72]   The requisites were 'a spacious and airy classroom, proper materials for instructions, and active thinking teachers'.[73]   In addition, almost as important as the school itself, there should be a large playground attached.   The schoolroom, Wilderspin advised, should be 80 feet long and 22 feet wide, with an inclined gallery at one end (on which the children sat in ascending order of age), a master's desk at the opposite end, benches around the walls, and lesson-posts at which monitors instructed children 'in that part which is purely mechanical, and in that only'.[74]   There were classrooms opening off the main hall in which advanced scholars were taught in small groups.   After early experiments with a light cane and 'shaming' in the manner of Lancaster, Wilderspin introduced the jury system and reliance on the gradual cultivation of the best dispositions of the pupils and abolished corporal punishment.[75]   Place-taking, emulation, rank, rewards, and prizes, as practised extensively

---

[70] S. Wilderspin, *The Infant System* (London, 6th ed., 1834), p. 15.
[71] *A System of Education*, pp. 27–28 ; *Importance of Educating the Infant Poor* (2nd ed., 1824), p. 40.
[72] S. Wilderspin, *Infant Education* (3rd ed., 1825), pp. 273–4, 277.
[73] Ibid., p. 273.   [74] Ibid., p. 275.
[75] Ibid., p. 276 ; *Importance of Educating the Infant Poor* (2nd ed., 1824), pp. 30–32, 144–5, 150.

in National and British Schools of the time, were forbidden. Wilderspin believed that it was on the one hand absurd to demote a child
because his natural abilities did not lie in a particular direction, and
that on the other hand children were quite able to perceive merit and
worth without the addition of outward signs. 'We have no badges
of distinction,' he wrote, 'no crosses on the button holes, no bits of
ribbon attached to the child, no medals or anything of the kind ; we
do not think it necessary to deck a child with as many orders and
degrees as an Austrian fieldmarshal.' [76]

Outside the classroom was the playground, which was not only a
place for exercise and recreation but also a centre of moral education,
where the children unconsciously revealed the effects that their classroom instruction had produced. It thus presented an excellent opportunity for the master to observe and, if necessary, correct bad behaviour
on the child's part. 'It is here alone', wrote Wilderspin, 'he will
show you what he really is, and thus enable you . . . to crush those
bad propensities.' [77] The playground, he advised, should have a sur-
face of brick, fruit trees in the centre, and a flower border round the
walls. Two rotatory swings similar to maypoles, vaulting-ropes,
and blocks of wood for building were the main pieces of equipment, and all the children should be actively engaged in some
physical occupation, as in the modern 'adventure playground' (see
illustration facing p. 289). The choice of play, however, should be
left to the children themselves ; 'if they play at what they choose they
are free beings, and manifest their characters ; but if they are forced
to play at what they do not wish, they do not manifest their characters,
but are cramped and are slaves, and hence their faculties are not
developed.' [78]

With regard to the infant-school teacher, Wilderspin considered that
his character and ability were all-important. He denied that any clever
National School boy would do for an infant teacher, as some believed.
Wilderspin's ideal teacher had 'a tenor voice, a good deal of vivacity
and a pleasant countenance', and no physical disabilities.[79] He would
require 'much patience, gentleness, perseverance, self-possession,
energy, knowledge of human nature, and above all, piety . . .' [80] He

[76] *Select Committee on Education* (1835), p. 27.
[77] *A System of Education*, p. 27 ; *Select Committee on Education* (1835), p. 23.
[78] *A System of Education*, pp. xi–xii.
[79] *Select Committee on Education* (1835), p. 29 ; *Early Discipline*, pp. 57–58.
[80] *Importance of Educating the Infant Poor* (2nd ed., 1824), p. 196.

should never commit misdemeanours against which he had warned the children, promise what he was not able to perform, nor say one thing to a child when he meant another.[81]

This was bound up with Wilderspin's view of morality, which was essentially non-denominational Christian. In an age when morality was universally linked with Christianity, usually in one of its denominational forms, Wilderspin attempted to run his school on generalized ethical principles. The object of the school was 'health of body, activity of mind and piety and benevolence of spirit'.[82] Wilderspin's criticism of existing schools was that they almost entirely lacked a spirit of morality, and he insisted that 'the fundamental principle of the Infant School system is *love*'.[83] His system of morals encouraged all the simple virtues — unselfishness, love of neighbour, honesty — 'the pure and perfect morality of the Scriptures'.[84]

Finally, method, which was Wilderspin's chief area of innovation. This was worked out on the basis of a simple curriculum — the three R's, including simple geometry, the elements of geography and natural history, acquaintance with the characteristics of everyday objects, plus the 'leading facts of the New Testament'.[85] The outstanding features of Wilderspin's method were firstly the use of apparatus of a material and colourful nature — brass letters, wooden blocks, various kinds of ball-frames, coloured pictures, and so on — which fulfilled the purpose of stimulating and activating the child's five senses, and secondly the extensive employment of music, singing, and mime. Here he followed the Owenite tradition, but he attempted to invent and use apparatus in a more methodical manner and relate it closely to his theory of child development. It will be convenient to consider Wilderspin's method in connection with each subject in turn.

Wilderspin began by teaching children the alphabet, making use of a series of visual aids. The most important were large representations of the letters of the alphabet made of brass and fixed to a large baize-covered frame, stuffed with hay and quilted like a mattress. When they had recognized the letters the children then traced them on slates engraved with the alphabet.[86] He also used cards containing a letter of the alphabet and a picture of a natural object, for instance a capital A

---

[81] *Importance of Educating the Infant Poor*, p. 16.
[82] *Infant Education* (4th ed., 1829), p. 136.
[83] Ibid., p. 137.   [84] Ibid. (8th ed., 1852), pp. 90–94.
[85] *Select Committee on Education* (1835), p. 20.
[86] *Importance of Educating the Infant Poor* (2nd ed., 1824), pp. 45–46.

with the painting of an apple underneath, which had the merit of teaching the alphabet 'and giving ideas of things' at the same time.[87]

Having mastered the alphabet the children went on to words, which were printed on cards, repeating the words together in small classes or forming simple words by combining brass letters placed on runners in a frame. In his later work Wilderspin used transparencies as an aid to word recognition.[88]

Having gained familiarity with words children progressed to reading, and by the early 1830s Wilderspin had worked out what he called 'developing lessons', the object of which was to induce children to think and reflect on what they saw. Coloured pictures of insects, quadrupeds, general objects, had attached to them a short description about which the teacher asked questions. The object was to link reading and visualization in the child's mind and to check the apathy in learning to read that a straight narrative might give to the children.[89]

Wilderspin considered that it was impossible to simplify grammar sufficiently to make its rules comprehensive to infant-school children, but that enough could be imparted to make it more comprehensible than was usually the case. He thought that the great mystery about grammar arose from 'not making the children acquainted with the things of which the words used are the signs', and the use of words such as 'substantives' and 'adjectives' which were as unintelligible to the infant mind 'as the language of magical incantation'. Grammar teaching should, therefore, commence at the level of the child's understanding and children should first repeat the names of things they saw around them, then the qualities of these things (for example, 'the school room is *large, clean*'). Only after that should they be given the terms for the respective classes of names and qualities ; verbs and adverbs should be related to actions of the children themselves,[90] and then children could repeat Wilderspin's own rhymes, for example :

> English grammar doth us teach
> That it hath nine parts of speech . . .[91]

Wilderspin also used what he called the Elliptical Plan of teaching English, which he obtained from Dr. Borthwick Gilchrist, the Orientalist, who visited the school in 1825. The children were given

---

[87] Ibid., pp. 58–59.   [88] Ibid., pp. 38–39, 42.
[89] *Infant System* (6th ed., 1834), pp. 183–4.
[90] *Infant Education* (4th ed., 1829), pp. 249–51.
[91] Ibid. (6th ed., 1834), p. 287.

a passage with certain words missing and had to fill in the blanks themselves 'on rational principles of concatenated deduction'.[92] This
method has been used in one or another form through to the present
day, where it is an important feature in programmed learning.

The chanting of tables and other mathematical rules has been fixed
upon Wilderspin as his only method of teaching arithmetic, but he
regarded it merely as one process among many. His fundamental
principle was that arithmetical operations could best be taught by
translating concepts into terms of material objects before bringing
children to consideration of number. This, as he pointed out, reversed
the usual process of arithmetic teaching, in which children learned the
tables by rote before they were shown the realities, a course which
made arithmetic 'an abstruse, difficult and uninteresting affair to the
infant mind'.[93]

In conformity with his theory Wilderspin devised several pieces of
apparatus — a series of wooden cubes, a brass figure-frame, an arithmeticon, and a transposition frame. The cubes were one inch square
and a hundred would be placed on a table ; after a few simple operations by the teacher, the children would be taught to add and subtract
by manipulating the cubes themselves. The frames differed in detail,
but all were in principle similar to the abacus, and enabled children
to move brass figures of numerals or coloured balls into innumer-
able combinations. With these it was possible to show visually the
concepts of units, tens, and hundreds, as well as many other processes.[94]

Wilderspin was also much concerned with form. Once children
had learned the elements of natural form in geometrical terms, it was
possible, he considered, to get them to apply the knowledge to objects
around them — plates, dishes, tables, streets, houses, rooms, fields,
ponds, and so on, which he added were neither useless, beyond their
capacity, nor displeasing :

> How it happened that a mode of instruction so evidently calculated
> for the infant mind was so long overlooked, I cannot imagine . . .
> the various forms of bodies is [*sic*] one of the first items of natural
> education, and we cannot err when treading in the steps of Nature.[95]

---

[92] *Infant Education* (3rd ed., 1825), pp. vii-ix.
[93] Ibid. (4th ed., 1829), pp. 186–7.
[94] Ibid. (6th ed., 1834), p. 193 ff. ; *Early Discipline*, p. 7.
[95] Ibid. (4th ed., 1829), pp. 200–1.

He familiarized children with simple form by printing geometrical figures on paper and pinning them to a board, or by letting them build houses, bridges, etc., with brick blocks. In all this he strove for simplicity, beginning with first principles and proceeding step by step

Wilderspin's Arithmeticon

from there, exactly in the manner of Pestalozzi.[96] 'There is scarcely anything of which children are not capable,' he maintained, 'if we so simplify the things that they can comprehend them.' [97]

Armed with the belief that 'geography is to children a delightful

[96] Ibid., pp. 201–9 ; (3rd ed., 1825), pp. 95 ff.
[97] Ibid. (4th ed., 1829), p. 209.

study', he tried to get away from the lists of capes and bays and to teach elementary geography in a vivid and lively way. He showed the children pictures and costumes of various peoples of the world, located the respective countries on large maps, traced the travels of St. Paul on a map with the aid of a magnetic compass, demonstrated the points of a compass by means of the four corners of the playground, taught elementary meteorological knowledge with the aid of the school weathercock, had the children sing rhymes descriptive of the Earth, and so on.[98] His most exciting innovation, however, was to draw a map of England on the schoolroom floor, with each county clearly marked, and to set the children journeys from one county to another, making the route difficult or easy according to the knowledge of the child.[99]

Wilderspin made use of pictures mainly in natural history and religious instruction. He would show children pictures of animals, birds, fishes, and flowers, teach them their names, then how to distinguish them by their forms, following this with a series of questions on their qualities and uses. On other occasions he would use objects themselves, attaching to a board fragments of gold, silver, and copper in both their natural and manufactured states. Sometimes he would have various types of paper or textiles or even small models of animals attached to the boards. By this means he believed that children would recognize these things when they met them later in their reading. Religious knowledge was demonstrated with pictures illustrative of parables and other biblical themes.[100] Despite his attempts to make teaching methods simple, concrete, and interesting, Wilderspin did not always achieve the aims implicit in his analysis of the child mind and his theory of learning ; mixed up among his new techniques was a fair amount of the rote-learning and verbalism that he specifically condemned. The weaknesses in Wilderspin's practical work, as we shall see, were an invitation for less gifted teachers to pervert his teachings and weaken the status of infant schools.

Wilderspin believed that music was an important means of mental and moral improvement, and its use an indispensable aid to the teaching

---

[98] *Infant System* (6th ed., 1834), pp. 222–3 ; *Early Discipline* (3rd ed., 1840), p. 8 ; *A System of Education*, pp. xiv–xv.

[99] *Select Committee on Education* (1835), p. 27.

[100] *Importance of Educating the Infant Poor* (2nd ed., 1824), pp. 74–76 ; *A System of Education*, pp. 62–77 ; *Select Committee on Education* (1835), pp. 26–27 ; *Infant Education* (3rd ed., 1825), Appendix, pp. 249–53 ; *Infant System* (8th ed., 1852), p. 17.

of infants. A piano was a very necessary piece of school equipment,[101] and ideally a teacher would be able to play 'the violin, flute or clarionet'.[102] Wilderspin employed music 'to soften the feelings, curb the passions, and improve the temper'. On one occasion, by singing 'a simple and touching air', he says that he successfully changed the opinion of a small member of one of his juries who wished to punish a fellow pupil whom Wilderspin knew to be innocent.[103]

Wilderspin first discovered the value of music when he found that very young children had difficulty in pronouncing the letters of the alphabet ; as an experiment he set the alphabet to a simple tune, and found that this solved the problem.[104] Wilderspin used singing, together with mime, in the teaching of arithmetic ; the children sang or chanted simple rules, raising their hands in unison, walked round a tree in the playground hand in hand, singing a multiplication table, or stood in rows and on words of command formed themselves into parallel lines, squares, or triangles.[105] These methods were not always successful, however, and if he felt that they were insufficiently effective he would immediately change to instruction with the brass letters or some other system, adapting the lessons, in the Pestalozzian manner, to the feelings and capabilities of the child.

Wilderspin's theories and methods were worked out both in his own school and in the course of his work as a travelling missionary for the Infant School Society from 1824 onwards. This post lasted for about five years only. The Society then wound up, mainly, according to Wilderspin, because it failed to stand up to the prejudice and opposition that the new infant schools aroused.[106] He continued his career as a freelance educational missionary, supplementing his fees with profits from an Infant School Depot that he ran at Cheltenham for supplying apparatus.[107] In 1839 he accepted a post as head of the Central Model School in Dublin, but within two years he had returned to England and taken up residence in Warrington, where he resumed his propaganda for infant schools. In the middle 1840s, however, he retired to Wakefield in Yorkshire on a civil-list pension, and there he spent the remainder of his life, occupying himself with

[101] *A System of Education*, p. xv.
[102] *Infant Education* (6th ed., 1834), p. 282.   [103] Ibid., p. 283.
[104] Ibid. (4th ed., 1829), pp. 241–3, 246.   [105] Ibid.
[106] *Select Committee on Education* (1835), p. 32.
[107] *Infant Education* (4th ed., 1829), notice on fly-leaf.

rejuvenating the local Lancasterian school and lecturing at the Mechanics' Institute.[108]   He died in Wakefield on 10 March 1866.

Despite his great achievements, Wilderspin in his later life was a disappointed man.   Though infant schools, largely because of his efforts, were widely established and by 1835 no less than two thousand were in existence,[109] he felt that in many cases the kernel of his system had been lost and merely a shell retained, a feeling also shared by other observers.[110]   Infant schools had been made to harmonize with the 'monotonous, heavy, sleepy, system' of the day schools, rather than to transform it, as Wilderspin had hoped.[111]   This was partly due to the difficulties of finding and training suitable teachers.   Infant-teachers, on the whole, he realized, found the use of pictures and objects and material aids too difficult, or misunderstood their significance and relapsed into 'the parrot system' of memory work.   Teachers also liked to make an impressive show before visitors by putting on a display of singing or chanting by children, and too often this became the sole method of teaching.   Wilderspin himself, on his educational tours, had done the same, though he emphasized in print that these demonstrations were merely a subordinate part of his system, and that the education of the heart and senses was really the fundamental point.[112]   At the end of his career he stated his credo forcefully :

> The abuse of a plan is no argument against its use.   That it has been abused I am well aware — that the *parrot-system* has been revived and also applied in infant schools.   It was never intended to injure the young brain by over-exciting it, or to fill the memory with useless rubbish ; yet this is done.   I cannot help it.   I have done and will do my best to prevent such a violation of the very first principles of infant teaching.[113]

Whatever the shortcomings of his followers, however, Wilderspin had almost single-handedly created a country-wide system of infant schools and provided a theory and method by which they could be run, and his achievement must be measured against the standards of his time.   The institution that Wilderspin's infant schools were designed to replace was the dame-school, and to Wilderspin more than

[108] *Wakefield Free Press*, 17 Mar. 1866.
[109] *Select Committee on Education* (1835), p. 13.
[110] Cf. C. Baker, 'Infants' Schools', in Central Society for Education, *Third Publication* (London, 1839), pp. 1–48.   [111] *Infant System* (8th ed., 1852), p. 11.
[112] Ibid., pp. 15–16.   [113] Ibid., p. 18.

to anyone else do we owe the inauguration of professional standards in the education of young children. The key point about Wilderspin is that he started from the very beginning and had to overcome both hostility and indifference. Many of his contemporaries, however, recognized his worth, and his methods were particularly well received in Scotland, where he influenced among others George Combe and Stow. The most acute summing-up of his work was made by John Lalor, one of the most progressive educational theorists of the 1830s. Lalor recognized that Wilderspin's system was, in its best form, a realization of the principles of Pestalozzi and considered it to Wilderspin's credit that it should be so close to Pestalozzi's views despite 'being worked out by a mind in wholly different circumstances'.[114] The assessment is not unjust, and Wilderspin's achievement does not suffer by comparison.

[114] J. Lalor, Prize Essay in *The Educator : Prize Essays on the Expediency and Means of Elevating the Profession of the Educator in Society* (London, 1839), pp. 100–1.

Section Five

EPILOGUE: 1750–1850

BEFORE 1789 the channels of communication with France were open and the remarkable French intellectual achievements of the second half of the century gained the respect of many Englishmen. Montesquieu produced the *Spirit of the Laws* in 1743 ; Buffon wrote many of his forty-four volumes on *Natural History* between 1749 and 1789 ; Diderot and d'Alembert between 1751 and 1772 produced the thirty-five volumes of the *Encyclopedia*, which drew together so many radical contributors of great distinction. Voltaire wrote for nearly sixty years of the century and prized his English associations highly. Rousseau, who also came to England for a while, had many English acquaintances and admirers. *Émile* and *The Social Contract* were published in 1762, and La Chalotais produced his *Essay on National Education* in 1763. It is little wonder that French political and educational ideas were greatly esteemed by many of the intellectual and literary radicals in England in the second half of the century, despite the wars of the period. Wordsworth, Coleridge, Lamb, Hazlitt, Day, Edgeworth, Williams, Priestley, Percival, Erasmus Darwin, Godwin, Mary Wollstonecraft, are among those who were Francophiles and at first supporters of the French Revolution. However, the Reign of Terror, the Directory, and the rise to power of Napoleon turned nearly all of them against France, and the ensuing twenty years of war in Europe cut them off from the Continent. Yet the faith in social progress and individual rights that the Enlightenment seemed to presage were still the guiding lights for the English radicals whatever the political realities of the Revolution.

Gilpin, Manson, Williams, Day, and Edgeworth were educational innovators in the fifties, sixties, and seventies of the century. It is true that Gilpin and Manson were British pragmatists and that Williams, Day, and Edgeworth were influenced by the new men of science and philosophical speculation from Europe, but they all marked a period of educational change. Between the middle eighties and about the end of the first decade of the nineteenth century the influence of Rousseau and of France died away and the re-emergence of educational innovation after 1810 had a provenance that is more identifiably English or at any rate British.

In Switzerland, Pestalozzi in 1781 began to produce in writing his own reinterpretation of Rousseau and the school of nature. Where Émile was in the privileged position of having a tutor and no real ties to his family, Pestalozzi wrote, in the series for which *Leonard and Gertrude* is the origin, of the particular needs of poor and suffering members of society and the central significance of family life and mother-love. In 1799 he worked with beggars and vagrants at Stanz and infants at Burgdorf and in 1801 he wrote *How Gertrude Teaches Her Children*, his detailed exposition of how children learn, and began the Institute to which educationalists like Froebel, Herbart, and von Humboldt came, together with the Mayos, Greaves, Kay-Shuttleworth, Lady Byron, and many others from England until Pestalozzi's death in 1827. He profoundly affected Fellenberg, who in his turn worked with Wehrli, and these three, as we have shown in earlier chapters, reintroduced influences from the Continent to England. Where the educational influence of Rousseau was felt, from about 1765 to 1785, on the children of the liberal intelligentsia in the relatively privileged circles of Williams, Day, and Edgeworth, the influence of Pestalozzi and Fellenberg was experienced mostly in schools for the poor like Ealing Grove and in Kay-Shuttleworth's reforms of national education, and, exceptionally, in the affluent and successful school at Cheam.

If Rousseau, Pestalozzi, and Fellenberg between them brought to the attention of English education the claims of the child-centred curriculum both for well-to-do and poor children, the realities of economic and social life in this country produced their own educational effects. The two main viewpoints we have taken on this in the preceding chapters are summed up in the work of Owen and the Hill brothers. Owen's educational theory and practice sprang from a humane concern for his workpeople and their families which extended to become a general economic and political principle worked out with courage. He has been called at various times a humanist, a pragmatist, a socialist, and a utopian and in so far as classification helps us to understand him he was all four at different phases of his life. He knew something of teaching, for in the early 1780s he had been an usher before entering trade and working in Stamford and London, but he had also seen at first hand the mechanization of the cotton trade and had both manufactured and used the new spinning machines by the time he was twenty. The whole matter and manner of industry concerned him at New Lanark, but more particularly the health of the total community, from the infants and families of the workers to social welfare, housing, and adult education. More than that, he invented schemes of co-partnership and profit-sharing, and in the country at large began agitating to reduce working hours and improve working conditions, especially in the time of distress and poverty following the Napoleonic Wars. With Peel he helped to bring in the 1819 Factory Act, which he regarded as inadequate in itself, and he was a main leader in the beginnings of trade unionism.

His educational work was for poor children of all ages and was part of his secular humanism. He was a radical in politics, in religion, in social theory, and in education, and he provided innovations in schools that were supposed to lead to tolerant communities of children and to egalitarian opportunities. In the last twenty-five years of his life he had little political realism, but it was through him that Buchanan and Wilderspin, the London, Manchester, and Salford co-operatives of the early 1830s, and the Rational Religionists of the 1840s came to make their mark. It was Owen who really gave a major place to the influence of a working-class ideology, with its accompanying social and economic factors, in education. It was Owen who saw the school as a practical utopia both in its physical layout and in its curriculum and child-centred practices. It was Owen who understood the ethics of Pestalozzi's work and who discovered that Fellenberg and Wehrli did not regard education as the acquisition of knowledge so much as the harnessing of potential.

Owen was not a philanthropist in Lady Byron's sense, but he also inspired middle-class innovators like Pemberton and John Minter Morgan, who influenced a relatively well-to-do section of the community with utopian schemes and short-lived educational experiments. However, it is Owen's strivings for working-class educational theory that we wish to stress here. While Robert Owen did his own thinking and remained his own man he clearly bears a debt to Rousseau, Pestalozzi, and Fellenberg as we have seen, and it appears in his educational work. Scottish academics like Mylne and Jardine represent another facet of the European Enlightenment to which Owen responded, and those who responded to Owen in England and Scotland in education represent both practical working-class movements and idealist-utopian middle-class groups.

Lady Byron was also an educational innovator of a different kind, a Christian and a philanthropist who worked for the poor but who did not wish to change society fundamentally. Kay-Shuttleworth was an innovator of great range, a Christian and a tactician who worked for the poor and made educational change with compassion and an eye on the art of the feasible. Owen was the most radical and the most unpractical, an agnostic humanist who worked for the poor and had unrealistic plans for the transformation of school and society. Although his communities failed and his schemes were discredited, in the long run his effect on the social and educational crust was the most seismic of all.

We said earlier that besides the ideas of the Continental theorists the realities of economic and social life had produced their own educational effects in the first half of the nineteenth century, and that if Owen represented one main illustration of this truism, the work of the Hills represented the second.

Theirs was the middle-class rational plan for the sons of successful industrialists. It was a contemporary style, without tradition and custom-built, a direct descendant of utilitarian theory and practice. The plan had a place for the human qualities of dependability and humanity, but it also had the characteristics of a specification for an age that wanted value for money and efficiency without sentiment. It was no accident that Hazelwood began after the Napoleonic Wars at Hill Top in Birmingham, and while integrity and Christian values were unquestioned in the school, the innovations were appropriate for the children of affluent parents with an established future in a wide range of public, commercial, and professional life. The Hills made no attempt to spread their gospel into a system of schools and no one copied Hazelwood, which was probably the most remarkable piece of educational and social planning in the whole period covered by this book. If Owen is chiefly remembered for his contribution to working-class education, the Hills came from and aimed at the man of the new industrial middle class.

At the end of this summary of the period we can state again the four trends in educational innovation that have appeared. First is the rational stream of thought from the European Enlightenment, which flowed more or less directly into English schools through Williams, Day, and the Edgeworths, although there were idiosyncratics like Gilpin and Manson before them. Second, there is the period of assimilation by a man like Owen whose educational work bears traces of the Enlightenment and Pestalozzi and Fellenberg, but whose modulation of middle-class thinking to working-class problems is one of the remarkable contributions to change in this period. Yet it would be to over-simplify if it were not admitted that utopian experiments were not always working-class ventures. The point is, however, that Owen represents a second-generation version, a British adaptation of the Continental influences. Third, there is the straight line of thought from Bentham and Mill to the utilitarian theory and practice of the Hills at Hazelwood for the children of the urban intelligentsia. Fourth, there is the stream of thinking that flows from Pestalozzi and Fellenberg to the philanthropically-minded innovators like Lady Byron and Kay-Shuttleworth, whose work for poor children in the country and in the town made their schools far more liberal and enlightened than was the common practice.

These have been the main lines of educational innovation in the historical context of the hundred years 1750–1850. The story changes as we move into the middle and later years of Victoria's reign, to the era of the great educational Commissions and towards the emerging outlines of general compulsory schooling, the decay of voluntaryism, and the beginnings of a state-provided system of elementary and secondary education.

Part Two

1850–1880

Section One

THE EDUCATION MADNESS

15. New Influences and the Intelligentsia

I

WE live in a highly educational age. Although we have not yet got a system of national education, we are always talking about it, and we mean to have it, and no doubt shall have it some day.[1]

The Great Exhibition of 1851, itself described as a civilizing and educational influence, a 'school of cultivation' for the citizens of London,[2] opened an era of relative prosperity and political calm in which the discussion and elaboration of an unparalleled number of projects and schemes for the development and reform of education occupied public attention. Prominent among them were proposals for a national system of education. A writer in Charles Dickens's journal *All the Year Round* wrote in 1867:

> Probably, fifteen years ago, the national-education mania was at its height. In some curious way, scarcely now to be traced, that part of the nation consisting of the upper and middle classes had suddenly wakened to the necessity of educating the lower class.[3]

The year 1850 had opened with W. J. Fox bringing before the House of Commons a project, based on a proposal of the Lancashire Public Schools Association, for establishing a national system of schools on the basis of local representation and non-interference with religious instruction.[4] Though it was treated with respect by both parties, it

[1] [Harriet Martineau], 'Deaf Mutes', *Household Words*, no. 209, 25 Mar. 1854, p. 134.
[2] *Westminster and Foreign Quarterly Review*, vol. lv. (July 1851), p. 349.
[3] 'The Schoolmaster at Home', *All the Year Round*, no. 445, 2 Nov. 1867, p. 444.
[4] *Parl. Deb.*, 3rd ser., cix (26 Feb. 1850), 27 ff.

was heavily defeated. In October of that year, however, at a conference in Manchester, the Lancashire Association became the National Public Schools Association, announcing a programme of free schools, supported by local rates, managed by local committees elected by ratepayers, giving secular instruction only.[5] It was a programme for national education which after twenty years of discussion and with much modification finally produced the 1870 Education Act.

The theory and practice of education also received attention in the 1850s. In 1854 the Royal Society of Arts organized the first national Education Exhibition ever to be held in Britain. Patronized by prominent public figures from Prince Albert downwards, it gave the public a shop-window not only on the state of educational practice of the time, but also on new ideas and experiments that were then being undertaken. In addition, there were many public lectures by prominent educationalists that further helped to put educational progress before the interested man in the street.

There were many other less noticeable but no less significant manifestations of the educational interest of the period. The number of educational periodicals rose sharply. Visits to schools became a popular hobby ; titled ladies, clergymen, and those with nothing better to do thronged the classrooms, much to the puzzlement of the children and the annoyance of the teachers.[6]

Discussions on a national educational system, the proposals and counter-proposals of the educational reformers, the great Royal Commissions of the 1850s and 1860s, the growing responsibilities of the Committee of Council on Education in developing a national system, are too well known to be noticed in detail here. What is less realized is the development in this period of new attitudes and practices in education that were largely influenced by new and developing social and intellectual forces manifesting themselves in mid-century. Among the most important of these was the movement for a specific middle-class education with new values and a curriculum more fitted to the age ; the ideal of international peace and free diffusion of culture that would follow from the development of world-wide free trade ;[7] above all, the growth of science and the dissemination of the scientific attitude, exemplified in the work of Darwin and Wallace and the writings

---

[5] S. E. Maltby, *Manchester and the Movement for National Elementary Education, 1800–1870* (Manchester, 1918), pp. 67 ff.

[6] *All the Year Round, loc. cit.*, pp. 445–7.   [7] Cf. below, Chap. 19.

of Spencer and Huxley. Nor must we forget the influence of the American system of common schools, which greatly impressed the radical intellectuals,[8] or the great school of Scottish educational reformers in Edinburgh and Glasgow — George Combe, Professor James Simpson, and their followers — whose activities during the generation preceding 1850 were a well-spring of ideas for progressive English educationalists. We shall first consider, however, the general movement for improved and independent middle-class education.

II

The middle class, in this context, were the strata of society associated with Britain's expansion as a world power in technology and commerce in the period of the Industrial Revolution, who had won an instalment of political power in 1832. In 1864 Matthew Arnold included in his definition of the middle class the middling manufacturers, retail tradesmen, and professional classes, in addition to the traditional groupings of clergy, gentry, and Army officers ; in economic terms they were those able to afford from £25 to £50 a year for their sons' education.[9]

The education for which the middle class was willing to pay was widespread but variable. In 1851, some 500,000 children of the middle and upper classes were being educated in 12,000 'superior' and 'middling' schools.[10] Proprietary schools, untrammelled by ancient statute, among the best of which were King's College School (founded 1829), University College School (1830), and Blackheath (also 1830), were created specifically for middle-class needs. The Grammar Schools Act of 1840 opened the way for the development of a wider curriculum in endowed grammar schools by reversing the Eldon Judgement of 1805 which had prohibited Leeds Grammar School from using its endowments to further the study of arithmetic, writing, literature, and modern languages.

Despite these developments, and the fact that the first half of the nineteenth century was the golden age of the private-venture school,

[8] Cf. Harriet Martineau, *Society in America* (London, 3 vols., 1837), iii, pp. 162–78 and App. D, pp. 333–42 ; G. Combe, *Notes on the United States of North America* (Edinburgh, 2 vols., 1841), i, pp. 159 ff., 355 ff.; ii, pp. 40–214.

[9] M. Arnold, *A French Eton ; or, Middle Class Education and the State* (London, 1864), p. 47.

[10] *Census of Great Britain, 1851 : Education* (London, 1854), pp. xxxiii, xliv.

the more articulate members of the middle class were becoming increasingly aware that the education available to them was unco-ordinated, inadequate in content, and variable in quality. As early as 1835 the Rev. R. J. Bryce, Principal of Belfast Academy, complained that the education of the middle classes was less provided for than that of either the higher or lower classes, and urged the formation of schools in which 'the mercantile and professional part of the population' would receive 'an enlarged general education'.[11]   Four years later John Wharton wrote :

> As it must be allowed, that the chief wealth, strength, and vigour of the nation is with the middle-classes . . . the education of that class demands the most serious attention, not only of parents individually, but also by the legislature at large.[12]

The growth of a more or less co-ordinated body of opinion with well-defined objectives on the kind of schools and curriculum acceptable to the increasing number of professional, commercial, and industrial groups, did not really begin until the late 1850s. The Tractarian Nathaniel Woodard's schools, inspired by his pamphlet *A Plea for the Middle Classes* published in 1848, proved something of a false dawn ; his concern, according to his biographer, was for the conversion of 'tradesmen and hucksters' into 'pliable and obedient children of the Church'.[13]   The founding of the National Association for the Promotion of Social Science in 1857 gave the initial impetus to, and provided a forum for, the advocates of organized middle-class education.   The Social Science Association also had links with the contemporary and parallel agitation for raising the status and improving the educational provision for women.   George Hastings, the secretary of the Association, had helped to promote the Married Women's Property Bill of 1857, and worked with Emily Davies, Barbara Bodichon, and others to open up opportunities in higher education for middle-class girls.[14]

In the following decade various aspects of the subject — examinations, the training of teachers, the curriculum — were discussed.   A

---

[11] *Report from the Select Committee on Education in England and Wales*, P.P. (1835), vii, p. 96.

[12] J. Wharton, *The Education of the Middle Classes* (London, 1839), p. 4.

[13] K. E. Kirk, *The Story of the Woodard Schools,* 2nd ed. (Abingdon, 1952), p. 25.

[14] Josephine Kamm, *Hope Deferred : Girls' Education in English History* (London, 1965) pp. 184–6.

number of books and pamphlets appeared in the same period, including T. D. Acland's *The Education of the Farmer, Viewed in Connection with that of the Middle Classes in General* (1857), Earl Fortescue's *Public Schools for the Middle Classes* (1864), Matthew Arnold's *A French Eton*, published in the same year, and J. N. Molesworth's Prize Essay on *The Great Importance of an Improved System of Education* (1867). These authors, with other writers and speakers on middle-class education, put forward a fourfold argument : that the upper classes had their own system of education provided by the universities and great public schools ; that in recent years provision had been made for the education of the working class ; that private schools catering for middle-class children were often of low quality and on the whole tied to a traditional syllabus ; and that these facts pointed to the necessity for an organized provision of middle-class schools that should include the sciences and modern languages in their curriculum. Robert Lowe was merely summing up ten years of debate when he suggested in 1868 that desirable subjects for the middle-classes to study would be the English language, modern languages, mathematics, and the physical sciences.[15]

With the moral weight of Matthew Arnold and Robert Lowe behind the agitation, some practical successes were registered. In 1857 the Oxford and Cambridge Middle Class Examinations were inaugurated, which attempted to introduce a measure of uniformity into the standards of private schools, and in 1866 a private Corporation for Middle-Class Education was set up in London, financed by City merchants and bankers, with the object of building 'a system of education of a practical character, based on sound religious principles, such as shall be calculated to fit the scholars for the industrial and commercial work of life'.[16] William ('Hang Theology') Rogers was its leading spirit, William Ellis lent his aid, and schools were opened by the Corporation at Bath Street, Cowper Street, and elsewhere.

A wider and more up-to-date curriculum was the chief feature of the movement for independent middle-class education, and it was to include science, as might be expected in an age that welcomed Spencer's *Education : Intellectual, Moral, and Physical*. Apart from Spencer's considerable powers of argument, his readability, and the passion and logic with which he put his case, the success of the book can only properly be explained in terms of its fulfilment of the aspirations of a

15 R. Lowe, *Middle Class and Primary Education* (London, 1868), pp. 3–18 *passim*.
16 W. Rogers, *Reminiscences* (London, 1888), p. 164.

large section of educated public opinion. Spencer's text, that the teaching of classics should give way to the teaching of science, and his constant linking of the former with old-fashioned despotic traditions of life and thought and the latter with progress, enterprise, and individuality, could not fail to appeal to his readers. These were largely the Liberal-orientated industrial and commercial middle classes who were in favour of *laissez-faire* and free trade and who welcomed an emphasis on science in education, which distinguished them from the supporters of the classics — mainly the religious and political Establishment, Conservative and protectionist in general outlook.[17]

III

One of the most neglected factors in the rise of the mid-century progressive movement is the influence of the Scottish educational renaissance of the 1830s and 1840s. The schools of Stow and Wood, the secular-school movement in Glasgow and Edinburgh, the development of infant schools, the radically progressive theories of Professor James Simpson and George Combe, were unmatched in the rest of the country. George Combe, the most active propagandist of phrenology in Britain, was the father-figure of the movement. Born in Edinburgh in 1788, he had trained as a lawyer but became a phrenologist in his late twenties after hearing Spurzheim lecture in Edinburgh.[18] He also developed a passionate interest in education and associated himself with a belief in its importance for human development, the formulation of psychological theories based on a rational assessment of the function of the human mind, the fashioning of a wide curriculum in which science would have pre-eminence over the classics and religion, and the advocacy of equal educational opportunities for women. All these propositions can be traced to, or at least were stimulated by, Combe's phrenological theories.

Phrenology was based upon the researches into the localization of brain function of F. J. Gall, the German anatomist, and systematized by his follower Spurzheim.[19] At the lowest level it was represented by the fairground quack with his phrenological chart of the thirty-

[17] A. Price, 'Herbert Spencer and the Apotheosis of Science : I', *Educational Review*, vol. 14, no. 2 (Feb. 1962), pp. 87–97.

[18] C. Gibbon, *The Life of George Combe* (London, 2 vols., 1878), i, pp. 1–115.

[19] J. D. Davies, *Phrenology : Fad and Science* (New Haven, Conn., 1955), *passim*, for a recent account.

seven faculties of the mind, his plaster cast of the human head, and his offer to read a person's 'bumps', characterized in W. S. Gilbert's words:

> Observe his various bumps,
> His head as I uncover it,
> His morals lie in lumps,
> All round about and over it.

That the mind can be analysed into a number of faculties or functions ; that these are localized in different parts of the brain ; that the excess of one faculty is correlated with an enlargement of that particular part of the brain ; and that these variations have a corresponding effect on the exterior formation of the skull may have little scientific validity today.[20] In the scientific climate of the early nineteenth century, however, these propositions brought the mind within the operation of natural laws and up to a point enabled it to be studied objectively. Disorders of the mind, which hitherto had been ascribed to demoniacal possession, witchcraft, or miraculous agency, were now studied in relation to the whole human organism. Psychology was removed from the realm of introspection and metaphysical speculation and the way cleared for a rational observation of human beings. As a modern historian of psychology has said, phrenology was 'an instance of a theory which, while essentially wrong, was just enough right to further scientific thought'.[21] It is hardly accidental that the two immediate forerunners of the Darwinian theory of evolution, Robert Chambers, author of *Vestiges of the Natural History of Creation*, and Alfred Russell Wallace, were both convinced phrenologists.[22]

The possibilities opened up for education by phrenology were farreaching. At the lowest level it provided a sort of ready-made selection test ; one had only to find out the faculties in which one was deficient and then set out to exercise and develop them. In this sense it was well suited to the age of Smilesian self-help, in which the application of science to industry had progressed sufficiently to interest the thinking

---

[20] Cf. G. Combe, *Essays on Phrenology* (Edinburgh, 1819), pp. 1–28 ; *Elements of Phrenology* (Edinburgh, 1824), pp. 18–20 ; *A System of Phrenology* (Edinburgh, 1825), pp. 25–35.

[21] E. G. Boring, *A History of Experimental Psychology* (New York, 2nd ed., 1950), p. 57.

[22] Cf. C. Darwin, *On the Origin of Species* (London, 1859), pp. 1–4 ; R. Chambers, *Vestiges of the Natural History of Creation* (London, 1844), *passim* ; A. R. Wallace, *The Wonderful Century* (London, 1898), pp. 160, 193 ; A. R. Wallace, *My Life* (London, 1905), pp. 255, 355, 362.

man, but in which education was insufficiently developed to have established a widespread scientific response. To the practising teacher phrenology was of service, in the words of W. B. Hodgson,

> not merely in enabling him to form rapid and correct judgement of individual characters, but from its clear and simple philosophy of mind, the light it throws on the nature of the being to be instructed, and consequently on the true aim and wisest methods of education.[23]

On the highest level also phrenology, with its humanism, its scientific basis, and spirit of rational inquiry, opened up new opportunities for the investigation of the mind of the child, for criticism of educational orthodoxies, and a revaluation of traditional disciplines.

J. D. Davies, in a recent American study of the subject, has pointed out that the educational aims and objects of the early nineteenth-century phrenologists sound today remarkably like those of twentieth-century progressive education,[24] and this is apparent. The main impression one gets from reading Spurzheim's *A View of the Elementary Principles of Education*, published in 1821, and Combe's *The Constitution of Man*, which came out seven years later, is of a wide-ranging and comprehensive belief in rational progress, the perfectibility and educability of man, and the necessity of scientific and universal education.[25] The healthy and harmonious development of the individual for the duties of life was the true aim of education, and Combe held that the universe and man were governed by natural laws. All that had to be done was to ascertain the faculties of man, exercise each so as to bring them all into equilibrium, and a happy and useful life would result. It is not difficult to hear the echoes of the European Enlightenment in these ideas.

Combe divided the educational process into two parts — training (the exercise of the faculties) and instruction (the acquisition of knowledge for the tasks of life). Knowledge was of two kinds, instrumental and positive. Instrumental knowledge consisted of the three R's and useful languages, which were in themselves merely a means of acquiring positive knowledge, which consisted of a study of the world and man's place in it.[26] The emphasis on the usefulness of language necessarily

[23] *Phrenological Journal*, vol. ix, n.s., no. lxxxvii (1846).   [24] Davies, p. 81.
[25] J. G. Spurzheim, *A View of the Elementary Principles of Education* (Edinburgh, 1821), *passim* ; G. Combe, *The Constitution of Man* (Edinburgh, 1828), *passim*.
[26] W. Jolly, *Education, Its Principles and Practice as Developed by George Combe* (London, 1879) pp. xxxi–xxxvi.

meant that Latin and Greek were given a subordinate place in Combe's educational scheme. The prevailing faculty theory which was often quoted in support of the classics was rejected on phrenological grounds ; the mind was not a unitary organism that could be trained by study in one discipline only, but consisted of numerous faculties only a few of which were suitable for language training.[27]

In religion, Combe took the deistical position that the Divine Ruler governed through the constitution and laws with which he had endowed the material world, and that man could best apprehend Providence through a study of that world.[28] He rejected the supernatural elements of religion and in true phrenological fashion maintained that religion and morality sprang 'from distinct and independent sources in the human mind'.[29] The teaching of orthodox Christianity was not included in his proposed curriculum.

In an age when the content of education could almost be described as classics for the classes and religion for the masses,[30] Combe's attack on the supremacy of Latin, Greek, and Christianity in the curriculum placed him among the radicals and brought him inevitable criticism from the Churches, who alleged that his partly behaviourist psychology meant a denial of the human will and implied the release of man from moral responsibility for his actions.[31] Owen's environmental theories had come under attack on similar grounds.

Combe's detailed proposals for a curriculum followed logically from his pedagogical principles. The study of anatomy, physiology, and phrenology would give the child a knowledge of man's physical and mental constitution. The physical and moral sciences, including chemistry, natural history, social science, human geography, and political economy, would enable the pupil to place man in his relations to nature and society. The three R's were to be acquired for utilitarian purposes, but neither the classics nor religion was completely excluded.[32] The former was given a subordinate place, along with modern languages ; the latter was termed 'natural religion' and was implicit in

[27] Ibid., pp. 69–86 ; G. Combe, *Discussions on Education*, in *Select Works of George Combe*, vol. iv (London, 1893), p. 34.
[28] Jolly, pp. 123–67 *passim*.   [29] Gibbon, i, p. 198.
[30] Cf. Rev. J. S. Hodgson, *Considerations on Phrenology* (London, 1839), *passim*, an opponent of Combe's who supported this position.
[31] A. C. Grant, 'Combe on Phrenology and Free Will : A Note on Nineteenth-Century Secularism', *Journal of the History of Ideas*, vol. xxvi, no. 1 (1965), pp. 141–7.
[32] Jolly, pp. 23–200 *passim*.

the progressive unfolding of knowledge of the material world. Though this programme was seriously thought out on philosophical lines, Combe was aware that it lacked a humanist element, and in adding the study of literature, poetry, painting, and sculpture he was pioneering liberal studies, possibly to fill the gap formerly supplied by the study of classical cultures.[33]

Combe's position as a pioneer can be appreciated if his proposals are compared with those of supporters of the Central Society of Education, who were active in the late 1830s. Though the Society had been founded to study education with the object of giving 'the theory of education a more scientific character than it has yet assumed',[34] and though its leading member, Sir Thomas Wyse, and the winner of its Prize Essay, John Lalor, were familiar with the methods of Pestalozzi and the latest Continental reformers,[35] the thinking of the Society always had affinities with the philanthropic ethic of the eighteenth and nineteenth centuries. Duppa, the secretary, was, as we have seen, a supporter of agricultural schools, and Wyse's picture of 'the educated labourer', independent, contented, sober, industrious, and religious, could stand as the classic early-Victorian image of what the educated classes hoped to make of the 'lower orders'.[36] It was worlds away from the free, rational, scientifically-orientated individuals of Combe's ideal.

Like all who proposed encyclopaedic, scientific curricula at this period, Combe's schemes were heavily weighted with inert knowledge. The pupils were expected to familiarize themselves with masses of fact and information, and Combe assumed that this knowledge would be of direct practical use to everyone.[37] Although his intention was to supersede the narrowness, obscurantism, and reverence of the past for its own sake which he felt was strangling education, he was limited by lack of understanding of the value of experimental science. Nevertheless, Combe's educational writings in the period when the battle against the dominance of religion and the classics was first being joined

---

[33] A. Price, 'A Pioneer of Scientific Education: George Combe (1788–1858)', *Educational Review*, vol. 12, no. 3 (1960), p. 225.

[34] Central Society of Education, *First Publication* (London, 1837), p. 2.

[35] T. Wyse, *Education Reform ; or, the Necessity of a National System of Education* (London, 1836), *passim* ; J. Lalor, Prize Essay, in *The Educator : Prize Essays on the Expediency and Means of Elevating the Profession of the Educator in Society* (London, 1839), *passim*.

[36] Wyse, pp. 313–23.   [37] Cf. Price, *Educational Review*, pp. 224–5.

on a large scale, directly affected the work of public men such as Richard Cobden [38] and of English educators such as William Ellis, whose ideas, as we shall show in Chapter 20, were diffused widely in the 1850s and 1860s.

Combe's educational thinking was mainly in the philosophical and theoretical sphere, although he supported universal free state education, co-education, and improved training and status for teachers,[39] and radically new and interesting proposals for the reform of the organization and structure of education were put forward by his associate, Professor James Simpson. A Scottish lawyer and writer, born in 1781, and a friend of Sir Walter Scott, Simpson had helped Combe to establish the *Phrenological Journal* in 1823.[40] Simpson made his mark on English educational thinking with a marathon performance as a witness to the Select Committee on Education in England and Wales in 1835. He was examined over a period of eleven days and his evidence, affixed to the Report as an appendix, occupies eighty-five folio pages.[41]

Simpson had also been touched by the Enlightenment. As a young man in Edinburgh he had addressed the Speculative Society on the philosophy of William Godwin, and heard his fellow lawyer John Jardine talk on 'Rousseau's System of Education'.[42] Simpson was the earliest advocate of what today we call comprehensive education. He wished to give to boys and girls together, 'for all ranks without distinction', an elementary education that would be 'as perfect as possible'. This was to be given in co-educational schools for children between the ages of six and fourteen years as a precursor of a selective higher system.[43] 'It would make the whole nation,' he argued, 'in point of education and of light, one family, and tend materially to aid the whole by the exertions of all.' [44] This education would be compulsory, free, and state-aided, and administered by a Minister of Public Instruction and Board of Education, aided by a corps of Inspectors.[45] The content of the education would be similar to that advocated by Combe, distinguished by the absence of corporal punishment, the separation of secular and religious instruction, and the postponement of language learning until after the age of fourteen.[46] This was the

---

[38] J. Morley, *The Life of Richard Cobden* (London, 2 vols., 1881), i, p. 93.
[39] Jolly, pp. xliv–xlvii.   [40] *Dictionary of National Biography*.
[41] *Select Committee* (1835), App. 3, pp. 121–206.
[42] *History of the Speculative Society of Edinburgh* (Edinburgh, 1845), p. 220.
[43] *Select Committee* (1835), pp. 121–3, 135–7.
[44] Ibid., p. 125.   [45] Ibid., pp. 135–51.   [46] Ibid., pp. 167–8.

most advanced educational programme of the first part of the century, and pointed the way to new perspectives in organization and administration.

III

The innovators whose work in founding, organizing, or aiding experimental schools will be considered in detail in later chapters consisted of William Ellis, businessman and philanthropist and founder of the Birkbeck schools ; Barbara Bodichon (*née* Leigh Smith), educational reformer and feminist ; Henry Morley, sometime general practitioner, journalist on Dickens's *Household Words*, later a professor at London University but early in life the head of a progressive school ; and Johannes and Bertha Ronge, German refugees and founders of the first kindergarten on English soil. All could be described as middle-class intellectuals, all were influenced in varying degrees by the advanced thought of their age, and all moved in a circle that brought them a wide range of professional and social contacts.

There were two foci that gave cohesion to the intellectual life out of which these educational experiments grew. One was the periodicals of Charles Dickens, whose interest in education was reflected in his novels to a greater extent than with any other nineteenth-century novelist. He was always willing to open the pages of *Household Words* and *All the Year Round* to accounts of anything new and unorthodox in the educational field. His interest in education was shared by contributors and members of his staff, including W. H. Wills, Harriet Martineau, and Henry Morley. The last of these three gave up the headship of a highly original school to join Dickens as a journalist. A study of Bruce Castle School, another of Morley's establishment, one of Ellis's institutions, and a fourth of Ronge's kindergarten appeared in the pages of Dickens's periodicals.[47] Dickens himsel frequently visited Ronge's school, which was a few minutes' walk from where he was living in the early 1850s.[48]

The second focus was the house of George Chapman at 142 Strand. Chapman, a friend and associate of Dickens, was a magnificently handsome publisher of great charm and energy, the ideal host for the intellectual coterie he gathered around himself in the early 1850s.

[47] P. A. W. Collins, *Dickens and Education*, Vaughan College Papers, no 3 (Leicester, 1957), *passim*.
[48] P. W. A. Collins, *Dickens and Education* (London, 1963), p. 41.

Critical of organized religion and eager to embrace new scientific and intellectual ideas, he published chiefly advanced religious and philosophical works, including volumes of Emerson and George Eliot's translation of Strauss's *Das Leben Jesu*. From January 1852 he edited and published the radical *Westminster Review*, with George Eliot as assistant editor.[49]

142 Strand became famous for its social gatherings, usually held on Monday evenings. Thackeray, Dickens, Carlyle, and Mrs. Gaskell were among the literary figures who were occasionally present. The most frequent attenders were George Eliot (who lodged there), Herbert Spencer, who lived nearby at 340 Strand and was then sub-editor of the *Economist*, William Ellis, Barbara Bodichon, who was Chapman's mistress for a short while in the mid-1850s, William Ballantyne Hodgson, R. W. Mackay the Biblical critic and disciple of Strauss and Bauer, J. A. Froude the historian, Francis Newman (a brother of the Cardinal), Harriet Martineau, W. R. Greg, Sir David Brewster the physicist, George Combe, Thornton Hunt (son of Leigh Hunt), and George Henry Lewes.[50] During the 1850s Hunt and Lewes conducted the *Leader*, which was managed by the veteran Owenite and Co-operator G. J. Holyoake. It gave regular news of Continental revolutionary activities, sought changes in the economic system in the direction of a rather vague socialism, criticized the Established Church in the light of humanistic 'true religion', and in education advocated a secular state system and the ending of the hold of the Established Church on elementary schools and of the classics on higher education.[51]

Hunt and Lewes were described by Mrs. Lynn Linton, the novelist, who had been a boarder in Chapman's house in Clapton in the middle 1840s, as

> essentially free thinkers — not on theological questions to which the term is usually narrowed, but on all moral and social matters whatsoever, beginning at the beginning and working up towards the apex.[52]

To a greater or lesser extent this description could be applied to the whole group. Among their concerns were the improved status and

[49] G. S. Haight, *George Eliot and John Chapman* (New Haven, Conn., 1940), pp. 3–41 *passim*.

[50] Ibid., pp. 43, 137, 217; E. S. Haldane, *George Eliot and Her Times* (London, 1927), p. 69.

[51] A. T. Kitchel, *George Lewes and George Eliot* (New York, 1933), pp. 63–89.

[52] Mrs. Lynn Linton, *My Literary Life* (London, 1899), pp. 22–23.

higher education of women, greater freedom in personal relationships
both within and between the sexes, a critique of orthodox Christianity,
and a fervent belief in the importance of science in education and the
national life. To an extraordinary degree the scientific aspect of phrenology had provided an intellectual leaven for several of the group even
before their later friendship with Combe. Herbert Spencer had been
influenced by Spurzheim's lectures at an early age ; [53] Combe's *Moral
Philosophy*, read in her teens, had permanently influenced the thinking
of Barbara Bodichon.[54] Ellis's determination to open schools that
would teach social science was inspired by a re-reading of Combe,[55]
and Hodgson had been lecturing on phrenology in Scotland in his
early twenties,[56] while George Eliot had been sufficiently impressed
by the arguments of the Coventry Owenite and phrenologist Charles
Bray to have a cast made of her head.[57]

In the sphere of education, the sympathies of several members of
the Chapman circle were with the general aims of the movement for
middle-class education, particularly those concerned with the incor-
poration of science and modern languages in the curriculum. In
addition, they evinced a general distrust of Christianity and of classical
culture in the traditional system. It is no surprise to discover that
Spencer, Ellis, Combe, Hodgson, Hunt, and Lewes had not attended
an English public school or university. The details of the foundation
and organization of the various schools with which the members of
this group were later connected differed widely, though each was a
product of the age and could not have existed in that form at an earlier
time. Besides emphasizing the place of science as against religion and
classics in the curriculum, and developing new teaching methods and
substitutes for corporal punishment, these schools demonstrated innovations such as co-education, the mingling of different social classes
in the schoolroom, the teaching of social science, education in the ideals
of international co-operation, and a new approach to infant development. All of these were of immense importance to the future, as we
shall see in succeeding chapters.

[53] H. Spencer, *An Autobiography* (London, 2 vols., 1904), i, p. 200.
[54] Hester Burton, *Barbara Bodichon* (London, 1949), pp. 14–15.
[55] Cf. below, Chap. 20.   [56] *Dictionary of National Biography*.
[57] Haight, pp. vii, 168 n.

James Buchanan

Samuel Wilderspin

The infant school playground as visualised by Samuel Wilderspin

16. Henry Morley's School

HENRY MORLEY'S reputation rests mainly upon his professorship of English Literature at University College, London, and on his editorship of Morley's Universal Library, a series of popular literary works of the late Victorian period. His academic apprenticeship was varied and unusual. He trained and practised as a doctor, worked as a journalist on Dickens's *Household Words*, and for two years from 1849 he conducted a very successful progressive school at Liscard in Cheshire. This school had several features that were quite unusual even for schools of this type, and Morley's original ideas on education entitle him to a leading place among the experimental educationalists of his time.

Morley's portrait shows a broad face with intelligent eyes and a steady gaze ; in appearance he was somewhat like the conventional *Punch* drawings of John Bull. His independent and somewhat pugnacious character had been formed during his youth when he attended as unpleasant a collection of private boarding-schools as ever was satirized later by Charles Dickens. His educational development took a more pleasant turn from a fortunate decision of his father to send him to school in Germany, to an institution kept by the Moravian Brethren at Neuwied on the Rhine. This school had a European reputation and accepted large numbers of English boys. Morley spent the years from 1833 to 1835 there, preceding by a decade another English pupil, the novelist George Meredith.[1] Neuwied had an important effect on Morley's whole future.[2] He ceased to regard schoolmasters as natural enemies, dropped his aggressive habits, and reshaped his attitude to education.[3]

At Neuwied the emphasis was upon freedom and the development of the imagination :

The heart was stirred, the soul was roused, the affections were satisfied, no check was set upon the fancy, and we were abundantly provided with material for voluntary exercise of thought. What if we did learn little Algebra and little Greek ! Every one of us was

[1] S. M. Ellis, *George Meredith* (London, 1919), pp. 41–45.
[2] H. S. Solly, *The Life of Henry Morley, LL.D.* (London, 1898), p. 25.
[3] [H. Morley], 'Brother Mieth and His Brothers', *Household Words*, no. 218, 27 May 1854, p. 345.

E.I.—U

being humanised in the best way, and trained to become a thinker and a student for himself, thereafter.[4]

There were a hundred and fifty boys in the school in groups of twenty, each supervised by two Brothers ; they ate in one refectory, and slept in one huge dormitory. They lived together, in Morley's phrase, 'as a sort of federal republic'. The classes were arranged in sets according to attainment and there was no corporal punishment, merely nominal punishments to guide errant scholars. The Moravian teachers themselves, Morley remembered, had 'a childlike simplicity of mind and purpose', and Morley quickly identified himself with the purpose of the school. With his fellow-pupils he collected bees and butterflies, acted out dramas of robbers among the rocks and nearby woods, and devoured book after book of folk-tales. He became the official poet and story-teller for the school, able to produce verses on birthdays and school feasts and to tell miraculous stories to his fellow-pupils to order.[5]

On his return from Neuwied he went to another school at Stockwell in London, and then, at the age of sixteen, he transferred to King's College, London, a few years after it had opened, to study medicine. He matriculated at London University in 1839 and continued his studies for another four years. In 1843 he took up a medical practice in Dunster, Somerset ; a year later he went to Madeley in Shropshire, where he became involved with a fraudulent partner and fell heavily into debt. During these years he began to take an interest in public health and wrote several tracts on the subject and contributed to the short-lived *Journal of Public Health*.[6] He also began to interest himself in education and read widely on the subject. Realizing that there was no living to be made in sanitary reform, he decided 'to work out in real life my ideal of a teacher's calling'.[7] His early school experiences both in England and Germany had given him ideas and convictions of his own on what should be done in education.

He left Madeley in 1848, the year of revolutions, and he was greatly influenced by the events in Europe and by the educational reforms of Pope Pius IX. Morley embodied the ideas on education that these reforms had suggested to him in a book of poems called *Sunrise in Italy*. It contains several poems and sonnets in praise of the French Revolution of 1848, but the major part consisted of the eponymous 'Sunrise

[4] [H. Morley], p. 346.　　　[5] Ibid., p. 347.　　　[6] Solly, pp. 34 ff.
[7] H. Morley, *Early Papers and Some Memories* (London, 1891), p. 25.

in Italy', which was in effect a dissertation on the principles of education in which Morley had come to believe, and the influence of the Moravian environment was clearly visible. The poem shows that he believed in the innate goodness and capacity for development of children, given a natural environment and no coercion from a stern parent or schoolmaster. The world of intellect was open to the growing mind, but natural science ought to be the foundation of study, supplemented by history and languages to facilitate international co-operation.[8]

With these principles as a basis Morley decided to open a school of his own at the earliest opportunity. 'This was my own small Revolution of 1848', he recalled.[9] He decided to start his school in Manchester and he arrived there with 7s. 6d. in his pocket, rented an unfurnished room, slept on a packing-case, and sold his books to keep alive. Despite the privations his prospects seemed exciting and stimulating :

> I rejoice in the prospect of a life of uninterrupted study, gained upon the condition that I earn my bread and fulfil my use in the community by teaching what I learn. Jenny Lind in 'Elijah', February 6 — won't I be there ! I'll sell my books to buy a ticket.[10]

In January 1849 Morley issued a prospectus, the first sentence of which read :

> THE PLAN OF EDUCATION will differ very much from that which is in common use.[11]

The school would include, apart from the usual elements of commercial education, a laboratory for practical instruction in the elements of chemistry, a reading-room, and a library. The teaching would be on an individual basis as far as possible ; 'Pains will be taken to give life to the study of the Ancient Classics', and the English language, literature, and composition 'will be taught somewhat more elaborately than is usual'.[12]

Despite, or possibly because of, the promise of individual instruction, the advertisement produced nothing. No pupils whatsoever arrived for tuition. Possibly the fees frightened off the parents of prospective pupils ; they were 10s. 6d. a week for a forty-eight week year, or over £25 a year, exclusive of books, school material, and dinners. In

---

[8] H. Morley, *Sunrise in Italy* (London, 1848), pp. 1–63 *passim*.
[9] Morley, *Early Papers*, p. 27.   [10] Solly, p. 108.
[11] Ibid., p. 101.   [12] Ibid., p. 102.

addition, the course in chemistry cost an extra twenty guineas a year.[13]
This was an extravagant charge for a day school — William Ellis was
running his schools at a cost of 6d. a week and no extra charges.
Despite his entry into Manchester society — he was friendly with the
Gaskells, G. H. Lewes, and Dr. Hodgson — Morley decided to leave
the city and pursue his future further west, and still poverty-stricken,
he walked to Liverpool to seek out the possibilities of opening a school
in that district :

> For want of money to spend upon railway fares, I walked from
> Manchester to Liverpool, fell among friends, and walked back from
> Liverpool to Manchester with my best hopes fulfilled.[14]

His 'best hopes' had been an offer by Charles Holland, Gaskell's
brother-in-law, a Liverpool merchant living in Liscard, Wallasey.
With a group of other merchants he guaranteed Morley a salary of
£100 a year if he would start a school to educate their sons. Morley
agreed and opened a school at 2 Marine Terrace, Liscard. It was a
tall, red-brick building that is still standing, with large windows looking out on to the sands, the river with its shipping, and Liverpool on
the opposite shore. Opened in the spring of 1849, in Morley's twenty-
seventh year, it was a co-educational school taking children from eight
to fifteen years of age.

What Morley tried to do can best be understood if we follow the
theories he sketched out in an article for Dickens's *Household Words*
called 'Schoolkeeping'.[15] He explained that he had four 'crotchets'
upon which he thought all school organization should be based. The
first concerned general principles of teaching. 'There is only one set
of right principles,' he maintained, 'but there may be ten thousand
plans.' The key was for each teacher to sort out the principles that
suited himself, assimilate them to his own nature, and then throw the
whole of his personality into his work. Above all, whatever method
he chose, it should be animated by his heart and brain, and be completely
alive and spontaneous.[16]

Secondly, the ideal qualifications for a teacher were integrity, an
utter opposition to falsehood, quick apprehension, and a lively imagination. Most important of all, the teacher should be fond of children

13 Solly, p. 102.   14 Ibid., p. 122.
15 H. Morley, 'Schoolkeeping', *Household Words*, no. 200, 21 Jan. 1854, pp. 499–
504.   16 Ibid., p. 500.

and have faith in the essential goodness of childhood — 'A main point which many teachers will refuse to uphold'. In addition the teacher should be a man of high culture and attainment, able to show the interconnection between various disciplines. Morley's list of attainments for a teacher would seem staggering even today ; his ideal teacher would have a knowledge of classical languages, at least two modern languages, mathematics, a command of world history, a good acquaintance with the latest travel books, a full elementary knowledge of 'the entire circle of the sciences', and a familiarity with the political and social movements of the day. 'All this will be too much for one man,' conceded Morley, 'but it is not too much for one man and a library.' This was not all. When a teacher had acquired the necessary breadth of cultivation, Morley insisted that 'depth must be maintained by constant and habitual study'. He was setting his standards high, but it is only fair to say that he reached them himself. In fact, much of the basis of his later learning seems to have been laid in preparations that he undertook for teaching in his Liscard school.[17]

As his third 'crotchet' Morley had great faith in the educability of children ; 'children are good', he maintained, 'and they are so created by Divine Wisdom as to be wonderfully teachable'. On the other hand they were also created to be active, restless, and incapable of continuous exertion. Teachers should take this into account and avoid making the children sit still on forms for hours on end.[18]

Morley's fourth 'crotchet' concerned the constitution of the school. Remembering perhaps his own early experiences, he wanted to abolish corporal punishment from schools altogether. If children were interested in their lessons and led by their affections, he believed that the whole work of the school could be carried on entirely without coercion, given perfect openness of speech and conduct throughout the school. He made each pupil sign a book, formally promising in all his dealings with the teacher and with his companions 'to act openly and speak the truth'. On this act he based a 'fundamental law' — that the first falsehood would be forgiven but that the second would mean instant expulsion. In practice he found that this worked admirably and he had occasion to expel only one boy, a youth of sixteen who had been 'blunted in feeling by the long course of mismanagement'.[19]

Morley was well fitted by temperament and attainments to carry out the ideals that he laid down. A man of great physical energy —

[17] Ibid., p. 501.   [18] Ibid.   [19] Ibid., p. 502.

as we have seen, he thought little of walking from Liverpool to Manchester and back — he had remarkable facility in writing. He claimed that he could compose an article faster than anybody in Fleet Street and rarely had to correct or alter what he had written.[20] He had an ebullient nature, was fond of charades, games, and romping with children, and with his schoolchildren he would often 'dance like a wild Indian, roll on the floor or in the sand, make such a child of myself'.[21] He had, in addition, a streak of unconventionality which fitted him for his self-appointed task of founding an experimental school; he had been, he claimed, 'educated into an exaggerated and somewhat false taste for outraging over-propriety'.[22]

Morley believed that the schoolroom should be the best room in the house and he spared no pains to give it a cheerful and elegant appearance. The floor was carpeted and the children sat on chairs and had tables instead of desks; the walls were covered with a richly decorated wallpaper and the mantelpiece was always covered with vases of freshly cut flowers.[23]

Morley broke with the usual routine of schooling, and attempted to introduce as much flexibility as possible into the organization and curriculum. The school day was divided into two parts, and in the first part the children studied what Morley called the means of education, mathematics, and languages, mainly from books. The second part was devoted to history, geography, science, and similar studies. Monday mornings, however, were given over to talk and discussions on current affairs and the children were encouraged to bring their knowledge of history, geography, and other subjects to bear on the events of the day. After some experience of this the children were able to relate past and present events in a way that would have warmed any teacher's heart:

> They bewildered me by their minute acquaintance with the recent discoveries at the North Pole, which they had acquired while their hearts were full of sympathy for Sir John Franklin. There was a new scientific discovery of which they were endeavouring to understand as much as possible, and they were criticising social movements in a startling way.[24]

When news was scarce, Monday mornings were given over to

---

[20] Solly, pp. 151, 205.   [21] Ibid., p. 132.   [22] Ibid., p. 156.
[23] Ibid., pp. 119, 123, 126.   [24] Morley, 'Schoolkeeping', p. 503.

lessons on common things — explanations of everyday words and objects.

One of the most important features of the school was the system of mutual examinations. Morley instituted this partly because of the limitations inherent in oral lessons given by the teacher, and partly as a check on the progress of the children. The school was divided into two sides, Greens and Blues, 'after the two factions of the Roman Circus', and each side asked the other a question in turn on a subject recently learned, every question being noted in a book by Morley himself and scores calculated on a fixed scale.[25] He soon noticed that the children began with thoughts rather than things. For example : 'Why does China stand still in her civilization ?' ; 'Why did our civilization begin on the shores of the Mediterranean ?' ; 'Why is England so particularly prosperous — why not some other island ?' Later on, however, questions began to be asked on natural history, meteorology, astronomy, geology, and other subjects.[26] Morley found that these lessons encouraged children to take notes and to search through books of reference.

Morley did not entirely abandon lectures. He would master a subject thoroughly, give a formal lecture, and follow it with a period for questions and answers. His own researches gave these lectures a high value ; for his history lectures, for instance, he studied the works of Champollion, Sir William Jones, Milman, and Gibbon.[27] He also made himself acquainted with a wide range of elementary sciences.

Grammar was taught systematically and included study of the sources of the language and the leading facts of philology. The technicalities of Latin were not insisted upon, an attempt being made to approach the language for the thoughts that it contained. Arithmetic was based on William de Morgan's recently published textbook. History covered the history of man, beginning with Nineveh and Babylon and carrying on up to the present day, the idea being to present a complete history of mankind in a three-year course. There was a great deal of reading of literature, particularly of Shakespeare, whom Morley considered to be a poet suitable for children as well as for adults,[28] and occasionally he would invent a story of his own, reviving his boyhood skill at Neuwied. The first hour of every

---

[25] [H. Morley], *A Defence of Ignorance* (London, 1851), pp. 17–18.
[26] Morley, 'Schoolkeeping', p. 504.   [27] Solly, pp. 127, 166.
[28] Ibid., p. 127.

afternoon was given over to the study of natural science and natural history, beginning with the creation of the world.

Morley had little time for denominational religion. He began by teaching from the Bible, but in his own words 'I was tired of hopping round the vulgar literal reading of the Cosmos in Moses'.[29] Finding that study of the Bible stood in the way of the children acquiring a knowledge of science, he tried a more critical approach to religious studies, taking courage from some works of higher criticism that had recently been published. He pointed out to the children the evidently legendary character of much Old Testament history, and showed how the advances of human knowledge had made it possible to reinterpret these events in a rational manner. Morley himself took a deistical view of religion but taught nothing that was inconsistent with any Christian belief. However, his school gained a reputation for heterodox theology and he lost one or two possible pupils because of it.[30]

Nevertheless, the number of children increased and when they began to exceed twenty, Morley found that it was impossible to carry on without some system of rewards and punishments, mainly because of the difficulties associated with 'the joyousness and restlessness of youth'. He abjured corporal punishment, scorn or sarcasm, and competition solely for material reward. He worked on the principle of making the penalties consist of a gain or loss of credit and of getting the pupils working for their own sake to a common standard of application and attention. Rewards were limited to the half-yearly presentation of books. Each pupil received one book, marked either first, second, or third prize, but the difference between them was not expressed in money values. Penalties were in the form of tickets; any interruption of school work counted as one penalty mark, three penalty marks were equivalent to the loss of half a day, and six to the loss of a whole day, which was represented by a ticket. At the end of a half-year the number of tickets and fractions of days lost were counted for each pupil and this total helped to determine whether or not he received a first, second, or third prize.[31] It was theoretically possible, of course, for every pupil to receive a first prize.

Punishment under this system derived from failure to be included in the prize-list. Morley's supreme punishment was based on the same principles of deprivation and consisted of nothing less than the com-

---

[29] Solly, p. 127.   [30] Ibid., pp. 133, 165, 185.
[31] Morley, 'Schoolkeeping', pp. 502-3.

plete abandonment of lessons. Such a sensational reversal of traditional educational practice was possible on one condition — that the children enjoyed lessons so much that their loss was keenly felt :

> Now and then it happened that some great event outside, such as the freezing of a pond, produced an irrepressible excitement. Common restraints would not check talking and inattention. The punishment then introduced was horrible to tell :—There was no teaching. All lessons were put aside. Instead of extra lessons for a punishment, no lessons appeared to me the best mark of supreme displeasure. Lessons were not to be regarded as their pain, but as their privilege ; when they became too unmanageable the privilege was for a time withdrawn.[32]

Morley's educational experiment unfortunately lasted for only two years. Despite the fees of ten guineas a year, he was unable to get out of debt. He gave up the school to work with Charles Dickens in London, mainly in order to pay off his debts. In June 1851 he was offered a position on the staff of *Household Words* at five guineas a week.[33]

His success in London needs little telling. He remained on *Household Words* and its successor *All the Year Round* until 1865. During this time he became a lecturer in English Literature to evening classes at King's College. In 1861 he became editor of the *Examiner*, a post he retained until 1867, and in 1865 he succeeded to the chair of English Language and Literature at University College, London, in which post he became the foremost popularizer of English literature, particularly of Shakespeare, of the late Victorian era.[34]

Of all the progressive and experimental educationalists of the mid-nineteenth century Morley had the highest ideals, the most impressive natural qualities and abilities for teaching, and the courage to introduce a great range of innovations. He had penetrating insight into what education might really become and the ability to mould school organizations and curricula in order to bring this about. He affirmed that the key to the improvement of education was to raise teachers' ideals :

> They must not look upon the child's mind as a thing to be impregnated with Latin verbs, and trained into a deep distrust at Cicero,

---

[32] Ibid., p. 503.   [33] J. W. T. Ley, *The Dickens Circle* (London, 1918), p. 308.
[34] Solly, pp. 226, 251, 355 ff.

and sickening horror at Herodotus. It is a spirit to be trained to
thoughtfulness, and to be furnished with materials of thought. . . .
The teacher who shall send a child into the world thoughtful,
observant, seeking knowledge, and not shrinking from a little difficulty in obtaining it ; a youth with a free mind, taught to reason,
and determined only upon truth, by whatever process he has come
to that result ; he is the enemy of Ignorance.[35]

17. Johannes Ronge and the Humanistic Schools

'THE first great English student of the Kindergarten', said J. L.
Hughes, an ardent Froebelian, in his book describing Charles Dickens,
Dickens as an Educator.[1] Dickens has had more than his share of praise
and attribution, but a fair appreciation can scarcely support this.
Hughes based his case not only on an article on the kindergarten in
Household Words in 1855, but on the similarity between Dickens's
humane aspirations for children, his desire to free them from the kind
of education represented by Squeers, the Blimbers, and Gradgrind,
and Froebel's theories of the free development of the infant through
creative and congenial play activities.

This conception of Dickens as the first English Froebelian has been
put into perspective by P. A. W. Collins in an article in the *National
Froebel Foundation Bulletin*. Collins shows that, although Dickens was
cognizant of the first English kindergarten, which was founded in
Hampstead in 1851, and publicized its work in his journals (his attention having been drawn to it by Mrs. Gaskell, the novelist), he was no
theoretical Froebelian, nor did he write the article in *Household Words*,[2]
which was the work of Henry Morley, his staff writer and also a friend
of Mrs. Gaskell. Nevertheless, Dickens deserves recognition as the

[35] [Morley], *A Defence of Ignorance*, pp. 22–23.
[1] J. L. Hughes, *Dickens as an Educator* (New York, 1900), p. 3.
[2] P. A. W. Collins, 'A Note on Dickens and Froebel', *National Froebel Foundation
Bulletin*, no. 94 (June 1955), pp. 15–18.

first English editor to put Froebel's name and achievements before the public.

The kindergarten referred to in *Household Words* was run by Johannes and Bertha Ronge, German refugees from the reaction in the German states that followed the failure of the revolution in 1848. Like Morley's school at Liscard, their kindergarten could be considered as an indirect offspring of the year of the revolution. Johannes Ronge had a reputation in his own right as the leader of a breakaway from the Roman Catholic Church in Germany, an act that won him the title of the 'Luther of the nineteenth century'. The affair of the Holy Coat of Trèves, and Ronge's part in it, now totally forgotten, was one of the sensations of the 1840s.[3]

In 1844 Bishop Arnoldi of Trèves, wishing to raise money for the repair and embellishment of the cathedral of that city, put on display a relic, reputedly the seamless coat said to have been worn by Jesus Christ at the Crucifixion. Between August and October of that year, between half a million and a million pilgrims (the accounts vary), mostly peasants, the poor and the ignorant, left their land and their homes and gave up their savings to make pilgrimage to Trèves in conditions of greatest hardship and squalor to see the Holy Coat hanging high above the Cathedral altar, and to offer their pence to the cathedral. Plenary indulgence for ever was granted to those who made the pilgrimage, confessed their sins, and contributed to the repairs of the cathedral. During the whole summer there were ceremonies, hymns, processions, and the sale of prints and medallions ; reputed cures of serious illnesses effected by the sight of the Holy Coat increased the number of pilgrims. But starvation and disease were rife among those crowded into and around the city.

Before the exhibition had been in progress a month Johannes Ronge, an obscure chaplain from Breslau, acted. He was humiliated not only by the open appeal to credulity and superstition but also by the acceptance of money from the poor and starving. Ronge issued a manifesto that declared that such practices degraded Germany in the eyes of the world and led to her mental slavery and the strengthening of the tyranny of Rome. This appeal to nationalist feeling, and the plea for

[3] The following account is based on A. Andresen, *Luther Revived* (London, 1845) ; *A German Catholic's Farewell to Rome*, by an English Resident in Germany (London, 1845) ; J. Fretwell, ' Johannes Ronge and the English Protestants', *Unitarian Review*, Jan. 1888.

the preservation of the spirit rather than the observances of the Church, evoked an immediate response. Ronge became almost a national hero, and within a few months the Catholic communities in no less than eighty-nine towns had severed their ties with the Church and a German Catholic Church had been set up which renounced the authority of Rome, rejected all the doctrines and practices introduced by the priesthood, declared the Bible to be the sole source of their faith, and extended toleration to all other confessions.

The similarity between this schism and the Reformation of the fifteenth century need hardly be pointed out, but Ronge himself was no Luther. He was a courageous and energetic reformer, but he evinced no extraordinary personal qualities, nor was he an outstanding theologian. His manifesto had started an avalanche that was ready to fall, but he failed to dominate the movement.

Ronge was elected to the Frankfurt Parliament in 1848, but within two years had been forced to flee in the face of the persecution of the democrats. But before he left Germany he had married Bertha, a daughter of the wealthy Meyer family, and an energetic and enthusiastic disciple of Friedrich Froebel, the founder of the kindergarten movement. She engaged Froebel to live with her and a number of friends for a period of six months, to teach them his doctrines before they went to different parts of Germany to set up kindergartens themselves.[4] Bertha's educational principles fused with the new religion of humanity being preached by her husband. Schools were set up in connection with the Reform communities, whose broad general aims — the development of individual character and the removal of undue restraints upon its growth — harmonized well with the principles upon which Froebel organized his kindergarten. The German Reform communities were thus both religious and educational societies, and they organized several excellent schools, a feature of which was the direct co-operation between parents and teachers in the running of the institutions.[5]

The Ronges left Germany for England with a hatred of creeds, priesthoods, and governmental despotism, but like many exiles they found adaptation to their new country initially very difficult. They

[4] B. Ronge, 'On Infant Training', *Journal of the Society of Arts*, vol. ii, no. 94, 8 Sept. 1854, pp. 711–12.

[5] 'At Home and at School', *All the Year Round*, vol. i, no. 24, 8 Oct. 1859, pp. 571–3.

spoke the language badly and their habits puzzled their friends. William Bell Scott, poet and painter, and friend of D. G. Rossetti, who gave the Ronges hospitality, described their meeting thus :

> A short, strongly-made man, with an expressive, well-formed face and thick black beard, advanced to meet us with the worst possible attempt at English, ending in unmixed German. We received an exuberant welcome, and were introduced to a lady of goodly presence, the noble Bertha, who had cast in her lot with the apostolic Johannes. . . .[6]

Scott saw Ronge as a simple, open character, physically strong and courageous, but his Teutonic habits scarcely endeared him to the household. He rose at five o'clock in the morning, called for coffee, lit his fire, and deluged the whole room with water from his bath. He had, in fact, an addiction to cold water, hanging out his wet sheets in the morning to dry on the rail at the head of the stairs.[7] But both Bertha and Johannes Ronge gradually improved their command of English, modified their habits somewhat, and settled in London, first at Hampstead and then at 32 Tavistock Place, St. Pancras, and they set up a kindergarten and later an Association School, which attempted to present to senior pupils the principles of Froebel fused with Ronge's new religion of humanity.

Froebel was one of those reformers who succeed in permanently changing the face of education. W. H. Kilpatrick, one of Froebel's most critical American admirers, considered that he had made education take 'a complete about face', in that he altered people's whole way of looking at childhood.[8] Though Rousseau and Pestalozzi, Froebel's spiritual and educational ancestors, had initiated the idea of 'child-centred' education, Froebel was the first to apply it, on an elaborately worked-out theoretical and practical basis, to those children normally educated in infant schools. He demonstrated that children's normal and natural play activities, guided and stimulated by the teachers, were an essential element of the learning process.

Friedrich Froebel was born in Thuringia in 1782, and after an apprenticeship to forestry, studied at the University of Jena, became a teacher at Frankfurt, worked under Pestalozzi at Yverdon, and after

[6] W. B. Scott, *Autobiographical Notes* (London, 2 vols., 1892), i, p. 336.

[7] Ibid., p. 337 ; W. J. Linton, *Memories* (London, 1895), p. 170.

[8] W. H. Kilpatrick, *Froebel's Kindergarten Principles Critically Examined* (New York, 1916), p. 207.

further study, teaching, and writing opened his first kindergarten in
1837 at Keilhau. Fundamentally, Froebel developed and expanded
one of Pestalozzi's key ideas — that all development comes from
within, that there are forces within a child that move him towards
those activities that aid in his development. A child is physically and
mentally restless, active, and seeking, and instead of ignoring or re-
pressing his natural activity the teacher should sustain and direct it.
Essentially, Froebel reversed the usual role of the active teacher and
the passive class. The children were provided with a wide range of
materials and objects and encouraged to undertake various kinds of
creative and expressive handwork. The child's self-activity became
the means of education.

It was this aspect of the kindergarten that impressed one of the first
British observers, the Rev. Muirhead Mitchell, one of Her Majesty's
Inspectors of Schools, and a pioneer enthusiast for the kindergarten,
who had seen Froebel's methods demonstrated at the Society of Arts
Educational Exhibition in 1854. In one of his Reports he wrote:

> The grand feature of the system is 'occupation', such as suits a child.
> He is taught little; he simply creates for himself forms and fancies.
> He has toys given him of the simplest sort, straight bits of stick,
> peas soaked in water. He is shown how to use them, and he becomes
> an architect, an inventor; churches, towers, houses, mechanical
> adaptations swarm from his excited brain; again, with cubes of
> wood, his ideas take a more solid form; he learns the weight and
> size of articles, he adapts them to their places, he fits them together
> with strips of coloured paper, he weaves webs of varied beauty, and
> of certain significances of form, he pricks out patterns with a needle,
> he even cuts clay and models it. . . .[9]

Froebel's theory of infant training was built on a complex system of
philosophical and psychological principles. He had an almost pan-
theistic belief in the immanence of God in nature and man, and his
aim in education was to develop the consciousness of the divine in
man.[10] Upon this basis Froebel built a number of philosophical
theories — among others, the 'parallelism' of human and natural
development; the doctrine of 'correspondences' between spirit and
body; the 'law of opposites' by which all development took place;

---

[9] 'Inspectors' Reports: General Report by Rev. M. Mitchell', *Minutes of the Committee of Council on Education, 1854–5*, P.P. (1855), xlii, p. 473.
[10] F. Froebel, *The Education of Man*, trans. Josephine Jarvis (New York, 1885), p. 3.

the recapitulation of the moral history of the race by the individual ; the belief in innate ideas, from all of which he made certain educational deductions. Many of these theories are now discredited, but the validity of the educational practice remains. As Professor Kilpatrick noted, Froebel's psychology is strong in proportion as it comes from his sympathetic regard for the child, and weak in proportion as it originates in his general philosophical outlook.[11]

This truth can be seen in the materials and activities that Froebel prescribed for the kindergarten — his famous 'gifts' and 'occupations'. The former, six in number, consisted of coloured balls and cubes of various sizes ; the latter included tablet-laying, paper-folding, stick-plaiting, drawing, clay modelling, and similar creative manual activities. The ball, for instance, was a 'gift' for Froebel because it had a value symbolic of the related concepts of unity, an inclusive whole, and the All.[12] But these philosophical or metaphysical concepts did not prevent the child, in practice, from using the ball to develop his consciousness of colours and relationships. As Henry Morley noticed at the Ronges' kindergarten :

> As the child grows he can roll it and run after it, watch it with sharp eyes, and compare the colour of one ball with the colour of another, prick up his ears at the songs connected with his various games with it, use it as a bond of playfellowship with other children, practise with it first efforts at self-denial and so forth.[13]

In other words, for whatever abstract reasons Froebel chose the ball as a plaything, its value to the child was intensely practical. Nevertheless, Froebel would not permit his system to be reduced to a mere set of exercises ; these were strictly subordinated to the aim of the full and free development of the mental, spiritual, and physical resources of the child.

The Ronges, with their fierce belief in the necessity of the unhampered growth of the individual, were peculiarly fitted to be pioneers of the kindergarten. They were, however, ambitious not only to put Froebel's principles into practice in a kindergarten, but also to extend the principles of Froebel's teaching to a school for older children and to a training establishment for teachers. In doing this they introduced some reforms of their own.

---

[11] Kilpatrick, p. 108.   [12] Ibid., p. 111.
[13] [H. Morley], 'Infant Gardens', *Household Words*, no. 278, 21 July 1855, p. 580.

Johannes Ronge's Religion of Humanity was the basis and unifying principle in the whole edifice. According to a contemporary observer, he had two rooms converted into a chapel at his residence in Tavistock Place, and provided benches for his listeners and a desk from which he spoke. Here on Sunday evenings, surrounded by garlanded busts of Byron, Milton, and others, and with a blue-painted ceiling decorated with a plan of the solar system above him, he preached his 'religion', whose object was 'to bring into action the higher religious ideas which have sprung from the development of science, philosophy, art and civilization in general, to form the groundwork for a higher period of cultivation'. This religion opposed all creeds upheld by priesthood and government as impediments to the free development of man's being.[14]

The Ronges established their first kindergarten in Hampstead in 1851, but it attracted little support and in 1854 it was transferred to 32 Tavistock Place, where it was run by a committee whose members were associated with Johannes Ronge's religious community.[15] Soon afterwards the school received public acclaim at the Educational Exhibition organized by the Society of Arts. Specimens of pupils' work were sent to the exhibition, a prospectus was distributed, and Mme. Ronge was invited to lecture. In the following year *A Practical Guide to the English Kindergarten* was published and widely reviewed.

The prospectus announced a kindergarten for children of both sexes from three to seven years of age, and a training school for 'infant teachers and nursery governesses'. The system, it claimed, differed from that adopted in English infant schools in that it aimed 'to educe the creative powers of the mind', and gave in some detail how the methods used would accomplish this. Children thus trained would, it concluded, always possess within themselves a source of enjoyment, have the power of self-control, and have a sound foundation laid for learning the more difficult arts and sciences.[16]

The description of the kindergarten given in the Ronges' manual *A Practical Guide to the English Kindergarten* shows the extent to which

[14] Christopher Crayon, 'A "Dangerous Reformer"', *Christian World*, 3 Nov. 1887.
[15] *Kindergarten and Humanistic Schools* ('A Monthly Paper for Promoting a Reformed System of Education and the Harmony between Home and School'), no. 1 May 1856), pp. 4–5.
[16] Prospectus entitled 'Kindergarten' in Society of Arts Educational Exhibition, Collection of Prospectuses, 1854.

above left :
 Henry Morley

above right :
 William Ellis

right :
 Barbara Bodichon

The Prince of Wales opening the International School at Isleworth

The Gospel Oak Schools, built by William Ellis in 1865

the layout and appointments of the school improved upon existing schools, and anticipated later practice with regard to space, light, and air. The children had two 'good, spacious, healthy and well arranged rooms'. One was used for seated exercises and furnished with forms and tables at each of which six children could sit. Great stress was laid on arrangement and order, with each child having a number which was marked on his own box, slate, drawing-book, and plaiting-mat. The second room contained no furniture except a piano and had access to a garden. Here the children were arranged for their musical and gymnastic exercises according to height and number and they sometimes selected their own games. In the garden they tended their own allotments in which they planted seeds and flowers.

The children attended for three to four hours in a morning only ; they continued their play at home, thus strengthening the bond between parents and teacher which was an essential feature of the Ronges' system. The teachers had to be women of high cultivation, sympathetic character, and intelligent training, each, in fact, a 'spiritual mother' to the children [17] and, given the social conditions of Victorian England, this meant that kindergarten teachers were drawn from the daughters of the upper classes. Karl Fröbel, Friedrich's nephew, then resident in Edinburgh, could see no other source of recruitment : 'Excepting mothers, no other class of persons can be fit or worthy to reign in the Kindergarten but the well-educated and accomplished young ladies of modern society.' [18] These would preserve the children from making contact with servants, whose alleged low moral standards, abusive language, and vulgar sentiments were held to be harmful to children.[19]

Games were a great feature of the work, and an anonymous visitor described a game called 'The Pigeon's House'. A number of the children represented pigeons ; the remainder joined hands with Mme. Ronge in a circle and sang :

> We open the pigeon house again,
>   And set all the happy flutterers free ;
> They fly through the fields and the grassy plain,
>   Delighted with joyous liberty ;

[17] J. and B. Ronge, *A Practical Guide to the English Kindergarten* (London, 1855), pp. vi-viii.
[18] K. Fröbel, 'The Kindergarten', *Museum* (Edinburgh), vol. x (July 1863), p. 184.   [19] Ibid., p. 183.

E.I.—X

And when they return from their merry flight
We shut up the house, and bid them goodnight.

Away flew the pigeons, waving their arms like the wings of a bird, out through the open door into the garden, round the grass plot, then back into the circle before it closed again. 'One little pigeon', says the chronicler, 'was all but too late and would have had to sleep in the fields, had not the other pigeons pulled her in as the door was closing.' [20] This dance is illustrated opposite p. 225.

The garden gave an opportunity of demonstrating Froebel's principles. It contained flowers and seats, but a few weeks after the school was opened the children had trampled the whole thing down, though they had been told to be careful. The Ronges did not restore it, however, but went on with the work of the school, until the children came to them and said: 'O, Mrs. Ronge, my father could give us some flowers, or my father will give us some seeds, and if you will allow us we will dig up the garden and put in the flowers because we should like to have it in order.' This, claimed Mme. Ronge, was the best of all education, because it proceeded from the inward feeling of the child. 'It is of no use forcing right precepts and practice upon children,' she continued, 'you must try to get them to see the necessity of knowing and doing that which is right.' [21]

When the children had finished their play they returned to their tables, where they played with their cubes; when they tired of these, they turned to their sticks and coloured balls and other gifts, singing all the time. The lesson was not lost on the visitor: how the games, songs, and handwork were the means by which the intellect was awakened, an elementary sense of mathematics and mechanics formed, the perceptions of colour discovered, and sense of harmony aroused. 'The system differs both in principle and practice', he concluded, 'from that adopted in the English infant schools. . . .' [22] In fact, one is reminded of the genius of Buchanan and of Wilderspin at his best. The Rev. Muirhead Mitchell, writing in 1855, believed that infant schools had failed in their object; their work was too mechanical, there was too much drill and rote-work having little relation to the life of the child, who was treated more as a machine than as a thinking

[20] 'A Visit to the "Kindergarten"', in B. Ronge, '*Kindergarten*' : *An Address on Infant Training* (London, 1854), pp. 7–8.
[21] J. and B. Ronge, *Addresses on the Kindergarten System* (Manchester, 1859), p. 27.
[22] 'A Visit to the "Kindergarten"', pp. 7–8.

human being. The quality of the teachers was poor, few had an understanding of child nature, and the schoolrooms were drab and badly cared for. Mitchell hailed the introduction of the kindergarten system 'with undisguised delight'.[23]

The *Practical Guide* was an illustrated exposition, done with Teutonic thoroughness and detail, of the ways in which Froebel's gifts and occupations could best be put to practical use. Though it was one of the best of the early kindergarten manuals, it suggested by its very detail and ordered arrangement how easily the system might degenerate into a routine devoid of the very spontaneity it aimed to cultivate. The Ronges had a passion for 'order' and 'development' and the whole school was arranged, in true Froebelian fashion, 'in accordance with the laws manifest in the human mind and organism'. The kindergarten occupations fell into three definite stages : building with solid bodies, work with linear bodies, and the artistic and manual occupations. Then followed a series of steps designed to make the transition from the kindergarten to the school, based on Froebel's conception of 'transition classes', in which teaching by words, leading on to abstract instruction, was introduced.[24]   The Ronges claimed as an improvement on the kindergarten system the introduction of a reading- and spelling-book, containing coloured pasteboard slips, with which the children made letters of the alphabet themselves, later forming them into words, and these operations were assumed to respect 'the law of motion in the human organism'. Together with drawing the fundamental forms — angles, the cube, the circle — and elementary arithmetic based on counting balls and cubes, these exercises made up the preparation for an Upper or Association School.[25]

The founding of a school for children older than the seven-year limit of the kindergarten, but run on similar principles, was perhaps the Ronges' most interesting innovation. The two institutions, taken together, were called the Humanistic Schools. The idea had first been mooted by the parents of the children attending the Tavistock kindergarten. In 1855 they formed a committee and financed and organized

---

[23] *Minutes of the Committee of Council, 1854–5*, pp. 471–3.
[24] Baroness Bertha von Marenholtz Bülow, *Hand Work and Head Work* (London, n.d.), ch. iv *passim*.
[25] The account of this school is based upon J. Ronge's written evidence to the Newcastle Commission, included in the Rev. J. Wilkinson's Report, *Reports of the Assistant Commissioners Appointed to Inquire into the State of Popular Education in England*, P.P. (1861), xxi, pp. 463–5.

a school for older children, called an Association School, which opened on 16 April of that year. At first only four pupils could be found, but within a year the numbers had risen to nearly sixty.[26]

What were the essential features of this branch of the Humanistic Schools ? It aimed to replace the rigidities of discipline and the strictly defined 'subject' nature of the curriculum found in most schools by the encouragement of the imaginative and creative faculties of the child through a range of studies in the humanities and the sciences. The Association School fostered 'respect for the individuality of the child, resulting from the conviction that it is a child of God and man, endowed with gifts and qualities requisite to enable it to lead a useful, noble and happy life, for which the parents and teachers have prepared it'. The teaching of the school aimed at the free and complete development of the child's heart, intellect, and physical powers. Corporal punishment was forbidden, discipline was maintained by 'love guided by reason and wisdom', and punishment consisted of being deprived of play with other children, or banishment from the class for one or more hours. The Rev. J. Wilkinson, an Assistant Commissioner, who dealt with the school in his Report, described it as 'an attempt to bring the cultivation of taste and imagination into education still more closely than has hitherto been done', and classed it as an interesting experiment, which, if it succeeded, might materially influence popular education.

The principles of the kindergarten were applied to the higher branches of learning, which included geography, natural science, 'human culture', social economy, and languages. Unfortunately this part of the memorandum, in which Ronge explained the scope and presentation of these subjects, was not included by Wilkinson in his Report, but presumably they were taught in the way indicated by Froebel in the section of *The Education of Man* entitled 'Man as a Scholar', which stressed the interconnection of phenomena and knowledge, the necessity of working outwards from the immediate environment of the child, with each new subject of instruction falling into place 'as firmly and necessarily as the ramifications of symmetrically arranged plants'.[27]

An unusual feature of the organization was the large part that parents took in the day-to-day running of the school, forming what

[26] *Kindergarten and Humanistic Schools*, no. 3 (July 1856), *passim*.
[27] Froebel, *The Education of Man*, p. 174.

must have been one of the earliest Parent–Teacher Associations. A Committee of Directors was responsible for the financial side and the general maintenance of the principles of the school, but under this a committee of parents and teachers planned and guided the general programme of the school, the curriculum, timetable, and the rules of discipline. These committees met every month, and a general gathering of parents met quarterly. In addition, monthly lectures were given to the parents in the winter and committees of other schools were invited. This organization had grown up gradually, for when the school first opened, with fees at a maximum of £1 a quarter, it had not paid, partly because the parents who were interested regarded it as too much of an experiment, but on raising the fees a better-educated class of parent was attracted and, with the help of favourable press publicity, the 'experiment' began to thrive.

The kindergarten movement was one of the few nineteenth-century experiments in education that established itself on a permanent basis. In 1857 the Ronges had visited Manchester, where they helped to form the Manchester Committee for the Extension of the Kindergarten System. Several German teachers resident in Manchester helped to found kindergartens there. In 1873 the Manchester Froebel Society was founded, followed in 1874 by a similar organization in London, and in 1893 the Home and Colonial School Society, which in the middle of the century had accepted Froebel's principles, was incorporated in the National Froebel Union which still flourishes today.[28] Yet the Ronges' schools lasted for only ten years from 1851, but they undoubtedly started the movement in England.

The Humanistic Schools did not last beyond 1861, when Johannes Ronge returned to Germany under the amnesty of that year to join his wife who had gone there shortly before because of ill-health. She died in 1863 and after her death Johannes went to Austria, where little more is heard of him before his death in 1887. Their schools in England were taken over by the Misses Rosalie and Mina Praetorius, who came from Nassau,[29] but the reforming impetus had gone out of them.

[28] P. Woodham-Smith, 'History of the Froebel Movement in England', in E. Lawrence (ed.), *Friedrich Froebel and English Education* (London, 1952), *passim*.
[29] Ibid., p. 43.

18. Barbara Bodichon's School

I

ON 6 November 1854 a day school for boys and girls was opened in
Portman Hall in Carlisle Street, off Edgware Road. The Hall was
used in the evenings for temperance meetings, and the benches and
temperance texts had to be put back at the end of every day. The
school was run by Barbara Leigh Smith, a woman of twenty-seven,
better known under her later married name of Bodichon. Her friend
Elizabeth Whitehead (later Malleson) was in charge of the teaching,
assisted by Barbara's sisters Isabella and Anne, and Octavia Hill, the
housing reformer.

The experimental nature of the school caused initial difficulties. In
the words of her biographer, 'Barbara's school was like nothing any
of her contemporaries had ever seen before . . . grave doubts about
the propriety of the school and the religious convictions of its founder
were held by people otherwise open to reason and reform'. Octavia's
sister, Miranda Hill, for instance, was warned not to teach there by the
Rev. F. D. Maurice, the Christian socialist, because of his dissatisfaction
with the religious *bona fides* of the establishment.[1]

The school broke with tradition in many ways. In the first place
it educated young boys and girls together. Co-education, in the eyes
of the mid-Victorian middle class, was permissible for working-class
or very young children, but was supposed to present peculiar problems
in the case of children of a higher class. Barbara Bodichon's belief
that girls should be treated in schools on equality with boys was
bound up with her advanced views on the social position of women.
She told the Newcastle Commission in 1861 that the education of
girls would always be neglected until women had received better legal
and social rights ; if the education of women was to improve, then
women in the educational world must have equality with men.[2] In
Barbara's school the alleged difficulties and dangers of co-education
were either ignored or faced, and the experiment, one of the earliest
ventures in this field, was highly successful.

[1] Hester Burton, *Barbara Bodichon* (London, 1949), p. 50.
[2] *Report of the Commissioners Appointed to Inquire into the State of Popular Education
in England*, P.P. (1861), xxi (5), pp. 103-4.

Portman Hall School further outraged Victorian propriety by mixing together different social classes. Children of middle-class parents sat side by side with boys and girls of the neighbouring tradesmen and artisans. The school was also a demonstration of racial tolerance ; children of various nationalities were welcomed as pupils there. For a short while Ricciotti, the young son of Garibaldi, attended the school. He was a crippled child, but he was more active on his crutches than most of the normal children were on their legs, and he used to terrify the younger ones by leaping wildly across the benches.[3]

The greatest opposition to the school came, as might be expected, from the clergy, who objected to the undenominational religious teaching upon which both Barbara and Elizabeth Whitehead insisted. At the morning assembly, instead of prayers and hymns, there was a reading of a parable from the Bible, a poem, or perhaps a story of some heroic deed. These ethical readings were intended to set the tone of the whole school day. 'They took the children out of the smaller or troubled atmosphere of their homes', wrote Elizabeth Whitehead later, 'and opened to them possibilities of life on higher moral planes.' [4] Barbara Bodichon herself believed that religion in schools was 'generally utterly useless' and ought to be the province of parents and pastors rather than that of teachers. The great advantage of secular schools, she maintained, was that children of different faiths would learn together 'toleration, forbearance, and charity'.[5]

The discipline of the school was based on a desire to do away with the normal use of rewards and punishments. As far as possible punishment was not administered and few prizes were given for school work. The aim was to make lessons short and pleasurable and use attainment and a sense of acceptance as the stimulus to improvement. As one of the main features of her control and discipline, Elizabeth Whitehead tried to get the children to side with her against all behaviour that she considered contrary to the spirit of the school. In such cases she attempted to show the pupils that they owed allegiance to her as the embodiment of right principles and counterposed this to the children's own code of honour, which she believed was a mistaken one. That she ran a risk is obvious, but sheer force of personality enabled her to be successful most of the time.

---

[3] Elizabeth Malleson, *Autobiographical Notes and Letters* (London, 1926), p. 49 n.
[4] Elizabeth Malleson, 'The Portrait of a School', *Journal of Education*, 1 Sept. 1886, p. 358.   [5] *Commission on Popular Education*, p. 104.

Several innovations were made in teaching method. The teachers made great efforts to work out for themselves the most rational way of teaching arithmetic and English, and in arithmetic many of the reforms of William de Morgan were anticipated, mainly, as Miss Whitehead recalled, by 'infinitely hard work'. Much attention was paid to what were considered by some to be educational extras — visits to museums or picture galleries, and the use of a school lending library. Physiology and the laws of health were an important part of the curriculum,[6] an innovation deriving from the work of Combe and Ellis.

Many of the children were impressed by the thoroughness with which high standards were encouraged. In reading, a high level of expression was aimed at, their handwriting had to be done in the most beautiful style, and their behaviour during dinner and playtime was carefully supervised. An old pupil wrote :

I felt I was surrounded by refinement, though I could not, of course, have expressed it, but the impression of it came to me from all sides. I had always been brought up in habits of obedience ; but, until then, reverence and obedience born of love had not been called forth.[7]

One possible fault of the school was a too slavish adherence to the monitorial system, which had been copied from William Ellis's school. It was used almost entirely in reading and arithmetic, but even the careful instruction of the monitors and the close supervision of the Head could not eliminate the mechanical monotony inherent in this form of teaching. On the whole, however, the general spirit of the school was sufficiently strong to overcome certain deficiencies of method. It was the atmosphere of the school that old pupils tended to remember. A former pupil who later became a teacher at Portman Hall wrote :

The chief thing that I remember, as having impressed me in those days, was the gentle influence which pervaded the school, and the capital order which was obtained without a shadow of corporal punishment, and but rare punishment of any kind except the strongly felt displeasure of our grieved teacher. There was a feeling, too, of cheerful alacrity and pleasure in the work, both on the part of the teacher and pupils, and the lessons were so varied that they never

[6] Burton, p. 51.   [7] Malleson, *Journal of Education*, p. 359.

became wearisome. In looking back upon the school, my feeling is that the children were really educated, rather than merely taught ; by this I mean that their minds were developed, and love and interest in knowledge were nurtured while gentle manners and kindly feelings were fostered by example.[8]

The devotion that the school secured from both pupils and staff enabled it to prosper, despite the difficulties and opposition it faced. The progressive schools of the previous generation had either disappeared or, as in the case of Bruce Castle, were lapsing into orthodoxy. Behind the challenging practices of her school stood Barbara Bodichon's own strong predilections for radicalism, rationalism, internationalism, feminism, and freedom in personal relationships. She clashed head-on, both personally and through her school, with the strongest of the Victorian prejudices, and to do this required independence and courage of a high order. Who was Barbara Bodichon and what influences had combined in the creation of her personality ?

II

Barbara Bodichon was born Barbara Leigh Smith in 1827. Her father was Benjamin Leigh Smith, a Unitarian and a Radical, and M.P. for Norwich at the time of the repeal of the Corn Laws. Her grandfather had been William Smith, a noted Abolitionist and ally of Wilberforce, and a sympathizer with the ideals of the French Revolution.[9] The family had a reputation for supporting advanced and unpopular ideas. Her father objected to sending his children to a traditional school, but since they might meet Richard Cobden, Harriet Martineau, or Henry Brougham discussing free trade, philosophy, or economics at the dinner table, this hardly seemed a disadvantage. The education of the Smith children largely consisted of private tutoring and private reading, interspersed with journeys in Britain and abroad in a large family coach, well supplied with books and sketching materials. For holidays they might go hop-picking, fishing, or walking in Scotland. When in London Benjamin Leigh Smith made his daughters attend Westminster Infant School and assist James Buchanan, the master. The Leigh Smith family gave money to build schools, endow hospitals, finance students, and help refugees ; their house in Blandford Square was often full of exiles from Poland, Hungary, Italy, and France.[10]

[8] Ibid.   [9] Burton, pp. 1–2.   [10] Ibid., pp. 3 ff.

On her twenty-first birthday, in April 1848, Barbara's father settled on her £300 a year. She celebrated her independence by enrolling, in 1849, at the newly founded Ladies' College in Bedford Square, where she became particularly interested in drawing and painting. The following year she made a tour through Europe with Bessie Parkes, great-granddaughter of Joseph Priestley, and later the mother of Hilaire Belloc. She became friendly with many of the leading women intellectuals of the day, including Mrs. Somerville, Mrs. Opie, and Lady Noel Byron. In 1852 she was introduced to George Eliot at one of Chapman's evening parties, and the novelist later made her the model for Romola :

> The hair was of a reddish gold colour, enriched by an unbroken small ripple, such as may be seen in the sunset clouds on grandest autumnal evenings . . . there was the same refinement of brow and nostril . . . counterbalanced by a full though firm mouth and powerful chin, which gave an expression of proud tenacity and latent impetuousness ; an expression carried out in the backward poise of the girl's head, and the grand line of her neck and shoulders.[11]

Barbara's independent outlook and her love of freedom led her to concern herself with the emancipation of women, and in 1854 she published *A Brief Summary in Plain Language of the Most Important Laws Concerning Women*. This was written with the help of Matthew Davenport Hill, the Recorder of Birmingham, an old family friend of the Smiths, who thus had connections with Hazelwood, and stressed the complete absence of rights of the married woman. It created a sensation at the time and was one of the first shots in the campaign that resulted in the Married Women's Property Acts of the 1880s and 1890s.[12]

In 1857 she published *Women and Work*, a plea for women to be accepted into the trades and professions, and the following year she helped to found *The English Woman's Journal*, which campaigned for the rights of women.[13] She felt, however, that this activity neither absorbed her whole energies nor was of sufficient practical benefit. Gifted, unconventional, restless, Barbara Leigh Smith was bound to be dissatisfied with the lot of the mid-Victorian middle-class woman, with its narrow range of possibilities : marriage, the running of a household, or the lot of a governess or teacher. She believed that all

11 G. Eliot, *Romola* (London, 3 vols., 1863), i, p. 79.
12 Burton, p. 61.   13 Ibid., pp. 99–100.

women should have the advantages in life that she herself had enjoyed, and her dissatisfactions with the Victorian conventions led her into an affair with John Chapman and at a later date to marry an unorthodox Frenchman. She assessed herself thus :

> I am one of the cracked people of the world, and I like to herd with the cracked . . . queer Americans, democrats, socialists, artists, poor devils or angels ; and am never happy in an English genteel family life. I try to do it like other people, but I long always to be off on some wild adventure, or long to lecture on a tub in St. Giles, or go to see the Mormons, or ride off into the interior on horseback alone and leave the world for a month.[14]

It was this dissatisfaction with what seemed to her the stifling morality and artificiality of Victorian middle-class social life that attracted her to Eugène Bodichon, a French doctor domiciled in Algiers, a socialist, republican, and self-styled eccentric, who was not above scandalizing London society by arriving at parties accompanied by a group of desert sheikhs in full Arab dress.[15]

Barbara Bodichon's school embodied many of the ideas that she had acquired during her lifetime, and was in consequence a protest against educational convention. The three main influences on her educational thinking were James Buchanan, George Combe, and William Ellis, although she was also well acquainted with all the current literature on education and, before opening her school, had visited various National, British, Secular, Catholic, Ragged, and other schools and taught in some of them.[16] Combe she had come across in her late teens, and from his *Moral Philosophy* she had derived much of her faith in rationalism and social progress.[17] The assistant teacher at Portman Hall came from Edinburgh and had been trained at George Combe's school there.[18] In addition to these influences, the moral atmosphere of Portman Hall School owed much to the example of Owen and Buchanan. 'My school . . . was the child of Robert Owen's, child of James Buchanan', she confessed.[19] She was also impressed by her friend William Ellis's Birkbeck School at Peckham, which she considered to be the most advanced school in London, and she suggested

---

[14] Ibid., p. 92.   [15] Ibid., p. 94.
[16] *Commission on Popular Education*, p. 103.   [17] Burton, pp. 14–15.
[18] [B. I. Buchanan], *Buchanan Family Records* (Cape Town, 1923), p. 18.
[19] Ibid., p. 25.

that Elizabeth Whitehead should spend some weeks there before taking charge of Portman Hall.

Elizabeth Whitehead, whom Barbara had met through a friend of her father's, William Johnson Fox, M.P. for Oldham, was born in 1828 and came like Barbara from a Unitarian and Radical family. She later played a leading part in the founding of the College for Working Women in 1864, and campaigned against the Contagious Diseases Acts and for women's suffrage and other causes.[20] At the Peckham School she observed the teaching, took classes, underwent criticism, and even gave a public demonstration of Shields's system in a lecture room of the Jermyn Street Museum before a large audience of advanced educationalists, using children lent by Mr. Shields. She did not think very much of the fellow trainee-teachers whom she met, being shocked at their manner and tone and finding them 'utterly distasteful', but she liked Shields very much and had many talks and discussions with him, and he in turn thought very highly of Elizabeth, telling Barbara that she was not only a teacher but 'an educationist'.[21]

Elizabeth Whitehead was forced to give up full-time teaching after one year because of overwork. It was due to her vitality and ability as a teacher that the school had been placed on the road to success. After her marriage to Frank Malleson in 1857, she retained the Inspectorship of the school for some years and her husband gave generous subscriptions to it. Barbara Bodichon herself finally gave up the school after her marriage to Eugène Bodichon in 1857. She spent half the year in Algiers and found she could not give the close superintendence that she felt the school needed. She donated the school equipment to Mrs. Malleson for the newly founded Working Women's College.[22] Her school lasted just over three years, preceding the great Commissions of the 1860s and the Revised Code.

Barbara Bodichon was a social radical who sought innovations in education and a hundred related activities. The Commissions led to many educational modifications in the 1860s and 1870s, but Portman Hall was in the genuine progressive, radical succession.

[20] Malleson, *Autobiographical Notes*, pp. 39, 55 ff.
[21] Ibid., pp. 46–47.   [22] Burton, p. 52.

19. The International School: Free Trade and Education

IT was a widely held belief, associated particularly with the name of Richard Cobden, that the unrestricted flow of commodities between nations must eventually lead to the disappearance of international rivalries.[1] Cobden's views on trade, in the words of his biographer Morley, 'were only another side of views on education and morality'.[2] Many leading advocates of free trade hoped to realize their vision of international harmony by the creation of a new type of education which would enable the citizens of different countries to become international ambassadors. Free trade was breaking down barriers between nation and nation, but they were, it was felt, still divided and kept apart by ignorance of each other's culture and language.[3] The provision of boarding-schools in the major industrial countries, which pupils could visit in turn to study the language of the country, was put forward as a means of bringing nations together. The one genuine and successful attempt at international education in the nineteenth century was made at the height of the free-trade era.

These views found a response in France, and were stimulated by the conclusion of the negotiations for the Anglo-French Commercial Treaty of 1860, in which Richard Cobden played an important part. The leading French exponent of the Cobdenite vision was Michel Chevalier, engineer, political economist, and erstwhile St.-Simonian, who was imbued with ideas of the free circulation of trade and culture between nations.[4] Chevalier had backed the Treaty of 1860, and was to play an active part in the preparations for the founding of international schools.

---

[1] 'I believe that the desire and motive for large and mighty empires, for gigantic armies and great navies — for those materials which are used for the destruction of life and desolation of the reward of labour — will die away; I believe that such things will cease to be necessary, or to be used when man becomes one family, and freely exchanges the fruits of his labour with his brother man': (J. Bright and J. E. T. Rogers (eds.), *Speeches on Questions of Public Policy by Richard Cobden, M.P.* (London, 2 vols., 1870), i, p. 363).

[2] J. Morley, *The Life of Richard Cobden* (London, 2 vols., 1881), i, p. 93.

[3] 'International Education', *Reader*, vol. v, no. 129, 17 June 1865, pp. 678–9.

[4] A. L. Dunham, *The Anglo-French Treaty of Commerce of 1860 and the Progress of the Industrial Revolution in France* (Ann Arbor, Mich., 1930), pp. 28–33.

It is significant that specific proposals were made independently on three occasions between 1855 and 1862 in favour of international education, two by Frenchmen and one by a Scot. The first proposal was made by Eugène Rendu, Inspector-General of Public Instruction, in France in 1855, but for political reasons it was not published until 1862. Rendu argued that in the sphere of politics, science, and industry a European outlook was necessary, and that the growth of communications and the gradual fall of customs barriers could pave the way for international education. He proposed four colleges, each having an eight-year course, attracting pupils from the ages of eight to sixteen years, with the pupils moving from school to school. The colleges would be sited in Paris, Rome, Munich, and Oxford.[5]

The next person to put forward a similar proposal was James Lorimer, a Scottish lawyer. In two remarkable articles in the Edinburgh *Museum* in the summer of 1861, he outlined a scheme very similar to that of Rendu.[6] There was no doubt, however, that the latter's proposals were completely unknown to Lorimer. Like many thinking men of his generation he deplored international antagonisms, and his articles were a plea for the rational study of languages and the use of travel in the service of international understanding.

Lorimer was concerned with the vast amount of time and energy spent on classical languages in modern European education, and writing soon after the Anglo-French Treaty, he proposed a form of reciprocal naturalization between Britain and France. Colleges should be established by the respective governments under the superintendence of the ambassadors, the studies should reflect the cultural background of the country in which the college was situated, and should terminate by the granting of mutual citizenship. Lorimer concluded :

> The expense of maintaining a single ship of war, to say nothing of a regiment of the line, far exceeds what would probably be required for the support of such an establishment in every capital town in Europe.[7]

In his second article Lorimer answered some of the objections that were urged against his scheme, notably that it might save Europe from

[5] E. Rendu, *Note sur la Fondation d'un Collège International à Paris, à Rome, à Munich et à Oxford* (Paris, 1862).
[6] J. Lorimer, 'Reciprocal Naturalisation. I : International Education', *Museum* (Edinburgh), no. 1 (Apr. 1861), pp. 77–87 ; 'II : The International School the Complement of the International Exhibition', ibid., no. 2 (July 1861), pp. 174–81.
[7] Ibid., no. 1 (Apr. 1861), p. 87.

the horrors of war at the expense of the eradication of national spirit and national character, to which mankind was so indebted for progress. In reply Lorimer insisted that war was still the greatest evil and that in considering national character one had to remember its double nature : on the one side was the moral life of a community which gave each country its own distinctive character, and on the other was prejudice, bigotry, and narrow-mindedness, particularly prevalent among the least travelled and least educated sections of the community, and which often formed the basis of so-called public opinion. This constriction of national character, Lorimer believed, could be released by the right type of education.

The third proposal for international schools was made in 1862 by a French manufacturer, Aristide Barbier of Clermont-Ferrand, on the occasion of the International Exhibition held in London that year. Barbier donated five thousand francs to the French Committee of the Exhibition as prizes for the best essays on the means of establishing international education in Europe. Though he had mooted his plan the previous year, he felt that the Exhibition provided a good opportunity for public men of different nations to meet and discuss plans for a form of education that would be the intellectual counterpart of the Exhibition's objects.[8]

Barbier suggested the creation of four colleges, one in each of four countries, for children of ten to eighteen years of age, and invited specific and detailed proposals on these lines.[9] He reiterated his views to the Education Section of the 1862 Congress of the National Association for the Promotion of Social Science.[10]

To judge the essays an international jury was set up, which included Sir James Kay-Shuttleworth, Richard Cobden, and M. Michel Chevalier. The first prize was won by Edmond Barbier, a French tutor resident in England (not related to his namesake Aristide) and translator of the definitive French edition of Charles Darwin's *Origin of Species*. His prize-winning essay was in all essentials a detailed working-out of the main ideas put forward by Rendu, Lorimer, and Aristide Barbier. Briefly, he suggested that four colleges, of about 120 pupils each, should be set up in Paris, London, Berlin, and Florence. The children should

---

[8] 'Proposed International Schools', *Journal of the Society of Arts*, vol. xi, no. 540 (27 Mar. 1863). [9] A. Barbier, *Éducation Internationale* (Paris, 1862), *passim*. [10] *Transactions of the National Association for the Promotion of Social Science* . . . *1862* (London, 1863), pp. 354–6.

start at eight or nine years of age and study the languages of the four countries concerned. They should spend one year in each country in turn, thus visiting each country twice in the course of their eight years of school life.[11]

The first response to Aristide Barbier's initiative was the organization of a European Association for International Education, with Eugène Rendu as secretary and with sub-committees to be set up in the four countries concerned. The first sub-committee was set up in France, consisting of leading educationalists and public men, and the prototype school was founded in France in 1862, in Saint-Germain-en-Laye, a few miles from Paris, with Jules Brandt as Director.[12] It combined modern languages and advanced classical studies, with the object of preparing pupils for professional work in the major European countries. Two hours a day were devoted to courses in English, French, German, and Italian, and religious instruction was barred from the curriculum. The pupil–teacher ratio was low and classes did not exceed twenty pupils. The individual responsibility of the pupils was fostered as far as possible and sport played an important part in the curriculum. A doctor visited the school daily to look after the health of the pupils.[13] The pupils were drawn from the upper classes of society and were expected to bring with them at the beginning of each academic year 'four linen sheets, twelve table napkins, twelve shirts, twelve linen handkerchiefs, twelve pairs of cotton socks, three pairs of shoes, three black silk ties, collars, brushes, combs, etc.' [14]

In England the scheme did not get under way until 1863. A provisional committee was set up that included Richard Cobden (who died before the school was opened), Dr. W. B. Hodgson, Thomas Twining, later an advocate of technical education, Sir John Bowring, and Alexander Panizzi of the British Museum. Cobden's place as chairman was taken by A. W. Paulton, his friend and collaborator of Anti-Corn Law days. The scientists John Tyndall and Thomas Henry Huxley also became members, and Edmond Barbier acted as secretary to the committee.

Another member of the provisional committee, the Rev. J. A. Emerton, though less illustrious than some of the other members,

---

[11] Barbier, pp. 49–78.

[12] 'International Education', *All the Year Round*, no. 281, 10 Sept. 1864, pp. 106–8.

[13] Prospectus entitled 'École Internationale de Saint-Germain-en-Laye', dated Feb. 1867.   [14] Ibid., p. 3 n.

deserves mention as an example of the wide influence of Cobden's ideals. Emerton was the Principal of the English International College at Hanwell, a post he had held for several years. The school building had been purchased by a friend and disciple of Robert Owen who had unsuccessfully tried to run a school there on Owenite principles. When the school failed Emerton was called in as principal, and he ran the school on his own lines. His claim to fame was his invention of a new method of teaching the French language by means of the Bible, which he called the Emertonian system. Students in each country read an English and French version of the Bible simultaneously, using one version as a means of translating the other.[15] A friend and admirer of Cobden, Emerton believed that the learning of languages was the best means to international peace and in 1859 he had given a prize for the best essay on the importance of a close union of England and France. In 1866 Emerton inaugurated the Cobden Memorial Classes, for teaching French by his method, at Rochdale and Hanwell, and at the beginning of 1867 the Rochdale class had five hundred members.[16]

The Committee sent out a circular letter in 1863 outlining the aims of the college as described in Barbier's prize-winning essay. The circular also attempted to answer various criticisms of the project, particularly the charge that the pupils would, during their time at an international school, lose all sense of national feeling. The circular also pointed out that, although the curriculum was very wide — in addition to six languages the pupils would have to study a range of scientific subjects, modern politics, and political economy — 'complete' instruction would be given in the three R's and languages and only 'the elements' of the rest would be taught.[17]

Sufficient support was forthcoming for the school to be opened three years later. The main benefactor was William Ellis, who advanced a very large part of the money required for the purchase of the site at Isleworth in Middlesex and the erection of the buildings, which were opened on 1 May 1866.[18] It was not until 10 July of the following year that the college was completed and the formal opening

---

[15] J. A. Emerton, 'The Inaugural Address on the Formation of the Cobden Memorial Class', in W. N. Molesworth, *Prize Essay on the Great Importance of an Improved System of Education for the Upper and Middle Classes* (London, 1867), pp. 56–61.

[16] Ibid., p. 97.

[17] *Brief Statement of the Proposed Plan for International Schools* (London, 1863), *passim.*   [18] E. K. Blyth, *Life of William Ellis* (London, 1889), p. 266.

E.I.—Y

was performed by Ellis's old pupil, the Prince of Wales, with great ceremony, amidst flag-poles from which fluttered the flags of different nations.[19] The first headmaster was Dr. Leonard Schmitz, who had been Rector of the High School in Edinburgh and a former associate of George Combe.[20] The official name of the school was the London College of the International Education Society.

In 1867 there were twelve day scholars between the ages of ten and fourteen years and fifty-eight boarders. Both day scholars and boarders were described as 'sons of clergymen, merchants, professional men, etc.' The fees were extremely high even for this class of school; boarders paid eighty guineas a year and day scholars twenty-four guineas. The amenities of the school, however, were on a high level. There was one master to every ten pupils, each boy had his own bed-room with, it was claimed, 970 cubic feet of breathing-space and the catering arrangements were similarly generous. The school stood in eight acres of ground, and the boys had fifteen hours of playtime a week in the winter and eighteen hours in summer. There was no corporal punishment and discipline was maintained by confinement during play hours, the imposition of extra lessons, or the deprivation of privileges.[21] In 1871 the college buildings were extended to include a new wing and a gymnasium at the additional cost of £10,000.[22]

Apart from the pupils from France, Germany, and Italy, the College attracted a number of scholars from all over the world, including Spain, Portugal, the United States, India, Brazil, Chile, and Nicaragua. Among its most distinguished English pupils were Frederick Delius the composer and Maurice Hewlett the novelist. The gentle and sensitive Hewlett never settled down at Spring Grove. He saw only conflict and hostility in the clash of different nationalities:

There were no traces in my time of the Brotherhood of Man about it. . . . The raw Brazilians, Chilians, Nicaraguans and what not who were drawn from their native forests and plunged into the company of blockish Yorkshire lads, or sharp-faced London boys, were only scared into rebellion, and to demonstration after their manner. They used the knife sometimes; they hardly ever assimi-

---

[19] C. Bibby, 'A Victorian Experiment in International Education: The College at Spring Grove', *British Journal of Educational Studies*, vol. v, no. 1 (Nov. 1956), p. 27.
[20] C. Gibbon, *The Life of George Combe* (London, 2 vols., 1878), ii, p. 243.
[21] *Report of the Schools Inquiry Commission*, vol. xii: *South Midland Division, Special Reports of Assistant Commissioners*, P.P. (1867–8), xxviii (10), p. 526.
[22] Bibby, p. 33.

lated; and they taught us nothing that we were the better of knowing.[23]

The initial prospectus of the school defined the curriculum as follows :

English language and literature ; modern languages ; Latin, Greek ; mathematics (arithmetic, algebra, geometry, etc.) ; natural sciences ; history ; geography ; moral science ; religious instruction ; military drill ; gymnastic exercises ; vocal music ; and drawing in its several branches.[24]

An analysis of the first year's syllabus shows that a proportionately greater amount of time was given to the classics than any other subject, followed by modern languages and science. Ten lessons each week were devoted to Latin and Greek, eight lessons to French and German, and five to the various sciences, though the science classes were on the average three times larger than those for ancient and modern languages. Mathematics and book-keeping, with four and five periods a week respectively, also figured prominently in the syllabus.[25]

The Schools Inquiry Commission described the general character of the school at the beginning of 1867 as 'classical',[26] though the *Illustrated London News* had in the same year drawn attention to the prominent place given to the physical sciences in the curriculum.[27] The original aim of making modern languages the core of the curriculum was obviously not being carried out; Italian, for instance, was not taught at all in the early years. The leaning towards the classics was due to Schmitz ; unless a large proportion of time was given to their study, he felt, they were not worth studying at all.

Thomas Henry Huxley, on the other hand, despite the general aim of making the College an international language institution, wanted to make science the backbone of the curriculum and proposed an ambitious scheme that would include physics, chemistry, biology, advanced social science, and the natural history of man,[28] but this was not accepted by Schmitz. In addition to its relatively low place in the curriculum, science was apparently not very well taught. In 1872 Charles Hooker, one of the pupils there, described the science teaching

---

[23] Ibid., p. 35.   [24] *Schools Inquiry Commission*, p. 525.
[25] Ibid., pp. 527-8.   [26] Ibid., p. 526.
[27] *Illustrated London News*, 20 July 1867, cited in Bibby, p. 28.
[28] Bibby, pp. 28-31.

at Spring Grove as 'an utter sham, worse by far than nothing and calculated to bring the thing into contempt'.[29]   By 1880, however, the science teaching had been improved by the provision of two laboratories for practical scientific work.   The teaching of modern languages had also been improved and extended, and five years after the opening it was reported that the pupils could converse equally well in English, French, German, and Italian, and on the first day of the new term gave scenes in the appropriate languages from Goethe's *Iphigenia* and Goldoni's *Villeggiatura*.[30]

According to the Memorandum of Association of the College, the fundamental principle of all educational institutions under the direction of the International Society was that no theological studies should form part of the general course of education, but arrangements were made for giving all pupils such special religious instruction as their parents or guardians desired.   There were two lessons of religious knowledge a week at which the Bible was read and explained, but no boy whose parents objected was compelled to attend.   The school day began and ended with prayers (presumably undenominational) composed by the headmaster.[31]

There is little information as to the way in which the various subjects were taught, and it is obvious that the most grandiose plans for a wide curriculum were of little use unless the subjects were taught creatively and imaginatively by teachers of high personal merit.   Some indication can be found, however, in an account written in 1886 by Jules Brandt, the Head of the French College.   According to Brandt, the basis of the school was the study of modern languages and the rest of the curriculum was founded upon the study of the sciences, with great stress laid on personal work by the pupils.   Teaching was to be based on the principle of intensive periods of work followed by fairly long breaks for recreation.   The watchwords of the school were 'moral austerity and religious toleration' and the pupils were to be given as much liberty as possible.[32]

Modern languages were taught for their practical utility.   Natural methods of reading and speaking, with frequent revision, were preferred to mechanical repetition, the abstract study of grammar, or

---

[29] Bibby, p. 33.   [30] Ibid., p. 34.
[31] *Schools Inquiry Commission*, pp. 525-6.
[32] J. Brandt, *Exposé du Principe et des Travaux de l'École Internationale* (Paris, 1866), pp. 4-5.

excessive use of the dictionary. The original circular for the school stressed that history would be presented 'with the utmost impartiality', and according to Brandt, teaching concentrated on the progress of civilization and the development of knowledge ; political history was taught only in so far as it threw light on the special characteristics of nations. Science teaching received equivocal treatment from Brandt ; he hoped that it would would fall somewhere between the 'scientific' and the 'popular', a view that cannot have helped science teachers at the schools to demand a higher standard of work.[33]

In his own school at Saint-Germain-en-Laye, Brandt abandoned ordinary classes and put his pupils into 'sets' according to their ability, assigning two tutors to each pupil, one for literature and one for science. Each subject was divided into three courses, graded according to the ability of the pupils.[34] It is not clear how far this method of organizing the pupils was carried out at the Isleworth International School, nor, indeed, how far the methods and organization of each school were copied by the others. It can only be assumed, since all the schools were under the direction of one committee, that some cross-fertilization of ideas and methods took place.

By the early 1870s the Isleworth College had established itself very much on the lines of the original aims of the founders. It had become truly international in scope, teaching the languages of four of the most important countries of Europe — England, France, Germany, and Italy — to a wide variety of nationalities. It continued its work throughout the 1870s and 1880s, and in 1874 H. R. Ladell replaced Schmitz as headmaster. In its last years it had a hundred pupils and fourteen masters and had several scholarships tenable at English universities. In 1889, however, the College came to an end and in 1890 the buildings were occupied by Borough Road Training College.[35] No reliable information has been obtained as to the reasons for its closure.

During the twenty-three years of its life the College had given in some degree a practical experience of internationalism to many hundreds of pupils. In addition, by giving science and modern languages a prominent place in the curriculum, it had, despite Schmitz's preference for classical studies, carried forward the movement for curricular reform. The Isleworth International School was in many ways far ahead of its time. If its original impetus in the 1860s had lain in visions of universal peace and prosperity arising from free trade and

[33] Ibid., pp. 5–7.   [34] Ibid., pp. 7–9.   [35] Bibby, pp. 35–36.

the spread of culture, in practice it had to adapt to the era ushered in by the Franco-Prussian War of 1870, which replaced the calico millennium of Richard Cobden. Dickens's journal *All the Year Round* had welcomed the project in its earliest days as 'the truest expression of the law of education in the nineteenth century', and saw in it a revival of the republic of letters of the medieval universities.[36] Perhaps the most remarkable feature of the English College was that it lasted so long in an atmosphere of war and international rivalry.

The idea of a linked group of schools has been revived from time to time, notably by Cecil Reddie of Abbotsholme and more recently by Kurt Hahn. It has usually foundered on the difficulties of practical arrangements, and the chief form that the principle has taken is of the parent school with direct links with similar schools in other countries. By any standards the International School of 1866–89 was a remarkable achievement, a product of the liberal intelligentsia for their children.

20. William Ellis and the Birkbeck Schools

WILLIAM ELLIS, businessman and educationalist, tutor to Queen Victoria's children, praised as a teacher by Florence Nightingale ('the best and most effective teaching I have ever heard'),[1] the friend and patron of William Lovett, the veteran Chartist, was the founder of a series of remarkable schools during the mid-Victorian period which attempted, as no other schools had done, to make the education provided correspond closely to the economic and social life of the times. This involved changes in curriculum and teaching method that were of interest and value for education as a whole, and it is fitting that he is the last educational innovator to be considered in detail.

Ellis exhibited traits following from utilitarian philosophy and mid-century *laissez-faire* capitalist ethics. He had little time for the conventional curriculum and did not believe in the neutrality of the teacher or in keeping politics out of the classroom. He thought it 'quite within the scope of school instruction' to persuade children of the follies of joining unions or of taking part in strikes, and to teach them

[36] *All the Year Round*, 10 Sept. 1864, p. 107.
[1] E. K. Blyth, *Life of William Ellis* (London, 1889), p. 98.

a morality based upon the doctrines of classical political economy to which he gave the general name of social science.[2]

Ellis, born in 1800, the son of an underwriter at Lloyd's who was ruined by the blockades of the Napoleonic Wars, was forced to leave school at thirteen and live a frugal life as a clerk ('we were allowed a penny a day each for lunch', he recalled. 'We used to buy a small biscuit with seeds in it for the penny ; but corn was dear and it was not much for a hungry boy . . .').[3] By self-denial and hard work, however, he progressed in the true Smilesian manner, becoming manager of the Indemnity Marine Insurance Company at the age of twenty-six. Under his guidance the company rapidly became one of the largest of its kind in the country.

'I met Mr. James Mill', he said, 'when I was about twenty, and he worked a complete change in me. He taught me how to think and what to live for.'[4] He became a member of John Stuart Mill's Utilitarian Society and later of George Grote's discussion group, where he read and discussed the works of James Mill, Ricardo, and Hartley. The views he formed strongly affected his attitude to education, which he believed should be brought into a closer relationship with life :

> I consider it a disgrace to our civilisation that a boy should leave school at the age of 13 and not have something like a clear perception of the world he is going into, and the duties that he will have to perform, and I consider that he cannot have that unless what I understand by the name of elementary social science is taught.[5]

Ellis was disturbed by the gap between the traditional subjects of the school curriculum and the nature of the expanding industrial and commercial society that formed the environment of the school. He strongly criticized 'all curricula of study founded upon the notions still prevalent in the seventeenth century'.[6] The curse of education in England was, in his opinion, that it was much more concerned with 'how to aim' than with what to aim at.[7] The target, Ellis had no doubt, should be a thorough acquaintance with industrial capitalist society and an appreciation of the place of the individual, particularly the working-class and lower-middle-class individual, in it.

[2] W. Ellis, 'Combinations and Strikes from the Teacher's Point of View', *Museum and English Journal of Education*, vol. ii, no. 8 (June 1865), p. 81.

[3] Florence Fenwick Miller, 'William Ellis and his Work as an Educationist', *Fraser's Magazine*, N.S., vol. xxv (Feb. 1852), p. 234.   [4] Ibid., p. 236.

[5] *Schools Inquiry Commission*, P.P. (1867–8), xxviii (4), p. 507.

[6] Blyth, p. 63.   [7] Ibid., p. 209.

Society, however, was plagued by social discontents, which Ellis divided into two groups — permanent evils, among which he included destitution, bad housing, crime, and improvidence, and intermittent upheavals such as commercial panics, combinations, and strikes.[8] Ellis was particularly interested in the last of these intermittent discontents, and much of his work was designed to improve relations between masters and men. He did not condemn strikes with the horror common to many of his middle-class contemporaries, for he took the view that the real causes of industrial and social unrest lay in error and maladjustment on the part of the workers themselves. The causes of human misery, he maintained, could be shortly summed up : 'Four names will suffice to embrace them all : ignorance, unskilfulness, depravity of disposition and bad habits. . . .'[9]

Ignorance and ill-conduct were, of course, removable by the general spread of education, but the special kinds of ignorance that Ellis saw manifesting themselves in society needed special kinds of instruction and disciplines to overcome them, and it was in this connection that social science, particularly the economic part of it, was relevant. It could teach the working class about the sources of wealth, the connection between capital and labour, the importance of respect for property, and 'the suicidal folly' of organizing combinations, strikes, and turnouts, of impeding the introduction of new machinery, and of opposing the free movement of capital and labour.[10]

Ellis envisaged a stable and expanding economy, on the lines of a perfect classical model. Employers would refrain from panics, crises, lock-outs, and other avoidable contingencies, workers would not misuse the powers of unions or co-operatives, and both would recognize and not hinder the free play of the market.[11] The alternative, in Ellis's view, was a population 'steeped in prejudice and writhing in misery, coveting their neighbours' wealth, declaring against capital, demanding more paper-money or the repudiation of debts, breaking machinery . . .'.[12] This cataclysmic opinion of the future was clearly influenced

[8] *Report of the Commissioners Appointed to Inquire into the State of Popular Education in England*, P.P. (1861), xxi (5), p. 181 ; W. Ellis, 'On Economic Science', *Journal of the Society of Arts*, vol. ii, no. 91, 18 Aug. 1854, pp. 667–9.

[9] W. Ellis, *Thoughts on the Future of the Human Race* (London, 1866), p. 133.

[10] *Commission on Popular Education*, xxi (5), p. 181.

[11] For Ellis's advice to the workers with regard to trade unions and co-operatives, cf. [W. Ellis], *Reminiscences of an Old Operative* (London, 1852), *passim*.

[12] W. E[llis], 'State of the Nation', *Westminster and Foreign Quarterly Review*, vol. lii (Oct. 1849), p. 109.

by the economic and social troubles of the immediate past, and Ellis felt called to positive action. After twenty years of attending to his business interests he turned to education, and the occasion for this was a reading of George Combe's *The Constitution of Man*, which revived his interest in population restraint (a favourite theme of Combe's) and related aspects of political economy. He wrote to his friend W. B. Hodgson in 1847 :

> Combe dwells more than once on the importance of a rational restraint upon population, and my conviction of this, more than anything else, led me last year to resume actively what I had laid aside for twenty years — the teaching of political economy.[13]

Ellis's strategy was to found and equip a number of schools in which social science would not be merely another subject in the curriculum but the very staple of the education given. He was not the first to advocate the inclusion of political and economic doctrines in the curriculum of elementary schools. The economist John Wade and Sir Thomas Wyse had, in the 1830s, suggested political economy as a suitable ingredient in working-class education.[14] Ellis, however, was the first to found and equip schools for this purpose.

Two further things were necessary — suitable textbooks and well-trained teachers — and with typical thoroughness, Ellis wrote his own books and set about training his own teachers, who had to have not only an enthusiasm for the doctrines of social science but also the skill to impart the knowledge in a manner favoured by Ellis. He despaired of finding an agency that could train suitable teachers, and for many years during the 1850s he carried out the job himself, giving weekly instruction to a class of about fifty teachers,[15] using the first Birkbeck School in Southampton Buildings as a sort of training college for teachers in other similar schools.[16] Ellis did, however, discover some teachers who fully shared his views and who could, without much further instruction, conduct his schools as he wished. The two most able were John Rüntz, a former working man, and W. A. Shields, both of whom became headmasters of Birkbeck Schools.

In producing textbooks in the social sciences that were suitable for

---

[13] Blyth, p. 58.

[14] Cf. J. Wade, *A History of the Middle and Working Classes* (London, 1833), pp. 494 ff. ; T. Wyse, *Education Reform ; or, the Necessity of a National System of Education* (London, 1836), pp. 313–23.

[15] *Commission on Popular Education*, xxi (5), p. 407.   [16] Blyth, p. 96.

children Ellis was, of course, following the practice of others, including Mrs. Marcet and James Mill. Mrs. Marcet's *Conversations on Political Economy*, designed for the edification of young people, had been published as early as 1816 and had appeared in five editions by 1824. Mac-Vickar's *First Lessons in Political Economy for the Use of Elementary Schools* had a similar aim, and James Mill's volume on the subject was intended for use as a school book.[17] In his own works Ellis presented the material of political economy logically and rationally, commencing with the simplest geographical postulates and proceeding through the economic structure of society to the complexities of social relationships. *Questions and Answers Suggested by a Consideration of Some of the Arrangements and Relations of Social Life* was published in 1848 and dealt with financial and monetary affairs in the form of a dialogue. *Progressive Lessons in Social Science*, published two years later, contained a graded series of sixty propositions followed by questions, covering the production and distribution of wealth and the kind of social relationships that Ellis considered should prevail. One would gather from the book that he accepted the existing economic system, the division between capital and labour, the necessity of the protection of property, the benefits of competition, and the theory that destitution was the result of moral failings rather than of economic causes.[18]

Was Ellis, in fact, attempting to indoctrinate the children at his schools with the capitalist ethic ? One of his disciples, William Mattieu Williams, a teacher at the Edinburgh Secular School, had been accused by the parents of his children, all skilled artisans, of being 'a special pleader for the capitalists', and had been informed that the political economy lessons would be refuted at home in the evenings. However, Williams believed that it was easier to convince children than parents of the truth of social science, for the parents would give such terms as 'wealth', 'capitalist', 'labour', and 'value' meanings derived from their experience of industrial life, which were not necessarily those of the political economists.[19]

Ellis, it is clear, was primarily a political economist of the classical capitalist school who turned to education in the first place because he saw the teaching of social science in schools as the quickest way to

[17] J. Mill, *Elements of Political Economy* (London, 1821), p. iii.

[18] W. Ellis, *Progressive Lessons in Social Science* (London, 1850), *passim*.

[19] W. M. Williams, 'On the Teaching of Social Economy', *Transactions of the National Association for the Promotion of Social Science, 1857* (London, 1858), pp. 512–15.

convert people to his views. Paradoxically, the very intensity with which he pursued his aim produced, almost as a by-product, some very unorthodox educational practices. As everything was in sacrifice to the god of utility, many of the traditional school subjects and methods that did not further Ellis's aim he excluded. In this pruning of the curriculum, classical languages and denominational religion, the twin pillars of orthodox education, were cut out and the gap was filled by the sciences and political economy. The old didactic teaching methods gave way to what Ellis called the Socratic method, a dialogue between teacher and pupil. Corporal punishment, to a great extent the accompaniment of the old learning, was abolished in Birkbeck Schools. In these and in other ways, Ellis's schools were ahead of their time, anticipating much of the outlook associated with Spencer and his associates in the 1860s.

Ellis began his educational work by taking a class in a British School in the autumn of 1846, and opened his first school two years later. During the following seventeen years he founded further schools in Finsbury, Westminster, Bethnal Green, Peckham, Kingsland, and Gospel Oak, and they were all known as Birkbeck Schools in honour of Dr. Birkbeck, pioneer of Mechanics' Institutes. They were all day schools and were intended to be self-supporting, the master's salary being paid out of the fees of the scholars. Boys and girls occupied the same building and were educated separately, but the attached infant schools were co-educational. The average leaving age was thirteen years but some children stayed on two or three years longer.[20] The schools were intended for the children of 'the labouring classes, the mechanics, but including also the children of some of the smaller shop-keepers'.[21] The fees were deliberately adjusted to exclude the undeserving, in Ellis's definition of the term. The 6*d.* that the children paid weekly was 'a charge which, while it is within the means of all provident parents, necessarily renders the school inaccessible to the children of the destitute, or of the improvident'.[22]

The main drawback of the schools was the ugliness and unsuitability of the buildings. It was Ellis's habit to buy up disused chapels, old halls, and abandoned school buildings and convert them cheaply to his uses, and the motive for this was not mere economy, for Ellis did not contemplate his schools becoming permanent institutions. He

---

[20] *Schools Inquiry Commission,* xxviii (4), pp. 502–3.   [21] Ibid., p. 502.
[22] E. E. Ellis, *Memoir of William Ellis* (London, 1888), p. 69.

believed that the example of his methods would be contagious and that in a short space of time all other school managers would put his methods into practice and he would thus succeed in changing the face of middle-class and elementary education and move into better buildings in the process.[23]

The first Birkbeck School was opened on 17 July 1848 in the theatre of the Mechanics' Institute in Southampton Buildings, Chancery Lane. John Rüntz was the headmaster, the Earl of Radnor became a patron, and several other prominent men subscribed to it, and a grant was also obtained from the Corporation of London. The main cost, however, fell upon Ellis, who guaranteed an annual sum to cover expenses for five years.[24] Rüntz had started life as a cabinet-maker, trained as a teacher at Borough Road College, became head of the British School at Finsbury, and later studied at University College.[25]

The wording of the prospectus showed that, in curriculum and method, the school was far ahead of its time. In addition to the basic subjects of the curriculum, mechanics, the physical sciences, the laws of health, and social economy were also taught. The last of these was defined in detail in a later circular :

1. Instruction in the means by which wealth or the comforts and necessaries of life are produced ; this inquiry leading to the conviction in the minds of the pupils, that industry, skill, economy, and security of property must prevail in society, in order that this production may be abundant :—
2. Instruction in the advantages of the division of labour, of the co-operation of labour and capital and in the arrangements which facilitate interchange ; the study of these subjects furnishing the pupils with arguments which demonstrate beyond all doubt how honesty, sobriety, punctuality, and moral discipline must obtain amongst a people for these arrangements to be fully serviceable :—
3. Instruction in the influence upon the general well-being, of the prevalence of parental forethought or of parental improvidence.[26]

Great attention was given to this moral training, the circular stressed, because the school was necessarily secular and open to children of parents of all denominations. The system of education, the prospectus continued,

[23] Blyth, p. 99.   [24] Ibid., p. 91.   [25] Ibid., pp. 89–90.
[26] Circular entitled 'Peckham Birkbeck Schools, for Boys, Girls, and Infants : Willow-Brook Road', in E. E. Ellis, pp. 67–68.

is that which modern science and experience have shown to be most in accordance with the constitution of the human mind, and best calculated to strengthen, develop, and rightly direct all its faculties, by presenting to them the objects naturally adapted to call them into varied and healthy activity.[27]

The 'objects' included material for object lessons, arithmetic textbooks and reading-books, maps, geographical models, and a globe. In addition there were physiological diagrams 'for lessons on the organs of animal and vegetable life', and experimental apparatus for teaching the elements of physics and chemistry. Each pupil had to supply the cost of a slate, an English grammar, a geographical primer, a writing-book, and various mathematical textbooks.[28]

The methods of teaching were eclectic, and made use of several innovations of the preceding generation. These included 'the monitorial system of Bell and Lancaster, the collective-lesson system of Stowe, and the arrangements incident to the object-lesson system of Pestalozzi'. Instruction was 'an exercise and a training of the intellect, rather than a tasking of the memory'. Reading was taught in connection with lessons on objects, and spelling and grammar from the words and sentences met with in reading. Arithmetic began with principles rather than rules, geography emphasized the physical features and political divisions of the countries before anything else was learned, and in physiology the functions of parts of the body preceded the learning of the names. The study of the physical sciences was introduced by lessons on industrial processes and equipment, and all teaching was carried out 'in a natural order and by the method of analysis'.[29] In the teaching of science itself experiment and lectures together with blackboard work were preferred to instruction from books. Physiology, as an example, was taught with the aid of Kensington Museum diagrams and sometimes the lungs and hearts of animals were obtained from local butchers for experiment and dissection.[30] This approach showed a determined attempt to present lesson material concretely, vividly, and in an unorthodox manner.

Similar organization and methods were in operation at Shields's school in Peckham. This was opened in April 1852, and was the first of Ellis's schools to be specially built for the purpose. It had three departments for boys, girls, and infants, and the average length of

[27] Blyth, p. 92.   [28] E. E. Ellis, p. 66.   [29] Ibid., pp. 66–67.
[30] *Schools Inquiry Commission*, xxviii (4), p. 507.

school life in the senior school was five years, from seven to twelve years of age.[31]   The prospectus indicated the width of the curriculum :

> The course of instruction in these schools will include reading, writing, arithmetic, grammar and composition, history and geography, drawing, algebra, geometry, vocal music, the elements of physiology, natural philosophy and chemistry.   The children will also be instructed in the conditions of human well-being.
>
> N.B.   The girls will be taught needlework.[32]

The circular already quoted stated that the Peckham schools would be 'spacious, thoroughly well-ventilated, furnished with objects for lessons, with reading books, maps, geographical models, globes, diagrams of physiological and natural history subjects, and with philosophical apparatus'.[33]

The hours were from 9.30 a.m. to 1 p.m. and from 2 p.m. to 4.30 p.m. Lessons were forty-five minutes long with a break between each lesson, but Shields introduced voluntary evening lessons twice a week from 6 to 7 p.m., which were attended by some eighty children.   As far as possible lessons were of a practical nature and books were reserved for private reading only.[34]

Shields, who had a free hand with the curriculum, introduced certain subjects, such as vocal music and drawing, which had little appeal to Ellis.   He also enlarged the concept of social science, including, besides political economy and 'systematic lessons in morals', some elementary physiology — lessons on digestion, circulation, respiration, the brain, and the nervous system, and their connection with general laws of health.   Pupils would thus be prepared, he hoped, when leaving school, to co-operate in forward-looking measures of sanitation and public health.[35]   However, the work of the school was handicapped by a shortage of teachers, and the pupils had to be split up into five divisions, each containing from fifty to a hundred pupils, with one master in charge of each division, assisted by a number of pupil teachers.[36]

Shields had left a small business to take up teaching, had trained under Rüntz, and after a short spell as a headmaster of the Oddfellows' Secular School in Manchester had taken over at Peckham.   He was a

[31] *Commission on Popular Education*, xxi (6), pp. 531–2.
[32] Blyth, p. 106.   [33] E. E. Ellis, p. 69.
[34] *Commission on Popular Education*, xxi (6), pp. 596, 599, 603.
[35] Ibid., xxi (5), p. 409.   [36] Ibid., xxi (6), p. 603.

forceful personality and a brilliant speaker, with a great gift for apt illustration. Some of his public lectures upon education, according to Ellis, 'created a sensation', and E. K. Blyth, Ellis's biographer, believed that had Shields been master of a school for the upper classes he would have been ranked with Arnold or Thring.[37] Under Shields the Peckham school, though originally built for four hundred, was enlarged to accommodate nine hundred pupils and successfully held its great reputation in the face of competition from Board Schools until 1887, when it closed. Shields himself died, supposedly of overwork, in 1878 after twenty-five years of remarkable achievement.[38]

Peckham School was, like all Birkbeck Schools, a secular institution, and this inevitably drew the fire of the supporters of denominational Christianity. An Anglican clergyman, president of the nearby Camden National Sunday Schools Committee, distributed handbills to the congregation at Camden Chapel, alleging that Peckham School was, like all the Birkbeck Schools, founded upon 'Socinian principles', and attacking 'this "godless" scheme' as 'one which seemed only calculated to spoil children for usefulness in this world, and avowed the most entire indifference to all preparation for the next'.[39] The great criticism made of the Birkbeck Schools was that morality was taught without reference to any religious basis. Ellis's contact with the Utilitarians had left him with little faith in organized religion, and denominational instruction was not given in his schools. He was concerned with the practical and the secular, and the transcendental and ritualistic aspects of religion he left severely alone. Practical religion, in Ellis's view, was concerned with the duties of common life and the principles of conduct. These, he believed, were the essence of true religion and he was opposed to burdening children with specific religious beliefs until their intelligence had developed sufficiently for them to understand them. Parents and pastors could teach their beliefs according to conviction, but in the Birkbeck Schools not even the Bible would be used. Ellis maintained that, with its sublimities and profundities on the one hand and its ambiguities and contradictions on the other, the Bible was a study for mature minds. To read it as a class book 'without note or comment' was even worse than trying to explain it to immature minds, for the Bible above all works required note and comment. Ellis believed that the current view in Church circles that education should be based on the Bible

[37] Blyth, p. 106   [38] Ibid., p. 107.   [39] E. E. Ellis, App. H, p. 197.

inverted the main issue. The study of the Bible, he maintained, should be based on education.[40]

One of the key features of the Birkbeck Schools was the Socratic teaching method. This was apparently adapted from the question-and-answer technique that had been a common feature of elementary textbooks on history, natural history, and economics since the late eighteenth century, though Ellis was influenced by the work of the Continental educationalist, Joseph Willm, who favoured the method in his *The Education of the People*.[41] W. B. Hodgson, a friend of Ellis, believed it was a superior method because the children had to think and speak when using it, which he thought was better than merely listening,[42] but Pestalozzi warned that Socratic teaching was too advanced for both teachers and children :

> The superficial and uneducated man cannot fathom the depths which were the source of the true Socratic spirit. His failure is therefore certain. The mind behind the questions is wanting, nor have the children the necessary background of knowledge and experience from which answers might be drawn.[43]

Ellis had no such reservations, but the extent to which the method was successful can best be judged by eyewitness accounts. One of the most comprehensive was written by Henry Morley and W. H. Wills of *Household Words*, who described a Socratic lesson on money on a visit to the Birkbeck School in Southampton Buildings in 1852 :

> 'What are wages ?' Answers vary in form : 'The reward of labour', 'Capital employed to purchase labour', and so forth. 'When you become men, and work, and receive wages, will you all receive the same amount of money for your labour ?' — 'No, very different' — 'Why different ?' — 'The price paid for labour will depend among other things upon the value of it, and that differs in different people' — 'How ?' — 'Some are more skilful than others'. . . . 'The rate of wages depends then on the skill and industry of the labourer. On

---

[40] Blyth, pp. 229–37 ; E. E. Ellis, ch. vii, *passim* ; W. Ellis, *A Few Questions on Secular Education* (London, 1848), *passim* ; W. Ellis, *Philo-Socrates* (London, 1862), pt. iii, pp. 104 ff. ; pt. iv, pp. 166 ff.

[41] J. Willm, *The Education of the People* (Glasgow, 1847), pp. 161 ff.

[42] Blyth, p. 337.

[43] J. H. Pestalozzi, *How Gertrude Teaches Her Children*, trans. L. E. Holland and F. C. Turner (London, 1894), pp. 45–46.

anything else ?' — 'Yes, he must be sober. He may be very skilful and work hard, but he may get drunk and be unable to turn his skill and industry to full account. . . .'[44]

They were particularly impressed with one boy, a 'little flaxen-haired statesman', who would, they believed, 'grow up to be a workman, skilful, industrious, sober, honest, and punctual . . . it is too much to hope that he will ever become Prime Minister'.[45] Richard Cobden was also struck by lessons that the Government might have learned with and from some of the children. On a visit to the same school with George Combe in 1852 he remarked that 'one half the House of Commons might listen to these lessons with advantage'.[46] A more experienced observer, however, reporting over a decade later, was more critical of the methods used in Ellis's schools. D. R. Fearon, one of the Commissioners of the Schools Inquiry Commission of 1867-8, reported that the lesson that he observed was not well delivered, far from interesting, and poorly illustrated, and was received by the children with decorum and propriety but no sign of real interest. The teacher's questioning was poor and he allowed too much irregular and simultaneous answering.[47]

Ideally, provided the Socratic method was successfully employed, it did not really matter what particular proposition was used as a starting-point; truth would be revealed at the end of the discussion, given a reasonable basis of agreement on terms and the degree of elementary knowledge. Ellis, however, in applying the Socratic method to schools, overlooked or ignored the fact that he was dealing with children between the ages of six and fourteen years who could not be expected to match the dialectical skill and knowledge of educated adults. Furthermore, he expected his pupils to supply answers that were largely in conformity with the material set out in his textbooks, and therefore much of the claim for the initiative of and genuine participation by the pupils was nullified. Nevertheless, the aim was a sound one — to try to overcome the verbalism and rote-learning of much current education and to stimulate the child's powers of thought. But everything depended on the skill and personality of the teacher.

---

[44] [H. Morley and W. H. Wills], 'Rational Schools', *Household Words*, no. 144, 25 Dec. 1852, p. 339.   [45] Ibid., p. 340.
[46] [G. Combe], 'Secular Education', *Westminster Review*, N.S., vol. ii (July 1852), p. 30.   [47] *Schools Inquiry Commission*, xxviii (6), pp. 534-5.

The distinguishing features of the Birkbeck schools were, therefore, as follows :

1. The curriculum revolved around social science, and the importance given to this subject (despite the criticisms that could be made of its content) brought the curriculum closer to the affairs of the outside world and the future lives of the pupils than was the case in almost any other school in the nineteenth century.

2. The curriculum included study of the natural sciences, and few schools of this type taught science on such a scale at such an early date. Ellis told the Royal Commission on Scientific Instruction in 1872 that one of his pupils who went to Oxford to study chemistry amazed the examiners by his knowledge of the subject.[48]

3. Traditional subjects that did not further Ellis's aims were excluded from the curriculum. The classics were not taught and Ellis dismissed classical scholarship as 'groping among the rubbish, the filth and superstition of by-gone times . . .".[49] Literature, poetry, and history were also excluded, poetry because Ellis considered that it led to undue exaggeration and history because of the unsatisfactory work of historians.[50]

4. The main teaching method was a Socratic dialogue between pupil and teacher, and this was considered by Ellis as the best way of presenting the principles of social science. In addition, the general mode of presentation of lessons was as far as possible practical, and it should be remembered that from 1862 onwards the National and British Schools had to work the Revised Code, which necessitated fairly rigid rote-learning.

5. The schools were completely secular. There was no religious teaching of any kind, and the Bible was not even used as a reading-book.

6. No corporal punishment was given, and in this Ellis demonstrated as other progressive educationalists had done that it was possible to run large schools without the use of the cane.

All these features clashed with the dominant educational spirit of the age in a way difficult to comprehend today. A contemporary of Ellis wrote that 'they formed astounding innovations, opposed by all

[48] *Royal Commission on Scientific Instruction and the Advancement of Science*, P.P. (1872), xxv (1), i, p. 597.
[49] W. E[llis], 'Classical Education', *Westminster and Foreign Quarterly Review*, vol. liii (July 1850), p. 409.   [50] Blyth, pp. 45–46.

the old wives of the political, social and theological worlds, as tending to subvert the order established by Providence for keeping us, in every sense, in our proper stations'.[51]

There were also obvious disadvantages in the schools, the main one being a certain bleakness of atmosphere and a semi-vocational bias, which the doctrines of social science did nothing to alleviate. 'Sentimental' critics of the Utilitarians had always opposed Utilitarian doctrines on the grounds of their inhumanity, as John Stuart Mill had pointed out : 'Utility was denounced as cold calculation ; political economy was hard-hearted ; anti-population doctrines were repulsive to the natural feelings of mankind.' [52]

Besides this, the schools and the curriculum lacked aesthetic sense and feeling. The buildings were ugly and there were scarcely any humane subjects in the curriculum. The monitorial system was used in the schools, mainly to save the expense of teachers' salaries, and it diminished the benefits that the personality of teachers such as Shields and Rüntz and the best of the Socratic teaching gave.

Ellis's approach was fundamentally different from the educationalists of the Enlightenment and their followers or even from an isolated theorist like Wilderspin. Ellis's point of departure was not the child, his interests, capacities, and potentialities, but society and its presumed necessities. Ellis assumed that if the curriculum and methods were in his view important and necessary for children to learn, then they were automatically appreciated by the children, an assumption he never fully demonstrated. He further assumed that if the facts of social science were given and what he considered the correct values stressed, the children would, later in life, possess a chart for self-guidance and adjustment in society. In the absence of records of pupils' after-school life it is impossible to tell if this happened, but it is likely that the majority found (as the parents of the children at the Edinburgh Secular School found) that the economic realities of life differed from the abstractions of the economists.

Ellis was probably the most influential educator of the mid-nineteenth century. Not only was he always ready to endow schools that followed his principles, but the success of his methods and the persuasiveness of his manner assured him of a number of disciples who endeavoured to put into practice all or some of his teachings. As we

[51] W. Jolly, 'William Ellis, Educationist and Philanthropist', *Good Words*, vol. 22 (1881), pp. 543-4.   [52] J. S. Mill, *Autobiography* (London, 1873), p. 111.,

have seen, he helped to finance the International School at Isleworth, Middlesex, and he found the money for the Edinburgh Secular School, started by George Combe and James Simpson, also providing a master, William Mattieu Williams, who was trained at the first Birkbeck School. Between 1850 and 1853 he helped financially two schools founded by the Glasgow Secular Society and in the same period provided much of the finance for the two schools in Manchester, the National Independent Oddfellows' Secular School and the Manchester Model Secular School, the last-named set up by the National Public Schools Association. Ellis also helped to found or assist other schools in London. Dorset, and Norfolk ; in 1858, for instance, he was helping and teaching in St. Thomas's Charterhouse, founded by the Rev. William Rogers.[53] As we have seen, Ellis gave practical training to Barbara Bodichon's schoolmistress, Elizabeth Whitehead, and he was the moving spirit behind William Lovett's National Hall School, opened in 1848, in which, Lovett claimed, he pioneered the teaching of physiology in English elementary schools.[54] Ellis not only underwrote the school financially, but also taught social science there. His influence extended abroad, for in 1864 Mme. Salis Schwabe, the widow of a German manufacturer and a strong admirer of Garibaldi and Italian freedom, founded schools on the Ellis pattern in Naples ; while in England she had become a friend and admirer of Ellis, and the headmaster of the Naples school, Quarati, had been trained under Shields.[55]

Ellis's influence was mainly in the sphere of the private school, but he also had an effect on the curriculum of state schools. Social science was introduced into London Board Schools in the 1880s by Rosamond Davenport-Hill, the daughter of Matthew Davenport Hill of Hazelwood, and a friend of Ellis ; she found that in some cases headmasters had already been teaching social science for some years on the Ellis plan.[56] Ellis's social science was the forerunner of the civics courses introduced into the elementary system by the Liberal Minister, Acland, in the 1890s, and the parent of all social studies courses that exist in schools and colleges today. The William Ellis School, the successor of the Gospel Oak School, the only establishment founded by Ellis in

[53] Blyth, pp. 111–19.
[54] *The Life and Struggles of William Lovett* (London, 1876), pp. 360 ff. ; W. Lovett, *Elementary Anatomy and Physiology* (London, 1851), *passim* ; W. Jolly, *Education, its Principles and Practice as Developed by George Combe* (London, 1879), pp. 224–30.
[55] Blyth, pp. 250–3.
[56] E. E. Metcalfe, *Memoir of Rosamond Davenport-Hill* (London, 1904), pp. 93 ff.

existence today, was still teaching social science, a combination of social history, geography, and civics, in the inter-war period.[57]

Most of the schools founded by Ellis, however, did not survive the competition of the Board Schools, and were either closed or absorbed into the state system. The process of time had also changed Ellis's views in the new educational climate after 1870. The writings of Ruskin (which Ellis, who was no utopist, typically called 'noxious rubbish') [58] had helped to humanize political economy, and Ellis's pamphlet *A Few Words on Board Schools*, published in 1875, showed that he had modified his conception of social science. It advocated that lessons on social life should be drawn from the surroundings of the children and include instruction on food, plants, streets, vehicles, natural phenomena, communications, and so on, illustrated where possible by objects, drawings, models, diagrams, and maps.[59] Thus even in Ellis's lifetime the content of social science had begun to change from classical political economy, to something resembling modern civics, a change that is symbolized in the decline of the Birkbeck Schools. This transition is notable in the work of the new wave of progressive schools that began in the 1890s, partly as a result of the rise of the Labour movement and partly from the concern of the liberal intelligentsia. However, Ellis had made a lasting mark in the period from roughly 1850 to 1880 as teacher, educational thinker, and philanthropist of a characteristically radical-capitalist stamp.

[57] T. D. Wickenden, *William Ellis School: 1862–1962* (London, 1962), pp. 144–231.   [58] E. E. Ellis, p. 165.   [59] Blyth, pp. 298–9.

Section Two

EPILOGUE: 1850–1880

I

In 1856 a Royal Commission under the Duke of Newcastle was instructed to survey the elementary educational system that had grown up since the first national grant of £20,000 in 1833 was shared between the National Society and the British and Foreign Schools Society. The Newcastle Commission recommended in 1861 that in future Government grants should be paid only to those schools that were reported by Her Majesty's Inspectors as efficient in the teaching of the basic subjects. A detailed schedule of work was laid down for each 'standard' or age-group by the Revised Code of the Education Department and on this children were examined by Her Majesty's Inspectors on a given date each year and grants paid on the standards achieved. This, while seeking to ensure some evenness of standard in the battle against illiteracy, began the long history of oppression, hostility, and organized deception in elementary schools that continued till 1902 and after, although the Revised Code began to break up in 1895. The reverberations in the attitudes of teachers in elementary schools lasted until well into the twentieth century and the thought of any experimentation in state-supported schools during the period from 1862 was quite killed.[1]

In 1861 the Clarendon Commission began its inquiries into the affairs of nine public schools — Eton, Harrow, Rugby, Winchester, Westminster, Shrewsbury, Charterhouse, St. Paul's, and Merchant Taylors'. By 1864 the Report was available and the Public Schools Act of 1868 ensured that reforms in the government and financial conduct of these schools as well as recommendations on organization

[1] See C. Duke, 'Robert Lowe — A Reappraisal', *British Journal of Educational Studies*, vol. xiv, no. 1 (Nov. 1965), pp. 19–35.

and practice were carried out. Many schools regrouped themselves, others were founded as new public schools, and for fifty years this kind of institution gained a firm hold on the public imagination.

The Endowed Schools Inquiry Commission reviewed the grammar, proprietary, and private foundations between 1864 and 1868, and in the twenty volumes of their Report included consideration of art schools, museums, natural science laboratories, girls' schools, and the extent of parents' co-operation. The Report revealed an alarmingly low standard in a large number of the nearly eight hundred establishments that were investigated, and Matthew Arnold's reports, in one of the volumes, on the educational systems of Continental countries showed England to have little understanding of the need for civic organization as compared with the educational forethought and design of France, Prussia, Holland, and Switzerland. All these countries had accepted the need for and principle of state participation in secondary and higher education, and the education offered in their schools was vastly superior in quality and range, especially in science, to anything offered in secondary schools in England. Arnold prophetically outlined the reforms called for in national and local government in order to end the chaos of *laissez-faire* in education and to provide reorganization of secondary and higher education. The Endowed Schools Act of 1869 recommended that countless bequests and educational benefactions should be brought under Endowed Schools Commissioners, who later became the Charity Commissioners. The first firm steps towards involving local and national government in education had been taken and the end of voluntary initiative as the basis of school provision was in sight.

In 1870 W. E. Forster introduced the Act that set up elected school boards and began to cover the country systematically with elementary schools supplementing the existing foundations. By 1880 it was possible to insist on compulsory attendance, at least for part of the day. By the end of the century Local Education Authorities and a national Board of Education had been set up with political accountability on one side and the structure of a permanent secretariat of officials on the other.

During the second half of the nineteenth century in England the population increased by more than seventy-five per cent, and the concentrations in cities became increasingly oppressive. The franchise, which had been narrowly extended in 1832, had by the end of the century become available to nearly all men in the town and in the country, and local government was sustained by the County Councils Act of 1888 and the Local Government Act of 1894. The industrial developments of the first half of the century in England were matched by the later, faster growth of industry and transport in Europe and the United States. Where in the eighteenth century foreign export was a minor feature for a self-supporting nation, by the nineteenth century overseas trade became a survival factor for England, and in the 1870s agriculture was starting upon its sharp decline and England began to depend on imports for its food, for which it paid in industrial or services exports.

II

Alongside the Royal Commissions, the Education Acts, the emerging state support, the accountability of payment by results, and the economic, political, and social changes in England, the work of the educational innovators considered in the last six chapters was done. What can now be said of it ?

These schools were institutions in protest and their distinctive features can show what was commonly thought to be wrong in practice. As we indicated in the first chapter of this book, the area of knowledge and curriculum is an obvious territory for innovation. Without exception Morley, Ronge, Barbara Bodichon, and William Ellis were interested in presenting a wide range of subjects. They rejected the three R's for poor children and they considered the classics, as they were commonly taught, an impoverished curriculum for well-to-do children, and in this they anticipated what the Newcastle Commission recommended for the elementary schools in 1861, the Clarendon Commission for the public schools in 1864, and the Taunton Commission for the grammar schools in 1868. Science, history, and very often the elements of economics and social science were thought to be necessary for children of what we should now call secondary age. All of the innovators mentioned above were concerned to see that children were taught to think about international matters, and Morley, Ronge, Ellis, and Schmitz of the Isleworth International School tried to approach this through world history in one form or another. These were the years when economic and political power both at home and overseas made the relevance of social science and international affairs obvious in schools. Yet very few followed the lead of Morley, Bodichon, Ellis, Lorimer, or Schmitz.

Foreign languages were another aspect of the same awareness of a world in which communications were becoming steadily more effective. In this whole area of knowledge the innovators showed in the second half of the century that the curriculum of a school was relevant, flexible, and changing, and that science, social science, history, languages, and the arts were more appropriate in educating children than the three R's or the classics.

The leaders in this were middle-class men and women, as they usually were in the first half of the century, but where between 1820 and 1850 there had been an Owenite working-class movement striving for educational innovation, there was nothing to correspond to this between 1850 and 1870. Simon says that 1850–70 were years of prosperity, rapid industrial development, and colonial expansion. He also says that in these years, by the Royal Commissions and Acts of Parliament, the Victorian upper middle class transformed the school system into an effective hierarchical structure in which the Forster Act established elementary schools for the working class in 1870, three years after the Franchise Act of 1867 had added a million artisans to the voters' roll. The connection between the extension of the franchise and mass popular education can easily be seen, and Simon's point is that from 1870 onwards the working class became more explicitly coherent and socialist as the crude tools of mass education and voting powers enabled them to organize political participation and exert pressure.[2]

In the first chapter we indicated that a teacher's concern for the interests and motivations of children is an index of the importance he attaches to the pupil in the learning process, and in this there is very little to choose between David Williams in 1776, Charles Mayo in 1836, or Johannes Ronge in 1856. The social context is different, the data are different, and Ronge taught younger children, but the willingness to encourage boys to be initiators is the same.

It is not often realized that co-education for older children was in existence in England before Bedales took it up in 1898, but Henry Morley and Barbara Bodichon accepted it fifty years earlier, although William Ellis did not. Mme. Bodichon was clearly an early champion of women's rights and a resilient opponent of convention whether in

[2] B. Simon, *Education and the Labour Movement, 1870–1918* (London, 1965), pp. 11–18.

education, politics, literature, or sex. Where she would appear, as a member of the affluent liberal intelligentsia, to be politically and socially to the left, Morley would appear to be a self-made man, a *laissez-faire* humanist whose public conscience combined his limited income with educational concern to produce practical and original results in his schools.

This interest in children as initiators is allied to a deeper concern for the quality of the relationship between the teacher and his pupils, and one revealing aspect of this is the kind of punishment thought appropriate. All of these schools rejected corporal punishment, but each of them retained a sanction of some kind, whether it was a school jury sitting in judgement and passing sentence, or fatigues, correction exercises, or the like. Equally, the competitive motivations stimulated by rewards, marks, ranking, and the snakes-and-ladders of a highly worked-out system, is the encouraging obverse of punishment. But in all these unorthodox schools of 1850–70 nothing has appeared in relation to methods of correction that has not already been seen in the earlier chapters of this book.

One other feature that is common to the innovators of 1850–70 is their radical views on religion. Henry Morley had been trained in a Moravian community and became what may be termed an ethically-minded theist who was not aligned to any doctrinal or ecclesiastical position. Something similar could be said of Johannes Ronge, whose Catholic allegiance was broken so dramatically in the late 1840s before he came to England with his wife and founded what he called the Humanistic Schools. Ronge not only preached his Religion of Humanity and denounced creeds and Churches, but he treated the children in his kindergarten, aged between three and seven, in the spirit of these numinal beliefs, which had many affinities with the spirituality of Froebel's understanding of childhood that Ronge did so much to proclaim. Barbara Bodichon was from a Unitarian family and had no Christian doctrine taught in her school. At the London College of the International Education Society theological studies were excluded from the compulsory course, but optional instruction was offered. William Ellis was more severe still, excluding religious instruction and the reading of the Bible even as an ordinary school book. John Stuart Mill and Bentham were the rationalist saints in Ellis's gallery, although he, together with Mme. Bodichon, knew of the esoteric Swedenborgian position of Buchanan and Wilderspin. Again,

Ellis and Mme. Bodichon knew of the theories of phrenology, an attempt at a rational theory of psychology that nevertheless had many irrational consequences of an almost religious kind.

This religious unorthodoxy was the cause of deep-seated hostility between the Churches, especially the Anglican Church and certain Free Churches, and the innovating schools. Whereas between 1780 and 1850 Dawes at King's Somborne was an Anglican cleric like Mayo at Cheam, and Kay-Shuttleworth was an influential layman, there is no instance of an Anglican among those we have considered from 1850 to 1870 as educational innovators. It is understandable that as one of the two main providers of schools Anglicans should attach great moral significance to the influence that radical institutions exerted on young people, and bearing in mind the intensity of the struggle during the two middle quarters of the century between the ecclesiastical and secular interests for the control of the nation's schools, the generally hostile response of the Churches to the educational radicals is to be expected and is an index of the changes in theological orthodoxy in the country in the second half of the century.

The powerful theoretical influences in education in the first half of the century were Rousseau, Pestalozzi, and Fellenberg, together with a generalized liberalism from the French Enlightenment and a combination of English eighteenth-century empiricism and nineteenth-century romanticism. We have tried throughout this study to avoid giving names to large-scale influences without pinning them down by example and illustration ; indeed, we have aimed at precise examples without a great deal of generalization in order to let the evidence speak for itself. The point to make here, however, is that the Continental theorists who affected English education directly between 1770 and 1850 had, as might be expected, receded by the third quarter of the century. Their theory and practice had been assimilated by the innovators and England had produced out of her own history and resources an indigenous progressive mode in education of which Henry Morley, Charles Dickens, and William Ellis, together with Combe and Simpson from Scotland, are illustrations in ways that we have seen. The Utilitarians like Mill and Bentham and later Herbert Spencer have more significance than the Continentals, and the theological and scientific arguments, at the centre of which were Huxley and Darwin, needed no imported fuel for their conflagration, although higher and lower criticism of the Bible brought material from Germany and elsewhere.

If any one Continental theorist in education had to be named whose influence grew in the second half of the nineteenth century it would be Froebel, and we have already shown how important a part in this was played by Johannes and Bertha Ronge. Buchanan and Wilderspin between 1820 and 1840 made the first real contributions in England to the enlightened education of young children at the kindergarten and infant-school levels, and these two were more influenced by Owen and their own teaching gifts and Swedenborgian beliefs than by Rousseau or Pestalozzi. The Ronges, on the other hand, made a formidable combination of theory and practice and were convinced of the truth of Froebel's educational principles. The organizations that were begun in Manchester, which led to the Manchester Froebel Foundation in 1873 and later to a London and national Froebel movement, represent an institutional continuity that Rousseau and Pestalozzi never properly achieved in England.

We have stressed the interest of the innovators in original teaching methods and the details are scattered through these pages. We have emphasized and illustrated their interest in moral education in the sense that Castle so excellently sums up at the end of his book :

> What matters is that those responsible for the moral education of the young should think more in terms of weaning and development and less in terms of shaping and inoculating.[3]

III

When all is said, however, the evidence shows that the variety and range of educational innovation in the first half of the nineteenth century are far greater than in the period 1850–80. Some of the reasons for this are obvious. Transition from an agrarian to an industrial society, from a powerful landed class to thrusting individualist capitalists, from a traditional to a *laissez-faire* order, made the first half of the century more inchoate. The values of the Enlightenment, of the Romantic movement, and of public-minded Christianity called for education in many forms and the schools were founded in great numbers.

By 1850 the needs of the urban masses were relatively clear and the embryonic organization of political and economic power in a working

---

[3] E. B. Castle, *Moral Education in Christian Times* (London, 1958), p. 337.

class was beginning to take shape. General compulsory education could not be evaded, must be paid for, and could be seen to be an instrument for cohesion, disruption, and power and at the same time, a matter of conscience, for Christians and humanists alike. But the main needs of the new era of mass education were for economic and social continuity without revolution, and the unique role of the middle classes in England is to be seen here. In education, organization of a kind was arrived at in the second half of the century and the elementary school, with a basic curriculum for all children whose parents did not want or were not able to pay for their schooling, was provided. The government of grammar schools and public schools was reformed, and all of this was done in the period 1850–80.

The cost of all this organization was that, while there is much evidence of intellectual, economic, and social ferment, the consolidation of Empire and industry spread schools across the land but produced only the kinds of unorthodoxy in education that we have seen in Morley, Ronge, Bodichon, and Ellis. Understandably it does not match the daring of Owen and the Hills and Kay-Shuttleworth or of David Williams, Lady Byron, and the Mayos. Rousseau, Pestalozzi, and Fellenberg are more massive in their educational influence and principle than Bentham or Mill or Spencer. In any case, after the Commissions of the 1860s the innovations were already indicated and the national house was swept and remained only to be garnished. It is more difficult for progressives to be seen to be so when the Government is practising some of their best theories.

Here then is a point of rest in this study of innovation in English education. The next point of departure in the progressive movement appears in 1889, when a new school was founded at Abbotsholme in Derbyshire, and significantly this new school looked first, but very briefly, at the Labour movement, and secondly, with intense, critical attention, at the public school.

But that begins another book.

Index

Punishment, corporal, abolition of—
contd.
at London College of the International Education Society, 322
at Birkbeck schools, 331, 338
Punishment, unorthodox :
at Cheam School, 5
at Belfast Play School, 17–18, 20–21
at Hazelwood School, 108–9, 234,
236
in Bell's monitorial schools, 226
in Lancaster's monitorial schools,
229–30
at Spitalfields Infant School, 258
at Morley's School, Liscard, Cheshire, 296–7
at Association School (J. Ronge), 308
at London College of the International
Education Society, 322
Pupil teachers, 179, 182, 197

Quaker schools : Bootham School, 117,
118 ; Ackworth School, 199 ;
Sidcot School, 199 ; Wigton
School, 199. *See also* Allen,
William
Quakers, Society of Friends, 17, 71, 72,
199, 217, 229, 233
Quarati, 340
Quarterly Journal of Education, 101
Queen Victoria, 146, 173, 252, 272,
326
Queen's Scholarships, 197
Queenwood College, 91, 131
*Questions and Answers Suggested by a
Consideration of Some of the Arrange-
ments and Relations of Social Life*
(W. Ellis), 330

Radicals, Radical tradition, 23, 25, 36,
41, 100, 112, 191, 196, 313, 316
Radnor, Earl of, 332
Raikes, Robert, 223, 226 ; and rewards
in Sunday Schools, 221–2
Ralahine, 79, 158, 159, 165, 166. *See
also* Craig, Edward Thomas
Rank in schools :
at Belfast Play School, 18
at Hill Top School, 100
at Hazelwood School, 109, 110,
235–6

Rank in schools—*contd.*
at Bruce Castle School, 119
at Pestalozzian Academy, South
Lambeth, 148
at Ealing Grove School, 162–4
at Brenton Asylum, Hackney, 208
at Barrington School, 231–2
Rasselas (Dr. Johnson), 172
Rational Religionists, Universal Com-
munity Society of, 84–5, 91, 270 ;
Congress (1840), 85 ; Congress
(1842), 85 ; Congress (1841), 149
Rational schools, Owenite, 85–6, 98
Liverpool : prospectus, 86 ; rules of
conduct, 87 ; curriculum, 87
Huddersfield, 88
Manchester, 88
Ashton, 88
Yarmouth, 88
Sheffield, 88
Hyde, *see* Ellis, John
Reddie, Cecil, 218, 326
Redhill, 218
Reeve, Henry, 189
Reform Act (1867), 345
Reform communities, Germany, 300
Reform Government, 82
Reformation, 300
Reiner, Charles, 152, 172, 178
life, 173
and Cheam School : teaching of
mathematics, 173–5 ; teaching of
science, 175
See also Mayo, Dr. Charles
'Religion of Humanity' (J. Ronge),
304, 346
Religious Instruction, modification of :
by M. Edgeworth, 34
at Laurence Street Academy, 50–51
at Salford Co-operative School, 82
by Rational Religionists, 85 ff.
at Ealing Grove School, 163–5
by G. Combe, 283
at Morley's School, Liscard,
Cheshire, 296
by J. Ronge, 304
at Portman Hall School, 311
at London College of the International Education Society, 324
at Birkbeck schools, 335–6, 338
Renaissance, 121
Rendu, Eugène, 318, 319, 320

Rational, Secular, Sunday. For
other schools, *see under* name, or
name of proprietor or head
Schools Inquiry Commission, 102, 118,
119, 323, 337
Schultess, Anna (Mme. Pestalozzi), 137
Schwabe, Mme. Salis, 340
Science teaching, as innovation, 279,
280
at Lawrence Street Academy, 47
by J. Ellis, 90
at Hazelwood School and Bruce
Castle School, 115–18
at King's Somborne School, 130–1,
132
at Cheam School (C. Mayo), 175–6
at London College of the International Education Society, 323–4
at Birkbeck schools, W. Ellis, 338
Scientific Educational Institution for the
Higher Social Classes (Fellenberg),
109, 142
Scotland, 55, 57, 181, 197, 213, 267,
271, 288, 313
Scott, Sir Walter, 130, 146, 285
Scott, William Bell, 301
'Scottish democracy', in university
teaching, 57
Secular schools : Edinburgh, 330, 339,
340 ; Oddfellows' School, Manchester, 334, 340 ; Manchester
Model School, 340
Select Committee on Education : 1834,
202 ; 1835, 240, 285
Select Committee on Scientific
Instruction (1868), 134
Self-government by pupils :
at Cheam School, 5–6
at Belfast Play School, 20
at Laurence Street Academy, 42–3
at Salford Co-operative School, 82
at Hill Top School, 100
at Hazelwood School, 108–9, 277,
233–4
at Bruce Castle School, 120
and Dr. Bell, 227
See also Juries, jury-courts, school
Shakespeare, William, 295, 297
Shelley, Mary, 146
Sherwood, Mrs., 220
Shields, W. A., 316, 329, 339, 340 ; and
Birkbeck School, Peckham, 333–5

'Silent Monitor' (R. Owen), 162
Simpson, James, 196, 277, 280, 340,
347 ; on rewards and punishments
in schools, 240–1 ; and 'compre-
hensive' education, 285–6
Singing classes at Exeter Hall, 189–92,
194–5
Smith, Adam, 57
Smith, Frank, 155
Smith, John, M.P., 246
Smith, Joseph, 83
Smith, Toulmin, 122
Smith, William, 313
Smithfield Market, 256
Smollett, Tobias, 13
Social Community of Friends of the
Rational System of Society, 75
Social Conditions in England, 1830s
and '40s, 197
Social Contract, The (J.-J. Rousseau),
268
Society for Bettering the Condition of
the Poor, 63, 199, 231
Society for the Diffusion of Useful
Knowledge, 246
Society for the General Encourage-
ment of Vocal Music, 193
Socrates, 48
Solander, Dr., 36
Somerville, Mrs., 314
Songs for Children (J. Ellis), 90
South Lambeth, 147
Southam, Warwickshire, 211
Southey, Robert, 26, 56, 230
Spain, 322
Spectator, 191
Spelling Book (D. Manson), 22
Spencer, Herbert, 277, 279, 287, 288,
331, 347, 349
Spirit of the Laws (Montesquieu), 268
Spitalfields, 243, 244, 246, 247, 256
Spitalfields Infant School, *see* Infant
schools
Spohr, 193
Spurzheim, J. G., 280, 282, 288
Stanz, 138, 269
Star in the East, 86, 166
Stewart, Dugald, 57, 157
Stock, Rev. Thomas, 221
Stockholm, 121
Stockwell, 290
Stow, David, 267, 280, 333

PRINTED BY R. & R. CLARK, LTD., EDINBURGH

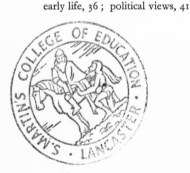

PRINTED BY R. & R. CLARK, LTD., EDINBURGH